The American Le[a...]
in Transition,
1965–1975

# The American League in Transition, 1965–1975

## How Competition Thrived When the Yankees Didn't

PAUL HENSLER

*For Lori & Lucy*
*Best,*
*Paul Hensler*

McFarland & Company, Inc., Publishers
*Jefferson, North Carolina, and London*

For Mom and Dad,
Pap, and Raymond,
who can only see this from the great beyond

All photographs are from the National Baseball
Hall of Fame Library, Cooperstown, New York

LIBRARY OF CONGRESS CATALOGUING-IN-PUBLICATION DATA

Hensler, Paul, 1956–
The American League in transition, 1965–1975 : how competition
thrived when the Yankees didn't / Paul Hensler.
p.    cm.
Includes bibliographical references and index.

ISBN 978-0-7864-4626-1
softcover : acid free paper ∞

1. American League of Professional Baseball Clubs — History.    I. Title.
GV875.A15H46 2013        796.357'64 — dc23        2012044196

BRITISH LIBRARY CATALOGUING DATA ARE AVAILABLE

Front cover photographs: *from left* Jim Palmer of the Orioles;
Harmon Killebrew of the Twins; Reggie Jackson of the Athletics
(National Baseball Hall of Fame Library, Cooperstown, New York)

Manufactured in the United States of America

*McFarland & Company, Inc., Publishers
Box 611, Jefferson, North Carolina 28640
www.mcfarlandpub.com*

# Table of Contents

# *Acknowledgments*

Since many disparate sources have been integral to the creation of this book, I am grateful to those who contributed in some way to this project with material or moral support. I have done my best over the years to ensure that no names were omitted during this journey, so I apologize for any oversights.

If a holy grail exists anywhere that enables both casual fans and serious students of the game of baseball to become completely immersed in the rich history of our national pastime, that place can be none other than the A. Bartlett Giamatti Research Center at the National Baseball Hall of Fame and Museum in Cooperstown, New York. Under the direction of librarian Jim Gates, the accommodating staff was most central for allowing access to the biggest trove of information available in a single place. I am thankful to research interns Lindsay Prescott and David Zhou, researcher Bill Francis, photo archivist John Horne, manuscript archivist Claudette Scrafford, research director Tim Wiles, and especially to research associate Freddy Berowski, my main point of contact who handled my appointments most efficiently and ensured that all material requested was at my fingertips. During my visits to Cooperstown, Hall of Fame senior vice president Bill Haase became a friend with whom it was a joy to share our experiences and love of the game.

Among the great secondary sources accessible with a computer is *The Sporting News*, which I found initially on the web site of the Paper of Record, a creation of R. J. "Bob" Huggins. "The Bible of Baseball" has now relocated to the web site of the Society for American Baseball Research (SABR), so I appreciate the efforts of former executive director John Zajc to bring *TSN* back online and also allow me to use selected oral histories and interviews housed in the SABR archives. Member services associate Eileen Canepari was helpful in the delivery of that requested material.

To demonstratively prove the point that one does not have to travel far to add great sources to one's work, my local library provided a route to out-of-town newspapers. At the Hall Memorial Library in Ellington, Connecticut, I appreciated the assistance of Mary Palomba, research assistant, and Susan Phillips, library director, but especially that of Gail Avino, the circulation supervisor and interlibrary loan coordinator who cheerfully and expeditiously processed my requests. As an extension of those requests, my sincere thanks go out to Sandy Date of the *Minneapolis Star Tribune*, Steve Nielsen at the Minnesota Historical Society, Dennis Halbin of the Kansas City Public Library, and Catherine Hanson at the California State Library for helping to bring their respective microfilm collections almost to my doorstep.

Because networking is vital to any endeavor, a bit of detective work via the Internet opened a few doors with fruitful results. In this regard, I extend my appreciation to Wanda Tucker and Helen Macdonald of the University of Arizona Outreach College and Elderhostel, Dan Mason of the Rochester Red Wings, and professor William Cohn at Trinity College in Hartford, Connecticut. These fine folks enabled me to interview Jim Bouton, Bobby Grich, and Jerry Kindall, who in turn led me to Sal Bando. A fan can have no greater thrill than to be able to speak one-on-one with players, especially those whose past careers and experiences can lend insight at key points to a book such as this, and I am in the debt of these men for taking the time to add their voices to the narrative.

Legal matters can be a daunting subject, but professor Edmund Edmonds of the University of Notre Dame eased the way through some otherwise rougher passages. For their help and encouragement — sometimes serendipitous — I acknowledge Brad Snyder, professor at the University of Wisconsin, Joan Claro of the New York Public Library, Monica Nucciarone of Pierce College in Washington State, fellow researcher Ken McIntosh, authors Tom Mahl and Bill Ryczek, and Dan Gentile, who offered a great tip that added a light touch to interviewing techniques. I tip my hat also to Kristen Shejen for lending her web site expertise to the mix.

Last but certainly not least, the two people most responsible for bringing me into the realm of writers merit most special attention. Eugene Leach at Trinity College in Hartford, Connecticut, was the professor who had the greatest impact and did more for me in the field of history and its attendant aspects of analysis and writing than words alone can express. His name became more than an answer to the trite question of "Who was the best teacher you ever had?" Although I could not accurately answer this question until I became a later-in-life graduate student, learning from Professor Leach was the highlight of my academic experience.

But my biggest debt is owed to none other than Donna, my loving wife who offered only encouragement during my return to the undergraduate and graduate classrooms that occupied so much of my time from 2002 through early 2007. Always proud of my achievements — and expressive of that pride — she furnished the strongest moral support anyone could hope for. That backing has been the foundation upon which my all my endeavors have been built. If this sounds hackneyed, so be it, but the saying is nonetheless true — I could not have done it without you.

# *Preface*

This book is vivid proof that once baseball is in a person's blood, it is often impossible to completely lose that passion. As a die-hard fan for over twenty-five years that endured the interruptions of numerous player strikes and owner lockouts, I found myself alienated by the debacle of the 1994 players' strike. The deadlock not only cancelled that year's playoffs and World Series but outlasted the winter and seemed likely to wipe out the coming season as well by the spring of 1995. More than seven months having elapsed since the strike began and still no sign of a resolution in the offing, I reluctantly concluded that it was time to move on to other pursuits.

But old habits do die hard, it seems. After the strike was finally settled, I still followed my favorite team, the Angels, occasionally on television and nearly everyday in the newspapers, checking the box scores and standings as eagerly as before. It was a habit that had endured many years of the Angels' outright failures and close calls, including the dreadful 1982 playoff loss to the Milwaukee Brewers and the humiliating one-strike-away loss to the 1986 Boston Red Sox in the American League Championship Series. If those heartbreaks hadn't ruined the game for me, maybe nothing could. By October 2002, when the Angels claimed victory over the Yankees and Twins to capture the American League pennant, and bested the San Francisco Giants to claim their first World Series title, I had lost even the pretense of resistance. My bitterness over the strike had seemed a thing too big to overcome, but was done away with little by little, almost without my having noticed. It was likewise in small, steady steps — several years' worth by the end — that this book came to be researched and written.

So why write a book about the American League from the mid–1960s to the mid–1970s? The answer is simple: Historians are always looking for a niche to fill, a new space to explore, or a chance to write about a tract of lesser-known territory. After finding myself drawn to the period and its teams, I was delighted to discover that there was indeed more to be written about both. I've since referred to it as "the Yankee interregnum," a decade in which the perennial American League champions suffered through losing or otherwise substandard seasons. If rooting for Yankees in the fifties had been, as Peter Golenbock suggests, like "rooting for U.S. Steel," by 1970 it had become a painful and futile exercise for even their most loyal fans.

But this book, unlike Robert W. Cohen's *The Lean Years of the Yankees, 1965–1975*, focuses not on the Bronx team's fall but on the rise of three franchises that briefly dominated the American League. The Minnesota Twins, Baltimore Orioles, and Oakland Athletics

1

each used their own talent and brand of baseball to win at least three league or division titles, and between them won five World Series. This after the Yankees had represented the American League in the Series for eight of the previous ten years. And fourteen of the previous seventeen years. My work contends that the decade represents what, for lack of a better descriptor, might be called a post–Yankees golden age. Whereas Cohen's book sought to rehabilitate a Yankee powerhouse gone soft, no such effort will be made in these pages, which instead focus on the rise of the Twins, Orioles, and Athletics. To provide a backdrop to the rise of these three teams, the book begins with detail on where each team came from — all three were relocated from other cities — and what was done to assemble the cast that led the teams into their best years of the mid–1960s to the mid–1970s. Using just enough traditional statistics to prove points without becoming burdensome to those leery of newer, arcane formulae and data, the story continues with a narrative describing what the teams did to maintain their positions of superiority at a time when the pressures of several sea changes significantly impacted the game of baseball. Among the alterations of the national pastime's landscape at this time were the creation of an amateur draft, rules changes following 1968's "year of the pitcher," expansion in both leagues in 1969, the addition of the designated hitter in 1973, and the vigor instilled in the Major League Baseball Players Association by its leader, Marvin Miller.

This era also produced three extraordinary new managers — Billy Martin, Earl Weaver, and Dick Williams — who led their teams to a succession of American League pennants unmatched by their contemporaneous rivals. While the achievements of this triumvirate were unparalleled at the time, the results came at a cost in terms of the trio's relationships with their players and, at times, even with their team owners.

The mid–1960s ushered in a new age of modernity in baseball. Fusty flannel uniforms gave way to polyester, in some ballparks real grass was supplanted by a new material called Astroturf, some plain black spikes were replaced by white baseball shoes, several franchises changed addresses in pursuit of move lucrative sites, and players began to command higher salaries. Meantime, the stodgy Yankees, who had always seemed to win, finally lost their place at the top of the American League standings and possessed only sporadic hope of recapturing their glory years.

Just as a forest fire clears the way for new growth to emerge, so too did the Yankees' immolation beginning in 1965 allow for a new crop of talented rivals to blossom. This story begins with the 1964 World Series, the Bombers' last postseason appearance before they went dormant for over a decade, and ends by recapping the demise of the storied Oakland Athletics at the close of the 1976 season, when most of Charlie Finley's best players took advantage of their economic freedom in the post-reserve-clause free agency era. In between these two milestones this book looks at how the three best teams in the American League were built and the success they enjoyed in the post–Yankees golden era.

While researching this book, I had the good fortune to interview former Oriole standout Bobby Grich. As we concluded our discussion, he told a story about a poignant experience he had following his departure from Baltimore after the conclusion of the 1976 season. During Grich's first year with the Angels, Kevin Uhlich, an Angel batboy, asked him what the difference was between the Orioles and the Angels. Grich replied that Baltimore had a winning tradition that was based on the team's development of its young players in the farm system as well as its ability to retain the services of its better players during their prime playing years. Unfortunately, the Angels had a history of acquiring many players in the twilight of their careers and farm teams that often produced few players capable of staying at the big league level for any length of time.

Twenty-five years later, when the Angels drove successfully all the way to a World Series title, the same bat boy, who had asked Grich about winning, had grown up to become the senior vice president of business for the Los Angeles Angels. Uhlich met Grich again and reminded him of that long-ago question. Wanting to put the Angels' past and present heroes in the public eye, Uhlich asked Grich if he would join the club as head of its alumni association and reconstitute the Angels' Hall of Fame. Grich assented to Uhlich's request and has remained in that capacity ever since. That was an important step in keeping a portion of baseball history alive and accessible for Angel followers, or any fan of the game for that matter.

In my own way, I, too, wish to bring the history of a small era of American League baseball not only to fans of the Twins, Orioles, and Athletics but also to that broad audience of diamond enthusiasts who may know little of the greatness those teams exhibited in the mid–1960s to the mid–1970s. This era was a dynamic and exciting time for the American League and its heritage. I hope that baby boomers enjoy reading this book by reliving some of their team's glory days; to those born after 1975, here is a chance to learn about three exceptional teams that shaped the American League as it moved into the modern era.

# 1

## *Long Live the King*

That the 1964 New York Yankees seemed to capture the American League pennant by going through the motions can possibly be attributed to the momentum generated by the team's astounding success during most of the previous two decades. Indeed, from 1947 through 1964, the Bronx Bombers won the league pennant fifteen times — and the World Series on ten occasions — so it was hardly a surprise that, as the author Peter Golenbock stated, "rooting for the Yankees was like rooting for U.S. Steel."[1]

Upon closer inspection, however, during the summer of 1964, the Yankees were hardly the indomitable team that had long reigned over the American League. Lethargic and limp, they finally righted themselves and moved briefly into their accustomed first place in late June, but a series of distractions and controversies then played hob with the club. An injury to shortstop Tony Kubek caused a predicament for rookie manager Yogi Berra, who elected to play Clete Boyer, normally the third baseman, at shortstop while moving Kubek's replacement, Phil Linz, to third. This ill-fated experiment, several players believed, contributed to several Yankee losses.

By late August, with the Bombers four-and-one-half games out of first, a shock wave rippled through the organization when it was announced that the fabled franchise was being sold to media titan Columbia Broadcasting System. Following a dreadful sweep at the hands of the contending White Sox in Chicago, Linz tried to inject some levity into the Yankees' gloomy bus trip to the airport by playing "Mary Had a Little Lamb" on his harmonica. The episode infuriated Berra and did nothing to enhance the skipper's relations with the team, as many of the players had for weeks been showering their manager with "a torrent of behind-the-back abuse."[2]

Come September, the Yankees finally overcame the ill fortune that had plagued them for much of the 1964 season. While the end result was a typically impressive 99–63 record and another American League pennant, the margin of victory was a scant single game over the White Sox and only two games over the third-place Baltimore Orioles. This Yankee squad was a team in transition, as promising youngsters such as Joe Pepitone, Tom Tresh, and Jim Bouton continued to supplant aging or injured veterans who had previously helped carry the club during the early 1960s.

Reflecting years later, however, Bouton saw the sale of the team to CBS as the turning point in the Yankees' fortunes because of the corporation's unwillingness to invest in more young talent. After Ralph Houk replaced the legendary Casey Stengel as manager and led the Yankees to pennants in his first three years at the Yankee helm from 1961 to 1963, he moved to the front office, where a policy of salary penuriousness prevailed. Players who felt they deserved better for continuing the Yankees' winning tradition were unhappy when they viewed their contract offers as sub-par. "The morale of the club disintegrated all at once when Houk became general manager in 1964," recalled Bouton.[3] Adding further discontent was the reality that Berra was not Houk's choice to continue as the field leader beyond the 1964 campaign. Thus the Yankees entered the World Series amid an ominous backdrop: sniping among GM, manager, and players; a false sense of superiority led by a corps of productive youths; and nagging injuries to a group of workhorse veterans, notably the leg trouble suffered by Mickey Mantle, Tony Kubek's season-ending sprained wrist, and Whitey Ford's ailing left arm.

The Yankees' opposition in the Series that October, the St. Louis Cardinals, were unexpected winners when the National League regular season concluded. The Philadelphia Phillies had a lead of seven-and-one-half games with fifteen games remaining but entering the last weekend of the season incredibly managed to lose ten of their previous twelve games. Even though the Phils were victorious in their final two games, they were unable to fend off the Cardinals, who finished with a 93–69 record, in one of the most memorable pennant races in National League history. Joining the Redbirds in the pennant hunt were the Cincinnati Reds, who like the Phillies finished one game out and tied for second place, and the San Francisco Giants, who ended the season just three games off the pace.

Instrumental for the Cardinals was Lou Brock, who arrived in St. Louis following a mid–June, six-player trade with the Chicago Cubs. Brock, who turned twenty-five years old three days after the swap and was just coming into his own as one of the best basestealers in the game, posted a .348 average in a Cardinal lineup that featured its own array of stars. Ken Boyer, who was named the National League's Most Valuable Player, drove in a league-leading 119 RBIs to highlight an offense that tied Milwaukee for best team batting average. The deft Bill White and graceful Curt Flood won Gold Gloves for their prowess in the field, and the pitching staff was bolstered by twenty-game winner Ray Sadecki, eighteen-game winner Curt Simmons, and a lithe nineteen-game winner named Bob Gibson, who was one of the game's most intimidating pitchers.

The Yankees were not alone in their postseason medical misery. For the Cardinals, shoulder woes hampered Brock, Boyer, and White, while Flood and catcher Tim McCarver nursed a variety of leg ailments. Though the Cards were physically hurt, their spirits were high thanks to the adrenal rush of the late September pennant run and the high jinks of Bob Uecker, the light-hitting, backup catcher whose antics provided much-needed levity to counter the stress of the season-ending finish.

When the World Series opened in St. Louis on October 7, "[t]here was some apprehension among the Cardinals about playing the mighty Yankees," wrote author David Halberstam, who noted that the Yankees "knew how to intimidate their opponents" and "always managed to seem like [they were] the home team."[4] Fearsome Yankee reputation notwithstanding, Flood realized that the Series would still be decided on the field and commented to his fellow outfielder Brock, "Hey, Lou, when they come down, they still have to play baseball."[5] Postseason games were a new experience for nearly everyone on the St. Louis roster; they realistically had nothing to lose since few observers reasonably expected them to eclipse the Phillies just a few days earlier.

Game One of the Series foreshadowed the demise of the Yankees' domination. Although

St. Louis relinquished an early 1–0 lead, and trailed 4–2 going into the bottom of the sixth inning, they confirmed what their scouting reports had indicated, that Mantle — whose lame legs had relegated him to right field and forced the move of Roger Maris to center — could no longer support the defensive ability he once possessed. This enabled the Cardinals, with their young, fleet runners, to take an extra base when the opportunity arose. Mantle's diminished skills afield personified the calcification of the older veteran Yankees, who were to be dethroned eight days later. In the home half of the sixth, the Cardinals chased veteran Whitey Ford with a four-run outburst, as the southpaw's ailing arm finally gave out and precluded his return for the remainder of the Series. St. Louis starter Ray Sadecki benefited from the rally, when his mates tacked on three more runs in the eventual 9–5 win.

Seeking to gain a split in St. Louis before the teams headed to the Bronx, the Yankees' hopes rested on the youthful shoulders of Mel Stottlemyre, short of his twenty-third birthday and already having proved himself as a rising star by averaging over seven innings in his twelve starts following his midseason arrival in New York. If the Cardinals failed to be intimidated by the Yankees entering the Series, neither was Stottlemyre taken aback when facing the hungry St. Louis lineup. In a duel versus Bob Gibson in the second game, Stottlemyre dispatched the Cards on seven hits and two walks in his complete-game victory, a performance punctuated by nineteen groundball outs. With the Yankees ahead 2–1 after six innings, the visitors padded their lead with a pair of runs in the seventh and added four more in the ninth against a trio of St. Louis relievers. This 8–3 Yankee win marked the first postseason appearance for Gibson, who, despite taking the loss, demonstrated that he was a force to be reckoned with.

In Game Three the Yankees turned to Jim Bouton, another young pitcher whose star was still on the rise. Facing the hard-throwing Bouton was a former Philly Whiz Kid, Curt Simmons, who at the age of 35 was no longer a kid but still won eighteen games and posted a respectable earned run average of 3.43 during the 1964 campaign. The October 10 tilt at Yankee Stadium was knotted 1–1 entering the ninth inning, during which Bouton overcame a Phil Linz error to extinguish a Cardinal threat. In the home half of the ninth, though, reliever Barney Schultz's first pitch to Mantle was tagged for a mammoth home run off the upper-deck facade in right for a 2–1 Yankee win. The homer recalled Yankee power of yesteryear. Prospects looked bright for the Bombers because another power pitcher, Al Downing, was slated to take Ford's place on the mound for pivotal Game Four.

If Sadecki looked unimpressive for the Cardinals in the Series opener, he was patently awful his next time out. The Yankees quickly scored twice by rapping out two doubles and two singles to chase him before Elston Howard, batting fifth in the lineup, even came to bat in the bottom of the first inning. The Yankee catcher then greeted reliever Roger Craig with another single to drive in a third run, before Craig settled down and combined with Ron Taylor to shut down New York the rest of the way. Although Craig walked three in four and two-thirds innings, he allowed only one other hit, while Taylor was simply superb in retiring every batter — save for a walk to Mantle — over the final four innings. Downing held the Cardinals at bay until the sixth, when two singles and an error by Bobby Richardson, the usually reliable Yankee second baseman, loaded the bases. Ken Boyer's grand slam into the left-field grandstand gave the Cardinals all they needed to secure a 4–3 win and even the Series at two games apiece.

Game Five featured a pitching rematch of Gibson and Stottlemyre, but this time Gibson, staked to a 2–0 lead, dominated until he was touched for a two-run homer by Tom Tresh in the bottom of the ninth that tied the score. McCarver avenged Tresh's clout by hitting a three-run home run in the top of the tenth off reliever Pete Mikkelsen, before Gibson allowed only a single in the bottom of the frame to complete his thirteen-strikeout performance and preserve the 5–2 victory. Moving back to Sportsman's Park in St. Louis for Game Six, the Cardinals were ahead three games to two and on the brink of achieving a remarkable upset.

Determined to not go quietly into the offseason, the Yankees sent Bouton to the hill in Game Six to face the veteran Simmons in a rematch of Game Three hurlers. Again Bouton provided a solid effort in holding the Cards to a single run through seven innings. A five-run outburst in the eighth, capped by Joe Pepitone's grand slam, gave the Yankees a safe cushion in the 8–3 final to force a seventh game to decide the Series. Despite yet another title being within their grasp, the Yankees had checked out of their hotel prior to Game Six in order to save the expense of another overnight stay in the event that they lost the contest and the Series. Hardly an expression of confidence by a team inured in a winning tradition, the surprising move impressed Bouton as an incident in which the Yankees' "parsimoniousness outweigh[ed] their arrogance."[6]

Game Seven on October 15 was the third Stottlemyre–Gibson matchup, in which Gibson prevailed despite pitching with just two days' rest. A pair of three-run innings in the fourth and fifth propelled St. Louis to a 7–5 win and a stunning championship. Even though Gibson allowed three home runs in that final game, his new record total of thirty-one strikeouts in three Series outings was a harbinger of what lay ahead in his own Hall-of-Fame career. Cardinal manager Johnny Keane exuded confidence in his ace and kept him in the game because "Gibson got a real good start ... I saw how strong he was going and how courageously he was throwing."[7] One may not have guessed that, according to Gibson's mother, Victoria Bolden, her son was so ill as a child that she "hardly let him out of the house until he was four years old."[8]

For the Yankees, it was another World Series seventh game in which the fans poured onto the field after the final pitch to celebrate victory, but as had happened in Pittsburgh four years earlier, the crowd greatly enjoyed the fact that the Yankees were on the losing end. Though they had lost their second straight Series for only the second time in team history, the Yankees may have felt no immediate cause to panic. Writing for *The New York Times*, Joseph Durso labeled the Cardinals' surge to the championship a "melodramatic climb," as if to imply that St. Louis had caught the Yankees in a momentary state of lethargy.[9] Because of the winning tradition long held by the Yankees, it was possible to view the loss to the Cardinals as just an anomaly, similar to the quirk that allowed the Los Angeles Dodgers to sweep them in 1963 or the 1960 upset by the Pirates, who scored fewer total runs in their Series win than did the Yankees. The postseason winning ways of 1961 and 1962 would surely return in 1965, and, as it had been for generations, it would continue to be a good time to be a Yankee fan.

Optimism for a bright Yankee future beyond 1964 hinged on the younger players already instrumental to the lineup. In the infield, Pepitone anchored first base with solid defense — his eighteen errors were offset by his league-leading totals in putouts, assists, and double plays — and was a welcome left-handed batter already proven capable of hitting over twenty home runs. Linz was the heir apparent for the injury-wracked Kubek and earned the nickname "Supersub" for his ability to play around the infield and in the outfield. Originally brought up as a shortstop, Tresh patrolled left field, committing only one error all season, and was a promising switch-hitter who, like Pepitone, could clout over twenty homers. The outfield stood to benefit further when six-foot three-inch Roger Repoz, another left-handed batter with power potential in the farm system, was ready to step up to the major leagues. With Yankee Stadium in its cozy configuration, the team emphasized left-handed batters, especially those who could produce the long ball.

The pitching staff featured a trio of hurlers around which any team could build a rotation: Bouton, who won twice in the 1964 Series; the hard-throwing Downing, the American League regular-season strikeout (and walk) leader; and Stottlemyre, the cool neophyte who quickly matured under October pressure. In the bullpen, Hal Reniff posted a 3.12 ERA to go with six wins and nine saves, and Pete Mikkelsen, a rookie with a good sinkerball, added seven wins and twelve saves.

Having already had the chance to develop in the glare of the Yankees' spotlight, Downing, Bouton, Tresh, and Pepitone were veterans of several World Series. Time was also on the side of all these young men, whose ages ranged from 23 (Downing and Stottlemyre) to 27 (Tresh). With health on their side, they were in position to become the mainstays who would perpetuate the Yankee dynasty for perhaps another five years.

But the *realpolitik* of baseball, on and off the field, precluded the attainment of any goals that once were within such easy reach of earlier Yankee clubs. Most glaring with the 1964 team was the string of injuries to key personnel who had borne the burden for much of the preceding five years. While it was reasonable to expect that offseason rest and recuperation would be invaluable to any injury-riddled team, the aches suffered by the Yankees were beyond the norm, and the calendar was not on the side of some of the stalwarts. Clearly on the downside of a spectacular career, Mantle could no longer hide his age and was destined to miss forty games in 1965; sadly he found too much comfort in drink over the span of his career in an attempt to assuage the pain. Maris, his outfield partner, took an even more precipitous fall, playing but 46 games and hitting a paltry .239.

While Maris was barely 30 years old, Whitey Ford was approaching age 40. Although he would pitch almost the exact same number of innings in 1965 as he had the previous season (244), he pitched only a combined 117 innings in his final two seasons. The middle infield manned so well by Kubek and Richardson was dissolved with the retirement of the shortstop following the 1965 season and the second baseman after 1966. And the man behind the plate, Elston Howard, soldiered on but also with reduced playing time and an attendant drop in offensive production.

Blame for the coming Yankee swoon can also be attributed to actions in the front office. Concerned about the manner in which the staff had prepared for the 1964 World Series, "Al Downing thought his team was being betrayed by the arrogance of its own scouting reports," which indicated to him and several of his teammates that the organization was suffering from a superiority complex.[10] Considering that the Yankees had barely won the American League pennant and their scouts were loath to forewarn the players about how tough the Cardinals — especially the black players, Flood, Brock, and Gibson — would be in the Series, the team was falsely assuming that its past, dynastic performance would continue pointing to a sanguine future.

The team ownership also suffered the ravages of its own aging process. Co-owner Dan

Topping, once a spendthrift when matters of signing good prospects were involved, suddenly developed fiscal sanity and by the very early 1960s he was reluctant to invest funds in new, quality talent. This caused the farm system to lack the many players necessary to carry on the accustomed winning tradition as prospects matured and moved up to the major leagues. Because Topping also suffered from a myriad of serious health issues, and his partner, Del Webb, was too pre-occupied with his construction enterprises, they agreed to put the Yankees on the market. At about the same time that the Yankees were trying to break out of their lethargy and reclaim first place in August 1964, the team was sold to CBS.

From a perspective of many years after the end of the Yankee era in the early 1960s, it is easy to chronicle the failings of the most storied franchise in sports history. Although the Yankees' star veterans seemed in a position to pass the torch to the youngsters like Tresh, Pepitone, Bouton, and Downing, Peter Golenbock summed up best the true finality of the championship heritage that was officially over in 1964 when he wrote, "The combination of no farm players, an inordinate number of injuries to Yankee regulars, and disastrous management ... brought the Yankee dynasty to its knees by 1965."[11] But even prior to the downfall, former Yankee general manager George Weiss, who was so instrumental in the development of young talent and overview of the ballclub's operations during his decades with the organization, had pronounced the Yankees to be a patient in critical condition when he was forced out of office in November 1960. Upon relinquishing the GM's seat to his longtime assistant, Roy Hamey — while Ralph Houk replaced Casey Stengel in the dugout — Weiss stated, "The Yankees have five more years at the most under the new management."[12] The veracity of Weiss's observation could not have been more telling by year-end 1964.

The Yankees' final pennant-winning season of the 1960s served as a microcosm of their ills despite the success they did enjoy in 1964. In 1965 the team inaugurated an eleven-year drought during which the Yankees would finish at least twenty games out of first place in six of the next seven years. In fact, this dubious skein proved to be their worst since a similar stretch from 1907 until 1917, the early years when the Yankees were still known as the Highlanders until 1913. Not until the arrival of George Steinbrenner as owner in the early 1970s was there much hope of the team rising from its torpor. Rather than the 1964 Yankees passing the torch to their young players who were trusted with continuing the dominance which they and their fans had taken for granted, the Bronx Bombers instead watched the Minnesota Twins, another offense-minded team, usurp the authority that the Yankees had held for most of the past fifteen years.

# 2

## *Calvin Griffith and the Birth of the Twins*

As industry in post–World War II America slowly migrated from the northeastern United States to the southern and western portions of the country, a number of major league franchises joined the movement to regions which promised new markets — and greater profits — for team owners. After decades of entrenchment in the Northeast, ball clubs such as the Boston Braves, Philadelphia Athletics, Brooklyn Dodgers, and New York Giants ventured to new homes in Milwaukee, Kansas City, Los Angeles, and San Francisco, respectively.[1]

By the beginning of the 1960s, some major league baseball officials recognized that the southern and western portions of the country were a mother lode of untapped opportunity for expansion by the American and National leagues. For many years in the first part of the twentieth century, about a dozen of the largest western cities had hosted minor league baseball franchises, but as new industry flourished beyond the upper East Coast regions, the baseball world was about to undergo its own transmogrification. The sanguine outlook for moving into new markets was deemed so great that one official with the St. Louis Cardinals envisioned the possibility of the creation of a "third Major League" to join its extant brethren: "The shift away from the Eastern Seaboard, not only in population but in industry and economic growth necessitates a cultural outlet for the people. Cities such as Houston, for instance, no longer are satisfied with minor sports.... Highly industrialized cities such as Minneapolis — St. Paul and Buffalo, find their people clamoring for Major League baseball to satisfy their sports desires."[2]

In an ostensible effort to stem the westward flow of baseball franchises and to quell rumors of his team's departure to Minnesota, Washington Senators owner Calvin Griffith pledged in January 1958 to keep his team in the nation's capital because "[t]he city has been good to my family and me.... As long as I have any say in the matter ... the Washington Senators will stay here, too. Next year. The year after. Forever."[3] Yet "forever" constituted a rapidly diminishing timeframe. Barely six months after issuing his stay-put edict, Griffith was actively seeking the opinion of his fellow American League club owners regarding a proposed relocation of the Senators. Because Griffith needed the majority of his colleagues to approve the movement of his franchise, a difficult road lay ahead for Griffith to convince enough of them to acquiesce. As 1958 melted into 1959, the Senators president was finding the siren song of the Midwest to be irresistible, but much effort was required before the moving vans could arrive at Griffith Stadium to begin packing for a move to the Twin Cities.

## Nepotism in the Most Literal Sense

The man who lorded over the Senators from November 1955 until he sold the Twins nearly thirty years later was Calvin R. Griffith. A native of Montreal, Canada, he was born Calvin Robertson in 1911 to a branch of the Griffith family tree and was later adopted by his uncle Clark Griffith, the owner of the Washington Senators and one of the founding fathers of the American League. Prior to reaching the age of 14, Calvin served as the Senators mascot during the team's drives to the 1924 World Series crown and the 1925 AL pennant. By his early twenties, he played baseball at several positions well enough to draw the attention of the Chicago Cubs, but in 1935 he was named treasurer and president of the Senators minor league affiliate in Chattanooga, Tennessee.

For the next seven years, he labored in those roles, moving to the Senators Charlotte, North Carolina, club in 1938, and by 1942 he "was recalled to Washington to serve as his

**Calvin Griffith (left) discusses business with his uncle, Clark Griffith (right).**

Uncle Clark's chief lieutenant."[4] Under his uncle's tutelage, Calvin continued to learn the responsibilities of baseball team operations, duties which eventually included player personnel administration and drawing up contracts with media outlets for the broadcast rights to Senators games. With so much experience accrued to his resume, Calvin became the heir apparent to the Washington baseball throne when Clark died in October 1955. Just short of his forty-fourth birthday, Calvin Griffith assumed the team's presidency in November. As he ascended to the top of the Senators organization, Griffith ironically had been exploring the possibility of purchasing the Philadelphia Athletics with the proviso that the team be allowed to relocate to Los Angeles.

During his tenure in the late 1950s, Griffith "charted a vigorous expansion of the team's farm operation and scouting departments," and the broadening of the player development portion of the organization sowed the seeds which would later be harvested in the form of players, both domestic and Cuban, who were among the integral members of the successful Twin teams of the 1960s.[5] Griffith served as his own general manager and was later praised by Harmon Killebrew as an astute evaluator of baseball talent. He was also the principal figure in engineering trades that filled voids in the Senators and Twins lineups, notably at catcher and first base. An active participant in all the affairs of his team, Griffith was not above making strong suggestions — if not outright demands — that influenced his field manager's policies and decisions.

By 1958, Griffith was being wooed by Minnesota baseball interests anxious to land a major league team to play at the new Metropolitan Stadium in Bloomington, which would come with an attractive lease and be expanded from 22,000 seats to 41,000 to accommodate the new tenant. Over the years, the Senators scheduled the occasional exhibition game on an offday during the regular season, with such contests often netting only a token fee to the club. But when the Senators were booked for a sold-out game in July 1958, Griffith gloated over how "Chet Roan (Met Stadium manager) practically bribed me with $10,000 for that game."[6] As an enticement for Griffith to relocate his team, Hamm's Brewing Company offered a $750,000 annual sponsorship for three years, while greater attendance than the Senators drew in Washington was guaranteed in Minnesota by other business supporters. Shortly after the fateful exhibition game, Griffith was "almost starry-eyed in reaction to the offers being thrown in his direction from Minneapolis."[7]

Along with a potential to gain over twice as much profit from the sale of television and radio broadcast rights compared to what Griffith earned in Washington, the major benefit to him would be guaranteed attendance of one million fans per season for the initial three-year period following the Senators' relocation, thus providing a revenue stream which would enable his club to increase the investment in new players and make his then-moribund team competitive.[8] Ironically, the Senators' home attendance had steadily increased from a post–World War II low of 425,238 in 1955 to 743,404 in 1960, with part of that success attributed to the young talent that was reaching the big league level.[9] Some Senators expressed reluctance at a westward move because they genuinely enjoyed the ambience of playing in the nation's capital, where there seemed to be a celebrity, politician, or dignitary at every home game. But the lures of increased cash flow and the magical attendance figure of one million fans — achieved only once in Senators history, in 1946 — trumped keeping the team in Washington and persuaded Griffith that greener pastures lay beyond the District of Columbia.

Dollar signs were more likely than stars to be clouding Griffith's eyes, but another factor may have contributed to his decision to relocate. Minnesota's summers could be as frightfully hot as they were in much of the United States, but the climate in the upper Midwest tended to be cooler in the spring and autumn. By escaping the notorious heat and humidity of the Mid-Atlantic region, Griffith believed that his players would be less enervated over the course of a lengthy season and thus more capable of increasing the totals in the team's win column.

As Griffith deliberated over whether to move the Senators west, opposition arose from both the local media and Griffith's wife, Natalie, who was not inclined to pull up stakes after becoming enmeshed with the capital-area social scene. In early July 1958 Griffith "sought [American League club executives'] reactions to the possibility of moving the team's franchise [*sic*] to Minneapolis territory. He was promptly battered down, especially by [Yankee owner Del] Webb and President Tom Yawkey of the Red Sox, who called such a move 'unthinkable.'"[10] Griffith was a baseball man, but he also was a businessman who well understood the need to improve the bottom line of his club's balance sheet.

As the 1959 season concluded with the Senators in last place for the third year in a row, Griffith openly stated his intentions that, pending league approval, he would transfer the Senators from Washington to the Minnesota twin cities of Minneapolis–St. Paul. To facilitate the change in attitude among those who at first staunchly objected to Griffith's proposal, Griffith began to carefully play politics within the group of AL owners and finally won their tentative backing if only on an unofficial basis.

Griffith also faced a challenge from the United States Congress, which threatened to strike down major league baseball's anti-trust exemption should the Senators relocate. But this obstacle was overcome by the American League's multifaceted expansion plan for the 1961 season. Concerns over leaving the city of Washington devoid of a baseball team were put to rest when, early in the fall of 1960, the league granted Griffith permission to move his Senators to Minnesota while it simultaneously awarded the city of Los Angeles a new AL team and another brand new franchise for the nation's capital to immediately fill the vacancy created by the departing Senators. "The news startled the baseball world," reported the *New York Times*, noting that American League officials "apparently were determined to beat the National League to the punch" by enacting an expansion program before the senior circuit could do likewise.[11] Only nine days earlier the National League had announced its own plans to add new teams in Houston and New York for the 1962 campaign.

As the new corporate citizen of the Twin Cities business community, a smiling Griffith posed with members of the Minneapolis area Chamber of Commerce for a photo opportunity before a welcoming banner emblazoned with the franchise's new logo, which featured two burly, handshaking baseball players perched above the lettering of the transplanted club's new moniker: *Minnesota Twins*.[12] Mindful of the new clientele to whom Griffith was now catering, the cover of the team's 1961 media guide displayed the slogan "Representing the American League in the Upper Midwest."[13]

Over the course of the Twins' first ten seasons, the team set the pace for attendance in the American League, owing much of its early success to the quality of talent that the Senators' system groomed in the late 1950s. Griffith hoped that the Senators' arrival in Minnesota would kindle winning in a franchise that rarely appeared in the first division and had not seen any glory days for nearly three decades since the team's last pennant in 1933.

Several years following the Twins' arrival, a team publication accurately summarized the state of baseball in the Land of Ten Thousand Lakes: "With his decision to transfer the Senators to Minnesota, on October 26, 1960, Mr. Griffith brought to baseball's New Frontier an era brimming with the promise of victory and excitement in concert with the boom of the Upper Midwest."[14] The word "nepotism" often carries an unfavorable connotation, but in the waning years of the original Senators and the emerging years of the Twins, the diligence of Clark Griffith's nephew won him accolades for building a solid contender capable of challenging the perennially dominant New York Yankees. The talent that Calvin Griffith assembled in the twilight of the Solons' stay in Washington and during the dawn in Minnesota enabled the Twins to eventually assume the throne as American League champions following the collapse of the Yankee dynasty after the 1964 season. The inaugural roster of new hometown heroes that arrived at Metropolitan Stadium in 1961 would improve in a few seasons to transform into a club that would win an American League pennant and fall just one game shy of winning a World Series.

## The Formation of the Twins' Powerhouse

With the lone exception of 1956, when they rose to a mere seventh place in an eight-team league, the Washington Senators finished in the American League basement all other years between 1955 and 1959. Despite the Solons' dreary performance during this time, the team signed several key players who would later mature and then anchor the offense by the time the club arrived in Minnesota. In laying the foundation that would pay the dividends they sought from new players seasoned in their farm system, the Senators — and the Twins after 1960 — scouted young talent under the watchful eye of Clark Griffith and, after his death in 1955, Calvin. Before the institution of the amateur draft in 1965, individual teams could negotiate with any amateur player they wanted to and then sign him, usually for a bonus which varied in size depending on the amount of interest that player commanded. For those prospects deemed by major league club officials to have significant potential to become top big league stars, bidding wars erupted among teams anxious to sign the best amateurs.

Because the Senators and Twins spent their share of bonus money to attract the players necessary to shake the team from its lethargy, the Twins' success of the 1960s was built upon several signees who could hit for a solid batting average, hit with power, and occasionally swing the bat for both average and distance. These players coalesced in 1965 into the team that unseated the New York Yankees and laid the foundation for Minnesota's subsequent success that carried through the 1970 season.

Chief among the signees was Harmon Killebrew, the pride of Payette, Idaho, who overcame a tepid start to his major league career to become in 1984 the first Minnesota Twin to be elected to the Baseball Hall of Fame. The stocky slugger may not have been discovered by the Washington Senators had it not been for the recommendation of a United States senator from Idaho, Herman Welker, who was serving in the nation's capital in 1954. When Clark Griffith was bemoaning his team's lack of offense early in the 1954 season, Welker told him of a constituent's family whose athletic prominence back home was well known. When Griffith sent former Solon infielder Ossie Bluege to scout one of the youngsters,

Bluege returned with a favorable report on Killebrew. Following his high school graduation, Killebrew was ticketed for the University of Oregon with a baseball scholarship, but Griffith authorized Bluege to sign Killebrew, who then joined the Senators for the remainder of the 1954 season.

Barely eighteen years old when he joined the big league club, Killebrew saw very limited playing time as a third baseman with the Senators through the 1958 season. Contract stipulations then required large bonus recipients to spend two years with their major league team; Killebrew was finally sent to the Washington farm system for seasoning in 1956. By playing at a level more suited to his raw talent, Killebrew logged several seasons in the minor leagues, where his impressive batting averages and power production served as a precursor to his bright major league future. At the conclusion of his last stint in Chattanooga, Killebrew was finally able to land a permanent spot on the Washington roster in his breakthrough season of 1959.

Despite being only six feet tall, Killebrew admitted that his tremendous power was generated by the strong wrists and shoulders that he developed while painting houses. Midway through the 1959 campaign, which Killebrew described as a "magical season," there was speculation in the baseball world that Killebrew was capable of hitting 50 home runs after the burly Idahoan finished with an American League–leading 42 homers and 105 runs batted in.[15] Calvin Griffith, who "insisted that someday Killebrew would be one of the great home-run hitters in the league," felt vindicated by the display of power.[16]

More changes in position to first base and then to the outfield did not hinder Killebrew at the plate in the early 1960s, as Griffith's prophesy continued to be fulfilled when his left fielder hit at least 45 homers in four of the next five seasons, leading the league on three occasions. Speaking years later of his performance in 1964, Killebrew mused, "I put more pressure on myself to hit 50 home runs ... but didn't get the job done."[17] By the conclusion of that season, however, the four-time All-Star was ensconced as the Twins' dominant veteran and clearly was the anchor of their power-laden batting order.

Despite an elbow injury that threatened to end his season, Harmon Killebrew returned in time to play in the 1965 World Series.

Also amassing impressive credentials of their own were several of Killebrew's teammates who socked at least twenty home runs in the season leading up to the Twins' first championship in 1965. While winning the Senators' center field job in spring training as a rookie in 1959, Bob Allison belied pre-season comments in the press that he "is not a power hitter as such, although he gets good wood on the ball."[18] The fleet, wispy, six-foot, three-inch, 205-

pounder was a former fullback at Kansas and brought a fine set of all-around skills to the Senators, with Griffith claiming "he has the best arm that has come to our outfield since Jackie Jensen was with us."[19] Allison went on to capture the American League Rookie of the Year Award thanks to his 30 home runs, league-leading nine triples, 85 runs batted in, and .261 batting average.

After having his home run production cut in half during the Senators' last season in Washington, Allison regained his form in Minnesota, where he hit no less than 29 homers and drove in an average of 96 runs in each of the next four years. With more outfield prospects maturing in the Twins farm system during the early 1960s, Griffith was comfortable with a plan to move Allison to first base. In 1964 the Twins took advantage of Allison's versatility and brought him to the infield, where he displaced Gold Glove winner Vic Power.

When Jimmie Hall burst on the scene in Minnesota as a 25-year-old from North Carolina, his arrival came only after the left-handed hitter toiled with very little success in the minors and had failed twice in bids to secure a job with the Senators in 1959 and 1960. Two stints in the United States Army in the early 1960s interrupted Hall's baseball career, but upon being discharged in the summer of 1962, he re-entered the baseball world by batting .313 for Vancouver of the Pacific Coast League and followed up with a .351 average in the Florida Instructional League. When Hall joined the Twins roster in 1963, his playing time increased due to early-season injuries to Killebrew and Allison. He muscled his way to a more permanent spot in the lineup as his surprising power stroke came to the fore.

In 1964, Hall made the American League All-Star team en route to a 25-homer season while increasing his batting average to .282. The perseverance shown by Hall paid off handsomely for both himself and the Twins, yet he gave credit to his father for not letting him quit when he faced doubts about his future. "I guess I might be working in the cotton mill, but my daddy wouldn't let me," said Hall late in the summer of 1963.[20]

Another newcomer to the Twins outfield was a native of Cuba who, along with Hall, provided another dangerous left-handed bat to complement the right-handed-swinging Killebrew and Allison. Born Pedro Oliva y Lopez in 1940, Tony Oliva came to the United States as Fidel Castro ascended to power on the Caribbean island-nation. At the age of 21, Oliva entered the United States by using his brother Antonio's passport — thus the change in his first name — and once in the country, Oliva played for Wytheville in the Appalachian League, where he crushed opposing pitchers for a .410 batting average and 81 runs batted in — both best in the circuit — and belted ten home runs in only 64 games.

Maintaining a strong pace over the next two years in Double-A and Triple-A, Oliva made the big league roster in 1964. One month into the season, Griffith was lauding his new right fielder by predicting that "Oliva could become another Mickey Mantle or another Al Kaline."[21] So early in Oliva's career, the only commonalities between Kaline and Oliva were the right-field position they played and the number six that adorned their uniforms.

Griffith's expectations ran high in Oliva's case because, unlike Killebrew and Hall who both had spent protracted periods of time maturing before performing well enough to hold down a major league job, Oliva quickly developed into one of the most dangerous hitters of the 1960s. Oliva's first full year in the majors in 1964 evolved into a small record book of its own as he breezed to Rookie of the Year honors from both the Baseball Writers' Association of America and *The Sporting News*. His league-leading figures in runs scored (109), hits (217, which were also the most by a rookie), doubles (43), batting average (.323), and total bases (374, tying a major league record for rookies) were augmented by nine triples, 32 homers, and 94 runs batted in.

Indeed, the exploits of Oliva outshone those of many of his teammates, including a fellow Cuban who had come to the team while it was still in Washington. During spring training of 1959, reporter Bob Addie noted, "The Senators are trying out a new shortstop named Zoilo Versalles.... It was inevitable that he should be nicknamed 'Zorro.'"[22] Since the quality of a shortstop affects every club, the Senators were hopeful that the diminutive Versalles could put an end to the parade of ineffectual players who tried to fill the gap at that position during the late 1950s. Born in Havana, the 150-pound Versalles was an all-star shortstop for the Senators farm team at Charleston in 1960, but Twins' manager Cookie Lavagetto observed in the spring of 1961 that Versalles needed "mental maturity to do the job."[23]

During the Twins' inaugural season in Minnesota, Versalles proved that he could stabilize the infield and bring improved offense to the shortstop position. At this time, he met an influential teammate who was completing what would be his final year as a major league player. Billy Martin ended his playing career with the Twins in 1961, and by the following spring training the ex–Yankee second baseman was eagerly mentoring his former double-play partner on the finer points of playing in the field. "Martin good advice man. He teach me to give signals. It gets me in the game," Versalles told *The Sporting News*, adding, "Billy is very good. He teach me little things. Make me better shortstop."[24]

Versalles also demonstrated that he could hit for power — he set the single-season club record for home runs by a shortstop and led the American League in triples for three consecutive years beginning in 1963 — but there was concern in the Twins organization about his work with the glove, as he unfortunately committed an average of nearly 30 errors per year.

For the infielders on the corners, Versalles' supporting cast included another new face who joined the Twins during their inaugural year in Minnesota. Signed off the campus of Kent State University in 1960 as a second baseman, Rich Rollins developed skills that would land him at third base, but not without some difficulty in making the transition. Billy Martin told Rollins that he lacked the ability to move to his left. While the criticism stung the young infielder, Rollins worked at his deficiencies and succeeded in earning a spot as the Twins third baseman in 1962.

Finishing with a .298 average, 16 homers, 96 runs scored, and 96 runs batted in, Rollins also led the league in errors at third base with 28 but was second with 33 double plays. Proving that his first-year production was no fluke, Rollins continued to hit for power and maintained a healthy average at the plate, even though errors in the field were a persistent issue. Nonetheless, Rollins gave the Twins stability at third base during his first three years in Minnesota, creating the kind of depth that would be so vital in their drive to the pennant in 1965.

Playing opposite from Rollins across the diamond was Don Mincher, who saw limited playing time when he joined the Senators in 1960 as the heir apparent to Killebrew at first base. Acquired from the Chicago White Sox on April 4, 1960, with catcher Earl Battey and $150,000 in a trade for slugger Roy Sievers, Mincher brought fine batting credentials to Washington after compiling a .272 average with 22 home runs and 92 RBIs for Charleston in 1959. After earning a position on the 1960 National Association All-Star team, the tall, left-handed swinger from Alabama seemed ready to join the big league club but was lacking defensively.

Since Mincher's trials at the major league level revealed inconsistencies in his performance, the tentativeness of Mincher's status forced the Twins to look elsewhere for help at first base. Vic Power, who would win a pair of Gold Gloves for his fielding excellence, was acquired from the Cleveland Indians just prior to the opening of the 1962 season. However, Mincher still curried favor with the Twins because of his power hitting. By 1964, Mincher improved both offensively and defensively to the point where he platooned with the right-handed-hitting Power and rewarded the Twins with 23 homers in just 287 at-bats while committing only five errors at first base. Although Mincher made his mark by adding depth to the Twins at first base, the second player whom the Twins acquired from the White Sox in the Sievers trade was by far a more critical component.

It has never been a mystery to followers of baseball that one of the players most essential to how well a team performs is its catcher. Charged not only with the duties of guiding the pitching staff on a regular basis, a good catcher must also carry his weight at the bat. In 1959, the Senators were relying on two aged veterans, Hal Naragon and Clint Courtney, to handle duties behind the plate. In the spring of 1960, Griffith and White Sox owner Bill Veeck consummated a deal, with Sievers — who averaged 30 homers per season for the Senators and led the American League with 42 in 1957 — headed west while the ChiSox parted with Mincher, $150,000 of Veeck's cash, and Earl Battey, a twenty-five-year-old catcher from Los Angeles, who would go on to anchor the Senators and Twins defense for most of the next eight seasons.

Battey quickly earned praise from Manager Cookie Lavagetto and the pitching staff for his defensive work, with one columnist observing that "Battey's form behind the plate is reminiscent of the great Roy Campanella."[25] Not only was Battey throwing out potential basestealers at a rate seldom seen when the Senators were in the field, but the burly catcher contributed mightily — and unexpectedly — on offense, his 15 home runs and 60 RBIs during his first year in a Washington uniform far outpacing the paltry 1959 Naragon-Courtney tandem of two homers and 29 runs driven in. For the whole of 1959, the pudgy Courtney threw out two basestealers, but in Battey's first season for the Senators, he erased over two dozen would-be base thieves.

While it would appear that Battey's offensive and defensive skills were of greatest concern to Griffith, there was a fringe benefit at the box office that also enhanced Battey's arrival in the nation's capital. Washington sportswriter Shirley Povich reported that the new catcher "is expected to be a favorite with Washington's large segment of colored fans who never have had the opportunity to root for an American Negro playing regularly for the Senators."[26] In 1960 when Battey won the first of three consecutive Gold Gloves, it was no coincidence that the Senators began their escape from the American League basement by climbing to fifth place. As Battey jelled as one of the top backstops in the league, he also earned a place on the AL's 1962 and 1963 All-Star teams.

The Senators and Twins pitching staffs fully understood why Battey was honored for his defensive prowess, but he was also admired for his willingness to play with pain. Battey was forced to use a protective flap on his batting helmet to guard his face after a pitch broke his cheekbone in 1961, and he used a brace for his problematic right knee in 1963 and 1964. Thyroid gland and goiter problems also interfered with Battey through the early 1960s, but he labored arduously to remain the bulwark of the Twins defense.

Although these regular position players solidified the Senators and Twins lineup — or at least added to the team's depth — those who toiled at second base failed to maintain a firm grip necessary to hold down a full-time job with any degree of consistency. During the dismal days of the late 1950s, the Senators tried to make do with a string of forgettable second sackers. In 1961, the position fell to Billy Martin, an ill-tempered major league vaga-bond who had fallen out of favor with each of the six teams that had jettisoned him since 1957. Martin was happy to be re-united with Twins manager Lavagetto, his teammate from their days with the Oakland Oaks of the Pacific Coast League. When Lavagetto was replaced by Sam Mele, the Twins turned to Bernie Allen as their second baseman of the future.

A twenty-three-year-old Ohioan and former All-America quarterback at Purdue, Allen was signed by Floyd Baker, the same scout who had inked Rich Rollins. While Martin was tutoring shortstop Versalles during the spring of 1962, Allen "had the Twins' bosses licking their chops" when they saw his performance in spring training at Orlando, Florida.[27] Demonstrating poise that he carried from his collegiate football days, Allen rose rapidly in the Minnesota minor league system and suddenly seemed ready to break into the Twins lineup. In early April, Martin was released as a player and signed to become a Twins scout, while Allen became the new second baseman and hit a solid .269 with 12 homers and 64 RBIs.

Though he slipped to a .240 batting average in 1963, Allen still had his future in front of him. But with the second baseman's job his to lose, he did just that when a devastating knee injury ruined what looked to be a promising career. On June 14, 1964, while in the midst of emerging from a terrible batting slump, Allen suffered torn ligaments in a collision with journeyman Don Zimmer and thereafter endured a long road to recovery. Immediately assuming Allen's place in the lineup was Jerry Kindall, who had been acquired from the Cleveland Indians in a three-way trade that dealt first baseman Power from Minnesota to the Los Angeles Angels. The timing of Kindall's arrival could not have been more fortuitous for the Twins, who curiously had completed the transaction just two days before Allen's injury.

A native of St. Paul, Minnesota, who received a basketball scholarship at the University of Minnesota, the wiry Kindall was just two seasons removed from his role as the Indians regular second baseman. Although he had been relegated to utility duty for the Tribe, Kindall realized a dream when given the opportunity to play full-time for his hometown team. Kindall was sought for his work in the field rather than at the plate, where he hit an anemic .148 for the Twins in 62 games for the remainder of 1964. Minnesota's heady lineup could temporarily indulge Kindall's weak bat in exchange for the infield skills of someone the Twins dubbed "one of the greatest glove men in the game."[28]

Notwithstanding the quandary at second base, the Twins' everyday position players nonetheless presented a formidable challenge to the lineups of any of their American League rivals. During 1964, however, the redoubtable Twins offense and defense foundered at key moments, and the team was on the short end of 38 games decided by a single run and lost 13 of 20 extra-inning contests. Success was impeded also by Minnesota's faltering glove work in the field and the mediocrity of the pitching staff. To legitimately vie for the pennant, great teams need to balance offensive and defensive capabilities, but the Twins had yet to blend these assets in the correct proportions that would propel them past the reigning Yan-kees and their challengers.

## Twins on the Defensive

If the Minnesota lineup was stocked with an impressive array of offense, the same could not be said for its defense. With 91 wins in both 1962 and 1963, the Twins profited from the efforts of catcher Earl Battey, first baseman Vic Power, and pitcher Jim Kaat, who collectively won five Gold Gloves. Minnesota's team fielding average of .980 in 1962 tied Baltimore for second place in the American League — with the Chicago White Sox leading at .982 — as the Twins committed 129 errors (third least in the AL) while turning a league-best 173 double plays. The following year, the Twins slipped to a .976 fielding average, which was the third worst in the league.

Looking to return to a fielding standard commensurate with 1962 as the team continued to mature in 1964, "Mele set his sights on improving the defense. Through the first one-third of the season, the Twins were third with a .981 fielding average."[29] By late June, the Twins bettered the fielding, but "then it seemed the roof fell in on everyone."[30] As September loomed, the White Sox had won far more games than had the Twins thanks to their less porous defense: "During their first 140 games, the Twins made 121 errors and gave up 69 unearned runs. The White Sox, who scored 99 runs fewer than the Twins during that time, gave up only 47 [un]earned runs and won 14 more games."[31] The Twins stumbled badly, finishing 79–83 despite topping all AL teams with 737 runs scored and far outpacing either league with 221 home runs. Gold Glovers Kaat and Battey still toiled for the Twins, but Power had departed via trade after 19 games. At the conclusion of 1964, the Twins had tallied 145 errors — over a third of which were committed by the left side of the infield, Rollins with 24 and Versalles with 31 — and led the majors by allowing a total of 91 passed balls and wild pitches. After his move to the Angels, Power played perfectly in the field and again won the Gold Glove; it can only be speculated how many errant throws the first baseman would have spared the Twins' infield had he remained in Minnesota.

Rookie star Tony Oliva was burdened by the reputation he carried as a result of 44 errors committed during his three seasons in the minors. Oliva was tutored by Bob Allison and former Twin — and fellow Cuban — Julio Becquer to learn the finer points of patrolling the outfield. On the mound, several starters produced nearly perfect fielding records, with Kaat in the early years of his tenure as the finest fielding pitcher of the 1960s.

## Twin Twirlers

The age-old problem of teams never having enough pitching hampered the Twins as badly as it did most of their American League counterparts. Entering the 1964 season, a quintet of solid starting pitchers was available to Sam Mele, but as the season progressed it became necessary for the Twins to bolster the staff with the June acquisition of Jim "Mudcat" Grant from the Cleveland Indians. Following Minnesota's decline from 91 victories in 1963 to 79 in 1964, the Twins regrouped in preparation for 1965 but appeared to have only four reliable starters on hand.

The elder statesman of the staff was Camilo Pascual, a temperamental Cuban found in 1951 by scout Joe Cambria, who recommended that the young right-hander abandon his desire to play third base and take advantage of an arm Cambria believed to be of major league quality. Beginning his career in a Senator uniform during Washington's nadir of the mid–1950s, Pascual struggled mightily in his early seasons. Not until 1959 did Pascual harness his emotions and learn to stifle his anger in order to allow his commanding presence as a pitcher to emerge. As one commentator observed, "When [manager] Lavagetto speaks of Pascual's 'new control' he is not alluding completely to the Cuban's ability to hit the corners. He means control of his temper, which in past seasons was one of his chief stumbling blocks.... This season Pascual has been on better terms with his teammates whose errors formerly inflamed him when he was working a game."[32]

Benefits were reaped as a result of Pascual's new sangfroid, which was also attributed to his recent marriage to "a pretty Cuban lass [who] perhaps ... has had a steadying influence on the personable Camilo."[33] His growing comfort on the mound, where he spent so much time grooming the dirt that it caused a furor among opponents, became apparent as he led the AL with 17 complete games and six shutouts, and forged 17 wins accompanied by a 2.64 ERA. He also put many of his teammates to shame when he hit a robust .302 by going 26-for-86. By the conclusion of the 1959 season, his bevy of auspicious statistics gained the attention of Cincinnati Reds executive Gabe Paul, who claimed, "I consider Pascual the best pitcher in the majors."[34] So impressed was Paul by both the Cuban hurler and Killebrew, who had belted 42 home runs to tie Rocky Colavito for the best mark in the American League, that he tendered Griffith an immense offer of $1 million for the two Senators.

Once he reined in his frequently volatile emotions, Camilo Pascual became one of the American League's best pitchers of the early 1960s.

The following season, however, brought mixed results for Pascual as the Senators lowered the curtain on their tenure in Washington. He pitched well enough to earn a place on the AL All-Star team in 1960, but the onset of shoulder trouble after a brawl-related injury in late May limited him to just over 150 innings and a 12–8 record with a 3.03 ERA. When Pascual later made known his desire to pitch winter baseball in his home country, Griffith's ire was raised because the owner wanted his ace to recuperate fully during the offseason. However, Griffith was powerless to stop him from playing winter ball, especially due to the worsening U.S.-Cuban relations at the time. "Castro would make a cause célèbre out of any attempt by Griffith to stop Pascual from pitching in his native land," a club spokesman said.[35] Pascual eventually confessed to being too sore to pitch and passed up the chance to play winter ball, easing Griffith's concerns.

When the Senators moved west, Pascual immediately profited from the winter layoff, and in 1961 he led the AL in strikeouts for the first of three straight years. But in the midst of a personal six-game losing streak, Pascual flung a bat at Allison during a June spat in the Twins dugout. The team's faltering overall performance cost Lavagetto his job shortly thereafter. In an attempt to salvage some good from a season gone amok, Pascual responded positively to the managerial change with a strong finish that left him with 15 victories, eight of which were shutouts, a league-leading total. Employing a refined curveball and pacing himself better in the early innings of his starts, he reached the 20-win level in 1962 and hit a solid .268 with a pair of home runs.

In 1963, Pascual gained career bests in wins (21) and ERA (2.46) despite troubles with a midseason muscle tear near his right shoulder and periodic tenderness in his pitching arm. There was no postseason award for Pascual that year, as Sandy Koufax captured Cy Young Award honors, but Pascual was the Twins' unequivocal ace. In 1964, when he pitched his way onto the American League All-Star team for the fifth time, he knew how much diligence was required to reach the upper echelon among big league hurlers while also withstanding the hazards of pitching at home in Metropolitan Stadium, a venue that had acquired a reputation for being friendly to batters.

Another member of Minnesota's supporting cast, a young Michigander brought up by the Senators in 1959, was destined to ply his trade over the course of the next quarter century. Touted by Yankee manager Casey Stengel in the spring of 1960 as a "young Lefty Grove," Jim Kaat worked his way through Washington's minor league system after signing out of Hope College in Holland, Michigan.[36] Kaat gained management's attention during a stellar 1958 season with Missoula of the Pioneer League, where he logged a 16–7 record, led the league in innings pitched, shutouts, strikeouts, and earned run average, and tied for the most complete games. Meriting a promotion to the Chattanooga club the next year, Kaat was less impressive against Southern League competition yet pitched well enough to warrant a brief, albeit poor, audition with the Senators.

Another bleak trial with the Senators in 1960 inspired little confidence, but Kaat persevered and made the Twins roster in 1961, never to return to the minor leagues again. By 1962, the Twins were singing praises about "their late-blooming curver Kaat" when the Dutchman worked with pitching coach Gordon Maltzberger to enhance his pitch selection.[37] The results of this collaboration were a solid total of 18 victories and 3.14 ERA, and over the next two seasons they teamed up to include a slider in Kaat's repertoire as well as work on taming his control issues. Kaat led the league in hit batsmen and wild pitches for three straight seasons, while he endeavored to reduce the number of home runs he surrendered, especially in home games at Metropolitan Stadium. But Kaat vowed to rely more on the slider in 1964, and by keeping his pitches low — "And by low," Kaat emphasized, "I mean way below the belt" — he enjoyed several lengthy streaks during which he allowed few home runs and felt comfortable on the way to a 17-win season.[38]

Poised to solidify his place in the Twins rotation, Kaat entered 1965 as the number two ace of the staff behind Pascual. He was joined by two veterans who arrived in the Twin Cities via separate trades with the Cleveland Indians. In the May 1963 acquisition of starter Jim Perry, Griffith was betting that the 26-year-old North Carolinian would display the talent that the right-hander showed in 1960 when he led the American League in wins (18), winning percentage (.643), starts (36), and shutouts (4). For the 1963 season, Perry gave the Twins an even 9–9 mark in 35 appearances, 25 of which were starts, and an ERA of 3.74. However, 1964 was a lost year for Perry, who had been relegated to the bullpen from the outset of the campaign when the starting assignments were given to a host of other starters. Perry's bullpen fate was sealed when Griffith again consummated a trade with Cleveland, this time a mid–June deal for starter Jim "Mudcat" Grant, Perry's old Indian teammate. Perry finished 1964 having contributed but a single start and pitching only 65 innings. At that time, the only pitcher named Perry whose future looked bright was Jim's younger brother Gaylord, who was embarking on a career with the San Francisco Giants.

Jim Perry's predicament evolved into an opening for Mudcat Grant, a right-hander acquired in a recent series of deals between Minnesota and Cleveland who would contribute greatly to the Twins. Self-confident of his ability even as a youngster in Lacoochee, Florida, Grant played third base in an adult league. He was later signed by the Indians when a Tribe scout observed how hard Grant was capable of throwing. Upon his breakthrough at the big league level in 1958, Grant split time between starting and relief duties, and over six-plus seasons in Cleveland, the pitcher, who moonlighted as a successful jazz singer, also earned a place on the 1963 American League All-Star squad.

At the time of his trade to the Twins for pitcher Lee Stange and third baseman-outfielder George Banks, Grant had been demoted to the Indians bullpen to correct a problem with his delivery. Not comprehending why he had been shipped to Minnesota, Grant said news of his trade was "devastating," but the Twins perhaps had an ulterior motive in consummating the deal.[39] Virtually unbeatable when he pitched against the Senators and Twins, Grant possessed a dominant 22–6 career record against Griffith-owned clubs, so by adding Grant to the Minnesota roster, "Griffith eliminated this nemesis."[40] Years later, Grant expressed his gratitude to fellow starters Kaat and Pascual as well as to his new catcher Battey for helping him adjust to life with the Twins. That adjustment was facilitated by what Grant perceived as a Twin Cities population that was more accepting of its African American citizenry and less racially "polarized" than other American cities in which he traveled.[41] For the remainder of his first season in Minnesota, Grant solidified his place in the rotation as a control pitcher — roughly one walk issued every four and a half innings in a Minnesota uniform — and compiled an 11–9 record with an impressive 2.82 ERA.

Two other pitchers who worked exclusively out of the bullpen and became integral members of the Twins heading into 1965 also came from outside the Minnesota organization. Purchased by Griffith from National League teams, these relievers were aged journeymen, but their lengthy resumes gave Griffith reason to believe that their experience would benefit the Twins. The first of these was a tall, religious man from Birmingham, Alabama, named Al Worthington, a right-hander who apprenticed with the New York Giants in a career that began at the Polo Grounds in 1953. After stints in Boston, Chicago, Cincinnati, as well as a number of minor league cities, the starter-turned-reliever was at last purchased by the Twins in July 1964. Minnesota author Jim Thielman noted that the reason for Worthington's many address changes stems from the pitcher's deliberate decision to avoid playing for organizations that actively engaged in cheating, especially those that stole signs given by opposing catchers. Even at the risk of spending more time in the minor leagues, Worthington felt more at ease pitching with a clean conscience and for organizations whose ethics were more consistent with his moral values.

Proving that he had legitimate talent as a reliable reliever, Worthington was brilliant as a late-blooming fireman even though his efforts at times fell victim to the Twins' slipshod fielding. In his debut season for the Twins, Worthington registered a minuscule 1.37 ERA in 72⅓ innings, including a streak of 37⅔ innings without allowing an earned run. On the strength of a knuckleball that he added to his pitch inventory, Worthington suddenly found that he thrived with a heavier workload of innings. "Pitching about every other day has been the best thing for me," he said, while also voicing his opinion that the Reds had given up on him too early the previous season. "It always takes me a while to get going in the spring. I pitch my best in hot weather."[42] Meanwhile, Griffith, who at first balked at catchers being allowed to use oversized mitts, now encouraged his own backstops to use a larger glove to better handle Worthington's elusive knuckler.

The second veteran pitcher bought by Griffith was Johnny Klippstein, who had spent most of his career in the National League with the Chicago Cubs and Cincinnati Reds. Klippstein hailed from Washington, D.C., broke in with the Cubs in 1950, and worked as a starter and reliever during his first eight years at the major league level. By 1958, he had virtually become a full-time relief pitcher, and thereafter moved about to several clubs. In 1960 at Cleveland, he led the American League in saves with 14 while playing with fellow Tribe pitchers Mudcat Grant, Jim Perry, and Dick Stigman, with whom he would be reunited a few years hence.

Klippstein's success with the Indians was ephemeral, however, so he was drafted by the expansion Senators, for whom his ERA ballooned to 6.78 in 1961. Traded back to the Reds in 1962, he later landed in Philadelphia, where he rediscovered how to retire batters efficiently. In the early weeks of the 1964 season, he was touted by *The Sporting News* as the Phillies' "bull-pen bellwether," but by June found himself supplanted by Jack Baldschun and Ed Roebuck for critical relief duty.[43] Once again expendable, Klippstein was sold to the Twins and joined Worthington in the Minnesota bullpen, where he nearly equaled his earned run average of the previous year by logging an efficient 1.97 ERA in just over 45 innings. Offering more proof of Griffith's deft hand in personnel moves, Klippstein and Worthington formed a unique tandem of elder statesmen who laid the cornerstone for the Twins' bullpen success in 1965.

## The Twins' Cuban Connection

When the Senators relocated to Minnesota and adopted the new interconnected "TC" logo on their baseball caps, one writer quipped that the letters did not stand for "Twin Cities" but rather "twenty Cubans," so vast their numbers seemed to appear on the team's roster. This is certainly hyperbole, but it is safe to say that Griffith was enthusiastic about mining the United States' offshore southern neighbor for baseball talent, since several key players on the Twins' roster in the early 1960s were natives of Cuba. However, the flow of Cuban players to the Twins and all other major league clubs came to an abrupt halt shortly after Fidel Castro assumed power in Cuba.

Victimized by the same prejudice that barred African Americans from the major leagues until Jackie Robinson's 1947 debut for the Brooklyn Dodgers, Latino players, especially those of dark pigmentation, were excluded from the American and National Leagues. Once Robinson had broken the color line and cleared the way for other minorities to join him, this heretofore untapped source of personnel became a valuable fountainhead from which teams drew integral players in growing numbers. In addition to Pascual, Versalles, and Becquer, the Senators in the years before their move west also had Pedro Ramos, Sandy Valdivielso, and Ossie Alvarez on the roster. Griffith's willingness to sign Cuban players eventually returned handsome rewards when Pascual and Versalles were joined later by Oliva as outstanding American Leaguers. As scout Joe Cambria evaluated young Cuban players and achieved success in furnishing Griffith with worthy major league candidates, the owner was confident in continuing the search for the best players in Cuba. However, world events in 1961 quickly squelched the ability of all baseball teams in the United States to seek players from Cuba.

When the Cuban revolution of January 1959 removed dictator Fulgencio Batista in favor of Fidel Castro, the new Cuban leader abolished professional baseball in favor of amateur baseball, with Castro defending his policy as "the triumph of free baseball over slave baseball."[44] Castro, a former pitcher who ironically had been scouted by Cambria in the early 1940s, survived an overthrow attempt during the Bay of Pigs crisis. When an American trade embargo against Cuba was enacted in 1962 — the year of the frightful Cuban Missile Crisis — economic and diplomatic relations between the United States and Cuba became irretrievably broken. Major league baseball, which had enjoyed unfettered access to Cuban players, was now forced to explore more fully other Latin American venues for foreign talent to stock their franchises. Only when Castro is officially out of office — in 2012 his brother Raul was in charge of Cuba's affairs — will Cuban players again possibly be freely scouted and signed to American contracts as they had been in the 1950s and early 1960s.

In the pre–Castro 1950s, the Senators availed themselves of the opportunity to bring into their organization Cuban players such as Pascual and Versalles, who helped to build the club into a contender; with Oliva's arrival to the Minnesota fold in 1962, the Twins had secured the services of one of the greatest hitters to come from Cuba. Griffith could not have known the aftermath of the Cuban Revolution, but the diligence of scout Cambria had delivered the final ballplayer harvest to the Twins before Griffith and all other club owners were shut out of the Cuban talent market.

## The Skippers in the Dugout

When the Senators vacated the nation's capital following the 1960 season, the man in charge of the players on the field was Harry "Cookie" Lavagetto, a former National League All-Star. Lavagetto took over as the Senators manager in the midst of the team's worst throes of 1957. Already saddled with a 4–16 record at the time Calvin Griffith sacked manager Chuck Dressen, the Senators were faced with the nearly impossible task of gaining any sort of competitive spirit, yet Griffith kept Lavagetto at the helm despite the struggles of that year and the next two seasons. An unexpected surge during the Solon's last campaign in 1960 saw not only a boom in home attendance but the club also placing an astonishing fifth, just three games behind fourth-place Cleveland.

The new Twins of 1961 appeared to be primed for contention, with the nucleus of Allison, Battey, Killebrew, and Pascual now maturing and beginning to realize their potential. In spring training at Orlando, Florida, Lavagetto was delighted by the vision of a youthful

Versalles as his regular shortstop, beaming, "We're ready to play .500 ball right now, and we could be an even bigger surprise than we were a year ago."[45] Unfortunately, just 49 games into the first season at their Minnesota address, an 11-game losing streak put the listless Twins at 19–30, thereby prompting Griffith to send his manager on a paid, week-long furlough in the hope that Lavagetto would return freshened for the remainder of the season. Cookie's stand-in, third-base coach Sam Mele, could fair little better, guiding the Twins to only two wins over the next seven games. Upon Lavagetto's resumption of duty — he even briefly tried his hand coaching first base in an attempt to shake the Twins from their doldrums — the tailspin continued and reached a low point when Allison and Pascual engaged in a physical confrontation in the Twins dugout during a contest in Chicago.

Clearly exasperated by the team's ignominious play, Griffith had exhausted his patience and on June 23 re-instituted Lavagetto's furlough, this time permanently, while putting Mele back in charge. Mele's longevity depended on his ability to right the listing ship while also adhering to Griffith's prescription of using younger minor leaguers from the Twins farm system — Versalles, Rollins, Oliva, Mincher, and Hall, to name a few — to cure the ailing Twins.

Born in 1922 in Astoria, New York, Sabath Anthony Mele had baseball roots that ran through his family tree. Two of his uncles were Al and Tony Cuccinello, the former having spent a brief season with the New York Giants, the latter playing a total of 15 years, mostly in the National League. A fine athlete in his own right, Mele earned a scholarship to New York University, where he lettered in baseball and basketball, and was later signed by the Boston Red Sox organization. He played well enough to earn a spot in the Boston outfield with Ted Williams and Dom DiMaggio, but in the summer of 1949, Mele, a fine defensive outfielder, was traded to Washington. Subsequent stops with several American League teams as well as the Cincinnati Reds rounded out his major league career. He joined Griffith's Senators as a scout in 1959.

Reassigned to become Lavagetto's first-base coach midway through that season, Mele moved to the third-base box in 1961 and was handed the reins of the Twins when Lavagetto was axed. Upon appointment to his new post, Mele swore an oath of loyalty for the obvious reasons. "I intend to work closely with Calvin Griffith," said the rookie manager. "Calvin said whenever I've got anything on my mind, come up in the office and feel free to discuss it."[46]

The best that Mele was able to salvage from the wreckage of the 1961 season was a seventh-place finish in the standings with an overall 70–90 record. But Mele's personal record for the year was a 45–49 record, which indicated that the players had responded positively to Mele, so the new pilot had secured, however tentatively, Griffith's confidence in his leadership. In early October, a satisfied Griffith signed Mele to a one-year contract for 1962. "He proved he can manage," observed Griffith, adding, "Now it's my job to get him some ball players to improve the club for next season."[47]

Griffith allowed Mele the privilege of personally selecting the members of his coaching staff for his first full year. In addition to George Strickland, Floyd Baker, and Ed Fitzgerald, all of whom were chosen to handle the regular players, the manager tabbed former White Sox reliever Gordon Maltzberger to mentor the pitching staff. Maltzberger found much to like in a rotation that included Pascual, Kaat, and Jack Kralick, as the new coach worked in the spring of 1962 with prospects Lee Stange and Billy Pleis.

Featuring a solid starting lineup — each regular logged at least 522 at-bats and 11 home runs — and a pitching staff and defense that topped the American League in several key categories — notably, 53 complete games, 173 double plays, strikeouts (948), and the fewest walks allowed (493) — the Twins stormed to a second-place finish in 1962 with a remarkable 91–71 record, a scant five games behind the Yankees. Fireworks from Twins' bats, led by Killebrew's league-best 48 homers and 126 runs batted in, fueled the offense, whose 798 runs scored trailed only New York's 817. Mele finished runner-up to Angels pilot Bill Rigney in Manager-of-the-Year balloting, while a trio of Twins — Vic Power at first base, and batterymates Earl Battey and Jim Kaat — won Gold Gloves for fielding excellence. Suddenly the future looked very bright in Minnesota.

Griffith had to have been ecstatic over the improvement not only on the field, where the Twins increased their victory total from 70 to 91, but at the box office as well. In their inaugural season in Minnesota, the Twins drew 1,256,722 spectators, but heightened interest in the team due to their bid for the pennant in 1962 encouraged 1,433,116 fans to come to the Met. With perhaps a few minor adjustments, it was well within the realm of possibility that Mele could vault the Twins to the top of the American League and join the 1959 White Sox and the Indians of 1948 and 1954 as the only teams since 1947 to break the Yankee stranglehold over the league.

With great expectations prevailing for 1963, *The Sporting News* immediately prior to Opening Day trumpeted on its front page the headline, "'Fluke' Label on Twins Burns Up Mele," as its lead story noted that the skipper claimed how "we have too much going for

**Catcher Earl Battey's grit earned him four All-Star Game appearances and three Gold Glove awards.**

us" to be concerned about failing to repeat as contenders.[48] Griffith's maturing talent was very much working to his team's advantage, but the club's improved play also drew the attention of their American League rivals. Fearful of a slow start that could cause the Twins to lose ground early in the season, Mele's unease became a self-fulfilling prophecy as Killebrew went down due to a knee injury only a month into the schedule. Another skein of health issues led Mele and Maltzberger to cobble together a pitching staff after losing at least five hurlers at various times. Although the offense was as potent as ever, the faltering start to the season did indeed put Minnesota in a hole from which it did not recover. Their 91 wins against 70 losses in 1963 — which was the same number of victories and one less defeat than a year earlier — demonstrated that the Twins could win consistently over the length of a season.

Although the offensive output for the entire season was actually less than in 1962 — the Twins scored 31 fewer runs in 1963 — they led the league in runs scored with 767, but prominent among the statistics was the reduction in runs allowed. The Twins pitching staff surrendered 602 runs compared to 713 in 1962, and the drop was reflected by an attendant reduction in the team ERA, which went from 3.89 in 1962 to 3.28, good for third best in the American League. For the second year in a row, Killebrew won the AL home run title (45), and his prodigious supporting cast contributed significantly: Bob Allison clubbed 35, rookie Jimmie Hall hit 33, Earl Battey belted 26, and Don Mincher added 17 in his limited playing time. The fielding achievements of three Twins were rewarded with Gold Gloves, Kaat and Power as repeat winners, with Versalles breaking Luis Aparicio's streak of five straight awards at shortstop.

Minnesota's early season swoon cost them dearly, but in fairness, it can not be assumed that the Twins would have improved to the degree necessary to win 105 games to overtake New York for the 1963 pennant. Twins players and coaches were better for the experience, which affirmed Minnesota's status as a legitimate contender. However, the team's failure to improve markedly irked Griffith. The owner acidly approached Mele late in the season to tender a contract offer for 1964. To the consternation of many observers, Griffith "ushered in what looms as an austerity program for 1964 by renewing Manager Sam Mele's contract for one year at a slight reduction in salary.... It was believed that the pay cut was unprecedented in owner-manager relations."[49] In an era during which lawyers and agents were all but absent from contract negotiations, players, managers, and coaches — especially those whose recent track record did not measure up to expectations — had little choice but to capitulate to their team owner and his terms, be they generous or meager. In earlier years, Charles Comiskey and Branch Rickey were among the prominent owners and executives who reluctantly parted with a dollar. In his own miserly ways, Griffith had surely found company with his front-office predecessors.

The owner's penurious act clearly was an insult to a skipper who took his post with no managing experience and had worked barely two seasons as a coach at the major league level. This would not be the last time that Griffith galvanized his reputation as a skinflint; since Mele had equaled his win total of 1962, he was entitled to at least the same salary he had received in his first full season as the Twins pilot. The pejorative "fluke" tag now became a rallying point for Mele and his men, because 1964 promised to be a pivotal year for the whole organization.

Trying to assuage the sting of 1963's shortfall, Mele waxed optimistically the following winter, claiming that the Twins "have the best potential in the American League," but he admitted that the White Sox and Tigers were also prepared to vie for the pennant against the incumbent Yankees.[50] Despite his reputation as a player's manager, Mele, who did not levy a fine against any of his players in 1963, might find occasion to mete out punishment should he feel pressure to keep his charges in line during the coming season.

Prognosticators still viewed the Yankees as the team to beat in 1964, as *Sports Illustrated* felt that "granted improved fielding, the Twins have the pitching and hitting to fight *for the runner-up spot*."[51] Mele and the Twins collectively held their breath in the hope that Killebrew and his knee, which was surgically repaired in December 1963, would be ready for action once spring training concluded. Mele figured to reap the benefits of having up to six pitchers available for starting assignments, but several problems developed within the first six weeks of the new season.

As deep as the Minnesota pitching staff was purported to be, the relievers in particular had developed an annoying penchant for squandering leads. The only hope the Twins had of climbing out their self-inflicted predicaments was through reliance on their trademark offensive power. Mele became hesitant about turning to the bullpen, thus putting added pressure on his starters to deliver more innings. The midseason arrivals of Grant, Klippstein, and Worthington were intended to shore up both the starting and relief corps.

Another situation concerned rookie Tony Oliva, who was showcasing his immense talent at the plate by hitting just below .400 as the month of June approached. When the young Cuban was beaned by Baltimore's Steve Barber — the seventh time that Oliva had been hit or pitched too far inside for Mele's comfort — the manager issued an edict to the offending pitchers that retaliation was imminent, especially for the perpetrator of this latest incident. Mele warned, "Barber is going down the next time we face him. I told Barber he was going down and he will."[52] Already alarmed at the potential injuries that could result from inside pitches, Mele and the Twins were dealt a severe blow when second baseman Bernie Allen tore ligaments in his left knee in the collision with Don Zimmer in mid–June. Fortunately, Jerry Kindall was on hand to step in as Allen's replacement, but he frustrated the Twins with his weak bat.

Although Grant gave the rotation a great dose of stability and Killebrew again was on his familiar torrid home run pace, the Twins endured an ostensibly endless string of roster moves in an effort to keep alive their pennant hopes. As they limped into August, however, Mele found his club in sixth place with a 50–53 record. If the losses weren't exasperating enough, one writer noted that sloppiness on offense and defense was causing much angst for the manager: "Mele fined Rollins for getting picked off base, and he started a policy of extra practice drills after bonehead fielding plays. He gave right fielder Tony Oliva special instructions after he missed a cutoff man with a high throw."[53]

As the losses mounted, Mele feigned concern regarding his employment status, saying, "I haven't had time to worry over rumors about my job. I'm just worrying about winning. If we start winning, all will be okay."[54] A glance at Minnesota's daily record throughout 1964 shows that at no time did the team gain any traction that would have allowed them to move away from the middle of the American League standings. Because the Twins could not forge a winning streak to give them sustained momentum to rise above the .500 mark, the campaign curdled into a long, desultory march to a 79–83 record and a sixth-place finish, 20 games behind the Yankees.

That Mele's tenure survived the Twins' sub-par showing of 1964 was testament to Griffith's hope that his manager would return the team to the form it showed in 1962 and 1963 when it battled for the AL crown. Some rumors indicated that Mele would be moving to Boston to assume leadership of the Red Sox, but Griffith squelched the gossip in October by inking Mele to his 1965 contract. Mele's continued employment with the Twins came at a cost, however, as Griffith forced out pitching coach Maltzberger and two of Mele's other lieutenants, Baker and Fitzgerald.

The post-mortem of 1964 fingered shoddy fielding as the prime culprit for the Twins' demise: "They lost 24 games directly by the margin of unearned runs…. Of those 24, 18 were one-run losses, and six were lost in the final inning…. So it was *when* the Twins made their errors this year, not how many."[55] Fourteen losses were directly attributed to infield errors, but in spite of this prevalent problem handicapping the Twins throughout the season, Mele felt no compunction about the plight of his ill-fated squad, as indicated in this exchange in *The Sporting News*: "Asked if he feels any guilt on his conscience for the Twins' losses and their poor defensive play, Mele replied: 'Not at all.'"[56] This is quite an astounding statement from a manager who in late July had found it necessary to re-introduce his players to baserunning fundamentals usually reserved for the month of March. Apparently his review of the basics should have included more time spent with the fielders in an effort to lower their error totals and improve their glovework in close contests.

Regardless of the excuses offered for the shortcomings just endured, the pressure was patently on Mele to put Minnesota back in hailing distance of the Yankees, who were again favored to repeat as champions of the American League. Because Griffith could more easily replace his manager than make wholesale roster changes, the year 1965 would be a watershed year in Minnesota, with Mele the master of his own destiny.

## The Twins at a Crossroads

The run-up to the 1965 season shows that the Minnesota Twins endured their share of hardships in trying to assemble and maintain a winning combination. Their quest for the formula necessary to dethrone the Yankees was not created in a vacuum, but the Bronx Bombers were not the Twins' sole rival. In the five seasons following their 1959 World Series appearance, the Chicago White Sox under manager Al Lopez fell short against the great Yankee teams of the early 1960s; they remained a constant threat to win close to 90 games per year and nearly captured the flag in 1964, finishing just one game behind New York. The ChiSox also sported newcomers Pete Ward and Gary Peters, who in 1963 won *The Sporting News* Rookie Player of the Year and Rookie Pitcher of the Year honors, respectively. The Detroit Tigers, featuring a potent offense led by Norm Cash, Al Kaline, and Rocky Colavito, proved they could break the 100-win barrier, as they did in 1961, and were now relying on youngsters Mickey Lolich and Denny McLain to become the workhorses of their pitching staff. In Baltimore, the Orioles finished only two games behind the Yankees due in large part to third baseman Brooks Robinson's Most Valuable Player performance in the field and at the plate as well as their "Baby Bird" pitching staff that included the formidable quartet of Steve Barber, Wally Bunker, Dave McNally, and Milt Pappas. Even though the newly-formed Los Angeles Angels were not considered pennant contenders, their young middle infield boasted Jim Fregosi and Bobby Knoop, as the fledgling franchise proved capable of overachieving under the direction of manager Bill Rigney. Lastly, incumbent champion New York had several positions occupied by stars now entering the twilight of their careers, but for every Whitey Ford, Mickey Mantle, and Elston Howard who appeared to be on the wane there was an Al Downing, Jim Bouton, Tom Tresh, Joe Pepitone, and Jake Gibbs waiting to fill the void.

The Twins had taken several major steps forward from 1961 to 1963, but after these years of progress, 1964 was an unpleasant turnabout. Griffith came a cropper with his transaction dealing away Power, as the infield defense suffered. Fortunately, an ample number of pieces to the Twins' foundation were in place. In an era that lacked freedom of player movement due to the reserve clause, Griffith could rely upon those players to continue in his service until such time as he saw fit to trade or release anyone on the Twins roster.

Griffith received an excellent return on his investments in Killebrew, Allison, and Kaat, all of whom transitioned from Washington to Minnesota and remained with the team through the 1970 season. While they may have been frustrated at times by having to shift some players to several positions, managers Lavagetto and Mele exploited the versatility of Killebrew and Allison by using them in the infield or the outfield as circumstances dictated. In the years since Killebrew became a full-time player in 1959, it became apparent that he was the superstar around whom the rest of the lineup would be built. More talent still in Minnesota's farm system in the early 1960s had yet to emerge, and those young players would be needed to sustain the Twins' ascent.

Owing much to the diligence of scout Joe Cambria, Griffith mined a quarry of Cuban talent in Pascual, Versalles, and Oliva. While Pascual's star was beginning to dim by 1965, he was the mainstay of the pitching rotation in the Twins' formative years; so great was his talent that earlier in the decade his name earned mention alongside that of Sandy Koufax, whose own meteoric rise as a pitcher was then in progress. That Griffith was offered $500,000 each for Pascual and Killebrew just as they began to gain footholds in the big leagues spoke volumes about the degree to which some other teams coveted the pair's potential.

On the trading front, Griffith proved a shrewd dealer in the acquisitions of Battey, a top-flight catcher second only to the Yankees' Elston Howard, and pitcher Jim Perry, whose best days on the mound in Minnesota still lay ahead. Mudcat Grant would yield a huge albeit ephemeral payoff in 1965, and relievers Klippstein and Worthington, both old enough to be seemingly past their prime, continued to produce when it was reasonable to expect less of them.

While the great strides made by the Senators and Twins from the hopeless years of the mid–1950s to the earnest promise of the early 1960s was reflected in the clicking of the turnstiles at Metropolitan Stadium, the reign of Clark and Calvin Griffith's ownership had not known the joy of celebrating a pennant-clinching since the throes of the Great Depression. Demonstrating that he was not much of a prophet, Mele felt that 1964 would herald the arrival of the Twins as champions of the American League, and had his club availed itself of more competence afield, his statement may have rung true. Whether the Twins would contend as they had in 1962 and 1963 or again suffer the frustration of 1964, nobody, least of all Mele, knew what 1965 held for the fortunes of the Twins.

# 3

## *"Sealing the Yankees' Tomb"*

The harshness of the Minnesota winter of early 1965 presaged the ill weather that would plague the state through much of the year. Camilo Pascual, adjusting to the cold climate in early January, "survived a week of snow and ice plus temperatures 15 degrees below zero — an earlier than normal wintry blast even in the land of 10,000 frozen lakes."[1] Surprisingly, the Twins ace and his family found the cold to be bearable at their new home in Bloomington, with the children enjoying playtime in the snow, before Pascual and his teammates were scheduled to retreat to the warmth of Orlando, Florida, in late February to prepare for the upcoming season.

The racial divide between blacks and whites in America was still very much in evidence as major league players headed to their spring training camps in Palm Springs, California, and across Arizona and Florida. The Deep South was reeling from the 1963 murder of civil rights activist Medgar Evers and the bombing of a black church in Birmingham, Alabama, the same city in which blacks, protesting over their right to enfranchisement, were set upon by police, German shepherds, and fire hoses. In 1964, a trio of civil rights workers who had endeavored to help blacks register to vote was slain in Mississippi, and on February 21, 1965, the radical voice of black independence, Malcolm X, was assassinated in Harlem. Weeks later in early March, police in Selma, Alabama, violently confronted peaceful black protesters who sought to advance their cause for voting rights by marching to Montgomery to deliver a petition to Governor George Wallace. These incidents were an ominous precursor to more violence and bloodshed that was to follow in the months and years ahead.

Segregation of black and white ball players in spring training for baseball teams training in Florida had been a long-standing problem. Earlier in the decade, *The Sporting News* implied that the burden was not on federal authorities to ameliorate tension resulting from the attempted integration of boarding accommodations. "There is an obligation on the part of both baseball and of the Negro players to be aware of what at any time could be a delicate situation," the publication editorialized. "It is to be hoped that baseball will meet such continuing issues forthright but with calmness and diplomacy."[2]

Against the backdrop of this strident time, the Twins had been attempting to force hotel facilities in Orlando to cater to all of their players, regardless of race. After years of tolerating segregated quarters, the team was at last able to house the entire roster at the Cherry Plaza Hotel for spring training of 1965 when the hotel's management acquiesced to hosting black guests. No longer would minority members of the Twins be obliged to sleep and dine separately from their white teammates. However, Minnesota was the last club in the major leagues to adopt this integrated policy for pre-season camp.

But any camaraderie instilled through integration at the Cherry Plaza was not apparent as the Twins opened camp to all players on March 2. Zoilo Versalles was harangued by trainer Doc Lentz to shed the weight the shortstop had gained over the winter. Don Mincher requested a trade when he learned of manager Sam Mele's decision to move Harmon Killebrew to first base. Mudcat Grant — who was not reluctant to speak his mind and was still stung by a racially-tinged incident with an Indians coach in 1960 — carped about what he perceived to be preferential treatment that the team lavished on Killebrew and Bob Allison.[3]

On the field, the Twins seemed to be in a sleepy state in the early days of spring training. Despite new coach Billy Martin's insistence that the lethargy would be broken once exhibition play began, problems lingered into the middle of March. As one writer commented, "The Twins' play on the field deteriorated, and as [owner Calvin] Griffith quickly noted, they not only lost games but lost them with uninspired and inattentive play."[4] The torpor reached its low point in the exhibition schedule when Versalles was pulled out of a game by Mele for failing to hustle after a groundball that went by the shortstop for a single. Entering the dugout, Versalles engaged his manager in a screaming match that cost the Cuban a $300 fine by the time the shouting ended. Using a different approach, Martin worked closely with Versalles and learned how to coerce and cajole his pupil, depending on the circumstances. "[Martin] coaxed him and blasted him to his face, but he was always sure to be alone with the temperamental shortstop when he gave him hell," Gene Schoor described Martin's approach. "Versalles couldn't take a dressing down in front of anybody else, particularly in front of anybody playing ball with him."[5]

With the Twins' state of affairs hardly propitious as the opening of the regular season approached — they lost 15 of 26 exhibition games — the prognostications of baseball fans and the sports media for the 1965 campaign foretold a gloomy season in the Twin Cities. Canvassing by *The Sporting News* found that among the Baseball Writers' Association of America and the 3,500 fans who offered their predictions on the pennant race, Minnesota would rank no higher than fifth place in the American League standings according to the writers, with the fans forecasting only a sixth-place finish for the Twins. Both blocs of voters maintained that the Yankees would remain the team to beat, followed by the White Sox and Orioles. Delivering a brutally frank assessment of Minnesota's chances of contending for the pennant, *Sports Illustrated* observed that "they are trying again with virtually the same club they had last year. Such curious optimism could reflect the Scandinavian stubbornness the Twins have been exposed to in Minnesota."[6] The team's "cornucopia of power" was praised by the magazine, but the Twins' penchant for failing to hit in the clutch and problematic fielding were causes for concern. While Minnesota had exhibited so much promise in 1962 and 1963, but with few corrective measures taken to counteract the regression of 1964, the venerable periodical ultimately concluded, "The Twins are impossible to figure out."[7] Even a column in an early April edition of the hometown *Minneapolis Tribune* succinctly summarized the forecast: "Yankees should win American League pennant again for sixth straight year."[8]

More aggressive baserunning had been added to the Twins' attack in 1964, and Mele planned on continuing to employ this asset in the new year. Despite the potential for more runners to be thrown out trying to steal or attempting to take an extra base on singles or long hits, Mele was willing to allow Martin, now coaching at third base and very likely to put his spurs to Twins on the basepaths, to exercise his best judgment when deciding if runners should be advanced in riskier situations. Never known for their overall team speed and having grown reliant on their home run power, the Twins were now intent on catching opposing defenses off-guard. But it remained to be seen whether this tactic would be of benefit to the perennially muscle-bound Twins.

While there had been few changes to the roster since the end of 1964, another new coach was present to guide the pitching staff in the wake of Gordon Maltzberger's departure. Johnny Sain was added to Mele's group of coaches when Griffith signed him following the 1964 season. The former pitcher came with an impressive resume.

As a cornerstone of the old Boston Braves pitching staff in the late 1940s, Sain was a four-time 20-game winner from 1946 to 1950. He pitched mostly out of the Yankee bullpen when he was traded to New York in 1951 for $50,000 and a young prospect named Lew Burdette. Sain became pitching coach of the Kansas City Athletics for the 1959 season, served the New York Yankees in that capacity from 1961 through 1963, and had taken a year off from the game when the Twins contacted him to replace Maltzberger. So valued was Sain for his leadership that in 1964 a group of Yankee pitchers, including Whitey Ford, petitioned the New York front office to bring Sain back to the Bronx fold when the hurlers fell on hard times.

But in 1965 the Twins became the beneficiaries of Sain's instruction and their pitching staff would respond positively. Reliever Johnny Klippstein praised Sain for the manner in which he advised his men, whereby "he would plant the idea" and "let you make your own decision" regarding pitch selection under a variety of game situations.[9]

Although Sain's tenure in Minnesota was short-lived, the guidance he furnished the pitching staff in the first of his two seasons there was integral to the Twins' success.

With spring training and the lackluster results of the exhibition schedule now a memory, the Twins confronted the regular season that lay ahead. The roster was comprised of veterans who formed the team's solid foundation and was augmented by a group of rookies who would make their mark in due time. Arriving in Minneapolis for the campaign's inaugural contest, the club was greeted by inclement weather, but the opener against the Yankees was now the primary focus, come rain or shine.

## Opening Day — Barely

The snow and ice that Pascual left behind when he departed for spring training still awaited him upon his return from Florida. Movement of the calendar from March to April had little ameliorative affect on weather conditions in the Twin Cities. At Metropolitan Stadium, Dick Ericson and his grounds crew removed nearly two feet of snow from the field in mid–March, cleared ten inches that had been deposited by another storm on March 27, and then had to rid much of the field of seven inches of ice. All manner of implements — Minnesota Loaders, shovels, flamethrowers, and pickaxes among the panoply of tools — was used to miraculously ready the ballpark in time for the April 12 opener. Frozen precipitation had been dealt with at the Met, but the first game of the season was nonetheless fraught with another peril: massive flooding caused by melting snow and ice beyond the bounds of the stadium itself.

Flooding across the region — indeed, the entire state of Minnesota — reached epic proportions, as three Twins requested the services of radio station WCCO's news helicopter to pick them up from their stranded location near the stadium and deliver them to the Met. So wretched had conditions become that a *Tribune* editorial cartoon of mid–April resorted to gallows humor when it featured a map depicting the entire state of "Lake Minnesota" as the newest member in the chain of Great Lakes.

Providing the Twins' Opening Day opposition were the New York Yankees, fresh off their exhibition game against the Houston Astros in the brand new, climate-controlled Astrodome, nee Harris County Domed Stadium. After the Yankees played before 47,000 fans who luxuriated in the comfort of the 71-degree environment of the ultra-modern ballpark, they and the Twins opened their official 1965 AL schedule in front of 15,388 fans who braved 44-degree weather. Many fans, faced with flooding problems of their own, either could not reach the Met or decided that it was easier to stay home and listen to Herb Carneal's play-by-play on the radio. The Twins prevailed, 5–4 in extra innings, despite a costly error by rookie Cesar Tovar that allowed the tying run to score in the ninth, an ugly reminder of 1964. But the third baseman redeemed himself by rapping a game-winning single with two out in the bottom of the eleventh inning.

In a poignant moment that boded well for the team, starting pitcher Jim Kaat consoled Tovar after the infielder's miscue. "The whole Twin club talked for a week about the way Kaat conducted himself after a ninth-inning error that might have broken the back of a lesser man," as Kaat's mature demeanor suggested how valuable an expression of forgiveness would be to the team's morale.[10] Tovar had been flawless in five fielding chances earlier in the game after he replaced Rich Rollins, and the little Venezuelan — he was nearly identical in height and build to Versalles — was grateful to be able to atone for the error in his major league debut.

The core of the Twins was built around players such as Pascual, Killebrew, Oliva, Hall, Versalles, and Allison, but 1965 was a new season that presented its own new challenges. These players captured most of the attention during the past few years, but now men such as Tovar, who were either new to the franchise or appeared to be relegated to subordinate roles in manager Sam Mele's overall plans, unexpectedly would be transformed into the "hero of the day" by making key contributions to Twins' victories. As the season progressed, clutch hits and pitching performances would be supplied by those thought to be foreordained to spend much time on the bench or in the bullpen.

Roughly one month into the new campaign, Minnesota's winning ways generated a momentum that the club was capable of sustaining. Later Kaat recalled that his roommate on the road, Klippstein, exuded confidence in the Twins' ability to overtake the reigning American League champions despite the fact that the new season was just a few weeks old. "All of a sudden we started winning series, two out of three, three out of four," said Kaat. "Meanwhile, the Yankees were having problems."[11] As the victories piled up, this positive attitude coalesced into a *sine qua non* that toughened this group of Twins. Although home runs were still a salient feature of Minnesota's attack, a better balance and blend of offensive and defensive capabilities outweighed the reliance on the long ball over the course of the season. In his assessment of the club's change in its approach, author Jim Thielman accurately described this improvement when he wrote: "As it turned out, a murderers' row wasn't as vital as dreamed because the 1965 Twins were no longer relying on power to win games. They won with pitching, base running, a bit more power than top contenders Chicago and Baltimore, and their tag-team of heroes."[12]

In the case of the Twins, "tag-team" was not used as a pejorative but actually became a fitting description that was applied in the most endearing sense. Just as rookie Tovar atoned for his miscue on Opening Day, another reserve player came to the rescue shortly thereafter. When Earl Battey was hurt in the April 23 game against the Tigers in Detroit, backup catcher Jerry Zimmerman took over behind the plate and capped a rally that enabled the Twins to overcome a five-run deficit by plating Killebrew with the winning run in the 8–6 victory. Few teams can ever claim to have two excellent catchers on their roster. While Battey was widely acclaimed as one of the best in the league, the light-hitting Zimmerman proved to be invaluable in filling the void created when Battey missed playing time due to an array of injuries. Over the course of the Twins' first 70 games, they compiled a record of 31–8 when Zimmerman substituted for Battey. The Omaha, Nebraska, native may have been Minnesota's most valuable reserve by imbuing the pitching staff with the same confidence the hurlers felt when Battey was behind the plate. Zimmerman, who hit a total of three homers in his entire eight-year major league career, may have seemed out of place in the Twins' power-laden lineup, but the modesty he exhibited in his work ethic made him a perfect fit in a clubhouse that was populated by gifted yet low-key stars like Oliva, Kaat, and Killebrew.

By the end of April, when two other rookies, Rich Reese and Cuba native Sandy Valdespino, added timely hits in limited duty, Mele was growing comfortable in relying on his bench not only when an offensive boost was needed but also as defensive adjustments had to be made on the field. "We have pinch-hitters who are good at getting the bat on the ball," said the manager. "Last year, our pinch-hitters were striking out too much. Valdespino is a relaxed hitter, good at coming off the bench. He and Reese hit to any part of the field. Frank Kostro showed last year he is good at coming off the bench to hit."[13] The season was but a few weeks old, yet already Mele boasted, "This could be the best bench we ever had, by far."[14]

Not to be outdone by the rookies, veterans Bob Allison and Jimmie Hall slugged opponents' pitching as expected, and Mudcat Grant also pitched well. Despite the early success, Mele's managing skill was being taxed because of a torrent of injuries of varying severity. Bernie Allen, the promising second baseman whose knee had been maimed the previous June, stayed with the club through most of spring training but was placed on the disabled list before the season commenced. Meanwhile, infielders Kindall and Rollins, and pitchers Pascual, Worthington, and Jerry Fosnow all were sidelined at different times with minor ailments.

Kaat's statement about the windfall of Twin victories by the second month of the campaign was unequivocal. After posting an 8–3 record for the month of April, which included a triumph over the White Sox on the final day of that month, the Twins split the series in Chicago, took two of three games against Baltimore, and won three of four against the White Sox after returning home from an eleven-game road trip. They finished May with a 19–12 record for the month and were 27–15 overall, which was good for a slim half-game lead atop the American League. The only "series" they lost was a single game at home against

Detroit on April 15. Not until their offense went virtually silent in Cleveland in early June did they finally lose a series in earnest, dropping three of four games to the Tribe. While Minnesota did not compile any lengthy winning streaks, they nonetheless eschewed the pitfalls of losing skeins that can stall any team in its quest to move up in the standings or maintain a lead it has built. Until the All-Star break in mid–July, the Twins suffered only a pair of three-game losing streaks. Although they did not put a lot of distance between themselves and their nearest pursuers, occupying first place was still preferable to any other position in the standings.

The Twins manager pointed to the third base coach's box to explain the reason for the surge in the club's competitiveness and its spirit. "You have to give a lot of credit to [Billy] Martin. He makes up his mind and goes with his decisions. We've scored a lot of runs because of that," said Mele.[15] Martin attributed his perspicacity to the tutelage of his former New York manager, Casey Stengel, who instructed Martin to observe how opposing outfielders were positioned in order to quickly evaluate baserunner situations.

The key player who was taking full advantage of Martin's mentoring was Versalles, whose game both in the field and at the plate was flourishing. Kudos flowed easily from Mele, who said Versalles "is thinking and playing hitters better than I've ever seen him," while by mid–June Martin was "on record as thinking Versalles can become the most valuable player in the American League."[16] Mele had positioned Versalles defensively in 1964, and with Martin now acting as infield coach, he, too, was making the shortstop more alert not just in knowing where to station himself against certain hitters but in simply throwing to

first base. Versalles felt "he has improved specifically in the routine business of throwing overhanded to first base whenever possible, instead of using his side-arm flip. That flip has resulted in throws in the dirt because it sinks."[17]

Whether Versalles's confidence in the field translated to success at the plate, or vice versa, is a moot point. Martin's tutelage had enabled the shortstop's offensive talent to meld with his defensive skills, now seemingly adjusted, at the right time for the Twins, so he truly had become a complete player worthy of MVP consideration. Enhancing Versalles's credentials were a pair of 12-game hitting streaks, even though he admitted to being too much of a free swinger at times and sought to reduce his strikeout totals.

Earl Battey, when he was healthy enough to play regularly, raised his average to .317 by early June, but then injuries to other players began to mount, with Battey again stricken with arm trouble. June found the Twins being hunted by a trio of con-

**The mercurial Billy Martin left his imprint on the Minnesota Twins as both coach and manager from 1965 to 1969.**

tenders, as Baltimore, Cleveland, and Detroit all jockeyed for position to remain in the pennant chase. Mele prophetically stated, "I don't think you can win a pennant these days with a nine-man lineup. It takes twenty-four or twenty-five players to win a pennant. You have to rest people, substitute others. No one on this team is going to play *every* game."[18] In what one scribe labeled as a "tragic month" for the Twins, Mele was once forced to use a jumble of players whose only apparent qualification to be put in the lineup was the presence of any trace of good health. Frustrated by the dwindling number of available Twins, the manager at one point quipped, "I might play one of the sportswriters … or the bat boy."[19]

Casualties were soon found among both pitchers and position players in frightening numbers. Knee, leg, and hip ailments played hob with Versalles, Hall, Oliva, Grant, and Kindall; Pascual was hindered by a back muscle problem; rookie pitcher Dave Boswell was struck down with a bout of mononucleosis; and Battey shuffled in and out of the lineup multiple times with leg and arm woes. Mele had little choice but to employ the full complement of the roster, in some instances fielding those players who were hurting the least.

The deluge of injuries did not escape the notice of Griffith as the mid–June trading deadline approached and aspirations to the pennant persisted, but the owner was more inclined to seek help from the organization's Triple-A affiliate in Denver. In his role as personnel director, Griffith sought a middle infielder and another pitcher to provide depth and flexibility to shore up Mele's decimated lineup. Jim Merritt and Gary Roggenburk were the favorites among the preferred hurlers eligible for recall. Bernie Allen seemed anxious to resume infield duties in Minnesota, although Griffith was more interested in employing Allen at third base instead of second, the better to protect Allen from having to make the double-play pivot on his newly-rehabilitated knee.

To clear at least one space on the current roster, Griffith considered waiving Frank Kostro, who proved to be a weaker hitter than originally forecast, but the owner was very reluctant to send third-string catcher John Sevcik through the waiver wire in order to clear him for a trip to the minors. The curious circumstances surrounding Sevcik's presence on the Twins roster were a result of the bonus system in place at the time the young catcher joined the organization. Sevcik, a former catcher for the University of Missouri, was brought to spring training by the Twins, who decided to keep him, along with Boswell, on the 25-man, big league squad. In order to protect Sevcik and Boswell, who were both classified as bonus players, from being claimed by another team, they had to remain on the Minnesota roster for the entire season. They could only be optioned to a minor league team in their organization if they cleared waivers, the chances of which were not likely to happen since another team could claim either promising young player for a mere $8,000. A third bonus player, who was not subject to the same restriction and was farmed out for seasoning, was a youngster from Panama named Rod Carew.

For all intents and purposes, Boswell and Sevcik were stuck on the roster; while the former did get to pitch on occasion, the latter was more of a handicap than an asset to Mele. Zimmerman was a reliable substitute for Battey, and other players filled in at positions around the infield and the outfield, but as a one-dimensional player, catcher Sevcik was consigned to a fate of interminable time on the Twins bench. Surely, the manager could have used the roster spot for another infielder or utility man to give Versalles or others a periodic rest. Thus Mele was burdened with a young backstop whose only chance to play appeared to be if and when both Battey and Zimmerman were unavailable. Defending

Sevcik's place on the roster, Griffith liked the potential he saw in the Missouri alumnus and anticipated the day when Battey would no longer be the starting backstop. "We can't risk losing Sevcik right now," Griffith said of his desire to keep the new receiver. "We need catching development at the top level and all the way through our organization. Sevcik and Ron Wojciak … are our two top young catchers. Besides, we need three catchers with the Twins. With Earl Battey susceptible to hand injury, we need Sevcik to back Jerry Zimmerman in an emergency."[20]

For the Twins to acquire help in the infield or on the mound, Griffith considered making a trade with another American League team whose place in the standings was in the second division. However, he found that Yankees infielder Phil Linz was not available, and Boston's Frank Malzone, rumored in the press to be coveted by Mele, was deemed too old and too high-priced to be of interest to Griffith. "We'd have to trade with contenders to [get] help," concluded Griffith, adding, "Maybe it's better to keep what we have—first place—and let the other clubs suffer with us."[21]

The pat hand that Griffith seemed resigned to play did have one advantage for the pitching staff. Jim Perry had been all but ignored in the Twins bullpen, but the veteran was quietly accumulating a trove of quality statistics in the first half of the season. After pitching a scant 65 innings in 1964, Perry was "the 28-year-old right-handed pitcher whom the Twins couldn't give away this spring," but in his few early appearances in 1965, he had won all three of his decisions and had fashioned a superb 1.69 ERA.[22] A Minneapolis sportswriter noted that Perry had twice been placed on the waiver wire the previous season for the purpose of sending him to Denver, but the Twins revoked them when the pitcher was claimed by other clubs. Perry's tenuous position had been enhanced because Allen was still rehabilitating his knee at Denver and was not yet ready to rejoin the Twins. By persevering at a time when so few others expressed faith in him, Perry secured his place on the Twins roster and would deliver an even greater payoff in a few short years.

As the Twins held the slimmest of leads for most of June—usually no more than one and a half games—the month also witnessed a signal event in baseball history, as the collective ownership of the major league franchises attempted to curb their appetite for spending enormous sums of money on young talent they needed to replenish their farm systems. By inaugurating a new process of selecting amateur players while guaranteeing clubs the right to negotiate exclusively with their draftees, team owners hoped to end the decades-long bidding wars between the more wealthy teams endeavoring to attract the best new players to their organizations. The concept of a draft to select high school and collegiate players was not unanimously popular among the major league franchises, but such a process would provide a new method of more fairly, to say nothing of more cheaply, assimilating young players into the world of professional baseball.

## Solving the Failure to Curtail Bonuses

In their excellent summation of the quest for talent prior to the implementation of baseball's first draft of amateur players in 1965, the authors of *The Baseball Draft: The First 25 Years* make abundantly clear that problems which had existed for decades in the signing of college and high school players now reached a crescendo. The time had come for major league teams to collectively devise a new method of choosing which players they wished to pursue while at once limiting the outlay of cash that they would spend in the chase for the young men who would constitute the foundation of their future rosters.

Three extant dilemmas confronted the big leagues as a new system was being debated. First, the New York Yankees, dominant for years over the American League, showed few indications that their reign was ebbing, their losses in the 1963 and 1964 World Series notwithstanding. No team before or since held sway over a sport in the manner by which the Yankees had a virtual chokehold over the league. The signing of the best new prospects and execution of shrewd trades by a diligent front office assured the Bronx Bombers of continued supremacy.

Second, the Los Angeles Angels had paid a bonus to a University of Wisconsin player that exceeded the salaries of some of the game's best-known players. When Rick Reichardt hit college pitching at better than .400 in 1962 and 1963, he drew so much attention from major league scouts that a bidding war for his services ensued between two club owners, Charlie Finley of the Kansas City Athletics and Gene Autry of the Angels. Despite Finley's last-minute attempt to trump Autry's offer, Reichardt signed with Los Angeles for the then staggering bonus of $205,000, an astounding sum for a player just out of college. The Reichardt signing indicated that the community of team owners had reached a critical mass in their financial extravagance with bonuses. Through the actions of some of their wealthier brethren, owners repeatedly failed to exercise any fiscal restraint. The solution, they believed, lie in measures to eliminate the internecine bidding for new talent and instead grant exclusive negotiating rights to the solitary club drafting a given player.

Lastly, the minor league system, once well-stocked by over 400 teams that supported the 16 major league clubs in the late 1940s, had dwindled by the early 1960s to about 120, a number that was in danger of diminishing further. If action was not taken to limit the spending for bonuses and ensure the viability of the minor leagues to furnish an arena where new players could adequately prepare to play at the major league level, then the entire support system for baseball would be at risk of collapsing. As Allan Simpson of *The Baseball Draft* wrote:

> Competitive balance, one of baseball's time-honored virtues, was seriously threatened. Teams — rich teams — were spending more and more to acquire the best amateur talent, and the more they spent, the more successful they became. The smaller-market teams were committing financial suicide to keep abreast. And the more everyone misspent on raw, unproven amateur prospects, the less there was to prop up a sagging development system.[23]

In 1946, the American and National leagues imposed a spending cap on bonuses that any single team could use to sign a prospect, but by 1957 self-enforcement of this rule had become ineffectual because player personnel directors ignored the regulation or otherwise sidestepped it to spend as freely as they desired. Another rule mandated that new players signed to a bonus exceeding a certain threshold were forced to remain on the major league roster for two seasons before they could be sent to the minor leagues. The reasoning behind this stipulation held that if a signee was deemed to be worth such an extravagant bonus, then he should be able to assume a place on his big league team with no break-in period in the minors allowed. If the newcomer showed himself to be incapable of performing after two years, only then could he be farmed out without being exposed to a waiver claim by a rival team.

In Harmon Killebrew's situation with the Washington Senators in the 1950s, he was a prime example of the unintended consequences of this rule. Killebrew had been signed in June 1954 for a $30,000 bonus, an astronomical sum at that time, and was thus obliged to remain with the Senators because his payment exceeded the $4,000 threshold. Barely 18 years old, Killebrew was planted on the far end of the Washington bench, where he waited until August — by which time the Solons had long been eliminated from the pennant race — before his name appeared as a starter on manager Charlie Dressen's lineup card. If Killebrew had been given the opportunity to play every day in the minors from the inception of his professional career until he had been given sufficient time to hone his craft, he likely would have been able to become a full-time major leaguer in 1956 or 1957. Killebrew was not sent down to the minors until 1956 and then spent parts of the next three seasons on both the minor and major league levels. Over the course of the first five years of his career, Killebrew collected only 57 hits and a .224 average in the 113 games he played for the Senators. Had he served a proper apprenticeship at lower levels of the Senators franchise in a more timely fashion, Killebrew's development would less likely have been retarded, and he could have made an impact in Washington at least by 1957.

At the conclusion of the 1957 season, major league teams reached an accord that allowed bonus players to be sent to the minors without risk to the signing club, and a year later clubs imposed a draft of unrestricted minor-league players who did not make the 40-man major league roster upon completion of one year at the lower level. From 1959 to 1964, various amendments to the maximum bonus size and first-year restrictions were introduced, but the rise in the totals of money spent for the best prospects continued unabated, not least of which was the $1.5 million spent in 1961 by the brand-new Houston Colt .45s of the National League.

Fearing an ensuing debacle should other clubs attempt to keep pace with the nascent Houston franchise, American League officials encouraged commissioner Ford Frick to implement a draft of amateur players, but the idea stalled over trepidation that doing so would expose the sport to a government investigation. "If it is illegal to put all the kids in a pool, let's find out why it is illegal," one AL official said, who implored that "the commissioner should concentrate on nothing else but this for the rest of the summer. We will be bankrupt unless something is done."[24]

By January 1964, Lee MacPhail, the Baltimore Orioles general manager who originally had been the first-year rule's biggest proponent but then soured on its viability, now championed the instituting of an amateur draft. Team owners in both leagues acquiesced to the creation of a draft, pending the adoption of a formal means to implement such a plan, and in August, team and league officials met to discuss a proposal which featured a selection system already employed by other major sports. Following an ironic dearth of support in the American League, where only two teams favored a draft, by late October the reluctance to embrace a new selection process — including Calvin Griffith's abstention in a vote taken that month — gave way to new groundswell of support. With the proposal recast in a favorable light during the annual winter meetings in December, baseball was at last ready to proceed with, as *The Sporting News* referred to it, "the new player recruiting setup."[25]

After much wrangling among the major league clubs, 19 of the 20 major league clubs finally agreed to the concept, and in early December 1964, the National Association of minor leagues, whose assent was necessary to ratify the plan, gave its unanimous support to make the draft a reality. As Simpson described it, "All eligible talent would be placed in a common pool with every team given an equal opportunity to select in turn. When a team selected a player, it would gain exclusive rights to negotiate with him."[26] With inter-club haggling now expunged, the inaugural draft was slated to take place on June 1, 1965, with each club — alternating between American and National League — choosing in the reverse order of its won-lost record of the previous season. Many baseball executives delighted in achieving the goal of elimination of bidding wars and curbing large bonus payouts through the implementation of a controlled process.

On the day of the first draft, Charlie Finley of the Athletics tabbed Robert James "Rick" Monday, an outfielder at Arizona State University, as the number one selection. Monday had just completed a fine season at ASU to help the Sun Devils win the College World Series, but his signing bonus with the Athletics of $104,000 was considerably less than the amount commanded by Reichardt a year earlier. The first draftee had no regrets about the new system despite the fact that it favored the team by having removed any bargaining advantage — other than holding out — that players once enjoyed.

Satisfied with the deal he had struck with Monday, Finley crowed, "The fact that we signed Monday for $100,000 showed that Kansas City did not attempt to take advantage of the youngster in the draft."[27] However, in 1990, Reichardt stated that as he was about to commit to signing with the Angels in the year before the draft, "At the eleventh hour, Finley basically doubled his offer, which put it much, much more than what I signed for."[28] If Finley was ready to commit well in excess of $200,000 for Reichardt, there is no reason to believe that the Athletics owner would not have been willing to spend in excess of $104,000 for a player whom he believed was the best available amateur. For Finley to claim that he had no intention to shortchange Monday was typical of his bombastic nature and representative of his fatuous disingenuousness.

Monday's perspective was perhaps a bit skewed as well. At the time he commented that the draft had not "made much difference" to him, he did so with the benefit of hindsight and the comforting knowledge that he had spent 19 seasons in the big leagues. Had he not played in the majors as long as he did and thus been enriched with the financial rewards he earned over those years — or had he become a virtual non-player in the manner of the Twins' Sevcik — he may have wished for the higher signing bonus that any number of teams in 1965 would have offered for his services.

Another opinion of the draft was expressed by one of Monday's Arizona State teammates who was also chosen by the Athletics in 1965. Sal Bando, who was named the most valuable player of that year's College World Series, believed that he profited from the new selection system. Years later, Bando looked back on his own situation and said that rather than money being of utmost importance in the negotiations with the team that drafted him, he viewed his own career development as the key factor. His selection by a franchise lacking in quality players meant that solid performances in the Kansas City farm system would earn him a quicker trip to the roster of a major league club whose needs were many and whose overall talent was thin.[29]

As draft day of June 1965 approached, Twins minor league director Sherry Robertson — who was Calvin Griffith's brother — prepared to make selections for the organization; following the advice he received from a trio of scouts, the Twins chose shortstop Eddie Leon, an 18-year-old sophomore at the University of Arizona. After seeing the bonus that Monday commanded, Leon was a bit more modest in his request, but he frankly stated,

"Unless I'm offered considerably more than $20,000, I will stay in school."[30] Although Minnesota allocated $300,000 for the 52 players they drafted, the Twins and Leon could not reach an agreement, so he returned to Arizona and was drafted in 1967 by Cleveland.

Although the Twins failed to sign Leon, by making him their first choice in the new draft, the Twins demonstrated that they were planning for a day in the future, perhaps three to four years away, when Zoilo Versalles would be considered past his prime and in need of replacement. With the position of shortstop being critical to holding any team's defense together, grooming a candidate to step in when Versalles was no longer capable of playing up to his standards was essential to the Twins maintaining the winning edge they worked so hard to attain. Leon was an experienced college player who had the potential to move more quickly up the minor league ladder than the average collegian and reach the major leagues by 1968, but the Twins' loss of Leon became the Indians' gain two years later. The Twins' cognizance of their constant shuffling of infielders not only led them to take a chance with Leon but also prompted them to draft a third baseman with their fourth-round pick. Graig Nettles of San Diego State University did sign with Minnesota. He ultimately reached the Twins' big league roster in 1967 for a handful of at-bats, but the left-handed-hitting infielder was destined for fame in venues beyond Metropolitan Stadium.

The new amateur draft became a reality at a critical juncture in baseball's history. Since the importation of talent from Cuba was virtually halted, baseball development directors wasted little time in training their sights on a fresh source of players in other parts of the Caribbean. In early 1963, Robert Cantwell reported in *Sports Illustrated* that the Dominican Republic had become the new wellspring of Latin American players, but the vast majority of future major leaguers still came from high schools and colleges across the United States.

Challenges would arise for the Twins in finding players worthy of drafting and in choosing how best to allocate funds to spend on bonuses for their draftees, but such hardships were common to all personnel directors. The opportunity for equitable selection afforded by the draft had to be conflated with prudent evaluation of talent to be drafted. Beginning in June 1965, teams in both leagues had fresh guidelines to follow for procuring players, and the sequence whereby teams picked according to the reverse order of their place in the standings the previous year gave an advantage to those teams who were poorer performers. Despite the theoretical parity inherent in such a system, it remained incumbent upon each club to judiciously select the players it believed to be worthy of its investment and capable of helping carry the team to future winning seasons.

## The 1965 Pennant Race at Midseason

As Minnesota's Sherry Robertson spent June 8 and 9 busily drafting a total of 52 amateur players — at least one for every infield and outfield position, in addition to right- and left-handed pitchers — by the third week of the month the Twins and their 38–24 mark were one-half game ahead of both the White Sox and Indians. Baltimore was two games back, the Tigers trailed by only three, and the Yankees wallowed in an unaccustomed seventh place. Minnesota's thirteen come-from-behind wins certainly made a crucial contribution to their status atop the AL.

The trials of the Twins manager were exacerbated at the close of June when Mele was forced to employ different infield combinations on eight consecutive days, while at once reaching into the bullpen to find starters to replace the ailing Pascual and Kaat, who had a problem with his left forearm. Mele plugged the gaps in the rotation with Mel Nelson, Billy Pleis, and Dave Boswell; Bernie Allen was at last back in the Twin Cities following his recall from Denver. Behind the plate, Zimmerman was substituting once more for Battey, who was out with an injury to his non-throwing hand. Don Mincher, ostensibly relegated to the role of odd man out, was installed in the lineup against some of the tougher opposing right-handed pitchers and spurred the Twins to victory on most of those occasions.

Shortly before the All-Star break, however, other injuries began to overtake the Twins and challenged Mele's capacity to assemble a healthy lineup. A slump-ridden Bob Allison had his misery compounded in early July when he suffered a bone chip in his right wrist after being hit by a pitch. With help from the bench leaping into the fray, Sandy Valdespino and Joe Nossek alternated in left field to fill the void and became two more examples of the importance of the depth upon which the Twins relied to fill unforeseen vacancies in the lineup. Writing about the Valdespino-Nossek tandem, a Twin Cities sportswriter commented, "Not until this year have the Twins ever been in position to take the loss of such a star as Allison with less than disastrous results."[31]

The undercurrents of the "hero du jour" theme ran swiftly and luckily to the Twins' benefit. Mele was quick to spread credit for the surging Twins' prowess to all corners of the clubhouse. "It really isn't fair to name one player," said the skipper. "So many have played well and made possible our great season."[32] On the mound, Boswell, who was fourth among Twins hurlers in innings pitched in early July, aided a pitching staff that at times had difficulties in keeping a starting rotation intact. Undaunted, Mele and his cobbled lineup held first place at the All-Star break by five full games. If any good was derived from the travails endured in the season's first half, Mele learned that he could employ his bullpen more confidently, and the quality performance of those coming off the bench mitigated the impact of so many injuries.

Rewards were in store for Minnesota's standout players at the midway point of 1965, as six Twins were selected for the American League All-Star team, for which Mele was tabbed to serve as a coach for AL manager Al Lopez.[33] In recognition of the contributions they made to the Twins' ascension to the top of the American League, Killebrew, Oliva, Hall, Battey, Versalles, and Grant were named to the team, the second straight year that six Twins were accorded All-Star honors. The five position players all had Minnesota's best run-producing numbers, while Grant led its pitchers with a 9–2 record. All of the Twins selected for the 36th mid-summer classic saw action in the contest played at the Met, but the National League prevailed 6–5. According to a *Tribune* staff writer who penned his experience of working at the game as a peanut vendor, "The 46,706 spectators had guzzled 50,664 bottles of brew and munched 49,524 hot dogs, shattering all existing stadium records."[34]

Calvin Griffith's decision to field a team nearly identical to the 1964 version was rewarding his patience and proving the naysayers wrong, at least in the short term, about the exigencies of having to make roster moves to shore up a team that left much to be desired the previous season. Although Mele was taxed by health issues suffered by many of the Twins, Griffith's faith in his players returning from the previous season and confidence in a manager who could extract the best results from those players allowed the owner to shy away from the trade market during 1965. There would be no trade with Cleveland, which had nearly become *de rigueur* over the last several years, since the farm system had furnished several integral players for Mele.

Any stoicism and security inherent from the lead of early July rapidly evaporated less than a week after the All-Star Game. A four-game losing skid, the loss of Boswell to mononucleosis, and Allen's failure to hold his place in the lineup raised more concern for Mele to address.

The frustration of the short losing skein led to an eruption by Mele during a July 18 contest when he confronted umpire Bill Valentine following a controversial call. There was debate as to whether Mele and the arbiter made physical contact, but unfortunately for Mele, American League president Joe Cronin was in attendance at the game and personally witnessed the confrontation. Swift punishment in the form of a five-game suspension and a $500 fine was meted out for the manager; coach Hal Naragon was handed the Twins' reins for the period of Mele's banishment. There was a rumor that Billy Martin would be the choice to replace Mele, but one Minneapolis scribe opined that Griffith overruled Mele in the selection process. "There is no reason to believe that Mele had his choice. The owner of the club names the manager and probably named the interim manager," wrote Dick Cullum, who suggested that Naragon was chosen specifically to forestall any speculation that Martin was the heir apparent to Mele, however far into the future that succession might occur.[35] A day would come when Martin did assume the leadership of the Twins, but however ambitious Martin may have been to assume control of the team, several years would pass before that desire was fulfilled.

By the end of July, Minnesota had slowly crept ahead of the rest of the AL and sported a six-game lead, when another string of injuries threatened to derail the Twins. Continuing to suffer pain in his pitching shoulder, Pascual finally underwent surgery in early August and joined Boswell on the sidelines. But the biggest loss was sustained during a game against the Orioles on August 2. Killebrew was stationed at first base when he tried to field an errant throw from third baseman Rollins; in reaching for the ball he collided with Oriole batter Russ Snyder and severely dislocated his elbow. Because Pascual and Boswell were already assigned to the 30-day disabled list, the team was precluded from moving Killebrew to the DL until one of the pitchers could be activated. Boswell was the more likely candidate to return, so the *Tribune*, which gave front-page coverage of the Killebrew mishap the following day, gloomily predicted that Pascual would offer little value to the Twins after surgery so late in the season. Meanwhile, Twins physician Dr. Bill Proffitt initially predicted a mere two-week layoff for Killebrew after putting the first baseman's elbow back into place.

Upon further examination, however, the damage to Killebrew's joint was so severe that the slugger was feared lost for the remainder of the season. But the Twins' depth once more ensured that the void was filled. Taking inspiration from a sign hung in their clubhouse which read "A hero a day keeps the contenders away," Mincher took over at first base while Killebrew, with his team-leading totals of 22 home runs and 70 RBIs, was idled.[36] Mincher's presence was "so effective … that the Twins' drive toward the American League pennant picked up steam, in spite of the absence of Killebrew."[37]

Also stepping in to give Versalles an occasional reprieve was Frank Quilici, a rookie called up from Denver who quickly found himself in good stead with Mele. The Chicago native was not bashful about being vocal on the diamond as he gave the Twins a firebrand not seen since Billy Martin played second base four years earlier. Jerry Kindall, who was

**Harmon Killebrew shows the form that would launch 573 home runs in his career.**

struck down by "clean, hard slides" by the Chicago's Tom McCraw on consecutive nights in mid–July, became displaced at second base by the newcomer, who played well enough to keep his name on Mele's lineup card for much of the last ten weeks of the season.[38]

Mincher, Quilici, and a resurgent Oliva, whose average finally approached the .300 mark by late July, were among the regular players who kept the Twins' fire stoked. Perry's pitching exceeded expectations, as he was undefeated in his first seven decisions before finally losing a game in mid–July. Undaunted by the loss of Killebrew, Minnesota's margin had risen to a modest but important eight-game lead by the second week of August.

At this time, one of the most harrowing events in modern American history erupted in southern California, a calamity that caught the attention of the Twins as they were the first American League team to play in Los Angeles following the outbreak of rioting in the Watts section of the city.

## Smoldering Watts

Prior to their move to Minnesota, the Washington Senators had added the first black player to the franchise in 1955. Ten years later, despite the delay in integrating their spring training hotel, the Twins were among the more enlightened teams in the American League with an average of four blacks on the roster.[39] Minority players such as Pascual received earlier consideration for jobs with the Senators because their lighter pigmentation made for a more comfortable fit as the roster integration proceeded. When Battey joined the Senators in the 1960 trade with the White Sox, he became the team's first African American to play at the major league level. The integration of the Twins' spring training hotel in 1965 further instilled a sense of unity for the organization.

During his stint in Minnesota, Vic Power found residing among his white neighbors near Lake Calhoun to be a pleasant experience, and Kindall was of the opinion that the Twins clubhouse, which had long been populated with many minority players prior to his arrival from Cleveland in 1964, was "harmonious" in its acceptance of racial diversity. The infielder observed that Mudcat Grant "had a reputation as a militant, a very proud black man, but I loved being around him because he had the strength of his convictions."[40]

Labeled an "orgy of lawlessness" by the *Los Angeles Times*, the horrific rioting in Watts was attributed to the inattention to "a variety of discontents and grievances of long standing" that had been manifest in the black community.[41] A toxic mix of a high unemployment rate, persistent discrimination despite federal legislation aimed at eliminating the practice, and police brutality against alleged black criminals boiled to the surface. When the spree of looting, fire bombings, arson, and shootings desisted and an imposed curfew was lifted on August 17, much of an 18-square-mile section of the city had been ravaged or fed to the flames. Property damage estimates ran to $35 million, police had made 4,000 arrests in an attempt to curb the rioting, and 34 people — most of them black, most of them killed by other blacks — were dead.

On August 20 as the Twins flew into Los Angeles for their final trip of the season to California, the team's plane flew over what remained of the charred area. Although news of the riots had captured headlines across the country for days, not until the players saw with their own eyes the devastation did it occur to them how grave the situation had been. "We didn't know the destruction was that bad," recalled one player, who said that the club was "sobered" by the experience of witnessing the aftermath of the unrest.[42] Kindall had difficulty explaining the emotion that prevailed on the Twins, but he believed that witnessing the riot-torn area may have actually helped strengthen the personal bonds within Minnesota's racially diverse clubhouse.

Less than one month following the Watts riots, another racial barrier was broken when the American League introduced its first black umpire. Emmett Ashford, a twelve-year veteran at the AAA level, was selected to attend spring training in 1966 and become assimilated into the contingent of major league arbiters. Nearly two decades had passed since Jackie Robinson's appearance in Brooklyn, and major league baseball, long handicapped by the inertia of inaction, was gradually diversifying all of its ranks with men of color. Ashford's promotion was emblematic of the gains, however slowly obtained, that blacks were making in reaching baseball's highest ranks.

## The Final Drive to the Flag

Even though Killebrew was sidelined with his damaged elbow, Minnesota retained the high ground in the standings by sporting an eight-game lead in mid–August. The Twins were honored with a cartoon by the *Los Angeles Times*' Pete Bentovoja, who cheekily portrayed a Murders' Row of Oliva, Hall, Mincher, Allison, Versalles, and Battey as having plenty of power to conduct "mop-up operations" as the Twins continued their inexorable journey toward the crucial stretch drive.[43]

Six weeks remained in the regular season, but the margin held by the Twins over their nearest rivals prompted several baseball insiders to concede that Minnesota had all but sewn up the race. Angels manager Bill Rigney said, "The Twins are 'in' in the American League." Minnesota "could do no wrong," according to Mele's uncle, Tony Cuccinello, who saw similarities in the current Minnesota team and the 1954 Indians for whom he coached.[44]

However, some countervailing opinion was rendered by those whose minds were still fresh with the memory of the Phillies' inglorious stumble the previous September. Addressing those Twins' fans succumbing to "World Series hysteria," Minneapolis sportswriter Charles Johnson offered a blunt reproach: "Keep your shirt on! ... Too many right now are taking it for granted that the pennant is assured.... Remember what happened to Philadelphia in the National League! It had a commanding lead with only two weeks to go last year and missed the boat. Fan pressure can infect the players and wreck what could be a happy occasion."[45]

Minnesota continued to whittle away at the remainder of the schedule, and after enduring the drama of seeing their lead briefly shrink to four and a half games, the Twins righted themselves and padded their lead to ten games midway through September. When their magic number diminished to a precious handful of games, and though the Twins had yet to officially clinch the league crown, a local retailer generously gifted each member of the de facto champions with a cooler and a color television prior to their contest on September 19.

After posting a 30–18 record in Killebrew's absence, the recovered slugger was inserted at third base by Mele on September 21. A most welcome addition to the lineup, Killebrew went hitless in four at-bats, but of greatest importance was the fact that he reported no pain in his rehabilitated joint. Now it would up to Killebrew to get enough playing time during the ten games left in the season to restore his sense of timing at the plate. Meanwhile, Oliva continued to swing his own bat authoritatively and hiked his average to .320, good for a seven-point lead over Boston's Carl Yastrzemski in the race for the AL batting title.

On September 26, the Twins' dream of securing the pennant came true in a 2–1 win against the Senators in Washington. When Jim Kaat struck out Don Zimmer for the game-ending out, champagne flowed freely in the visitors' clubhouse at D.C. Stadium, as few on hand escaped a dousing of bubbly. "Mele, a thoughtful, conservative man," noted the *Tribune*, "remained in game uniform until the champagne sloshing was completed. His wife, Connie, had reminded him not to ruin a good suit of clothes."[46]

For denizens of the Gopher State, it would have been impossible not to know the joy of conquering the American League and ousting the dynastic Yankees: "The headlines on the front pages of every Minnesota newspaper were like they were on VE and VJ days. There was dancing on Hennepin Avenue. Plans were made for massive 'Welcome Back Twins' greetings at the airport."[47] Editorializing that the Twins had "won in a waltz," the *Tribune* lauded Mele's "manager of the year performance" in directing his players and praised the club's "triumph [as] an object lesson in courage and aggressiveness."[48]

For all the hard-won victories and effort expended by the personnel on many levels of

**Cuba native Tony Oliva, who won his second AL batting title in 1965, was one of the most fearsome hitters in the Twins lineup.**

the Minnesota organization, the man most responsible for orchestrating the affairs leading to this glorious moment in Twins history was conspicuous by his absence from D.C. Stadium. Calvin Griffith was quick to dial the manager's office and offer his congratulations to Mele for the splendid job he did in leading the Twins to the pennant, but the owner extended kudos from his private box at Metropolitan Stadium, where he watched the Twins on television while attending a Minnesota Vikings football game.

That Griffith remained at home did not reflect any indifference to his team but rather stemmed from an issue that vexed him for quite some time. When Griffith began investigating the viability of moving his Senators out of the nation's capital in the late 1950s, he incurred the wrath of H. Gabriel Murphy, a minority shareholder in the team who was determined to preclude the transfer of the club to another venue. Murphy was upset over his inability to purchase an additional twelve percent interest in the Senators when a relative of Griffith, in whose name the block was held in trust, died. Griffith refused to offer the shares to Murphy—which would have given the latter a 52 percent majority stake in the club—so he filed suit against the owner. With an outstanding subpoena awaiting Griffith should he ever return to Washington, the Twins owner well understood the counsel of his attorney. "I guarantee you we'll win every lawsuit he brings against you in Minnesota, but the price you (and [Griffith's wife] Thelma) have to pay is that you have to physically stay out of the District of Columbia," warned Peter Dorsey. "You can't expose yourself to a process server."[49]

At the Met, a steady stream of well-wishers kept Griffith company, but the owner, who regretted that Murphy's legal maneuvering held him at bay, nonetheless was most proud of his players for the simple reason that "they made it happen."[50] For Griffith, the Senators and the Twins were his life and love, but he would not suffer the humiliation of being served papers while accompanying his team during its finest hour. Not to be completely shut out of the festivities, Griffith made sure that he was among the three-thousand-strong crowd of well-wishers who greeted the Twins upon their return home from their road trip in the early morning hours of October 1.

A Twins player later remarked that Minnesota's fate for the 1965 season was presaged by the team's success early in the season against the Yankees, as they finished the campaign with a 13–5 record against New York. "Sam Mele and [Johnny] Sain knew they had great pitching and hitting, they just had to tighten up the defense," Kindall later observed, adding, "The 1964 team sounded the opening bell for 1965."[51] So much had been expended in keeping the Twins in first place for so long that some feared the effort might have been in vain when Killebrew was stricken in early August. The injuries to Killebrew and Pascual were weathered by Mincher's play at first base and the juggling of the pitching staff throughout much of the season by Sain. Killebrew's return for the last two weeks of the season gave more hope of continued success as the Twins prepared to face the National League pennant winner in the World Series.

## Next Stop: The Fall Classic

If the Twins and their comfortable lead in September produced minimal suspense in determining the American League pennant winner, the same was not true in the National League where a knot of teams struggled for the championship. By the third week of August, the Milwaukee Braves clung to a narrow half-game lead over the Los Angeles Dodgers, the San Francisco Giants were one game behind, the Cincinnati Reds were only three games out, and the Philadelphia Phillies—trying to atone for 1964's catastrophe—remained in the hunt, just 5½ games off the pace.

One month later and after a roaring 14-game winning streak, the Giants were atop the league by 3½ games over the Dodgers, the Reds trailing by 4½, with the Braves — claimed by former Giants hurler Jack Sanford to be the best hitting team in either league — now a distant third, eight full games behind. Not to be counted out, manager Walter Alston's Dodgers put their own pennant aspirations in high gear and reeled off thirteen straight victories in the latter part of September. Los Angeles clinched the NL pennant with a three-game series win against the Braves on the final weekend of the season, as their 97–65 record was two games ahead of the Giants.

Roger Angell, one of baseball's premier authors, demurred to call the 1965 World Series "a classic," citing the fact that the Twins-Dodgers match-up was a battle of two teams that had finished 1964 in sixth place in their respective leagues. But Angell was quick to point out that the tilt was "an entertainment of more than sufficient interest, and only the most thrill-surfeited fan could ignore its distinctive omens, curiosities, and pleasures."[52] One of those curiosities was the weather, with autumn appearing to bypass the Upper Midwest as the region experienced a cold snap that caused various forms of frozen precipitation to fall on Montana, the Dakotas, Minnesota, and Wisconsin in mid–September. Since prime-time television had yet to strip the sport of daytime World Series games, at least the home games in the Twin Cities would be played during the relative warmth of October afternoons rather than chilly evenings at Metropolitan Stadium.

When Mudcat Grant won his twentieth game of the season in his penultimate starting assignment on September 25, he became the first black American League pitcher to accomplish the feat. His one-hit taming of the Senators solidified his standing as the ace of the Twins staff and made him the logical choice to open the World Series for Minnesota. Of the overall prospects of defeating the Dodgers, who were installed as 7 to 5 favorites to win the Series, Mele said cautiously, "We may surprise them."[53]

The Twins received a break of sorts thanks to the Judaic calendar. Sandy Koufax was the nonpareil ace of the Dodger staff, but because Yom Kippur fell on October 6, the same day as the scheduled opening of the World Series, the left-hander elected to sit out his start and instead observe his religious obligation on the Jewish Day of Atonement. With Koufax's first assignment held off a day until Game 2, Don Drysdale was tapped for the Game 1 starting honors. When Mincher belted a third-inning homer off Drysdale, Mele credited the first baseman with "lighting the fuse" that set the stage for Minnesota's six-run explosion, which featured a subsequent three-run clout by Versalles.[54] Grant scattered nine hits over the last six innings, as the Twins chalked up an inspiring 8–2 triumph.

Determined to show that their opening-game victory was not an aberration, the Twins muffled the Dodgers and the fearsome Koufax in Game 2, 5–1, as Kaat limited Los Angeles to just seven singles. With the game scoreless in the top of the fifth inning, the Twins kept the Dodgers off the board when Allison made a fantastic catch in left field to save a run by robbing Jim Lefebvre of an extra-base hit with Ron Fairly aboard. In the bottom of the sixth, the Twins tallied twice to secure the win. Mele was buoyed by the Twins' two-games-to-none lead, and Griffith, who recounted his greatest thrill in baseball as having occurred when he was granted permission to move his Senators out of Washington, now claimed that the Twins' early lead in the Series was his second biggest thrill. Somehow, his franchise's clinching of its first American League pennant in over three decades did not pass muster or had at least fallen to third place among such momentous occasions, but the owner was obviously elated that his ballplayers had toppled two of the best pitchers in the National League.

With the Series shifted to Chavez Ravine in Los Angeles, Pascual was charged with keeping the Minnesota winning streak alive, after being deemed sufficiently recovered from his August surgery. But the Dodgers started left-hander Claude Osteen, a former Washington Senator from the post–Griffith era, who had a penchant for beating the Twins during his stint as a Solon. Besting the Twins five times over the previous two seasons before his trade from Washington to the Dodgers, Osteen again handcuffed the Twins, this time in a 4–0 shutout. Minnesota hurt their own cause with early baserunning miscues that kept them from capitalizing on Versalles' leadoff double to open the game. Pascual surrendered eight hits, half of which were doubles, and several long outs, prompting one columnist to speculate, "I think the outfield finally came to [Mele] with a petition" to remove their starting pitcher. "Two more innings of Pascual," he concluded, "and those guys would have been ready for the Olympic marathon."[55]

While Osteen was the hero of the day for vanquishing the Twins, Battey was the victim of the day. When Willie Davis fouled off a pitch in the seventh inning, Battey gave chase, and, as was shown in a ghastly sequence of photographs in the next day's *Los Angeles Times*, the catcher rammed throat-first into the railing near the Twins dugout. The intrepid backstop left the game after regaining consciousness and, incredibly, was in the lineup the next day.

Determined to shake off the ill effect of his start in the Series opener, Drysdale went the distance in hurling a 7–2 victory in the fourth game, enabling the Dodgers to square the Series at two games apiece. Drysdale yielded a pair of solo home runs, one each to Killebrew and Oliva, and limited the Twins to just three other harmless hits, while Los Angeles unleashed a wide-ranging repertoire on offense to put the Twins away. Besides six infield hits and a pair of stolen bases, Dodgers Lou Johnson and Wes Parker hit homers in a surprising display of power. Grant did not survive the sixth inning for Minnesota, and "obviously it went unsaid in the Dodger clubhouse, but there was an undercurrent of feeling that they left the Twins well shook up Sunday with their bunting and base running."[56] The ironwilled Battey started behind the plate for the Twins but was unable to speak because of his damaged throat, thus impairing his ability to communicate with his fellow fielders. Mele was rankled by his team's defensive lapses and his batters' total of eleven strikeouts, six of them on called third strikes, a statistic which stressed the control that Drysdale possessed that day.

As Drysdale atoned for his substandard opening game outing, Koufax also redeemed himself for his poor showing in Game 2. With an outpouring of offensive support for Koufax and a tour de force by the Dodger ace, Los Angeles swept its three games at home with a 7–0 rout. Perfect through the first four frames, Koufax allowed only two hits and one walk through eight innings before tiring a bit in the ninth.

Mele confessed to the Twins being "outplayed" at Dodger Stadium, but he struggled to find the source of his team's scoring drought on the West Coast.[57] With just two runs to show for the three Series road contests, Mele lamely cited the inability of the great Yankees to win in Los Angeles. History was also on the Twins' side in this regard, as they ended their 1965 visits to Dodger Stadium having scored an anemic total of 22 runs in nine games against the Angels and in the three Series contests versus the Dodgers.

The Twins returned home to brisk 37-degree temperatures. Almost as chilled as the Minnesota air was Tony Oliva, whose Series average in five games was a sub-par .158 on three hits in 19 at-bats. But the 1965 AL batting champion had much company among his teammates. In three games at Dodger Stadium, Battey, Mincher, Allison, Hall, and Quilici were collectively a moribund 2-for-37. The antidote to Minnesota's short losing streak was a return to the Met and the hope that the home-field advantage would sway the remaining two games — if indeed they would both be necessary — in their favor.

Osteen, the Dodgers' winner of Game 3, was trusted with the starting assignment in Game 6, but on the other side of the diamond, Mele was undecided whether to use Grant, Pascual, or Merritt, the rookie with the great pickoff move. Mele could have done worse than settle on his ace, and Mudcat came through in the biggest game of his career, a superb 5–1 victory that kept alive the Twins' chances in a seventh game.

Facing the minimum number of batters through the first four innings, Grant was staked to a 2–0 lead on an Allison homer, and Grant padded the lead with his own three-run shot in the home half of the sixth. In the crowded Minnesota clubhouse after the game, the ebullient victorious pitcher playfully chastised the reporters who seemingly deserted the Twins when they lost their winning ways out west, but Grant was truly elated by the home crowd's response to his heroics at the bat. "[That] meant more to me than the home run," he said of the standing ovation he received. "Imagine, looking up and seeing all those people cheering for you. I'll never forget it," beamed Mudcat.[58]

Unwittingly, the Dodgers provided an unexpected bit of incentive for the Twins in Game 6. When word reached the Minnesota clubhouse that Alston's crew had checked out of their hotel in anticipation of winning the game and immediately departing for Los Angeles, "Our boys were a little peeved," observed Mele of the Dodgers' arrogance. "It tickled us to have them take their bags back."[59] Although the Dodgers hoisted their own petard, they retained one last chance to redeem their impetuousness. For their part, the Twins retained the home-field advantage for the final game, but Los Angeles had the opportunity to put the best pitcher in baseball back on the mound.

Alston equivocated on his decision as to who his starter would be. Drysdale, troubled by a minor injury to his pitching hand incurred when he broke his bat while hitting a foul ball in Game 4, was the logical choice. But if weather were to force postponement of Game 7, Koufax would be the certain starter as he would benefit from an extra day's rest since hurling his Game 5 masterpiece. Pitching Koufax on two days' rest could prove risky, but the left-hander's elbow recovered sufficiently after his previous appearance, and the pitcher's self-assessment of his readiness exuded confidence. "I feel good," Koufax told the press. "There's nothing to save my arm for after tomorrow. If I'm asked to pitch, I'm not going out there to lose."[60]

After much deliberation and collaboration with both his aces, Alston gave the ball to Koufax. "Given my choice against Minnesota, I would prefer to use a left-hander," said the Dodgers manager, who further justified his final decision with the argument that he "can't think of anyone I would rather bring in from the bullpen in a tough situation than Drysdale."[61] Doubts about how Koufax would respond to the short layoff were put to rest as he allowed three hits and three walks while again fanning ten Twins en route to a 2–0 win to bring the World Series championship to Los Angeles for the second time in three years. When Twins starter Kaat surrendered a run-producing hit to Parker, Mele quickly pressed into service a parade of relievers to stanch the flow of Dodger runs, a move that achieved its purpose. But the Dodgers held fast and Koufax, with just two runs, had more than enough support and carried the Dodgers to the title while securing the Series' Most Valuable Player award on the strength of his showing in his final two starts.

The Twins were betrayed by the home-field advantage that had accrued to the winner of each of the first six games of the Series before that pattern was broken by Koufax. Mele tipped his cap to Parker — if the Twins skipper was "surprised" by the Dodger first baseman's .304 Series batting average, he should have been aghast at Ron Fairly's .379 average and .690 slugging percentage. But the manager dreamt of what might have been had Jim Gilliam not been protecting the third-base line in the fifth inning when he stabbed Versalles's line drive for a force play at third with two Twins aboard.[62] If the Twins had been able to break through against Koufax in that inning, the momentum could have shifted in their favor. Although the fates held to the contrary, Mele was gracious in defeat by commenting, "When you lose to a pitcher like Koufax, you don't have to be ashamed."[63]

The *Minneapolis Tribune* was laudatory in its post–Series editorial of the season-long effort put forward by the Twins. "Nobody but Coach Billy Martin thought Minnesota had a chance to win the pennant," noted the editors, who enunciated their pride for everyone in the organization from the owner to the batboys but emphasized that "without the support of the faithful [fans], the Twins would not be American League champions."[64] In his maiden postseason voyage, "'Money Bags' Calvin Griffith came in for nothing but praise for himself and for his organization," gushed another local columnist, "for the entire operation and the hospitality that was extended to all baseball people, press, and plain fans, even though he 'suffered' more than anyone else through losing four games."[65]

"I've always wanted to play in a World Series," said an expectant Allison prior to the commencement of Game 1. "I just hope I can make a contribution."[66] Allison's signal moment was his spectacular catch in the second game, but his strikeout in the bottom of the ninth to end Game 7 was a cruel denouement for a man who had done so much for Griffith's teams over the years. In that final game, Kaat said of Koufax, "He was so overpowering, I actually felt sorry for our hitters." Oliva expressed disappointment at his own failures by stating, "So many times I had stepped to the plate with men on base only to make an out; one or two hits at the right time might have made a difference in the Series."[67] A circumspect Griffith tersely summed up the harsh reality of the Series loss by observing, "We just didn't get the breaks, that's all there was to it. You can't cry over certain things."[68]

The Twins' winning of the American League pennant furnished a reason for their fans to feel euphoric and optimistic about the near future for the team. With the Yankees out of contention for at least one season, Mele and company could look forward to capitalizing on the formative experience of 1965. Because the Twins almost assuredly would not be wracked by as many medical problems as they just endured, they would be well-prepared to face the challenge of defending their title in the 1966 season.

## Rewards and Awards — and Expectations for the Future

The Twins need not have felt too upset despite their defeat at the hands of the Dodgers. Although the World Series could have ended on a better note in Minnesota, the time had come to pause and bask in the glory of postseason accolades that were hard-earned by players and management alike.

Paramount among the awards was the American League's Most Valuable Player, and the choice was a simple one for the voting members of the Baseball Writers' Association of America to make. Named first on all but one ballot of the twenty that were cast — two from each of the ten AL cities — was Zoilo Versalles. The Twins shortstop ended 1965 with a respectable .273 average — hardly an awe-inspiring statistic, which would have been better had he not led the league with 122 strikeouts — but from his leadoff spot in the batting order, he led the league in runs scored (126), doubles (45, tying Boston's Carl Yastrzemski), triples (12), total bases (308), and was second in hits (182) to teammate Tony Oliva. His 27 stolen bases in 32 attempts led the Twins, and he belted 19 home runs for good measure in the 160 games he played, missing only two contests the entire season. In the field, his 39 errors were, unfortunately, a league-leading total, but he was first in double plays with 105 and second only to Chicago's Ron Hansen in assists — 487 to 527 for the White Sox short-stop — the net result being a second Gold Glove for Versalles.

Taking a little credit for the fire that ignited his high-spirited Cuban infielder, Mele believed that his run-in with Versalles during spring training forced his shortstop to be more aware of the importance of intelligent play at all times. But coach Billy Martin con-tributed the most toward shepherding Versalles over the course of the six-month season: "[Martin] got him to be more aggressive when he was up at the plate. He got him to use his natural speed on the base paths. He taught Zoilo how to release the ball more quickly, throwing to first base and the short, snap throw to second base for the double play."[69] Ver-salles spent much time discussing opposing batters with Kindall, one of his keystone partners, and focused on the importance of the pivot when turning a double play. By inculcating Versalles with a methodology steeped in hus-tle while also emphasizing attention to detail, Martin spurred Versalles to the head of the class in the American League.

Zoilo Versalles, an All-Star shortstop, was nearly a unanimous selection as the 1965 American League MVP.

Recipient of the lone first place vote that kept Versalles's MVP award from being unan-imous, Oliva finished second in the ballot-ing but was named by *The Sporting News* as the AL Player of the Year in canvassing conducted among the league's players. On the strength of his defense of the American League batting championship and high finishes in several other offensive categories, Oliva won the *TSN* honor over Versalles, who was favored by the writers.

Top individual honors aside, Oliva and Versalles were but two of the five Twins named to *The Sporting News* postseason American League all-star team. Joining them was center fielder Hall, who had amassed a .285 average, 20 homers, 86 runs batted in, and 14 steals; catcher Battey, who ended his injury-wracked year with a .297 average, 6 homers, and 60 RBIs; and Grant, the top winner in the circuit with a 21–7 record, a league-best .750 winning percentage, and 3.30 earned-run average in his 270 innings. Had a Cy Young Award been given in both leagues that year — separate laurels for the best pitcher in each league did not come about until 1967 — Mudcat would have been the odds-on favorite, but Koufax was the natural selection as the best in all of major league baseball. For fielding prowess, pitcher Kaat was awarded a fourth Gold Glove for his excellence on the mound. Battey narrowly missed another such award when Bill Freehan of the Tigers edged the Twins backstop for honors among catchers.

Twins players other than the named winners also received their due from appreciative teammates. Kindall believed that Al Worthington, whom he called "a mountain of dependability," was the team's MVP because of the number of important saves he registered over the course of the season.[70] Jim Perry received praise for emerging from his lost season of 1964 to fill the void created when Pascual was injured. Zimmerman capably took charge behind the plate for the ill-fated Battey, who himself should have received a special citation for performing as well as he did with the multitude of injuries he suffered.

The coaching and managerial contributions of other uniformed Twins cannot be understated. The aforementioned Martin served as a catalyst in directing Minnesota's aggressiveness on the bases from his post at the third-base coach's box and made the most of his time showing the finer points of the craft of defense to the team's infielders. Martin's diligence and knowledge of the game — "His mind was *so* active," noted one of the players — won him the admiration of those he coached, as he worked hard to impress those club owners who would someday be searching for new managerial timber.[71] The Twins hit fewer home runs in 1965 than in 1964, but they stole far more bases and scored more runs, thereby vindicating the emphasis on the running strategy that worked so well as Martin helped crack the whip for Mele.

Making a tremendous impact on the pitching staff was Johnny Sain, who, after being coaxed from a one-year retirement, continued the fine tutelage he had bestowed on the Yankees' pitchers during his stint in the Bronx from 1961 to 1963. "It was no accident what happened to the Yankees and Twins when John Sain was there," said one of Sain's star pupils, Jim Bouton, who won 21 games in 1963.[72] Teaming with Mele to ensure that the entire bullpen could be as reliable as possible, Sain and his manager conspired to make the best use of the whole pitching staff. Of primacy was the relief duo of greybeards Worthington and Klippstein, who combined for 19 wins out of the bullpen and logged respective ERAs of 2.13 and 2.24, with Worthington's 21 saves commensurate with those of the best closers of the era. Enjoying a career year was Grant, the best pitcher in the American League in 1965, while Perry's dozen victories were both unexpected and vital to the Twins' cause.

After a midseason argument with Martin over a defensive lapse by a Twins pitcher, Sain expressed his distain for Martin by choosing to dress with his pitchers in the clubhouse rather than remain in the coaches' office. This was more a continuation of rancor between Martin and Sain that dated to their days when both were with the Yankees over a decade earlier, as the impact of the latest spat had a negligible effect on the pitchers. What mattered most was concord between pitching coach and his staff, the trimming of Minnesota's 1964 team ERA from 3.58 to 3.14 in 1965, and a lowering of opponents' batting average (from .243 to .235) and on-base percentage (.312 versus .301) from the previous season.

The ringmasters who brought players and coaches together to deliver at last a pennant to Minnesota lay at the top of the Twins' managerial command. For his masterful orchestration of the entire team throughout 1965 with its surfeit of injuries to many players, Sam Mele was hailed as *The Sporting News* Manager of the Year in voting conducted among his major league peers. Following the Twins' downfall of 1964, Mele's employment under Griffith was tenuous at best, but the manager prevailed thanks to his own prudence and skill in assembling the best lineup he could from the healthy players available on any given day. Knowing he was under close scrutiny and subject to dismissal if the club were to falter early in the season, Mele made a statement to his squad in spring training by standing up to Versalles, thereby making all ballplayers unequivocally aware of who was in charge. Mele's actions in the game against Cleveland, which netted him a suspension, convinced any doubters who may have believed that this "players' manager" lacked intensity. When Allison and Hall showed weaknesses, Mele did not hesitate to use Valdespino and Nossek for profit. The only forgotten man on the roster was third-string catcher Sevcik, who did no better than serve as a caddy when Zimmerman spelled Battey behind the plate.

For his own part, Calvin Griffith was named by *The Sporting News* as the 1965 Executive of the Year, a recognition that was well-earned in light of the years of work that the owner had invested to reshape the old Senators into a contending team in its new venue. Since the award was given to one recipient for all of major league baseball, Griffith joined the Angels' Fred Haney as the only AL executives *not* associated with the Yankees to win the honor since 1948.[73]

Mele, who was quickly rewarded with a rare two-year contract by Griffith following the World Series, was generous in sharing the credit with his top two coaches. Martin and his acerbic tongue were acknowledged for injecting a healthy dose of hustle into the Twins, while Sain won plaudits for convincing Mele that the starting pitchers should work every fourth day rather than every fifth. Victory totals produced by mainstays Grant (21) and Kaat (18) were augmented by Perry (12), Pascual (9), and newcomers Boswell (6) and Merritt (5).

Collectively, the Minnesota victory total reached 102, the first time in franchise history that the one-hundred-win mark was eclipsed, but the bumpy course to the pennant could not have been navigated without the exploits of trainer George Lentz. Had Lentz not plied his trade as ably as he did, Mele's job of patching together a lineup from a clubhouse which at times was ostensibly full of walking wounded would have been done only with far greater difficulty. A former boxer and health club operator who found his way to the Senators in 1945, Lentz "handle[d] his men with a lashing tongue and a careful hand" as he applied an assortment of treatments to the various maladies visited upon the Twins.[74] Oliva's and Grant's knees, Allison's wrist, Killebrew's elbow, Pascual's shoulder, and all of Battey's woes were among the challenges swiftly addressed by the trainer. Coddling the Twins back to health was Lentz's specialty, and his nursing of Killebrew's devastating elbow trauma put the Twins' star back in the lineup by late September. Indeed, the man who neither played nor coached for Mele had the greatest responsibility for keeping the enterprise viable with his medicinal and recuperative talents.

As the cheering faded in the winter of 1965-1966, the business of baseball had to again be tended to. Although the Yankees were dethroned for at least one year, they and eight other American League teams now became the hunters, while the defending AL champions assumed the role of the hunted. Griffith elected to play a pat hand on the trading front during the injury-related turbulence of 1965, and he had been fortunate to have personnel capable of stepping into the breaches that arose. Roster adjustments, however, would be necessary if the Twins were to retain their title and replenish the stock of players who were fatigued, injured, or otherwise not up to par during the 1965 season.

A major change was also in store for the upper echelon of major league baseball's executive office. During the summer of 1965, a select committee of major league team owners was in the midst of a search for a new commissioner, preferably "someone from the diamond ranks ... [who] can be the boss with power to wield a big stick," reported the *Minneapolis Tribune*.[75] However, the surprising choice in November to replace Ford Frick, who had occupied the post since 1951, turned out to be a retired Air Force lieutenant general with a weak background in baseball. William Eckert, a West Point graduate who later earned an MBA at Harvard, was named commissioner on the strength of the skills he displayed as a business leader while serving in the military. His admitted deficiency in baseball acumen ultimately hindered his tenure, but the dynamics of the game's top leadership were beginning to shift inexorably.

With one commissioner stepping aside and the long-running dynasty in New York left to answer questions about how to correct its course in the wake of its worst record in decades, the future of the game of baseball was open to much speculation. The growing popularity of professional football, whose own dynasty in Green Bay was in full flower, was diverting the interest of sports fans from the diamond to the gridiron. As teams in the American Football League matured and improved their quality of play by outbidding the National Football League for some of the better collegiate players entering the professional ranks — Joe Namath being a prime example — they also drew increasing numbers of fans to their stadiums.

There was concern that the potential demise of the Yankees, who had become the best gate attraction in the American League, would have a negative impact across the entire circuit. Larry Claflin of the *Boston Record-American* praised "Sam Mele's hustling team [for having] revived interest in a league that was threatened with strangulation by the Yankees." Charles Johnson of the *Minneapolis Tribune* claimed that fans would flock to see any winner play, offering his argument that with Minnesota's surge to the top of the league, attendance for Twins games at home and on the road was on a pace to allow Minnesota to supplant the Yankees as the best drawing team.[76] If the Twins demonstrated an ability to remain in contention in the near future, worries about faltering in the AL due to a poorly performing New York team would be unwarranted. Noting that the Yankees had too many aging stars who were closing in on retirement, Johnson added presciently, "This club has so little talent coming up that a return to dominance may be a long uphill fight that could take years. That doesn't mean the American League will collapse for lack of support."[77]

The comity enjoyed by so many of the 1965 Twins also provided a tangible bond among teammates that burnished their championship season with a special quality of camaraderie that was not soon to fade. Allison, Kindall, Kostro, and Quilici openly acknowledged an élan that buoyed the spirits of the players during the season and also contributed to long-term friendships that endured for decades after their playing days were over. Enhanced by this inter-personal chemistry, the Twins were able to survive the year's physical disabilities in great part due to the positive attitudes with which they regarded each other, as their banter worked well to diffuse tension, cheer up downcast teammates, or otherwise add vivacity to their clubhouse.

Twins' author Jim Thielman referred to Minnesota's great rally in a win against the Yankees just before the All-Star break as a victory that "sealed the Yankees' tomb and secured the Twins' status as the team to beat in the American League during the summer of 1965."[78] Today we have the benefit of hindsight in evaluating the trends of past teams' performances, but the Twins proved themselves worthy of the pennant they earned and of their place in the line of succession to the Yankees. Minnesota was indeed the first team to inter the New York Yankees, but the duty would fall to several other American League clubs to ensure that the vault remained shut for a long, cold decade.

# 4

## Rollercoaster: The Twins of 1966 and Beyond

As the defending American League champions entered the 1966 season, the challenge for the Minnesota Twins was to prove that the achievements of 1965 were an extension of the diligence the team exhibited in 1962 and 1963. Solid play in three of the last four seasons and a winter of recuperation for tired and injured players seemed to indicate that Minnesota would be prepared to take on all rivals. A fully recovered squad could allow the Twins to again rule the AL, potentially for the next few years if Sam Mele were given the right replacements to shore up problematic spots in the lineup and on the mound.

Although the word "dynasty" had been loosely floated in the press in the aftermath of their World Series appearance, the Twins ultimately showed in the five years after their thrilling 1965 season that talk of such dominance was premature. To be sure, few teams could field players of the star quality found in the Twin Cities, with some fine young players also on the way up from the minor leagues. Although Minnesota nearly won its second pennant in 1967 and did in fact win American League Western Division titles in 1969 and 1970, the Twins barely gained a modicum of dynastic traction in the waning years of the 1960s. To their enduring credit, Minnesota capitalized on the deeds of Jim Perry, Jim Kaat, Harmon Killebrew, Tony Oliva, and a newcomer named Rod Carew in maintaining a solid foothold among contending teams in the American League.

Yet after 1970, the inchoate semblance of any Minnesotan dominance lapsed into mediocrity as age took its toll on the veterans, while the latest farmhands proved to be adequate major league players but not up to par when matched against formidable challengers located in Baltimore and Oakland. The blend of veteran and youthful talent manifest in the lineup of the Orioles and the nucleus of the incipient powerhouse being formed by the Athletics relegated the Twins to the status of also-rans in the 1970s after a brief period highlighted by two division championships and the tempest of Billy Martin's debut as a major league manager.

## The Post-Series Swoon

The 1965 season, with its 102 victories, World Series appearance, and abundance of personal awards for the Twins also brought the certainty that Calvin Griffith's payroll would increase in 1966. Griffith acted swiftly to put his manager under contract for the next two seasons at $48,000 per year, and several players, notably the All-Star performers, were expected to demand salaries in the $50,000 range. Coach Billy Martin anticipated cashing in for his role in bringing out the best in Zoilo Versalles, stating, "I hope Mr. Griffith thinks I did a good job…. The raise I get — and I hope it's a big one — goes into the bank for a rainy day"[1]

Seeking new players to address problem areas, Griffith explored the trade market at the December 1965 winter meetings but was unable to consummate any deals. The owner was known at times to be a difficult trader, often accused by other general managers of habitually overstating the value of his own players. Jimmie Hall attracted the attention of the Athletics and the Giants, and Kaat, an eighteen-game winner, was the prize most coveted by other teams. However, as the meetings passed, the Minnesota roster remained static.

The Twins profited immensely in 1965 from a conscious effort to employ speed and derring-do on the bases; in the new year Mele wanted his fielders to be aware that their rivals were apt to try to mimic this strategy in order to beat the Twins at their own game. In Chicago, for example, new White Sox skipper Eddie Stanky was expected to pursue a course of spirited play reminiscent of the brawling days of a previous generation of major leaguers. Fully cognizant of his challengers' plans, Mele intoned, "We're going to be even more aggressive in our thinking than we were last year because the other clubs are going to bunt and steal and hit-and-run on us. We proved you can't sit around and wait for a home run to win a ball game and a pennant."[2]

After posting a strong 15–6 record over the last three weeks of spring training, confidence appeared to seep from every Twin pore. Fully imbued with bravado, Griffith proclaimed his club's 1966 edition to be "the strongest club I've ever been associated with."[3] But the bluster of Griffith's optimism and the gusto of a season-opening sweep at home against the Athletics suddenly deteriorated when the Twins were hampered by inactivity due to poor weather. A series of April postponements in the Twin Cities, Kansas City, and then for five straight games on a trip to Detroit, Baltimore, and Washington signaled a withering number of makeup contests to be played in the coming months. "We'll have to start all over to get into shape," griped Mele. "It would help if we could at least work out. But the field has been too wet everywhere."[4]

When the skies did clear, the Twins found that losses were piling up at an unaccustomed rate because of a collective slump by many batters and the underperformance by pitchers who were relied on to replicate their feats of the previous year. Less than two months into the season, one Twins' beat reporter unleashed his poison pen to implore Mele to "wake up" and give his men "a kick in the pants" to shake them from their lethargy, but they stumbled along as a .500 team already 14 games out of first place at the end of June.[5] Desperately needing to sweep a five-game series against front-running Baltimore if they were to show any sign of getting themselves into the pennant race, Minnesota dropped all five contests and thereby fell into a hopeless 19-game deficit. A writer from Minneapolis observed that the Twins had become "sagging losers," while Chicago's Stanky labeled Mele as "Benedict Arnold" for committing the "traitorous deed of handing Minnesota's 1965 pennant pattern to Baltimore."[6] Concurring with the accusation, Mele stated, "If the Orioles put on our road suits, I'd swear they were my Twins of 1965."[7] Baltimore was, indeed, enjoying its first of many fine seasons as one of the premier teams of the era.

While the defending American League champions were not to catch the front-running Orioles, they did use a string of modest winning streaks to slowly piece together a very respectable 54–30 record after the lost weekend in Baltimore. By averting losing streaks that would enervate their turnabout, Minnesota climbed into second place on the strength of key contributions by a host of regulars. Mudcat Grant, who was a woeful 5–12 at the All-Star break, won eight of his last nine decisions to tie Jim Merritt for second on the team with 13 victories, but perennial Gold Glove winner Jim Kaat was the true star on the Minnesota mound. The Dutchman outpaced AL starters in almost every major category: 25 wins, 41 games started, 304⅔ innings pitched, and 19 complete games, while his 205 strikeouts were second only to the Indians' Sam McDowell. Al Worthington missed action following an untimely mishap in which he caught the index and middle fingers of his right hand

In a career that eventually spanned four decades, Jim Kaat won 16 Gold Gloves for his fielding excellence.

in the garage door at his home, but he returned to the Twins bullpen in early August and inspired enough confidence for Mele to presciently declare, "We've got a good chance to finish second."[8] The rugged veteran finished with 16 saves and averaged just over one strikeout per each of his 91 innings pitched. Dave Boswell and Jim Perry, both showing signs of brighter days ahead in the Twins rotation, won 12 and 11 games, respectively.

On offense, Harmon Killebrew and Tony Oliva were their reliable selves, the former finishing with a solid .281 average and placing second to Triple Crown winner Frank Robinson in homers (39) and RBIs (110), the latter coming in second to Robinson in both batting average (.307) and runs scored (99). In his first full season with Minnesota, Cesar Tovar showed his true value during the 134 games in which he played. Tovar's speed fit perfectly with Mele's running game, and his ability to play virtually anywhere on the diamond allowed the manager the luxury of inserting him into the lineup to fill the most pressing need.

Several disappointing performances hindered the Twins and thus thwarted their title defense. Earl Battey, whose best days were clearly behind him, appeared in only 115 games as injuries continued to erode the erstwhile iron man. The 20 home runs hit by Hall appear to be a good year's total, but as Twins historians Rick Little and Bill Morlock observe with no small amount of exasperation, when this amount is matched against his RBI total of 47, "that means, not counting the times he tallied an RBI for knocking himself across the plate with a homer, he only managed to advance 27 players to the plate. That's almost beyond imagination."[9] Ted Uhlaender, Hall's stand-in, could not deliver on the promise he displayed in the minors, where he hit .340 on several occasions, as the rookie batted only .226 in his first full season in Minnesota. For Versalles, the catalyst who had propelled the Twins to the top of the American League, his descent was painful for many to watch, as the feisty Cuban could muster only a .249 average, seven home runs, and 36 RBIs. The shortstop was caught stealing more often than he was successful at swiping a base, with only ten thefts to show for his 22 attempts.

Another troubling question revolved around Bob Allison, whose value had plummeted in 1966. Playing poorly in spring training, Allison forced Mele to start the season with Sandy Valdespino in left field with the former Rookie of the Year on the bench. Allison pulled up lame in the month of May, and then lost more playing time after being hit by a pitch in mid–July and breaking a bone in his left hand. Slumps and injuries resulted in what Allison's biographer termed "the first really futile year in Bob's tenure as an American League star."[10] Bleak totals of eight homers, 19 RBIs, and a .220 average did not bode well for the veteran outfielder.

Griffith elected to make no trades to fortify weaknesses during the pennant-winning season, and his gamble paid off. But the pat hand of 1966 returned a second-place finish for the Twins, who landed ten games behind the Orioles in the loss column as Baltimore moved to the top of the league. For the upcoming 1967 season, new blood would be an essential element if Minnesota hoped to rebound. Personnel changes commenced 48 hours after the wearisome campaign drew to a close.

Coaches Johnny Sain and Hal Naragon were released following the culmination of a feud with Mele that had dragged on for over a year. From Sain's perspective, his input about the pitching staff was being ignored by Mele, whom Sain felt was making virtually all of the decisions regarding how the pitchers were to be handled. Mele had found Naragon to be an unequivocal supporter of Sain, thus rendering him expendable as well. By granting Mele's wish to have the two coaches removed, Griffith tersely hoped for an improvement in relations among Mele's staff: "This should clear the air. You have to have harmony in your leadership. Apparently we didn't have it."[11] Early Wynn, who spent three seasons as the pitching coach for Cleveland, was selected by Griffith to replace Sain. Pressure would be on Wynn to maintain the quality of the Twins' staff, a group which he himself claimed was "second to none" in the American League.[12]

Adding to the growing disenchantment was Kaat, who drew Griffith's ire when he issued a statement critical of Sain's dismissal, as the bonhomie that seemed so dominant a trait among the former league champions continued to dissolve. By virtue of his emergence as the winner in the Sain-Naragon debate, Mele had placed himself in a difficult position. As Max Nichols wrote, "Griffith left no doubt that Mele is on the spot next year — [he] must contend for the American League pennant or lose his job." The "player's manager" now found himself having to curry more favor with the owner than with his men on the field.[13]

Griffith also drafted a list of priorities to be addressed regarding player improvements, among them a need to "acquire a righthanded-hitting left fielder" who would force "Killebrew to the two infield posts" to which he was accustomed to playing.[14] Other exigencies demanded help in the middle infield as well as the bullpen, where the two eldest hurlers were a cause for concern. Worthington's return to the Twins was in doubt, and Johnny Klippstein, who pitched less than 13 innings in the last half of the season, was released shortly after the season. Ironically, Griffith deemed the catching trio of Battey, Zimmerman, and Russ Nixon as being "ample" and "not our trouble spot," comments which raise a fair degree of consternation when one recounts Battey's physical condition and the tepid batting ability of the latter two backstops.[15]

At baseball's annual winter meetings in December 1966 held in Pittsburgh, Griffith consummated a pair of major trades as if his intent were to make up for his inactivity over the past two years. Departing Minnesota were several Twins who had been instrumental in the rise of the club to its hard-earned 1965 pennant. Don Mincher, who had earlier groused about his lack of playing time, and Hall, the former All-Star who was benched when left-handed pitchers became difficult for him to solve, were sent along with relief pitcher Pete Cimino to the California Angels for Dean Chance. The Halos' right-handed ace had won the 1964 Cy Young Award by virtue of his 20–9 record and 1.65 ERA, but his performance over the last two seasons yielded a moderate 27–27 record. Speaking in reference to Chance's pairing with Kaat in the Minnesota rotation, the frugal Griffith suddenly became a spend-thrift when confronted with having to pay Chance a salary in the $50,000 range because he believed the Twins "may have the best right-handed starter and the best left-handed starter in the American League right now."[16] Bill Rigney, Chance's manager in California, felt that with his former ace now toiling for the offensively potent Twins, the pitcher's presence virtually guaranteed Minnesota the AL pennant.

Griffith further thinned the numbers of his longtime players by shipping Camilo Pascual, whose best years had also passed, and infielder Bernie Allen to the Washington Senators for Ron Kline, a 34-year-old veteran reliever who saved 52 games over the past two seasons. Enamored by what he viewed as a surfeit of pitching, Griffith felt comfortable moving forward knowing that Chance and Kaat were the anchors of a starting rotation that also included Grant, Boswell, Perry, and Merritt. Minnesota's best reliever had been Worthington, who wanted to continue pitching even as his 38th birthday approached, but Kline provided the Twins with another reason to feel that late-inning leads would be preserved. Griffith still lacked the new left fielder he desired, but Tovar, Oliva, and Killebrew formed a solid base for the top half of the batting order. Mele, like Griffith, exuded confidence about the depth of the pitching staff.

While 1966 was a down season in Minnesota, Griffith's willingness to revamp the roster with trades and fresh faces on the coaching staff indicated that he was poised to meet the demands of getting his team back into contention. Charles Johnson of the *Tribune* advised that the team be given a more prudent evaluation because despite the number of recent personnel changes, some "malcontents" still needed to be pared from the Twins, including "certain holdovers who have indicated that they are sliding downhill."[17] Although Johnson did not divulge the names of the less desirable players, it is easy to imagine that Versalles, Grant, and Allison were among those whom he believed to be in possession of a bad attitude, diminishing skills, or some combination of both. But of the three teams of major interest in these pages, the Twins were the only franchise among them to remain in the chase for the 1967 American League pennant until the last weekend of that exciting campaign.

## 1967—The Wildest Season

For anyone who witnessed firsthand the last few weeks of the 1967 season, a look at the final AL standings can quickly bring back a flood of memories. Twins' fans had good reason to cheer in the second half of that season, but for much of the early going, Minnesota hardly looked worthy of contending. However, some new blood in the lineup and a resurgence following a change of managers nearly carried the Twins to another American League crown.

Remaining as the *bête noir* in the Twins lineup as the opening of the 1967 campaign drew near, the second base position still had not been filled by anyone capable of providing a reasonable degree of quality play. Although Frank Quilici was the leading candidate to take over at the keystone spot in 1966, he did not secure a place on the roster and never appeared in a Minnesota uniform that year. In 1967, Quilici lost out to a rookie of Panamanian origin who had once so impressed a Twin scout with his superb play on a New York City sandlot team that the youngster was smuggled into and out of Yankee Stadium for a brief, clandestine tryout while Minnesota was in town for a series in the Bronx.

Few baseball players carry the distinction of having been born on a train, but that was exactly the case for Rod Carew. With his father and expectant mother en route by rail from Gatun, Panama, to a hospital in Ancón, the couple came up short in their attempt to reach the medical facility, as Olga Carew gave birth to a son while in transit. Named for the doctor who assisted with the delivery, Rodney Cline Carew lived a hardscrabble life in the Canal Zone before emigrating to New York City as a young teenager. During his final year of high school, Carew joined a sandlot group that played in the Bronx Federation League.

It was with the New York Cavaliers that he drew the attention of a Minnesota scout whose son coincidentally was a teammate of Carew's. After impressing Twins' personnel who saw him play in two BFL games, Carew was quietly ushered into Yankee Stadium for a very brief workout when the Twins visited during the summer of 1964. Impressing Sam Mele with a mere twelve swings in the batting cage, the manager demanded that Carew be removed from the plate, lest anyone from the Yankees catch a glimpse of the gem that the Twins had discovered and were now anxious to sign. Herb Stein was the New York metropolitan scout who brought Carew into the Twins' fold. Almost immediately following Carew's high school graduation, he began his climb through the Minnesota minor league system as a second baseman.

Bursting on the scene as the 1967 American League Rookie of the Year, Rod Carew went on to become the best pure hitter of the 1970s.

Carew's batting stroke seemed to never fail him — he hit .325 for

Melbourne in the short-season Rookie League and .303 for Orlando of the Florida State League in 1965 — but he also later admitted that he "developed an attitude" as a reaction to the racism to which he had been subjected in the South.[18] Also raising Carew's ire were "sly remarks" emanating from teammates envious of the Panamanian's success, and the moniker "Calvin's bobo" especially stung the sensitive Carew.[19] When minor injuries forced Carew to the bench, his absence from the lineup also drew the taunts of teammates who suspected he was more concerned with his own health than with helping the club. With Wilson of the Carolina League in 1966, Carew's average slipped to .292, but the Twins front office was hopeful that Carew's part-time service in the Marine Corps Reserves would mature their petulant infielder.

Originally ticketed for Denver of the Pacific Coast League in 1967, Carew accomplished the rare feat of moving from the Double-A level to the Twins roster. With former second baseman Billy Martin tutoring Carew on the finer points of playing in the field, Carew appeared in 134 games at second base and excelled with a .292 average, 22 doubles, 7 triples, 8 homers, and 51 RBIs while earning both the Baseball Writers' Association and *The Sporting News* honors as the American League Rookie of the Year. Despite his tendency to brood, Carew's ability with a bat enabled him to remain a fixture in the Twins infield for the next eleven years, as he developed into one of the greatest hitters of his era.

The transactions consummated by Griffith over the winter may have fortified the pitching staff, but it seemed the Twins could not shed the bugbear of poor play that haunted them for several years. Mistakes that did not necessarily appear in the Minnesota box scores were again plaguing the team, and time spent in spring training to work on the fundamentals of the game appeared to have been of little utility. When the regular season commenced, as one write characterized it, "the goofs were a continuation of the giveaway style of play the Twins displayed in Florida, where they gave up an average of one unearned run a game.... The supposedly pennant-contending Twins seem to be vying with each other to replace Charlie Brown's inept fictional idol, Joe Shlabotnik, as the most undesirable bubble-gum card in America."[20]

Beset by a torrent of misjudged fly balls, baserunning gaffes, and other assorted displays of ineptitude, the Twins stumbled out of the gate with an 11–15 record, good for a share of last place in the AL with, of all teams, the defending World Series champion Orioles. So horrific was their performance in one game that a bewildered Mele sent his men back onto the field after the stadium cleared out so that he could drill his players in basic execution. But Mele's punishment was to little avail, as by early June, with Kaat struggling on the mound and Oliva lost at the plate with an average in the low .200s, the Twins continued to drift near the .500 mark in the middle of the standings. Defending his earlier comment about Minnesota's assumed superiority, Angels skipper Rigney found reason to excuse the lapses of many clubs by lamenting, "More than ever teams are beating themselves by mistakes instead of beating opponents by pulling off smart plays. It's a common ailment and does not mean that the Twins should be quaratined."[21]

The Twins need not have been treated as lepers, but the consternation raised by their torpor at last became too much for Griffith to bear. On June 9, the owner belied his statements of just three weeks earlier, in which he scoffed at the notion of changing managers, and relieved Mele of his duties. Ushered in as the new pilot was Cal Ermer, the manager at Minnesota's Triple-A affiliate in Denver, who in the summer of 1965 was touted by

Denver general manager Jim Burris as being cut from the same cloth as Ralph Houk, Gene Mauch, and Johnny Keane. Ermer was now charged with setting the listless Twins back on a winning course, while the deposed skipper was at a loss to explain his dismissal and defended the manner in which he handled the club. "I managed the same this season as I did when we won the pennant," said Mele, whose capital among his players had fallen so much that only Killebrew and Kline stopped by to say farewell before Mele's hasty departure from the Twins clubhouse.[22]

Few players' tears were shed over the firing — unlike Martin, who was genuinely upset to see his friend be shown the door — but history shows that a new manager was exactly the tonic the Twins needed. By the end of July, Minnesota was still struggling in fifth place, but the fight for the league lead was contested by a clutch of teams so closely bunched together that the Twins were only 3½ games off the pace. Dean Chance was pitching in the manner that had earned him his Cy Young Award, by mid–August Allison rediscovered his batting stroke as did the nearly-forgotten Rich Rollins, and Jim Perry was employed as a fifth starter whose 5–1 record from late July through the following month helped boost the Twins into first place near the end of August. Although the Twins' power numbers were down slightly from 1966, Ermer's steady hand on the Twins' tiller furnished a calming influence which translated into more victories.

Minnesota was clearly on a hot streak, but with Boston, Detroit, and Chicago all very much in the pennant hunt, the Twins traded places in the standings with their rivals sometimes literally by the hour. At one point in August, the White Sox, Red Sox, and Twins each spent a few hours one evening in first place as they completed their respective games. By the first week of September all four were in a virtual dead heat for the league lead. Making a comeback of sorts was the "hero du jour" as Uhlaender, Merritt, Carew, and Rich Reese made timely contributions with a fielding gem, a well-pitched game, or a clutch hit. Oliva swatted his way back to the upper reaches of the league's hitters, Killebrew homered and drove in runs at his accustomed pace, and Tovar battled Oliva for the AL leadership in doubles. Excitement had indeed returned to Minnesota and was approaching a fever pitch with a few weeks left in the campaign.

Exuding the fervor of the day, the first page of the September 17 *Tribune* sports section shouted out good news and bad: "White Sox Rally for 4 in Ninth to Win"; "Twins Lose League Lead to Tigers"; "Orioles Tumble Red Sox"; "Tigers Nudge Nats." The scrum among the four leaders led some teams to nefarious attempts to gain whatever edge they could. Stanky's White Sox in particular drew the harshest criticism for the landscaping they performed on the Comiskey Park infield, which included several inches of sand in front of home plate and turf placed atop the grass just beyond. "They must have put a hundred gallons of water on top of all that stuff," beefed Cleveland manager Joe Adcock, who added, "I can see them wetting down the infield to slow grounders, but that was ridiculous.... It was a lousy mess."[23]

As the four contenders hurtled down the stretch in the last half of September, the Twins held first place by the narrowest of margins. On September 23, the "magic number" for Minnesota, Detroit, Boston, and Chicago was nearly equal to the remaining games that each of these teams had left to play. The first to fade were the White Sox, who won but two of their final eight contests. Of the surviving three clubs, the Twins clung precariously to the top of the standings thanks to Chance's 20th victory of the season, Kaat's personal seven-game winning streak — he was undefeated for the month — and an offense led by Allison and Killebrew, who vied with Boston's Carl Yastrzemski for the home run title.

In the last week of the season, the Tigers refused to cede ground, beating the Yankees on the road before returning to Detroit, while the Twins with their one-game lead over the Red Sox traveled to Boston for the season's final two games. Red Sox manager Dick Williams feared the worst when Boston lost twice in Cleveland with only a handful of games left — "Williams Says His Bosox Running Out of Tomorrows" ran one *Tribune* headline. In the climactic final weekend, the Tigers had to play back-to-back doubleheaders at home against the Angels and accomplish the envious task of winning at least three of their contests while also hoping that the Twins would lose at least once in Boston. The Tigers split both twin bills and were eliminated in the ultimate game of their schedule as Twins alumnus Mincher contributed a home run to one of the California wins.

At Fenway Park, the Twins were in control of their own fate but were denied a return to the World Series after neither Kaat nor Chance could deliver the blow necessary to subdue Boston. In the first game on Saturday, Williams gambled that his starter, Jose Santiago, would come through by pitching his regular turn in the rotation, thereby leaving ace Jim Lonborg available for the finale on Sunday. Years later Williams wrote that "*not* changing strategies worked. Once again, under-managing triumphed over over-managing."[24] Winning for the twelfth time in his last sixteen decisions by allowing two runs in seven-plus innings, Santiago saw his teammates accumulate six runs over the fifth, sixth, and seventh innings, with Yastrzemski and George Scott stroking key home runs to rally past the Twins. Kaat broke down with an injury to his left elbow while nursing a 1–0 lead, as Perry and Kline could not keep the Red Sox in check. Scott broke a 2–2 tie with his homer in the sixth, while Yastrzemski blasted a three-run shot to cap the eventual 6–4 win.

Boston and Minnesota were tied entering the final day of the season, as Lonborg and Chance, the respective starting pitchers, each sought to administer the *coup de grâce*. The Red Sox theme of "The Impossible Dream" was destined to become a reality, however, as they surmounted the odds against a ninth-place team rising to win the pennant the very next season. Staked to a 2–0 lead, Chance held the Red Sox at bay until Lonborg, who was winless in six decisions against the Twins during his three major league seasons, opened the fateful sixth inning with a bunt single. A pair of singles loaded the bases for Yastrzemski, whose single tied the game and further enhanced his credentials for the AL MVP award. A Ken Harrelson groundball scored the go-ahead run, Worthington wild-pitched in the fourth tally, and an error by Killebrew at first allowed the final Boston run to score. The Twins rallied in the eighth, cutting the lead to 5–3, but Lonborg completed his mission by shutting down the Twins after yielding a leadoff single in the ninth. When the last out was recorded, pandemonium erupted at Fenway Park as jubilant fans stormed the field and mobbed their heroes, while the disconsolate Twins escaped to the clubhouse.

At that moment, the Red Sox technically had clinched only a tie for the pennant, but when the Angels beat the Tigers in the second game of their Sunday doubleheader at Detroit, Boston officially became the American League champion. Griffith, who had traveled to Boston hoping to attend a celebration like the one he missed two years earlier in Washington, "wore a brown suit and a frown" and immediately promised changes for 1968.[25]

Among the anticipated moves to be made in the offseason were acquisition of a catcher and the removal of some of the suspected malcontents. Pleased by the manner in which

Carew responded to the challenge of moving from Double-A to the majors, Griffith wondered if Graig Nettles could also accomplish the feat. In addition to hoping Nettles could become a full-time Twin, Griffith viewed catching prospect George Mitterwald as a likely candidate to replace Battey behind the plate. Not to be overlooked for his role in breathing new life into the Twins was Ermer, the 43-year-old rookie skipper who guided the Twins to a 66–46 record after assuming managerial duties. His debut in the major leagues was a baptism by fire, but Ermer displayed the comportment necessary to withstand the pressure of a pennant race that was by any measure one of the most intense in baseball history.

The unfortunate conclusion for the Twins in Boston was also punctuated with a rancorous postscript over how potential World Series shares would be split among the uniformed personnel had Minnesota reached the Series. Players loyal to former manager Mele — a group led by Chance and Worthington — argued in favor of a split share for the ousted pilot, whereas a second contingent, led by Kaat, Allison, and Uhlaender, was adamantly opposed to any kind of monetary award. When details about the internal friction surfaced as the pennant race reached its final weekend, the discord astounded many. "We couldn't believe it," said one Red Sox veteran when he learned that some Twins wanted to deny Mele a cut, and one Twins player commented about the acrimony caused by the fiasco, "I've never been so ashamed of anything in my life."[26] The Twins clubhouse had become a domicile divided over a manager no longer associated with the team, as bruised feelings over money stung many players who worked so diligently through the mid–1960s to make Minnesota one of the better clubs in the American League.

Excruciating as the 1967 season had ended for the Twins, family squabbles in the front office compounded the difficulties for an owner who was intent on retooling for the next season. Calvin Griffith sought to bring his son Clark into the organization but wanted the young man to climb the same ladder that he once had. When Clark demurred about learning the craft of baseball management by starting in the minor leagues, the Dartmouth-educated scion's attitude drew the ire of several family members already entrenched in the Twins front office. Jon Kerr, Calvin Griffith's biographer, poignantly summarized what became of the team when he wrote, "Just as 1967 had ended in turbulence and disappointment on the field, the Griffith organization would never again be able to steer a course of sustained peace and security."[27] The key word is *sustained*. Although Minnesota did reasonably well in the three seasons beyond 1967, the Twins lacked the ability to keep the foothold they had established in their pennant-winning season.

## The Swoon Revisited

Cal Ermer's managerial debut was nonetheless encouraging despite the Twins' failure to secure the 1967 American League pennant. By reversing Minnesota's early-season swoon and leading the team to a remarkable turnaround, Ermer had earned the opportunity to continue at his post in 1968, but Griffith was less inclined to give some players the latitude he accorded his skipper.

Deciding that changes in two key positions were in order, Griffith traded Versalles and Grant to the Los Angeles Dodgers for pitchers Robert Lane Miller and Ron Perranoski and catcher John Roseboro. At the age of 34, Grant appeared to be on the downside of his career, and Versalles, still youthful at age 27 but whose stock had diminished significantly in the last two years, had an attitude that curried little favor among his teammates. By consummating this deal, Griffith gave the Twins bullpen some balance with the addition of the left-handed Perranoski to complement Worthington, as Roseboro was slated to fill the shoes of the departed Earl Battey, who appeared behind the plate in only 41 games and hit just .165. Versalles's replacement would be chosen from among a contingent that included some minor league infielders, the weak-hitting Jackie Hernandez, who, according to the Twins, "could prove to be every bit as valuable to the team as was Versalles," and should all else fail at shortstop, the team had nothing to fear because "there's always Cesar Tovar!"[28]

When the 1968 season began, Minnesota bolted out of the gate with a six-game winning streak but thereafter fell into a pattern of play that slowly submerged the Twins into the middle of the AL standings, where they remained for the rest of year. Twins hitters were held hostage to the forces currently affecting all of major league baseball, notably those characterized by dominant pitching performances and batting averages that in the AL had been in a steady decline for years.

In 1961, the Twins' first year in Minnesota, the league batting average attained its highest point of the 1960s, but immediately after the AL's expansion from eight to ten teams that year, hitting began a steady descent across the league while earned-run averages followed a parallel course. In the case of the Twins, the ability of their batters was reflected in averages generally higher than that of the league — Minnesota's average peaked in 1962 — but as league pitching strengthened, Twins batters suffered a decline in average. Beginning in 1962, the Twins' ERA was also better than that of the league and, except for 1964, dropped each season. When the American League expanded again in 1969, batting averages and ERAs experienced a marked increase.

| | AL Batting Average | Twins Batting Average | AL ERA | Twins ERA |
| --- | --- | --- | --- | --- |
| 1961 | .256 | .250 | 4.02 | 4.28 |
| 1962 | .255 | .260 | 3.97 | 3.89 |
| 1963 | .247 | .255 | 3.63 | 3.28 |
| 1964 | .247 | .252 | 3.63 | 3.58 |
| 1965 | .242 | .254 | 3.46 | 3.14 |
| 1966 | .240 | .249 | 3.44 | 3.13 |
| 1967 | .236 | .240 | 3.23 | 3.14 |
| 1968 | .230 | .237 | 2.98 | 2.89 |
| 1969 | .246 | .268 | 3.62 | 3.24 |

*Source: Gary Gillette and Pete Palmer, The ESPN Baseball Encyclopedia.*

This illustrates the state of the game in 1968, dubbed "the year of the pitcher." So overwhelming had pitching become in both the American and National leagues that it prompted one sportswriter to opine that "[a] 'big inning' occurs when a team scores once."[29] Indicative of the offensive dearth which placed Minnesota in a lethargic state were the games they played in early May. Beginning with a series in Detroit on May 1, the Twins went 5–8 and scored a total of just 24 runs in those thirteen games, hardly the type of production that had struck fear in Minnesota's opposing pitchers for much of the middle of the 1960s.

While Detroit dueled with Baltimore and Cleveland through the first half of the season, the Tigers used the heroics of 31-game winner Denny McLain to stay ahead of the pack. The fourth-place Twins lost precious ground in the standings when they were swept during a crucial mid–June series in Detroit that could have boosted Minnesota to within four games of the front-running Tigers. There followed the unfortunate distraction of Rod Carew's peevish threat to leave the team in Cleveland when Ermer told the second baseman that he needed more time to get into shape following a short stint with the Marine Corps Reserve. Although Carew never actually left the club, he later confessed that his attitude and immaturity got the better of him because he believed he was fit to play. While Carew pouted, he may have noticed that Killebrew and Allison, who had been temporarily benched by Ermer in Cleveland, were providing moral support for their fellow Twins rather than sulking about the manager's decision. Carew "could profit by observing his older and more experienced teammates," noted a Minnesota scribe, who chided the young infielder with the hope that "he learned a valuable lesson … that the team comes first."[30]

Killebrew's slump — he was batting only .204 with 13 home runs and 34 RBIs — prior to that season's All-Star break did not keep him off the American League roster for the mid-summer classic, but his appearance for the AL resulted in another devastating injury. Stretching for a throw at first base, Killebrew severely tore his left hamstring and was lost for much of the second half of the season. Standing in at first for the Twins, Rich Reese performed well in the short term but was hobbled by his own knee problems. Minnesota, already 15 games out of first place, was soon mired in seventh place with little hope of advancing.

Some fine individual performances kept the Twins from coming completely undone, as Tony Oliva hit .289 for the year and was closely followed by Uhlaender at .283, which were third- and fifth-best in the AL, respectively. Carew ended at .273, and Tovar, who batted .272, fully demonstrated his versatility by starting a late-season contest on the mound and played the rest of the game at all the other positions. Meanwhile, a rookie who was picked by the Twins in the 1965 draft gained attention during his September recall from the minor leagues. Graig Nettles, who had established himself as a power hitter in the minors, continued to show his muscle by clouting five homers in 22 games for the Twins. This was the kind of promise that Griffith was counting on to lead his club back into contention, but the owner chose to use Nettles as trade bait one year hence rather than keep him on Minnesota's roster.

On the mound, Chance (16–16, 2.53) and Kaat (14–12, 2.94) were the best among the starters, and the ageless Worthington logged 17 saves and a 2.72 ERA. If the pitchers had been as successful as Chance was against the formidable Tigers, perhaps the Twins' story would have had a happier ending. In his seven games against the eventual World Series champions, Chance pitched 50 innings and posted a 4–1 mark accompanied by a stingy 1.62 ERA. However, the collective team offensive output at times mimicked Chance's batting average of .054 to finish fifth in the league in runs scored, as Minnesota's final record came to 79 wins against 83 losses.

Wasting no time in clearing the decks, Griffith fingered the managerial shortcomings as the root cause for the Twins' woes and jettisoned his manager and the entire coaching staff one day after the conclusion of the 1968 campaign. "The main problem was that Ermer didn't have control of his players," reported the *Tribune*, as speculation abounded that Billy Martin would be named manager.[31] Lending credence to these rumors were Griffith's own comments about the former Twins coach, whose managerial apprenticeship was with Minnesota's AAA affiliate that season: "Billy did a heck of a job at Denver this year. The big thing is his temperament…. I'm looking for a take-charge type of manager. Martin was a tough coach."[32]

Neither was Griffith in any mood to excuse time lost by his players due to injury, and even the recuperating Killebrew did not escape his wrath. Reese would be available at first base, Nettles had a chance to take over at third, and Killebrew, coming off a season in which he barely hit his weight (.210), would not likely be able to play the outfield. Killebrew was on notice that he "would have to hit a ton" if he entertained thoughts of reclaiming a spot in the lineup.[33] Griffith felt that the underperformance of the Twins also hurt him at the box office, where the Twins drew over one million fans but nonetheless were 340,000 short of 1967's attendance.

Minnesota reached another crossroads at the end of 1968. The Twins were faced with the challenge of regrouping a cast of players, young and old, under a new manager who was no stranger to the Twin Cities, a firebrand whose desire to win — and pilot *his* team on *his* terms — would lead him to a successful but ephemerally stormy tenure under Calvin Griffith.

## *"A Keg of Dynamite"*

When Billy Martin became the Twins third base coach in 1965, the influence he spread among the regular position players became evident. Mentoring the infielders on defensive techniques and cracking the whip to make baserunners more aggressive, Martin made a vital contribution to Minnesota's pennant-winning season. When Griffith fired Mele midway through 1967, Martin lost out to Ermer in the Twins' managerial sweepstakes, but it seemed only a matter of time until Martin would at last be appointed a big league skipper.

In 1968 Martin was serving in his accustomed role as Twins coach, but Griffith offered him the manager's post at Denver in May when the Bears' record fell to 8–22. Reluctant to forfeit his current job in favor of one at the AAA level, where he feared he would become a forgotten man, Martin accepted the challenge of his first managerial assignment and put Denver on a winning track. After guiding the Bears to a 65–50 record, Martin seemed a natural fit to return to the Twin Cities to restore the luster to a Twins team only one year removed from its last serious run at the league crown. Griffith claimed that he wanted Martin to serve time in the minors "to see how well Martin could learn to control his volatile temper," but the eight times that the emotionally-charged Martin was ejected from Denver games indicated otherwise.[34]

As speculation continued to escalate about the selection of Martin to replace Ermer, support for him came from an unlikely source. Denying past animosities with Martin and now promoting the supposed mutual respect that existed between them, former Minnesota pitching coach Johnny Sain expressed his hope that Martin would be placed at the Twins' helm. In early October 1968, Griffith officially named Martin as the fourth manager of the Twins, thereby making him the latest in a series of young AL skippers who, along with Dick Williams and Earl Weaver, would leave an indelible mark on the league from the late 1960s through the mid–1970s. Upon the announcement of Martin's hiring, the new manager issued an edict that set the tone for his regime: his men were expected to hustle, act like men, and play the game of baseball with the demeanor befitting a winner. While at Denver, Martin forged a serious working relationship with long-time minor league pitcher Art Fowler, so it was no coincidence that Fowler became the pitching coach at the various stops along Martin's managerial travels through the American League in the 1970s and 1980s.

Martin's AAA stint won him Griffith's admiration — "Frankly, I doubted whether he had the ability to handle men," said the owner, "but he proved at Denver that I was wrong" — and reinforced his value to some players already on the major league roster.[35] Rod Carew admitted that Martin's departure to Denver had a negative impact on him, so the second baseman welcomed his return. As Martin's influence had been felt by other Twins, especially the infielders, a young Graig Nettles also received advice and instruction when Martin became his manager at Denver. Nettles shed his doubts about Martin after being inculcated with his style of managing. "When I saw the results, I stopped hating Billy Martin," said Nettles in a later interview, "and I began to see him for what he was: an extraordinary leader."[36]

Signed to a one-year contract, Martin was under pressure to live up to the expectations of those observers, such as Yankee manager Ralph Houk, who believed that the Twins were a virtual cinch to reach the World Series again. At Martin's disposal would be a new shortstop acquired in late November by Griffith, who put an end to the brief Jackie Hernandez experiment when he traded pitcher Jim Merritt to Cincinnati for Leo Cardenas, a National League All-Star four of the previous five seasons and a past Gold Glove winner. A starting lineup that now featured Cardenas, Carew, Oliva, Tovar, Uhlaender, and a recovered Killebrew created optimism for a bright season ahead.

Attached to this potential success was the cost of doing business with the autocratic Martin. Not only would Griffith inherit Fowler as one of Martin's coaches, but the owner also took on the baggage of Martin's inveterate combativeness, which had already reared its ugly head while Martin was a Twins coach. Among the more notorious incidents were the Sain-Martin spat in 1965 and Martin's fights with Howard Fox, Minnesota's traveling secretary, during the following summer, to say nothing of the alcohol-fueled reputation that preceded Martin's arrival in the Twin Cities. There was no small degree of trepidation on the part of Griffith, whose team's 1969 media guide described Martin as a "take-charge guy" who was "aggressive, colorful, [and] determined."[37] Yet for all the passion that Martin brought with him, he also inspired Griffith to feel "as if he were 'sitting on a keg of dynamite.'"[38]

With the fuse figuratively, if not also literally, lit, Martin and the Twins embarked on their maiden voyage in 1969 under a new format that resulted from the expansion of both major leagues. The addition of new clubs meant that Minnesota would have fewer teams to beat in capturing a divisional title, but it also entailed the necessity of winning a newly-created round of playoffs in order to win the pennant and advance to the World Series.

## Major Changes in the Big Leagues

Several important events impacted major league baseball during its most formative period in the modern era. The second expansion program of the 1960s and the removal of General William Eckert as commissioner of major league baseball thrust new venues and a new chief executive upon the game and gave birth to a new dynamic that, in fits and starts, positioned baseball not only to remain competitive against other major sports but also to scale new heights of popularity. Baseball also acted to put more offense into a game that by 1968 had grown moribund with dominant pitching performances that ultimately translated into too many low-scoring games.

Although major league baseball experienced growing pains at the onset of the 1960s, as the decade neared its conclusion, executives of both the National and American leagues deemed it necessary to again add more teams to attract fans, or, more precisely, paying customers. Baseball enjoyed a monopoly of sorts on sports fans' attention during the summer months, but competition from expanded professional football, basketball, and hockey seasons siphoned increasing numbers of fans and revenue during the spring and autumn. By adding franchises to four cities for the 1969 season, baseball hoped to rekindle fan interest in Kansas City, which had been abandoned by Charlie Finley's Athletics after 1967, and to establish new fan bases in Montreal, San Diego, and Seattle.

While the additions of San Diego and Seattle provided outposts in the extreme northern and southern reaches of the Pacific Coast, the awarding of the Montreal franchise was controversial because of the rebuff of those hopeful of baseball's return to Milwaukee, which had lost the Braves in 1966, or the creation of teams in Dallas or Buffalo. As Joe Durso wrote, reflecting another angle, "The losers in the [selection process] were disconsolate with strong overtones that cities in the United States had been bypassed for a Canadian city."[39] Regardless of which cities the new teams would reside in, both the AL and NL were now stocked with twelve teams each, Kansas City and Seattle becoming part of the American League with Montreal and San Diego joining the National.

By the summer of 1968 the leagues had agreed on splitting into east and west divisions of six teams each, with a new best-three-of-five-games series to be played to determine the respective league champions that would then advance to the World Series. The assignment of teams to their new divisions was controversial in its own right because the American League literally adhered to a geographic split of its teams, placing both expansion clubs Kansas City and Seattle in the western division with California, Chicago, Minnesota, and Oakland. The AL East was comprised of holdovers Baltimore, Boston, Cleveland, Detroit, New York, and Washington. The league maintained its 162-game slate by scheduling teams to play 18 games against each opponent within their division and 12 games against every team in the other division. This configuration meant that the Twins had 36 contests scheduled against brand new teams that were expected to be weak competitors. If the 1968 standings foretold the possible outcome of the first season with the new divisional format, Oakland looked to be the only serious competitor capable of challenging Minnesota for the AL West title. Prognosticators who favored Minnesota also had to assume that Billy Martin could steer the Twins on a winning course.

A second major change in major league baseball came in December 1968 with the departure of Commissioner Eckert, whose resignation was forced by dissatisfied club owners headed by Baltimore's Jerry Hoffberger. This facilitated the naming of an attorney with baseball connections as Eckert's replacement. Bowie Kuhn, a Princeton alumnus who took his degree from the University of Virginia Law School, worked for a Wall Street law firm and personally tended to a variety of legal matters for the National League over a period of nearly twenty years. Better credentialed than his predecessor — Eckert earned an MBA but had no practical experience with baseball — Kuhn was a unanimous choice of the seven-member panel of owners charged with finding a new commissioner.

Named to the position in early February 1969, Kuhn assumed the executive leadership of a sport that faced an uncertain future but had taken steps to increase its fan appeal through expansion and rules changes designed to inject more offense into the game. Kuhn's term in office eventually lasted through September 1984, during which he locked horns with several owners — notably Charlie Finley — and pursued actions "in the best interest of baseball" that sometimes drew the ire of fans, players, and club officials. But when the empirical evidence of baseball's advances in the Kuhn years was gathered — not least of which were the introduction of the designated hitter, the return of All-Star balloting to the fans, league championship and World Series games played at night, and the symbiotic effect of free agency that enriched both players and team owners — the Baseball Hall of Fame Veterans Committee concluded in 2008 that Kuhn's accomplishments and the prosperity the national pastime enjoyed under his auspices warranted his induction into the Hall of Fame.

Lastly, the decline of offensive production was acted upon following the 1968 season when major league baseball's Rules Committee agreed to a pair of significant changes. For as maligned as Eckert was during his time as commissioner, he nonetheless was directly involved with proposals to lower the height of the pitching mound from fifteen to ten inches and to reduce the size of the strike zone, formerly measured from the shoulders to the bottom of the knees but now redefined to extend from the armpits to the tops of the knees. Both of these modifications were approved for the 1969 season and, along with the thinning of pitching talent due to the expansion in both leagues, brought about the desired effect of raising batting averages and the number of runs scored. In 1969, the league batting average in the AL jumped to .246, sixteen points over 1968 — the Twins enjoyed a 31-point spike — while the league ERA went from 2.98 to 3.62, as AL teams averaged 110 more runs scored for the season, rising from 553 to 663 runs. Batting averages were less dramatically inflated in the National League, climbing from .243 in 1968 to .250, but the league ERA increased from 2.99 to 3.59, as average runs scored per team went from 558 to 658.

As a revitalizing energy was beginning to influence baseball at a time when it was most needed, the Twins hoped their own changes, which added a proven shortstop to the infield and put a new manager in the dugout, would meld with the return of a healthy Harmon Killebrew to lead them to another pennant before the close of the decade.

## The Best in the West

Billy Martin began his managerial stint in Minnesota by exhibiting the same degree of intensity that marked his days as the Twins' infield and third base coach. But with his responsibilities now spread among all the players on the major league roster, as well as those making their way up from the minor leagues, Martin's fervor escalated not only to put victories in the win column but also to placate the owner who entrusted him with the fortunes of his team. Martin's philosophy of the game of baseball adhered to the simple premise which emphasized sound execution of fundamentals plus alert, aggressive play at all times. An extension of this philosophy implied that a winning team translated into heightened fan interest and ultimately more revenue for the club, which in turn translated into a contented Calvin Griffith. To carry out this mission successfully, Martin was obliged to instill the discipline lacking when Cal Ermer ran the club.

The Martin system of baseball began in earnest at the onset of spring training in 1969, when Martin drew criticism for directing his team as if it were in a pennant race rather than simply shepherding his players through the process of getting ready for the upcoming season.

For Martin, exhibition games seemed as crucial as the last contest of the World Series, but this gamesmanship was a manifestation of the only way that Martin knew how the game should be played.

Once the regular season commenced, some time was needed for the Twins to catch fire. To Martin's dismay, they lost their first four games and quickly dropped to the basement of the American League West, before they reeled off a seven-game winning streak in mid–April and shortly thereafter an eight-game winning skein that stretched into May. These victories put the Twins into first place, a position they would occupy for most of the season as they dueled with the Oakland Athletics for supremacy in the AL West. With the exception of three short-lived dips into second place, Minnesota remained atop the division after the Twins swept a series from Oakland that began on the Fourth of July. For the month as a whole, Minnesota's 23 wins against seven losses were its most productive of the season.

Despite strains on the pitching staff, Kaat and Boswell emerged as the two most reliable starters, as the bullpen was buoyed by Perranoski, who was becoming the best fireman in the AL. On offense, the hitters were slugging at a pace not seen since the halcyon days of 1965, and runners were en route to pilfering 115 bases, a Minnesota record that held until 1976. This total included seven steals of home by Carew, who was encouraged by Martin to cast aside any fears when attempting baseball's most daring theft. "You can't be afraid of being thrown out, because that's going to happen occasionally," said Martin. "You have to do it *recklessly.*"[40]

The Twins suffered no lulls of complacency with Martin lording over them, as he made sure his players remained focused at all times. When former vice president Hubert Humphrey visited the Twins clubhouse after a tough loss, Martin brooked no photo opportunity with Minnesota's popular politician, who was chased from the scene — tactfully so, at least according to Martin — because the players were supposed to be downcast over the defeat. Humphrey's banishment infuriated Griffith, however. The owner had more cause for concern in early August when Boswell, who also possessed a volatile temper and had a drinking problem, started a fight with Allison outside a bar after a game in Detroit and eventually ended up on the receiving end of a flurry of Martin's punches when the manager intervened. The bout went to Martin, who took seven stitches in his hand while inflicting 20 stitches' worth of damage to Boswell's face, as the episode became another embarrassment to the Twins' organization.

Following a suspension and recovery from his injuries, Boswell pitched so well that he won eight games over the last six weeks of the season to finish with 20 victories and tie Jim Perry for the team lead. Boswell's contribution was a huge factor in facilitating the growth of the Twins' lead from 1½ games on August 20 — the date of his return to the mound — to its nine-game margin over Oakland in the final AL West standings.

Unpleasant episodes notwithstanding, Martin's first year as a major league manager earned Minnesota the first American League West title with a 97–65 record, but credit was due many Twins for the stoic effort they turned in to keep the Athletics at bay throughout the summer. The lowest batting average among the regulars was John Roseboro's .263, which still led all catchers in the league. Oliva (.309, 24 home runs, 101 RBIs) and Carew (.332, 19 stolen bases) were joined in the .300 circle by first baseman Rich Reese (.322), who also clouted 16 homers. Uhlaender (.273) and Tovar (.288, 45 stolen bases) rounded off the outfield, but the left side of the infield infused the lineup with offense and defense that made Minnesota the best team in the west.

New shortstop Cardenas gave the dramatic improvement the Twins sought when he not only hit .280 with 10 home runs and 70 RBIs but in the field led the league at his position with 310 putouts, 570 assists, 126 double plays, and 5.7 chances per game. Mounting the greatest comeback following his terrible leg injury the previous season, the durable Killebrew appeared in 162 games and amassed league leading totals in homers (49) and RBIs (140) to capture AL Most Valuable Player honors.

For all that the Twins accomplished, they were no match for the powerful Baltimore Orioles in the inaugural American League Championship Series. In its first full season under manager Earl Weaver, Baltimore rode rough-shod over the entire league en route to 109 wins and made short work of the Twins when the Orioles swept the Twins three straight in the best-of-five series. The first two contests were low-scoring, extra-inning affairs, but then to the consternation of many observers, Martin elected to use spot-starter Bob Miller instead of a rested Kaat, who had beaten the Orioles twice in the regular season. The result was an 11–2 drubbing of the Twins. Rumors began to circulate immediately in the Twin Cities' press that Martin's job was in peril. According to Tom Briere, after the Game 3 loss, "Someone asked Martin what he thought the Twins needed next season. 'A new manager,' he said with a straight face."[41] Frustrated Twins fans vented with lusty booing during the final game in Minnesota, as Oliva was particularly stung by the spectators' behavior. "I had been booed on the road and didn't care…. To be booed at home is another matter," said the right fielder.[42]

Indeed, the turmoil generated by the imperious Martin throughout the year had become too much for the front office to bear. After taking several days following the Baltimore series to contemplate his club's future, Griffith decided that the way forward was better without Martin. Citing the stereotypical excuses of communication failures and violations of club policies, veritable as those reasons may have been, Griffith dismissed Martin, who had been labeled by one columnist as "one of the most popular figures in Twin Cities athletics."[43] Martin's winning ethic and gales of fan protest aside, the fact remained that Martin had badly worn out his welcome in Minnesota as Twins manager. When the Twins were quickly dispatched in the league championship series, Griffith's decision to fire Martin was easier to make.

## 1970—Different Manager, Same Result

"After an experience like the one I just had, maybe I'd be better off out of baseball," said Martin, who was offered up to $250 a night to perform as a nightclub singer in the Twin Cities region. Barely one week after Martin's Waterloo, his replacement was introduced by the Twins.[44] Named by *The Sporting News* as the 1962 Manager of the Year, former California Angels skipper Bill Rigney assumed managerial duties for the Twins. After running through three managers in the last three seasons, Griffith hoped that Rigney would lend some stability to a Twins team that Martin believed "could have won the pennant five years in a row."[45]

Flushed with the success of his swap with Cincinnati for Cardenas, Griffith looked once more to the trade market during the December 1969 winter meetings, this time to bolster the Twins' pitching staff. Reverting to his favorite trading partner, the Indians,

Griffith executed a major deal that sent Nettles, Uhlaender, Chance, and Miller to the Tribe for reliever Stan Williams and starter Luis Tiant. Griffith acquired Tiant with the expectation that he would hurl like the 21-game winner he was in 1968 rather than the 20-game loser he was in 1969. History tells us that the trade in the long term was a disaster for the Twins, but Griffith looked every bit the magician in the early going of the 1970 season when Tiant won his first four decisions and Williams, a 33-year-old veteran, won five games in April and May.

The Twins had a lot to prove in defense of their western division crown, especially after losing all but one of their first fifteen exhibition games of 1970 during spring training. But once regular season action began, the path they followed was strikingly similar to 1969. Minnesota embarked on a four-game winning streak which staked them to a lead in the AL West that the Twins relinquished only briefly, and on May 18 they moved into first place, where they remained for the rest of the season.

Rigney's first year at the Minnesota helm, however, was not without its perils. The starting rotation suffered greatly when Tiant spent June and July on the disabled list — he finished 1970 with a 7–3 mark but pitched only a fraction of the innings expected of him — and the fortunes of twenty-game winner Boswell turned completely sour when a detached muscle and torn rotator cuff led to a disastrous year (3–7, 6.39 ERA in only 69 innings). First baseman Reese's early slump was a cause for concern, and the club suffered a cruel blow in late June as Carew and his .366 average were erased from the Twins lineup when Milwaukee's Mike Hegan broke Carew's right leg during a play at second base. The catcher's position had become a challenge because George Mitterwald, who had played sparingly in several trials with the Twins since 1966, struggled to fill the void created when Roseboro was released after the 1969 season. A nine-game losing skid in August caused alarm — Minnesota was 14–18 for the month — as their first-place lead dwindled to three games, but the Twins recovered in September to pull away from the Athletics and the Angels.

Enabling the Twins to surmount these difficulties were the reliable offensive output of Killebrew, whose statistics in the first half of the season hinted at a possible triple crown, as he finished at .271, 41 home runs, and 113 runs batted in. Oliva (.325, 23 HRs, 107 RBIs) and Tovar (.300, 13 triples, 30 stolen bases) were key contributors, and new left fielder Brant Alyea (.291, 16 homers, 61 RBIs), acquired from the Senators in the spring, cooled down after a torrid start, but his bat again came to life and boosted the offense in September when the team badly needed a lift. Compared to 1969, Minnesota stole only half as many bases — 57, down from 115 — but the Twins led the division in runs scored with 744 and had the American League's best team batting average at .262.

On the mound, Jim Perry, whom the Twins could not give away just a few years earlier, had the most starts (40) in the AL and tied Baltimore's Dave McNally and Mike Cuellar for the most wins with 24 on his way to capturing the American League Cy Young Award, which came amid controversy that either of the two Orioles could have been the rightful winner. Tom Hall, the thin left-hander in his second year with the Twins, logged an 11–6 mark and 2.55 ERA; Perranoski was the best reliever in the league, posting 34 saves and a 2.43 ERA; Williams worked exclusively out of the bullpen and won ten games against a single loss with a 1.99 ERA; and rookie Bill Zepp was 9–4 with a 3.22 ERA in his dual role as starter and reliever.

The Twins pitching staff yielded only 605 runs, second in the division to Oakland's

593, and introduced a new wunderkind born in Holland who eventually immigrated to the United States via Canada and spent over two decades in the major leagues. Joining the Twins in early June 1970, Bert Blyleven was a lanky six-foot, three-inch right-hander who, at the age of eighteen, excelled with the Twins' Class A, AA, and Florida Instructional League teams after graduating high school in 1969. Blyleven earned a promotion to Minnesota after appearing in only eight games for AAA Evansville in 1970, and he quickly established himself as a strikeout pitcher who employed a curveball to devastating effect. Tabbed Rookie Pitcher of the Year by *The Sporting News*, Blyleven (10–9, 3.18 ERA, and 135 strikeouts in 164 innings) and Zepp seemed to be two pitchers on whom the Twins could build their future rotation.

A 98–64 record brought a second AL West championship to Minnesota. As glowing as Rigney's year had been, he, like

Twenty-four-game winner Jim Perry was the controversial recipient of the 1970 AL Cy Young Award.

Martin in 1969, had the dubious task of preparing the Twins for a rematch against the vaunted Orioles in the ALCS. Rigney lauded his team for the tenacity it showed in the face of adversity throughout the course of the season: "The players could have turned on themselves. They could have used the injuries to Carew, Boswell, and Tiant [as an excuse]. But they didn't. Somewhere, somehow, they found a way to win."[46]

The Twins again were no competition for Baltimore, who had won 108 games and outdistanced the second-place Yankees by fifteen games. Using seven-run outbursts in each of the two games at Metropolitan Stadium, the Orioles bested the Twins in Minnesota and then returned home to complete the sweep on Jim Palmer's complete-game victory. Although he batted .500 in the playoffs, Oliva viewed the second straight sweep at the hands of Baltimore with somber resignation. The right fielder had believed that the Twins were in the same echelon as the Orioles because the 1969 ALCS featured a pair of one-run contests that the Twins could have won. But when his team surrendered an average of nine runs per game to the Orioles in the 1970 playoff, Oliva said of his team, "Our attitudes changed. The Orioles had beaten us, and the games weren't even close. You couldn't argue with the results of six games."[47]

No one was aware at the time, but seventeen long years would pass before the Twins next appeared in the postseason. Neither was anyone aware that Bert Blyleven, whose major league journey coursed through a variety of cities, would re-surface in a Twins uniform to help Minnesota to its first World Series championship in 1987.

## The Throes of Mediocrity

Little was left in the wake of the Twins' loss to the Orioles in the second American League Championship Series, and in 1971 Minnesota began a very long journey through the American League as an average team. Staples in the lineup included the continued run production of Harmon Killebrew, Tony Oliva's hitting prowess, the continuing development of Rod Carew's mastery at the bat, and Cesar Tovar's stolen bases and versatility afield. The youthful Blyleven continued to shine as the leader of the pitching rotation, as from 1971 to 1975 he averaged 17 wins per season with an ERA that was never more than 3.00.

Unfortunately, the Twins' supporting cast was not of the caliber that was such a vital asset in the formative years of the 1960s. Prospects such as Lyman Bostock, Steve Braun, Steve Brye, Bill Campbell, Bobby Darwin, Dave Goltz, Larry Hisle, and Danny Thompson were commendable players in the Twin Cities through the early and mid–1970s, but the men further down the bench and the pitchers who filled out the rotation and bullpen lacked the quality of their predecessors. One can wonder what the future for the Twins may have held had they been able to retain the quarry of late 1960s draftees who went on to ply their trade with teams beyond Minnesota's borders: Steve Garvey, chosen as a third baseman in June 1966; catcher Rick Dempsey, who was traded to the Yankees in 1972; left-handed pitcher Al Hrabosky; and shortstop Rick Burleson, picked five rounds after Blyleven in June 1969.

Killebrew's hourglass became bottom-heavy with the sands of time, and the future Hall-of-Famer played his last game as a Twin in 1974 before taking a curtain call with the Kansas City Royals the next year. The fates were most unkind to Oliva, whose knee miseries relegated him to the role of designated hitter beginning in 1973. In his case, it is fair to speculate that a healthy Oliva may have earned credentials worthy of enshrinement in Cooperstown, but his career ended in 1976, as he fell short of amassing even 2,000 hits. In the summer of 1973, and with fifteen years of service in the major leagues, Kaat found that he had outstayed his welcome with Griffith and was placed on waivers. But to the owner's dismay, Kaat discovered a fountain of youth with his new team and his old pitching coach — the White Sox had Johnny Sain in their employ — and the Dutchman enjoyed two 20-win seasons in Chicago. Kaat later adjusted to the role of reliever and ultimately finished his yeoman 25-year career with the Cardinals in 1983.

By the mid–1970s, the Twins were a team that was consigned to winning roughly one-half of its games, and a managerial change in 1972 from Rigney to Frank Quilici inspired no substantial gains. As Minnesota's status as an also-ran became evident, fans grew increasingly reluctant to pass through the Mets' turnstiles, and attendance fell below one million for the first time in 1971 and plummeted to 662,401 in 1974. A vicious financial eddy engulfed Calvin Griffith as fewer customers brought on a shortfall in revenue, and some of the stars he had cultivated — Campbell, Hisle, and Bostock, who commanded salaries commensurate with the best players in the game — fled to teams with deeper pockets when the era of free agency arrived. Griffith suffered the salary squabbles of Blyleven, but the owner feared Blyleven's defection to free agency and traded him to Texas in June 1976. The only big-name star left was Carew, who as a perennial batting champion was the Twins' main gate attraction, but he too would be traded later in the decade.

In essence, the Twins rode a rollercoaster during their first twelve years in Minnesota, enjoying prosperity and disappointment in alternating spans of one or two seasons before mediocrity took hold in the early 1970s. The arc of the Twins' success was low and bumpy, but one pennant, two division titles, and one very close call still qualifies them as one of the better teams of the late 1960s. As the Twins' fortunes waxed and waned from 1965 to 1970, their tenuous reign was short-lived because two teams proved to be much more durable in the long run. Baltimore's juggernaut was about to reach a plateau in 1969 with enough strength to put them in three consecutive World Series, while Oakland, already nipping at the Twins' heels in 1969 and 1970, had a team about to blossom into a five-time AL West champion and three-time World Series winner.

Players and managers came and went, yet Calvin Griffith continued as the owner of the Twins until he sold the team in 1984. Minnesota's closest brush with glory after 1970 came in the year of ownership transition when the Twins finished in a tie for second place. The torch of the Yankee dynasty had been passed to the Twins, but it flickered briefly and dimly in Minnesota. Meanwhile, a force was coalescing in Baltimore that made the Orioles the envy of the American League as the 1960s came to a close.

# 5

## Salvaging Veeck's Wreck

If Calvin Griffith overplayed his hand with Minnesota by serving dual roles as owner and director of baseball operations, the Baltimore Orioles profited from the separation of those offices and from prudent judgment exercised by key figures in the team's front office. The divergence practiced by the Orioles enabled those concerned with the product on the field to concentrate on bringing together the best players and coaches, while the ownership tended to the economic and business aspects of the club's affairs. During the eleven years focused upon in this book, the Orioles became the American League's flagship franchise, winning 1,034 regular-season contests and making four World Series appearances. Scouting, player development, and shrewd trading became the hallmark of this team, whose management on the field and in the executive suite set the standard for success from 1965 to 1975.

From its modern-day inception as a team newly transplanted from the Midwest to the East Coast during the 1950s, the Baltimore Orioles charted a course to exorcise the demons that had plagued their forebears, the St. Louis Browns, whose ineptitude since the end of World War II was evidenced by its habitual finishes deep in the second division, usually in seventh or eighth place in the eight-team American League. Much work was required simply to transfer the Browns eastward, and rebuilding a hapless club into a pennant contender took an extraordinary effort.

### Amusing but Losing—The Browns Come to Baltimore

When Bill Veeck became the owner of the St. Louis Browns in June 1951, gimmickry rather than serious baseball became his modus operandi for drawing fans to Sportsman's Park. Famous for signing the midget Eddie Gaedel to be a pinch-hitter, occasionally doling out free beer to fans, and even allowing a select group of spectators to vote on strategic game decisions while the contest was in progress, Veeck had taken a chronic loser and turned it into an entertaining team, even if the results were not reflected in its won-lost record.

Declines in overall attendance in the American League were due in part to the stranglehold the New York Yankees had on the circuit, but Browns fans continued to file through the turnstiles in increasing numbers in the early 1950s thanks to Veeck's incessant promotions. Intent on forcing the Cardinals, who were co-tenants at Sportsman's Park, out of St. Louis, Veeck tried to endear himself to fans of his intracity National League rival by employing former Cardinal stars in various capacities for the Browns. Dizzy Dean worked in the broadcast booth, while Rogers Hornsby and Marty Marion served as field managers. Through these promotional and recruiting initiatives, Veeck sought to win over so many Cardinal fans that their defection would cripple the NL club and force them to vacate the city of St. Louis.

Regardless of the ploys and showmanship for the benefit of the fans, Veeck failed to endear himself to his fellow American League club owners. Following the 1952 season, Veeck was actively seeking a new home and greater income for his cash-poor Browns, but working against him were the feuds he had engaged in with other owners over issues such as revenue for broadcast rights to the Browns' contests. Antagonistic owners in Boston, Cleveland, and New York went so far as to "use their scheduling latitude to force the Browns to play eight extra day games rather than the more profitable night games."[1] Veeck was fighting a losing battle against a spiteful cabal that was determined to see him fail.

Veeck shopped his Browns to other venues, with Los Angeles, San Francisco, and Milwaukee among possible new homes. There was also a chance that a last-minute move to the city of Baltimore, which had just constructed Memorial Stadium, might be brokered before the opening of the 1953 season. But six affirmative votes were necessary among the league's owners to approve the shift, and four were solidly against the flamboyant "Sports Shirt Bill." They instead desired to preclude his move while engaging in the *schadenfreude* of watching the Browns inch closer to bankruptcy.

After the mayor of Baltimore, Thomas J. D'Alesandro, worked tirelessly "to bring baseball to the city to show that Baltimore was a big league town," agreement was finally reached in late September 1953 to transfer the Browns when a bloc of AL owners succeeded in forcing Veeck to sell his stake in the team to a Baltimore-based consortium that would then control the franchise.[2] The major figures in the acquisition of the club included D'Alesandro, attorney Clarence Miles, brewery moguls Jerry Hoffberger and Zanvyl Krieger, as well as a select group of real estate and investment experts.

While the drama of the negotiations played out during the 1953 season, Veeck broke a promise to fans by making no attempt to promote or conduct the Browns as "a first division club."[3] Predictably, attendance plummeted, and Veeck found his team mired in the basement of the American League. At the conclusion of the final Browns game in St. Louis, "Auld Land Syne" was played by a live band; two days hence on September 29 the group from Baltimore paid $2,475,000 to Veeck in exchange for the team. With Veeck having been purged from the ranks of the American League, the remaining owners approved the transfer without a single dissenting vote. After hosting Eastern League and International League minor league teams for over 50 years, the city of Baltimore was ecstatic over landing a major league baseball team for the first time since 1902.[4]

With the franchise now secured by the new owners, the burden of rebuilding a broken team, now known as the Orioles, fell to an assemblage of front-office staff who possessed varying degrees of talent. Jim McLaughlin, head of the Browns' farm system, was the sole St. Louis executive permitted to remain with the club, while fresh faces such as former Philadelphia Athletics general manager Arthur Ehlers and his assistant Jack Dunn were brought on board. Joining them was a former sportswriter, Harry Dalton, who was charged with organizing the minor league teams. Of the motley crew of 360 Browns farm-system players inherited by Baltimore, Dalton later recalled succinctly, "It was a humble beginning."[5]

## Enter "The Wizard"

The reincarnated Orioles were treated to a heroes' welcome for the home opener of the 1954 season in Baltimore, as a cavalcade of convertible automobiles transported the players to Memorial Stadium along a parade route lined by over 300,000 spectators. Although the crowd was pleased with the Orioles' 3–1 win over the White Sox, this game proved to be the high-water mark for the year. The ghost of the old Browns cast its shadow over the new Orioles, as Baltimore, whose lineup occasionally featured future Twins manager Sam Mele, inauspiciously duplicated the previous season's record of 54–100. Jimmy Dykes, who had replaced Marty Marion as the team's skipper, was fired after one season, and it was clear that drastic measures would be necessary to turn the Orioles into a serious baseball team. The club could only count on the novelty of major league fever for so long before Baltimore fans would exhaust their patience and abandon the new hometown team.

Having proved his ability to turn the Chicago White Sox from a lethargic second-division club into a respectable team capable of winning over 80 games per year in the early 1950s, Paul Richards was recruited by Ehlers and then entrusted with the duties of both field manager and general manager for the Orioles following the 1954 season. Under Richards's direction, the Baltimore foundation was constructed in a way that made it durable for decades to come. A strategic approach that Earl Weaver later described as "pitching, defense, and three-run homers" actually had its genesis when Richards assumed the reins of the Orioles. Known as the "Wizard of Waxahachie" in tribute to the Texas town in which he was born, Richards firmly believed in building a baseball organization in two ways: Trading for players he knew could fill weaknesses in the lineup — a process he carried out at times with reckless abandon — and, in the days before the amateur draft, spending lavishly to sign untested young prospects in the hope of landing the right talent who would develop into quality major league players.

Paul Richards was the architect of the foundation upon which Baltimore built its developmental system.

As a field manager, Richards had his share of supporters who appreciated his initiative and foresight to make the correct decisions at key moments in a ballgame. Although many of his players, including Brooks Robinson and Dave Philley, appreciated Richards's mental toughness and ability to instruct players on the finer points of the game, his detractors such as pitcher Hector "Skinny" Brown did not appreciate the aloof demeanor that Richards often exhibited. Others felt that he was obsessive about pitching and tended to micromanage every facet of his staff. So intensely involved was Richards with the business of building the team that some personnel believed that Richards was more concerned with teaching rather than actually winning games.[6] Conflicting opinions aside, Richards's incubation period of the late 1950s yielded gradual improvement in Baltimore's lot as an infusion of new players supplanted the rabble of 1954.

Sowing seeds for the future, Richards also ensured that the minor league system was consistent in its teaching methods at every level of the Orioles organization. By inculcating all subordinate teams with the same manner of instruction, players would not have to suffer a relearning process of the game's basics at each stop throughout the farm system. So durable was this developmental mantra that one Oriole player who later coached for the team was pleased to inform the Wizard that decades after his departure from Baltimore, Richards's basic methodology was still being followed.[7]

The Orioles' seventh-place finish in 1955 and their standing in sixth place in 1956 may not appear to be a marked improvement when measured against a Yankee team then in the halcyon years of its reign. But Gus Triandos, who was acquired in a trade with the Yankees, established himself as a reliable starting catcher, while Willie Miranda, who also had been packaged in the same deal with New York, anchored the shortstop position and became a favorite of Baltimore fans. By 1957, the Orioles continued to move forward, and they reached the .500 plateau for the first time with a 76–76 record — which was good for fifth place — as another future major league manager, Dick Williams, completed the first of his three tours of duty with the Orioles. Triandos earned recognition as an All-Star and continued to provide Baltimore with its best source of run-production and power hitting.

Joining the Orioles in 1957 was a youngster whose early travails in Baltimore belied the stardom to which he was destined. As an all-state basketball player at Central High School in Little Rock, Arkansas, Brooks Robinson was also a pitcher, catcher, and second baseman throughout his youth, but after attracting the attention of seven big league teams, Robinson signed with Baltimore in 1955 for a $4,000 bonus. Robinson declined a $30,000 contract that would have consigned him to a two-year stint on the Orioles roster, a period during which he likely would have spent precious time sitting on the bench rather than developing his skills in the minor leagues. He later admitted that Richards "sold me on the fact that if you've got any ability, you're gonna get a chance to play in the big leagues in a hurry."[8] By not subjecting himself to the circumstances that hampered Harmon Killebrew when he signed with the Washington Senators, Robinson began his journey to Baltimore by playing with "guys my own speed" on a Class B York, Pennsylvania, team whose manager, George Staller, believed that the newcomer's best position was third base.[9]

A full year of fruitful seasoning in the minors in 1956 enabled Robinson to crack the starting lineup a year later as the Orioles third baseman. Although he was set back by a knee injury in 1957, Robinson had become the cornerstone of the Baltimore infield and its most indispensable player for nearly two decades. By 1960, he began to galvanize his reputation as one of baseball's best fielding third basemen by winning the first of his many Gold Glove awards. Ever the gentleman, Robinson modestly ascribed his defensive prowess to "that little instinct [of] being where the ball was all the time."[10]

When the Orioles faltered in 1958 with a 74–79 record and a dip to sixth place, the letdown had serious ramifications for Richards. Unlike Calvin Griffith's Senators and Twins, whose player procurement and expenditures were both controlled by Griffith himself, Baltimore's organizational structure allowed Richards in his dual role as general manager and field manager to be less conscious of how the team's funds were disbursed, notably for new signees. Despite the Orioles ownership's willingness to absorb the sting of some red ink if short-term financial losses could be recovered by a winning team, Richards, according to Harry Dalton, "had an unlimited budget and [still] exceeded it."[11] Richards evolved into one of the primary contributors to the ills of the bonus system through the huge amounts of money he lavished on those players he believed to be the best amateur prospects he could sign. The hiring of William Walsingham as an executive administrator to watch over Richards's expenditures proved ineffectual because Richards simply balked at Walsingham's money-saving suggestions when he felt they proved contrary to his own wishes.[12]

By the fall of 1958, when the Orioles top executives had seen too much cash disappear without the anticipated quick return on Richards's investments, the only way to curtail the exorbitant spending was to remove Richards from the general manager's seat. Jim McLaughlin, a fine administrator who still headed the farm system at the time, sought to stock the major league club with players who navigated their way up the minor league ladder to reach Baltimore. His conservative approach, which included use of funds earmarked to improve the administration of an effective scouting network, eventually won out over the spendthrift ways of Richards, who was allowed to remain as the field manager.[13]

The unease arising from this multi-faceted management structure and clash of personalities within the Orioles baseball operations was further complicated by the changes in the team's ownership. In the year after the Browns moved from St. Louis, a consolidation commenced that by 1959 reduced the number of the Orioles' majority stockholders from seven men to just two, Zanvyl Krieger and Joseph Iglehardt. Actively seeking to purchase the club at this time was beer mogul Jerry Hoffberger of the National Brewing Company,

who intended to use the baseball team as a new platform for increasing sales of his company's product. Hoffberger's interest persisted, but years would pass before he purchased enough stock to control the Orioles outright.

When Richards was relieved of the general manager's role, Baltimore ownership realized that a calming influence would be most beneficial in removing the angst attributed to Richards's autocratic manner. Chosen to be the new GM was Yankee farm director Lee MacPhail, called by veteran Baltimore sportswriter Bob Maisel "one of the most underrated executives in Orioles history."[14] MacPhail brought excellent credentials to his new post, but he assented to join Baltimore only after being assured by club ownership that Richards, even in his role as field manager, would not be in a position to undermine MacPhail's authority. With a deft hand, MacPhail "showed a sure touch in dealing with important matters such as television, stadium facilities, race relations, and upgrad-

In contrast with some of his American League counterparts such as Calvin Griffith and Charlie Finley, Jerry Hoffberger allowed his front office to handle the Orioles baseball affairs.

ing the Orioles minor league system."[15] Calm in his demeanor, MacPhail also helped build morale, which was an indispensable asset to solidifying the whole organization with a feeling of trust and harmony.

There was little evidence during the 1959 campaign that all the shuffling in the front office had a positive effect on the playing field, as Baltimore finished in sixth place with a 74–80 mark. But some of the minor league seeds that had been sown by Richards were emerging as genuine major league prospects. Notable among these "Baby Birds" was a trio of 20-year-old hurlers, with Jerry Walker, Milt Pappas, and Jack Fisher each performing well on the mound. Pappas, who later recalled that Richards set a limit of 80 pitches per start so as not to overextend the youngsters, lauded Richards "for the way he nurtured and matured me," enabling him to embark on what became a 17-year career in the major leagues.[16] Capitalizing on the efforts of veteran knuckleball pitcher Hoyt Wilhelm, who was used almost exclusively as a starter in 1959 and tied Pappas for the team lead in victories with 15, the beginning of the 1960s looked to be very promising.

## The Fledglings Birds Take Flight

The new decade opened with a flourish as a profusion of rookies and young veterans claimed spots on the Baltimore roster. The burgeoning youth movement of the pitching staff was complemented by the appearance of new faces around the diamond who contributed greatly to the Orioles' astonishing success in 1960. On the left side of the infield, Brooks Robinson was paired with another 22-year-old, shortstop Ron Hansen, who would be American League Rookie of the Year after hitting .255 with 86 RBIs. At first base was the strapping left-handed Jim Gentile, plucked from the Dodgers organization where he had been buried in their farm system. Manning center field was Jackie Brandt, newly acquired from the San Francisco Giants and a player with a personality that justified his nickname "Flakey." New to the Orioles rotation was first-year hurler Chuck Estrada, who burst on the scene by tying Cleveland's Jim Perry for AL victories with 18. Five other Baltimore pitchers won at least ten games, including rookie southpaw Steve Barber, as Pappas again reached the 15-victory plateau. The plethora of green talent yet to arrive from the depths of the Orioles' farm teams — or who would make their mark with other major league clubs — included Dean Chance, Pete Ward, Jerry Adair, and John "Boog" Powell.

With nothing to lose and everything to gain in competing against the defending American League champion Chicago White Sox and the omnipotent New York Yankees, the upstarts from Baltimore audaciously bolted to the top of the league standings by the end of May. In June, by fending off the Yankees in an early yet important series at home, pennant fever had made an unlikely appearance in Baltimore. Though they possessed a team batting average in the bottom half of the league, the Orioles managed to lead the AL in runs scored. Richards's innovative side made its presence felt when he unveiled an oversized catcher's mitt — dubbed the "elephant glove" by one backstop — for use by Oriole receivers whenever Wilhelm was on the mound delivering his vexing knuckler.[17] Richards's rotation was so deep at midseason that he claimed eight different pitchers were capable of handling starting assignments, and he wasn't afraid to use a starter occasionally in relief.[18]

As September loomed, the Orioles refused to bow to the Yankees in their battle for first place, but in a crucial four-game set in the Bronx in the middle of that month, Baltimore was swept and never recovered. Criticizing Richards for "pitch[ing] the young blood," veteran hurler "Skinny" Brown later said, "You've got to go with your best at the end of the year."[19] Barber, Estrada, Fisher, and Pappas each failed to keep the Bombers in check, as the Orioles limped home after losing all four contests to a Yankee team intent on continuing their dominance over the American League. Disappointingly, the Orioles settled for second place at 89–65, trailing the Yankees by eight games at season's end.

However, the success enjoyed by Baltimore throughout 1960 vindicated Richards's emphasis on pitching and defense as the prime attributes of a team's foundation. Baltimore's overall ERA tied the Yankees at 3.52, the Orioles were charged with the fewest errors (108), and the season served as a precursor to the superb Baltimore teams that were to come later in the decade. MacPhail and Richards took the joint decision in the middle of 1959 to employ as many of the young crop of talent as was practicable. Although Baltimore came up short in their bid for the 1960 pennant, there was abundant optimism that the Orioles could soon surpass the mighty Yankees as the best team in the league.

## An Untimely Departure

As the drama of the September pennant chase unfolded, the Orioles front office was in the process of finding a new site for its Triple-A minor league affiliate. MacPhail, McLaughlin, and Richards moved quickly to secure Rochester, New York, as the home of Baltimore's top farm club when the Red Wings, disenchanted with the way in which the St. Louis Cardinals were handling their top minor leaguers, severed ties with the National League team. Because both Rochester and Baltimore ran their franchises as publicly owned community baseball teams, their working agreement was a very good fit in terms of operational style, which became another cornerstone in the Orioles' franchise.[20] This relationship proved to be yet another key element in the Orioles' minor league system by placing its highest team geographically close to its major league parent.

In 1961, the ranks of the American League grew by two teams, as a new version of the Washington Senators replaced Griffith's former club and Gene Autry's Los Angeles Angels became the first AL club based on the West Coast. Fresh from their success in 1960, the Orioles created high expectations for a repeat performance, but not all observers concurred with the Baltimore faithful. In its preseason review of the Orioles, *Sports Illustrated* commented that there was little chance of "luck and talent" blending as fortunately as it had the prior year, but admitted presciently that "the Baltimore club will be a power in the league for years to come."[21]

No "fluke" label could be attached to the 1961 Orioles as they improved by six victories over the previous season. But with the Yankees fielding a team that ranks as one of the best of all time and Detroit finishing in second place eight games out despite 101 wins, Baltimore could only continue to mature its youth at the major league level. The quartet of Barber, Estrada, Fisher, and Pappas combined for 56 wins, Wilhelm saved 18 games, and Hansen was third in the league for assists by a shortstop, batted .248 with 12 home runs, and drove in 51 runs. Hansen and Robinson, who led the league's third basemen in fielding percentage and batted .287, had a new infield partner, second baseman Jerry Adair, whose full-season

**Executive Lee MacPhail helped marshal Baltimore through its building years of the early 1960s.**

debut included a .264 average over 133 games. Among the veterans, Gentile had the best year of any Oriole at the plate, batting .302 with 46 homers and 141 RBIs.

The biggest surprise of the campaign came unfortunately for the Orioles in late August when, following months of speculation, Richards announced that he was leaving Baltimore to take the general manager's position with the expansion Houston Colt .45s of the National League. So hasty was the manager's departure that Richards left with one month remaining on the schedule, forcing third base coach Luman Harris to become the *pro tem* skipper. Harris guided the Orioles to 17 wins in his 27 games, as the team finished at 95–67. MacPhail cast about to find a permanent replacement for Richards, a man whom Pappas said "revolutionized the way and thinking of baseball."[22] MacPhail also dismissed McLaughlin as the farm director and replaced him with Dalton, another move that ultimately honed the team's focus for the future.

## An Unwelcome Setback

The new manager named by MacPhail to pick up where Richards left off was, by MacPhail's evaluation, "a wonderful man," but in the final analysis, it turned out that "he was a better guy than manager."[23] The promotion of Billy Hitchcock from the Orioles' former Triple-A team in Vancouver was made with the hope that MacPhail could also supplement the roster with a few veterans to balance the youth already present and take the burden off Gentile, who was at that time the Orioles' biggest offensive threat.

To Baltimore's chagrin, several factors worked in concert to unravel the strands that Richards had so carefully woven. The Orioles soon found out that Hitchcock with his more relaxed demeanor translated into less rigidity in making the players adhere to the rudiments of the game that had been imparted by Richards, as errors on defense, gaffes on the basepaths, and an inability to produce timely hits stalled the Orioles often in 1962. Ironically, Baltimore's pitching staff led the league in team ERA for the second straight year, and their fielding percentage was a repeat of the .980 achieved in 1961, but the Orioles that plated 93 more runs than they yielded the year before (691 to 598) were now victimized by a scoring deficit (652 to 680).

The developing political crisis in Berlin required a buildup of United States armed forces, which included mandatory military service for several young Orioles, Barber and Hansen being among those called to duty.[24] Although the addition of veteran Robin Roberts helped the pitching staff—he finished at 10–9 with a 2.78 ERA—Barber could not get on track when he rejoined the team for weekend stints and was further debilitated by mononucleosis. The infield was unsettled because Hansen's stand-in at shortstop, Adair, was a second baseman by trade who was now playing out of position.

One newcomer who joined the Orioles in 1962 and was destined to become a fixture in Baltimore was a hulking Florida native named John Wesley Powell. An outfielder/first baseman, Powell signed with the Orioles weeks before his eighteenth birthday and quickly rose through the minor leagues, arriving in Baltimore after posting very impressive statistics at Rochester in 1961 (.321 average, 32 homers, 92 RBIs). Nicknamed "Boog," he presented a maturity beyond his years by confessing in the spring of 1962 that his defensive skills in left field were problematic, but his 6'3" frame held 235 pounds of left-handed power that made him a most welcome addition to Baltimore's lineup.

During Hitchcock's first year at the helm, the Orioles were tenuously only five games behind the league leaders in early July, but the team soon fell out of contention. At times, the excuses for Baltimore's backslide ranged from the obvious, a noticeable lack of discipline was reflective of Hitchcock's friendly personality, to the absurd, such as the occasion when Hitchcock insisted that his frontline starters hurl shutouts as the best way to counteract the Orioles' offensive woes. "I was sort of easygoing with them," admitted Hitchcock, who as a player was innately determined to succeed and felt no need to be constantly prodded, but as a manager, Hitchcock wrongly assumed that all of his players were imbued with the same zeal that had driven him.[25] The net result of Hitchcock's inaugural season in Baltimore was a dive to seventh place due to a dreary 77–85 record.

However, the Orioles' farm teams continued to graduate matured prospects, and by the close of the 1962 season over half of the 33 men on the Baltimore roster were products of the system built by Richards.[26] This remained a good sign for the future, but MacPhail was sage enough to recognize that a dose of veteran help was needed to revive an Oriole team that was in danger of quickly turning from a legitimate contender into an also-ran. MacPhail engineered several trades that eased the Orioles' payroll, such as dealing Gus Triandos to the Tigers, and added some speed on the basepaths, which was exactly what the newly-acquired shortstop Luis Aparicio brought with him upon his acquisition from the White Sox. With Triandos gone, MacPhail also struck a deal with the San Francisco Giants for catcher Johnny Orsino and two pitchers, Mike McCormick and Stu Miller, the latter soon to become a most valuable reliever for his new club.

In order to land Aparicio, Baltimore parted with Wilhelm, who was the Orioles' best fireman, former Rookie of the Year Hansen, and Pete Ward, a third-base prospect who stood little chance of playing ahead of Brooks Robinson. Also gone were a pair in their early twenties, pitcher Jack Fisher and Dave Nicholson, a young outfielder whose failure to hit the breaking ball precluded his rise to a full-time major league job. On the positive side of the ledger, Aparicio became a second anchor in the Baltimore infield and continued to lead the American League in stolen bases as he had done each season since his debut with the White Sox in 1956. Combining with his new teammate at third base, Aparicio and Robinson gave the Orioles a virtually impregnable defense on the left side of the infield.

For 1963, two fresh faces were also added to Hitchcock's coaching staff, Luke Appling and, perhaps more threatening to the manager, former Kansas City Athletics skipper Hank Bauer, a World War II Marine veteran who suffered no fools. Along with a hardened attitude by Hitchcock, who pledged enforcement of a curfew on his players that was lacking the previous year, the revamped Orioles meant business when they charged quickly from the opening gate and sprinted to a 30–15 record, good for a 3½ game lead by late May. Conditions soon deteriorated, however, and an 8–22 swoon that stretched through much of June dropped Baltimore seven games from the league lead and, to all intents and purposes, out of the pennant chase.[27] Two young veterans being counted upon to deliver as they had in the recent past also disappointed. After a torrid start, Robinson, hitting in the number three slot of the batting order, drove in only 38 runs and hit .222 over the last four months of the campaign, while Estrada struggled with arm trouble until his last appearance on June 1 and was sidelined the remainder of the season.

Predictably, Aparicio and Robinson led the league in fielding percentage at their respective positions, while Gentile did likewise at first base. Barber became the first Oriole to reach the 20-victory plateau, Miller led the AL in both appearances (71) and saves (27), and another minor leaguer hurler, Dave McNally, found a spot on the staff and won seven of his 15 decisions. Powell's run-producing capabilities shone in his team-leading 25 home runs and 82 runs batted in, but even the Orioles' rebound to an 86–76 mark was not adequate enough to allow Hitchcock to retain his job. Long gone were the smiles from the faces of MacPhail and Hitchcock, both of whom mugged for the cameras when the general manager inked the amiable Alabaman to his first contract, as MacPhail was now tasked to find a disciplinarian who could firmly guide a team again at a crossroads of pennant contention and mediocrity.

## A Rebound Under Bauer

When Hank Bauer was named as an Orioles coach in 1963, MacPhail was perhaps anticipating the day when Hitchcock would need to be replaced. Bauer had nearly two years of managing experience with Kansas City, beginning in 1961, and having played in nine World Series for the Yankees from 1949 to 1958 had a background steeped in a winning tradition. By naming Bauer as the new Baltimore manager, MacPhail quite likely looked beyond Bauer's uninspiring 107–157 record as the Athletics skipper in part because Kansas City's eccentric owner, Charles O. Finley, had proven himself to be more interested in relocating his team than finding help for its horrific pitching staff.[28] Bauer's ascension from Orioles coach to manager also occurred because he was actually MacPhail's third choice for the post, following rejections by both Yogi Berra and Eddie Stanky to run the club.[29]

Bauer's presence was felt by anyone within earshot of his harsh voice, but, as one of his players noted, the ostensibly grating sound was simply the veneer of a man with a truly kind disposition. Intent on treating the players like adults but commanding the respective worthy of his position, Bauer revoked the curfew but enforced a coat-and-tie dress code on road trips.[30] Assisting the manager were new coaches Gene Woodling and Billy Hunter, both former Yankee players acquainted with championship teams. MacPhail again traded for infield help he believed necessary to make up for Jim Gentile's diminishing offensive production. Gentile was shipped to the Athletics prior to the 1964 season for his first-base counterpart, Norm Siebern, who was named to the AL All-Star team but whose season-ending totals (.245, 12 home runs, 56 RBIs) turned out to be worse than Gentile's (.251, 28, 71).

With a new manager, a revamped coaching staff, and a new cleanup hitter in Siebern, Baltimore dueled with the Yankees and White Sox for control over the American League. One month into the 1964 season, when the Orioles endured their own version of the Linz–harmonica incident, Bauer reinforced his reputation as a stern headmaster. When some of his charges made merry on the bus ride home from Washington following a defeat, Bauer aired out the offenders, and immediately thereafter Baltimore reeled off a 17–6 mark. Bauer let it be known that losing came with a cost and made it abundantly clear that he expected his players to take every loss as seriously as he did. Because this was a year that brought the Orioles ever closer to realizing that the pennant was within their grasp, the thought of letting the opportunity slip away was anathema to Bauer.

Near the end of June, the Orioles held the upper hand by 4½ games and then sporadically dipped into second place, while Robinson and Powell supplied much of the firepower that inspired Baltimore's drive. When the Yankees lost the climactic series against Chicago in mid–August, the Orioles marched into Comiskey Park and took three of four contests to regain the league lead, which they held until mid–September. At this time Baltimore was without the services of Powell, who missed fifteen games after breaking his wrist on August 20. Their ensuing 7–8 record, while not terrible, demonstrated that Powell's bat may have made a difference in the four one-run losses they sustained during this stretch. But when they later bowed to Detroit in a crucial series with less than a dozen games left, the Orioles fell from one game out of first place to four games behind and never recovered. New York found its stride and barely outlasted its two rivals, as the White Sox held second place one game out, while Baltimore, at 97–65, ended in third place, a slim two games away from tying the Yankees. Bauer's skill in keeping his team focused for so much of the season won him Manager of the Year, indicating that he was the best managerial candidate to expunge the sting of collapses brought on in the Hitchcock era.

Several performances spurred the Orioles during 1964. Brooks Robinson was the most complete player — defensively and offensively — to set foot on the diamond. In addition to his .317 average and 28 home runs, he led the American League with 117 RBIs; at third base, his statistics were nonpareil with league bests in putouts, assists, double plays, and fielding average, all at a cost of just 14 errors. This package of data, made even more palatable by Robinson's down-home, humble comportment, earned him AL Most Valuable Player

honors and the accustomed Gold Glove award. Although still rankled by having to play left field, Powell continued to mature and belted 39 homers while driving in 99 runs. Pappas recorded 16 wins, old hand Robin Roberts was victorious 13 times, and the bullpen boasted a trio of relievers — Stu Miller, Dick Hall, and former National League veteran Harvey Haddix — who combined for 40 saves and another 21 wins. The fruitful minor league system once more showed itself to be a well seemingly incapable of running dry, as two more prospects were promoted to the Baltimore roster and directly impacted the pennant run.

Breaking through in 1964 were rookie right fielder Sam Bowens, who contributed a .263 average along with 22 homers and 71 RBIs, and a right-handed wunderkind from California named Wally Bunker. Signed out of high school after being pursued by Baltimore and sixteen other teams, Bunker breezed through the California League and made one start for the Orioles in 1963, but he was aston-

**Peerless as a defensive third baseman, Brooks Robinson was the 1964 AL Most Valuable Player.**

ishing in his first full season as a professional, posting a 19–5 record and 2.69 ERA while securing the Rookie Pitcher of the Year award from *The Sporting News*. At nineteen years of age, Bunker was another fresh face in an Orioles lineup already brimming with young talent, as for the fourth time in team history, the Orioles surpassed one million in attendance.

When browsing the Orioles' 1964 media guide, one cannot escape the feeling of glimpsing the team's future lineups, even though several players were at least two years away from gaining significant playing time. Mark Belanger, Paul Blair, Curt Blefary, Andy Etchebarren, and Dave Johnson were all close to making the Baltimore squad, and another, Darold Knowles, would find success later as a reliever in various cities over the course of his 16-year career.

Entering 1965, Bauer added more new, young players to his lineup and found that there was overcrowding in the outfield and at first base. Boog Powell through the 1964 season had spent most of his time patrolling left field with limited success despite his efforts to improve his glove work. Bauer chose to ease the burden on the outsized Powell by alternating him between left field and first base, with the displaced Norm Siebern limited to part-time duty. Prospects Blair and infielder/outfielder Blefary found themselves in Baltimore after coming to the Orioles from outside the organization, Blair picked out of the New York Mets minor league system before working his way up through the Baltimore farm teams, while Blefary was claimed from the Yankees when they "put me on waivers ... so that they could sneak me to Triple-A."[31]

Adding to the saturated outfield were Russ Snyder, who was returning after spending half of 1964 on the disabled list, as well as holdovers Bowens and Brandt. Although Lou Piniella did not make the big league team, he appeared briefly in Baltimore in 1964 and went to spring training in 1965 before being traded to Cleveland one year later. Among the infielders, Blefary's minor league roommate, Dave Johnson, seemed on the verge of becoming a fulltime Oriole when he debuted in April 1965 but was subsequently sent to Rochester for further seasoning. On the pitching staff, New York native Jim Palmer was a bonus prospect signed out of Scottsdale (Arizona) High School in 1963 who joined the Orioles after spending but one season in the minors. Palmer's future batterymate Andy Etchebarren was another bonus recipient who was soon to land a permanent major league job.[32]

The sum of the above parts in 1965 returned 94 victories against 68 losses and a third-place finish, eight games behind the American League champion Minnesota Twins and just one game in back of runner-up Chicago. Neither Aparicio nor Adair won Gold Gloves in 1965, yet both excelled by leading the AL in fielding at their respective positions. The pitching staff led the league in team ERA at 2.98, six pitchers won at least ten games, and Hall and Miller combined for 36 saves. But the real shortfall for Baltimore was a lack of timely hitting, as the Orioles' team average of .238 and 641 runs scored ranked in the bottom half of the American League. Thirty-seven of their losses were by two runs or less, including eight one-run defeats from late August until the season's end.[33] Blefary finished with a .260 average, a team-best 22 home runs, and 70 runs batted in to cop Rookie of the Year honors in the AL, but only Powell (17 homers, 72 RBIs) and Brooks Robinson (18 homers, 80 RBIs) were up to the task of significant run production. Much was expected of second-year outfielder Bowens, but when his late-night escapades had an adverse impact on him, his career quickly waned after his initial display of great promise.

Compounding the travails of Baltimore's failed pennant quest was the steep, troubling decline in attendance at Memorial Stadium. Over 1.1 million fans had trekked to see the Orioles play in 1964, but the paid attendance for 1965 was only 781,649. A contending team was certainly an asset to Baltimore, but a small-market club incapable of winning a pennant was bound to struggle to lure fans through the turnstiles. This shortfall did not go unnoticed by the team's new owner, Jerry Hoffberger, who in June became the club's chairman of the board of directors. A way had to be found to put Baltimore at the top of the American League, which the front office believed would bring fans — and revenue — back to the ballpark at 33rd Street and Ellerslie Avenue.

MacPhail realized that the Orioles could use some of their surplus of pitching to acquire a power-hitting outfielder who would fill the void in the offense created by Bowen's deficiency. At the December 1965 winter meetings, the general manager completed two minor trades, one sending Siebern to the California Angels for outfielder Dick Simpson, and a second dealing Brandt and Knowles to Philadelphia for reliever Jack Baldschun. Having secured Simpson and Baldschun, MacPhail then proposed packaging them along with veteran Orioles pitcher Milt Pappas in a trade with the Cincinnati Reds for star outfielder Frank Robinson.

In essence, MacPhail had done everything to facilitate the Robinson transaction except consummate it, because he had resigned his position in mid–November and was transitioning his responsibilities in the Orioles front office to Harry Dalton. MacPhail was taking his expertise to New York to serve as an assistant for the newly-appointed commissioner of baseball, William "Spike" Eckert. Although MacPhail would be missed in Baltimore, he was entrusting his tasks to a man very familiar with the manner in which the Orioles operated. Dalton's promotion in early December from director of the minor league system to vice president of player personnel was part of Baltimore's executive restructuring that also saw Frank Cashen, formerly of National Brewing Company, join the Orioles as Hoffberger's executive vice president. Jack Dunn was the third vice president in charge of the team's business affairs, who, along with Dalton, reported to Cashen.[34]

The executive staff had been realigned, and with MacPhail set to depart, the erstwhile general manager delegated to his successors the decision on the trade of Pappas, Baldschun, and Simpson for Frank Robinson. MacPhail deserved the credit for assembling the pieces that led to the Robinson trade, but it was actually Cashen who gave the final approval for the deal. Conflicting versions of Bauer's opinion on whether the trade should have been made later revealed that the manager agreed with Dalton. "Bauer was with me, and we liked the deal," said Dalton, but the manager informed Cashen that he did not want to surrender his best starting pitcher for an outfielder reputed "as being a guy who disturbed everything."[35] The decision to sanction the trade, which was greatly influenced by the lobbying of Orioles scout Jim Russo, was a huge gamble on Cashen's part. But Robinson's ultimate emergence as the leader of the Orioles, as well as Jim Palmer's maturity in filling the vacancy created by the departure of Pappas, would vindicate Baltimore's newly-organized front office.

Thus on December 9, 1965, the Orioles and the Reds completed what Cincinnati president Bill DeWitt, Jr., termed "a million-dollar deal," and the removal of Pappas, Baldschun, and Knowles from the Orioles created spirited competition among a group of hurlers — including Palmer, Eddie Watt, and Moe Drabowsky, who had been drafted from the Kansas City Athletics — for starting and relief jobs on the pitching staff.[36] As the Robinson trade demonstratively placed the capstone on what would become the first year of the great Orioles dynasty, the era of Dalton's personnel management began in earnest at the major league level, using the Baltimore farm system that he helped develop to prepare high-caliber prospects for careers in an Oriole uniform.

## The Baltimore Method

In contrast to the Minnesota Twins with their relatively static lineup during the early 1960s, the Orioles were a team that seemed to be constantly adjusting their roster to accommodate the crop of players emerging from their minor leagues. Excoriated as Paul Richards was for his exorbitant spending on untested new players, he also codified the Orioles' standards that enabled the farm clubs to imbue newcomers with baseball's fundamentals in a consistent manner. Years would elapse before any judgment could be passed as to the degree of success that Richards's practice would attain, but as we have seen, in 1960 and 1964 Baltimore came close to winning its first pennant, with many vital contributions coming from players signed by Richards and then trained in the Orioles' system.

The popular real estate mantra of "location, location, location" has its own counterpart in the world of baseball, that being "scouting, scouting, scouting," so it is no coincidence that Baltimore's intense focus on this most essential process of finding talent to replenish its minor league teams led to the wellspring of quality players who later populated the Orioles roster. Jim McLaughlin ceded his role as Baltimore's farm director to Harry Dalton in 1961, and through the early years of the 1960s Dalton was responsible for oversight of the system that eventually delivered key players to Memorial Stadium.

Scouts scoured the United States to evaluate high school and college players not only for their ability on the diamond but also for their personality traits. As far back as early 1961, the Baltimore front office had enlisted "FBI agents to speak to scouts to show them how to uncover facts on prospects' attitude and potential."[37] Jim Russo worked as a national scout and served as the Orioles' chief talent assessor, and reporting to him was a coterie of regional scouts who comprised the second level of the department. Russo's associates included Dee Phillips, Walter Youse, Jim Wilson, Don McShane, and other scouts who pursued players that each believed to be suitable candidates capable of reaching the major leagues. After a player was signed — an event almost always preceded by rounds of bonus negotiations — he and perhaps as many as several hundred of his potential Orioles teammates would spend time at Baltimore's minor league spring training facility in Thomasville, Georgia.

Thomasville was to the Orioles franchise what Parris Island is to the Marine Corps, namely a boot camp where the rules and methodology of Baltimore-style baseball were imparted to the organization's newcomers. Future Baltimore coaches and managers such as Cal Ripken, Sr., and Earl Weaver were quasi–drill sergeants charged with leading practices and squad games, assessing the progress of the players, and offering input to a "handbook detailing the Orioles' philosophy on all phases of the game."[38] Each morning, players were roused from military-style barracks by reveille, meals were taken at the camp's dining hall, and at the conclusion of a day's activities, players could head into town for entertainment or relax at the local pool hall. When the lengthy training season ended, players were assigned to clubs at various tiers in the farm system to compete in their respective leagues from April through early September.

Shortly after the conclusion of the minor league season, Dalton convened meetings to review the performance of the prospects, notably those at Double-A Elmira of the Eastern League and Triple-A Rochester of the International League. Dalton's legal pads containing handwritten notes — now part of the Papers of Harry Dalton collection at the

**After assuming the control of the Orioles' front office in late 1965, Harry Dalton led Baltimore through the period of its greatest success.**

National Baseball Hall of Fame Library — offer a glimpse into the discourse among the compendium of minor league coaches, managers, scouts, and assorted officials who were solicited for their opinions on the strengths and weaknesses of any given player. For example, at the meeting of September 21, 1964, Dalton noted the following comments on Curt Blefary and his just-completed season at Rochester as critiqued by scouts Frank McGowan and Dee Phillips; minor league managers Cal Ripken, Sr. and Billy DeMars; former minor league manager Barney Lutz; minor league pitching instructor George Bamberger; and former Orioles skipper Billy Hitchcock, who served as minor league field coordinator following his departure from the Baltimore dugout:

> FRANK: Defensively don't like his hands at 1B — he likes OF better — has trouble in OF getting jump — comes in on ball well — arm may be adequate from LF — good hitter — power-goes to LF w/ power — good hustler — needs one more year in OF to play in Balt[imore] in '66 — great desire — arm is little weaker than Boog's at Roch[ester] — batting he [is] ready for Balt now — hits good pitching w/ authority — GOOD (due to bat)
> CAL: Good — greatest hustler I've ever seen — OK in OF — may be better OF than Boog — will be hitter, good LF — chance for Balt in '65
> LUTZ: Good — agile — arm improves every day — good on fly balls and ground balls — aggressive hitter — will be better OF than Boog — chance here [to play in Baltimore] in '65
> BAMBY: *EXC*[ellent] — play here now — looked good at 1B — play Balt '65
> HITCH: *EXC*[ellent] — good bat — great desire — will be adequate in LF — may stay here in '65
> DEMARS: Better OF than Boog was — going to LF w/ power — great hustler
> DEE: Great improvement at 1B in Fl[orida] since] '63 — will work[39]

For his own part, Blefary later stated that he "loved" Bauer even though the manager made him the last cut of spring training in 1964.[40] After coming so close to making the Orioles roster, Blefary, rather than sulk about his demotion to Rochester, took it upon himself to strive even harder and impress upon his superiors that he was intent on winning a major league job. His statistics for the Red Wings in 1964 (.287 average, 31 home runs, 80 RBIs, 102 walks) and the above critique by Orioles officials reflected this aspiration. Because Blefary performed well enough in the Rochester outfield, he helped facilitate the shifting of Boog Powell — to whom he was constantly compared — to first base.

Similar notations were made at that September 1964 meeting with regard to catcher Andy Etchebarren, whose appraisal was supplemented with feedback from former Hitchcock assistant George Staller, minor league pilot Earl Weaver, and coach Jim Frey. Five of six opinions offered on Etchebarren rated him as "good," and although several expressed concern about the catcher's hitting ability, Bamberger labeled him the "best catcher in [the] org[anization]."[41] Staller, Lutz, and Hitchcock pressed Dalton to protect Etchebarren from being drafted by another major league team, while Bamberger and Weaver gave the backstop top grades for his hustle.[42]

Other minor leaguers who soon made a huge impact in an Orioles uniform were written up with great anticipation. The young Paul Blair left little doubt as to his defensive ability, as Lutz remarked, "Real good jump, good on ground balls, arm true and acc[urate]."[43] Weaver, however, tempered Lutz's enthusiasm by noting a weakness Blair had at bat because he "went for high [fastballs] in his eyes," as several other evaluators agreed that Blair would benefit from an extended stay at Rochester.[44] A new infielder, Dave Johnson, was making a better impression at second base than at shortstop, but his "mental lapses" (in Bamberger's opinion) and a tendency to be "homer happy" (according to Hitchcock) hinted at a delay in Johnson's arrival in Baltimore.[45] After completing his first season in professional baseball at Aberdeen in 1964, Jim Palmer's record of 11–3 included an ERA of 2.51 and only 75 hits allowed in 129 innings, but his 107 strikeouts were offset by the 130 walks he issued. Still eighteen years old at the time of Dalton's meeting, the future ace drew curious mixed reviews from those gathered: "Lets up when he gets behind ... quiet, don't know if he has real good drive ... must play regularly — Palmer acts like [he's] 18 ... [will pitch in] majors in 2 yrs — protect [from major league draft] ... wildness due to mental block — they don't hit his good fastball ... why more walks than strikeouts[?] ... has ability to have good [curveball]."[46] These are some examples of unvarnished comments by baseball insiders who were paid not only to find and train the best talent they could bring to the franchise but also the candid remarks of those whose appraisals determined the fate of the prospects they at one time or another so eagerly sought to bring into the Baltimore fold.

Of course, not all the reviews were good, as Dalton's notes are also littered with the debris of players attempting to hang on, who, despite their efforts, simply had little or no chance of reaching the major league level. "Finished ... release ... over [the] hill ... sloppy ... reflexes not good ... question his desire and gumption" were some of the unflattering remarks found amid the often brutal assessments.[47] It was no accident that Lou Piniella was traded to Cleveland following the 1965 season, since his "bad makeup" prompted some members of Dalton's de facto jury to declare that he "won't play for Balt" because his uninspired play made him a "bad hustler, worst I've seen," as Lutz summarily stated, "Get rid of him."[48]

Dalton's extensive agenda included a discussion of which players the Orioles should protect in future major and minor league drafts, how best to stock the Rochester farm club for the upcoming season, ways to ensure proper coverage of geographical scouting regions, and the search for a solution to the difficulty in coaxing prospects to sign with Baltimore. Regarding the last item Dalton noted, "Discuss why we don't sign more players.... Point out that most players we sign get a full year trial!," and the value he placed on the input of his assistants was emphasized by a parenthetical reminder to himself to permit "each [scout to] list their [recommendations] in order — *Let all scouts talk as each rec is made.*"[49]

Also scheduled for review were potential improvements to make Baltimore's player rating system clearer and orders to minor league managers to check the progress of injured players who would be on the mend over the coming winter. The productivity of the Orioles farm system notwithstanding, Dalton was still compelled to ask his managers about "weaknesses in our instruction and development system!," and debate suggestions for enhancements to the Thomasville facility.[50]

Communication with the various farm teams was essential to disseminating information and news throughout the organization. The Orioles sent newsletters approximately once a month to provide statistical recaps of the best individual performers, medical updates — Palmer's back problems were already being chronicled in June 1964 — and citations for teams whose progress was tallied against their records at the same point one year earlier. The rosy text of some of these missives may appear to be overwrought with optimism, but, in truth, the results made by the lower ranks of the franchise became the threads which strengthened Baltimore's fabric in the years to come.

Not everything the Orioles touched turn to gold, though, as their first foray in the amateur draft of 1965 yielded virtually no help for them. But beginning in 1962, the Orioles spent well over a decade "achiev[ing] the highest won-lost percentage among all major league organizations," and the team-issued bulletins that contained descriptions and phrases such as "hottest team in baseball," "brilliant pitching and timely hitting," "brightest record for the Red Wings," and "Aberdeen's red-hot pace" had much substance backing up these glowing assessments.[51]

This glimpse of the Orioles' method is not meant to imply that all other baseball organizations were less diligent in their own scouting and player development endeavors. But in the context of the era, one cannot overlook the productivity of the Baltimore farm system in terms of the quality of its prospects and the number of key players who ultimately contributed to the Orioles' win column. Paul Richards, Jim McLaughlin, and Harry Dalton deserve credit for creating the framework of Baltimore's minor league organization and successfully nurturing its growth.

## A New Robinson

Unlike the Minnesota Twins, whose stable lineup headed by Killebrew, Versalles, Oliva, Battey, and Allison at last jelled to become a winner in 1965, the Orioles still lacked one ingredient in their formula to overtake the Yankees in 1964 and the Twins one year later. The arrival of Frank Robinson enabled Baltimore to add a fourth power hitter to the lineup and also let the leadership abilities of the former National Leaguer come to the fore.

A native of Beaumont, Texas, and the youngest of eleven children, Robinson grew up in Oakland, California, and played high school baseball for Bay Area coaching legend George Powles, whose teams in the early 1950s included future major league stars Vada Pinson and Curt Flood. As a youth, Robinson's tall, slender physique earned him the nickname of "Pencils," and following his high school graduation he was signed to the Cincinnati Reds organization by scout Bobby Mattick for a meager $3,000 bonus. Robinson excelled at his minor league assignments in Ogden (.348 average with 17 homers in 1953) and Columbia of the Sally League (.336 average and 25 home runs in 1954). After his playing time was limited due to an arm injury in 1955, he burst onto the major league scene with a spectacular rookie season with the Reds in 1956. Robinson's .290 average was fortified by the 38 homers he belted, and his 122 runs scored led the National League, all of which earned him Rookie of the Year honors.

Robinson's shyness off the field developed in these early years because, as the youngest member of the Reds, he had little in common with his older, veteran teammates. But this aloofness belied the intensity he brought to the diamond. Robinson's daring baserunning and hard slides instigated several fights with opposing fielders, and his penchant for crowding the plate in order to reach outside pitches invited many brushback pitches and opportunities to be hit by a pitch (he led the NL in HBPs six of his ten years with the Reds). His reputation as one of the toughest competitors in the game fostered animosity with some opponents — and occasionally among some of his teammates — who felt that he went out of his way to try to injure them, but he quickly proved himself to be worthy of the Most Valuable Player award he earned in 1961 and the six All-Star accolades he garnered while in Cincinnati pinstripes.[52] A Gold Glove recipient in 1958, Robinson slugged his way into the pantheon of National League superstar outfielders next to Hank Aaron, Willie Mays, and Roberto Clemente. Robinson also overcame the disgrace he brought upon himself in early 1961, the result of his arrest from an incident when he drew a gun in a restaurant, and soon realized that he needed to be a more responsible citizen as part of the burden he carried as a public figure and role model to youngsters.[53]

By the end of the 1965 season — his tenth with the Reds — and having accumulated a trove of imposing statistics (.303 average, 1,673 hits, 324 home runs, 1,009 RBIs), Robinson was deemed by Reds president Bill DeWitt, Jr., to be somehow showing his age. So DeWitt embarked on a mission to peddle the thirty-year-old Robinson — in his 156 games in Cincinnati during 1965 he hit .296 with 33 home runs and 113 RBIs — and found willing takers in the Orioles front office. Robinson was dispatched to Baltimore for Pappas, Baldschun, and Simpson, as DeWitt justified the transaction by noting that "[Robinson] is certain to slow down dramatically one of these days because, as a young man, he led a fast life."[54] Robinson suspected that his salary of $62,500, which was among the highest at the time, also factored into DeWitt's decision to trade him in an effort to trim Cincinnati's payroll. The assumption of Robinson's salary was a tremendous risk for the Orioles because of their revenue shortfall caused by a plummet in their attendance from 1.1 million in 1964 to less than 782,000 in 1965. A failure to increase the gate at Memorial Stadium with Frank Robinson now under contract to the Orioles would be a fiscal disaster.

But the early verdict on the new Baltimore right fielder was good. From the very beginning of spring training in 1966, Robinson imstilled his new teammates with the power of positive thinking to such an extent that Robinson's batting prowess in spring training prompted Jim Palmer to confidently state, even before the regular season had begun, that the Orioles had just locked up the American League title.[55]

## *"Awfully Good Awfully Fast"*

With Frank Robinson adding extra sinew to a lineup already containing the Powell-Brooks Robinson-Blefary contingent, Baltimore completed its 1966 spring exhibition schedule with 15 wins and 11 losses. More encouraging than that mediocre record, however, was the batting displayed by the Orioles' big four hitters, whose averages ranged from Frank's .373 to Blefary's .320, as prognosticators of several major national sports publications chose Baltimore as the favorite to win the American League pennant.[56] Coming through again was the farm system, which sent three more players — pitcher Eddie Watt, infielder Dave Johnson, and catcher Andy Etchebarren — to Baltimore, with rookie hurler Gene Brabender making the team after fulfilling a two-year military commitment.

Scout Jim Russo's observation years later — "We got awfully good awfully fast when Frank arrived" — certainly contained more than a kernel of truth when the Orioles bolted from the gate in April 1966 by winning eleven of their first twelve contests and stayed right behind the front-running Cleveland Indians.[57] Baltimore fans were not only witnessing exciting baseball; they also were being exhorted to yell "Charge!" whenever a bugle call blared over the Memorial Stadium loudspeakers. There was much to cheer this season, not least in early May when Frank Robinson launched a pitch from Luis Tiant completely out of the ballpark. This achievement was thereafter commemorated by the flying of an orange flag bearing the simple message "HERE," which was flown at the rear of the left-field stands where Robinson's clout exited Memorial Stadium and landed in the parking lot 540 feet beyond home plate.

The enormity of Frank Robinson's home run was not lost on those who saw it, but in the short term, the feat did little to inspire the team. Following that win over Cleveland on May 8, Baltimore lost ten of its next fourteen games, slipping from first place to third as Boog Powell was in the throes of a severe batting slump. However, over the next 25 games beginning May 24, the Orioles went 19–6, and after defeating the Yankees in Baltimore, 2–1, on June 14, they claimed the American League lead and never relinquished it for the rest of the season. To the credit of the busy bullpen, nine of those wins were earned by the relievers — Stu Miller was victorious on four of those occasions — while several leg ailments briefly forced Frank Robinson out of right field. But the Orioles continued to roll during the month of June when they went 25–8 and entered July by opening a homestand with a key, five-game series against the defending AL champion Twins. To the delight of the nearly 100,000 fans who flocked to Memorial Stadium, Baltimore swept all five closely-contested games — the Orioles outscored the Twins by a total of just nine runs — and cruised into the All-Star break with a 58–29 record, good for first place with an eight-game lead.

By playing .667 baseball for the first half of the season, the Orioles had a cushion against any potential doldrums over the latter portion of the campaign. This was especially important following the midsummer break, when Baltimore posted a tepid 39–34 mark because several key players had second-half slumps. Brooks Robinson was hitting .295 at the break but batted only .236 from that point until the end of the season, while Powell (.302 down to .267), Etchebarren (.249 to .163), and part-time outfielders Snyder (.347 to .262) and Bowens (.270 to .149) also declined significantly. Fortunately for manager Hank Bauer, Aparicio (from .257 up to .302), Blair (.234 to .324), and Frank Robinson (.312 to .321) picked up some slack to prevent a total collapse of the offense.

On the mound through the All-Star break, Barber's ten wins paced the Baltimore starters — Palmer had nine, Bunker eight, and McNally seven — but the 21 victories and 27 saves credited to the bullpen emphasize the role of the relief corps, which was strengthened by the mid–June trade acquisition of knuckleballer Eddie Fisher. Given the majority of playing time at second base, Johnson had clearly established himself with a .252 average and made Jerry Adair expendable. In return for Adair, the Orioles received an excellent value when Fisher posted five wins and 13 saves working exclusively out of the bullpen.

As Baltimore's win total grew, however, there were occasions when injuries taxed Bauer's ability to field a steady lineup. Of greatest concern, Barber suffered from a sore arm and failed to win any games following the break, Bunker was similarly stricken and also ineffectual, Etchebarren and Powell were both hit by pitches on their throwing hands, and Johnson was sidelined by a broken toe.

But Frank Robinson soldiered on and received a batting tip from Johnson to help him break out of a hitting slump in late July, enabling Robinson to resume his quest for the league's highest batting achievements. Frank's professionalism on the field led the team by the example he set, as his hard-edged play gave the appearance that the Orioles were trailing in the standings rather than occupying first place. The only sign of his laxity was evident in the clubhouse following many an Oriole victory — and only following victories — when he placed a floor mop atop his head and acted as the judge of the team's derisively comical Kangaroo Court.

The humorous proceedings of these tribunals in fact carried an instructional message. The levity in the clubhouse after a win furnished a suitable ambience for Judge Frank to impose fines of a few dollars on players for mistakes committed during the game just concluded. *Faux pas* by Oriole baserunners, fielders, and batters were brought before the court, and Judge Frank would then ask the jury of the offender's peers — that is, the rest of the team — for its verdict. If found guilty, the culprit was fined and forced to keep a golden baseball shoe, broken bat handle, or glove in his locker, even on road trips, until another miscreant was convicted of a similar offense. One former Oriole commented that the court was "a fun but effective way to send messages to your teammates" in order to make them learn from their miscues.[58]

Another Oriole whose antics gained attention regardless of a game's outcome was reliever Moe Drabowsky. Famed for his "hot foot," which was created by nefariously igniting lighter fluid that soon had flames licking at the trousers of any unsuspecting clubhouse visitor, Drabowsky was also known for hiding snakes in a teammate's locker and for using his team's bullpen telephone to call the opposing team's bullpen to request that one of their relievers begin warming up. Paul Blair, who fled the clubhouse during one of the reptilian episodes, referred to Drabowsky as "Mojo," and the pitcher himself justified his pranks as "a defensive mechanism to relieve tension."[59] Drabowsky added, "The perception of whether you were keeping things loose or acting like a clown depended on how the team was performing."[60]

In Baltimore's case during 1966, Drabowsky may have been the court jester, but he made sure that spirits were light as the Orioles' lead in the AL swelled to 13 games at the end of July. Although the margin was trimmed to 8½ games by the third week of September, time had expired for the Twins, Tigers, and White Sox to mount a threat to overtake the Orioles. On September 22 in Kansas City, Palmer went the distance in a masterful 6–1 win over the Athletics to clinch Baltimore's first American League pennant and touched off a huge celebration in the visitors' clubhouse. The revelry was followed by no small amount of angst when Baltimore won just two of its final seven games while waiting to see who their National League opponent would be in the upcoming World Series.

Bauer's team had made great strides in vaulting to the top of the American League, and there was much reason for the Orioles to be thankful because the script could have had a far different ending. Exactly one month before Palmer's pennant-clinching gem, the Orioles had gathered on the evening of August 22 for a team party — as it turned out, the Kafkaesque setting was the home of a funeral director — and lost in the festivities was the plunge of Frank Robinson into the residence's swimming pool. Thinking that Frank's struggles in the water were only a stunt, teammates ignored him until at last Etchebarren dove in to save Robinson, who was unable to swim.[61] The potentially catastrophic loss of the Orioles' leader would have doomed not only the 1966 team but those clubs of the following years to which Robinson's impact was so great. There was no substitute for a player who had come to Baltimore as what turned out to be the epitome of the right man in the right place at the right time.

Performing before a record home attendance of 1.2 million spectators, the Orioles' AL championship came on the strength of their 97–63 record and Frank Robinson's Most Valuable Player performance during the 155 games in which he appeared. On his way to winning the AL MVP award, Frank amassed league-bests in batting average (.316), home runs (49), and runs batted in (122) to become the first Triple Crown winner since Mickey Mantle had accomplished the feat ten years earlier. Robinson also led the league in slugging percentage

(.637) and runs scored (122), while teammates Brooks Robinson (.269 average, 23 homers, 100 RBIs) and Powell (.287 average, 34, 109) finished second and third, respectively, in the MVP balloting. Luis Aparicio stole 25 bases and scored 97 runs to augment his .276 average, Blefary belted 23 home runs and drove in 64 runs, and the center field platoon tandem of Snyder and Blair provided offensive support and yeoman work on defense. Earning a berth as Aparicio's keystone partner, Johnson proved he was ready to stay in the major leagues, and assuming the difficult duties at backstop was the rookie Etchebarren, who had been thrust into the role of front-line receiver because of injuries to Dick Brown and Charlie Lau. Brooks Robinson and Aparicio each won Gold Gloves for their fielding excellence, and Hank Bauer was named Manager of the Year by *The Sporting News*.

Baltimore's pitching staff was plagued by a shortfall of complete games — starters finished only 23 of their assignments — thereby putting heavy demands on the bullpen. The two best starters were Palmer, who finished with a 3.46 ERA and led the staff with 15 wins, while McNally was second with 13 wins. Bunker and Barber logged 10 victories apiece, but elbow ailments rendered both ineffective over the second half of the campaign. The pressing workload on the relievers, however, brought them a well-earned share of the spotlight. Collectively, the relievers were brilliant thanks to the notable efforts of Drabowsky (undefeated in six decisions with seven saves), Watt (9–7, four saves), Miller (9–4, 18 saves), Fisher (5–3, 13 saves), and Dick Hall (6–2, seven saves).

**Rejuvenated in his new Baltimore uniform, Frank Robinson won the Triple Crown on his way to becoming the 1966 AL Most Valuable Player.**

Bold as these statistics were, Baltimore was nonetheless installed as the underdog to the heavily-favored, defending World Series champion Los Angeles Dodgers. The oddsmakers, who put Walter Alston's team at 8-to-5 to beat the Orioles, had found much to like about the Dodgers. Los Angeles possessed the best pitching in baseball thanks to a rotation fronted by the redoubtable Sandy Koufax. Having won two of the last three World Series, the Dodgers had plenty of experience in championship competition, as they had yet to lose a World Series game at their home ballpark, Dodger Stadium.[62] As neophytes to postseason play, the Orioles were expected to bow quickly and quietly in four games. Although most professional prognosticators were correct in predicting the number of contests eventually played, they could not have been more wrong in forecasting the outcome of the Series.

## *Dodger Pitching Gets Its Comeuppance*

The World Series of 1966 was emblematic of the malaise that was creeping into the offensive output of major league baseball during the 1960s. When the statistics of the four games played in the Series were totaled, both teams produced an anemic 15 runs on just 41 hits, and the Dodgers, who managed to push only two runners across the plate, never scored a run after the third inning of the first game. If the Dodgers seemed feckless at the plate, the Orioles were not much better, but in the Series against Los Angeles, a scant, solitary run often made the difference.

Opening the World Series on the road at Dodger Stadium, Hank Bauer tapped McNally as his Game 1 starter, and the left-hander was staked to a quick three-run lead when Frank Robinson and Brooks Robinson belted back-to-back home runs in the top of the first inning off Don Drysdale. After trading single runs in the second inning, Los Angeles loaded the bases when McNally lost control in the third inning and issued walks to three straight Dodger batters, prompting Bauer to bring in Drabowsky for what became a long relief stint. Drabowsky walked in the second Los Angeles run, but then shut down the Dodgers the rest of the afternoon on one hit and finished with eleven strikeouts in the 5–2 Baltimore win. The *Los Angeles Times* tipped its cap to "Big D," but hastened to add that the pitcher being cited was Drabowsky rather than the home team's Drysdale.[63]

The trouble that beset McNally's control in the opener was more than matched by the horror experienced by Dodgers center fielder Willie Davis in Game 2. With Koufax on the mound for Los Angeles, the Dodgers hoped to even the Series despite their ace's elbow ailment, as he and the Orioles' Palmer hurled shutout baseball for the first four innings. But the Dodgers, and Davis in particular, came undone in the fifth, when they surrendered three unearned runs as the center fielder committed errors on three consecutive plays, a dubious performance consisting of two dropped fly balls and a throwing error after the second muff. Baltimore added runs in the sixth and eighth frames—by more conventional means—as Palmer was masterful in finishing his four-hit, three-walk outing in the 6–0 triumph. *Times*' columnist Jim Murray was unflagging in his sarcasm aimed at Davis and claimed the beleaguered outfielder may have been in line for a fourth error when he and Ron Fairly allowed indecision on each other's part to permit a fly ball by Frank Robinson to drop into the gap in right field for a triple.[64] With the Series now moving to Memorial Stadium, the chance that the Orioles might pull off an upset of monumental proportions became a distinct possibility.

The Series now had a heightened sense of urgency for the Dodgers entering Game 3. Shortstop Maury Wills refused to believe that Los Angeles was inferior to the upstart Orioles, and the Dodgers seemed capable of making up ground quickly against an Oriole pitcher whose season was interrupted by injury in July. However, Bunker endured lingering pain and pitched the game of his career when he stymied Los Angeles with his six-hit blanking of the Dodgers, 1–0, as Blair launched a 430-foot home run off Claude Osteen for the only run of the contest.

Baltimore's commanding three-games-to-none lead permitted Bauer to pit McNally, who lasted only two-plus innings in Game 1, in a rematch against Drysdale, who faced but twelve batters his first time out. Eerily, the result was another 1–0 Baltimore win, as Frank Robinson's solo home run in the fourth inning provided the margin of victory in the Series-clinching contest and brought him MVP kudos for the Fall Classic. McNally surrendered four hits and two walks yet was perhaps but one pitch better than Drysdale, who yielded four hits and one walk. The hitting star of Game 3 was the fielding star of Game 4, as Blair robbed Jim Lefebvre of a potential home run in the eighth inning. After a brisk one hour and forty-five minutes of play, the end of Game 4 touched off a wild celebration. In some instances in the city of Baltimore, riot police were called out to quell the actions of some over-exuberant fans.

Years later, Orioles reliever Dick Hall opined that the value of the Dodgers' Maury Wills, while undoubtedly important to the Los Angeles offense, may have been overstated. Although Wills was a great leadoff man and catalyst, Hall and his teammates learned before the start of the Series that Wills' on-base average was only fifth-best on the Dodgers. Realizing that Wills was not as redoubtable as they had been led to believe, the inexperienced Orioles had a sense of diminished intimidation.[65] For Baltimore's own part, their offense in the Series was hardly overwhelming, but the Orioles used it to their best advantage.

All the years of labor on the part of Paul Richards, Jim McLaughlin, Lee MacPhail, and Harry Dalton now bore the fruit of Baltimore's first World Series crown, and it was fitting that the man acquired from the Reds not only vindicated the trade of Milt Pappas but also won the Series finale with his bat. Despite his Triple Crown performance of 1966, Frank Robinson claimed that his best personal season, statistically speaking, was in 1962, but now as the owner of a championship ring, he had helped give the small-market team of Baltimore a stage presence it had previously lacked.

These were heady times in Baltimore, and with the Yankees having ignominiously fallen to the basement of the American League, at least one member of the media thought he saw the future when he sent a congratulatory note to Dalton as the season drew to a close: "Dear Harry, Now you've *really* got the pressure on you!" gushed the general manager of radio station WINS in New York. "All you have to do is keep the dynasty coming."[66] In a moment shot full of anticipation for a rematch, Walter O'Malley, the Dodgers' major domo, quipped to Bauer in the Orioles clubhouse after the Series finale, "We'll see you again next year."[67]

## Bauer's Dilemma

The Orioles and Dodgers did meet again in 1967, but not under the circumstances envisioned by O'Malley. Aside from several spring training matches scheduled in March, neither team performed close to expectations, as the season was a dismal failure that banished both the Dodgers and Orioles to the role of World Series spectators. Bauer's pitching staff in particular was wracked by a skein of injuries that directly led to the Orioles' decline. Starters Palmer, Barber, McNally, and Bunker were felled by arm or shoulder miseries, and the four combined for a total of only 17 wins for the 1967 season. Unexpectedly relying on several rookies to fill the void, the Orioles' top winners were Jim Hardin (8–3 record with a 2.27 ERA) and Baltimore native Tom Phoebus (14–9, 3.33).

Baltimore contended for the opening weeks of the 1967 campaign and spent the first half of the month of June in third place roughly four games out of first. But late that month in a home game against the White Sox, Frank Robinson suffered a severe injury, and the

Orioles were handicapped for the remainder of the year. Avenging a take-out slide that victimized Etchebarren the previous game, Robinson plowed headfirst into Chicago infielder Al Weis and was knocked unconscious when he struck Weis's knee. After the effects of his concussion subsided, Robinson thereafter was plagued with double vision, which he claimed took its toll on him for the remainder of his career.[68] Batting .337 at the time of the incident, Robinson was sidelined for 28 games and not nearly as effective upon his return to the lineup.

Blair cemented his place in the outfield with a .293 average and Gold Glove–winning defense, but Powell raised eyebrows when his production fell to a disappointing 13 home runs and 55 RBIs. Team harmony was further disrupted when Barber, who suspected he had become Bauer's scapegoat for the Orioles' swoon, aired out his manager and was subsequently dealt to the Yankees in early July.

The absence of Frank Robinson from the lineup, to say nothing of the persistent vision problems that dogged him, contributed to Baltimore's torpor, as the Orioles ambled along in eighth place until a modest winning streak in mid–September boosted them two notches in the standings. However, the spectacular pennant frenzy that gripped Boston, Minnesota, Detroit, and Chicago was missing in Baltimore, as the defending champions tied Washington for sixth place with a 76–85 record. In retrospect, bright spots were few, but the Orioles were able to give an extended tryout to a new infielder, Mark Belanger, who was soon to become a fixture as Baltimore's enduring shortstop. Additionally, two selections from the June amateur draft, Bobby Grich and Don Baylor, would yield a huge payoff a few years hence following their respective minor league apprenticeships.

The year 1968 loomed as a pivotal season in Baltimore. A winter of healing was expected to mend physical problems, and Bauer went to spring training with several new players and coaches on the roster, not all of which he welcomed. By expressing a vote of confidence in Belanger, Dalton traded Aparicio, along with Snyder and John Matias, to the White Sox for second baseman–outfielder Don Buford and two pitchers. Catching help was brought on board when former Rochester manager Earl Weaver insisted that the Orioles draft backstop Elrod Hendricks from the Angels organization after Weaver had seen Hendricks play in the Puerto Rican winter league.

Ominous for Bauer was a shakeup of his coaching staff, which had been initiated by Dalton. Harry Brecheen, the long-time pitching coach, was replaced by George Bamberger, whose belief that pitchers should throw even on their days off was vastly different from that of his coddling predecessor. More threatening to Bauer, however, was the appointment of Weaver as the new first base coach. In an interview long after his career ended, Brooks Robinson stated, "I think everyone thought that sooner or later Weaver would be the manager, simply because Weaver was Dalton's guy."[69] Whether Bauer liked it or not, pressure was brought to bear on him to make these pieces mesh, put the Orioles back on a winning track, and turn those victories into an increase at the box office, which in 1967 fell more than 340,000 fans short of 1966's gate.

Working with no margin of error, Bauer had the sword of Damocles hanging over his head as an imminent successor stood in the wings, and the manager's peril could only be removed by a rapid return of the Orioles to pennant contention.

# 6

## Soaring

Turbulent is the best adjective that describes the upheaval that beset the United States during 1968. In foreign affairs, the country was troubled by the capture of the USS *Pueblo* off the coast of North Korea, and the explosion of the Tet Offensive across South Vietnam during the war in Southeast Asia belied American military leaders' claims that the figurative light at the end of the tunnel there was growing brighter. On the home front, President Lyndon Johnson chose to forego a bid for re-election rather than subject himself to the frustrating rigors of his office, and the springtime assassinations of Martin Luther King, Jr. and Robert Kennedy evoked a sense of heightened despair that America was losing those who could lead it into an uncertain future. Anti-war demonstrations that climaxed with the August riots at the Democratic National Convention in Chicago seemed to offer further proof that the nation was coming apart with no relief in sight.

Amid this rampant turmoil, the Orioles tried to regain the form that had brought them a championship just two years earlier. On the heels of King's murder, and minus Pete Richert and Mark Belanger, who were briefly called to active military duty, Baltimore opened the 1968 season by lumbering along the month of April just two games above .500 until an eight-game winning streak vaulted the Orioles into first place. But the 16–6 record of May 6 was the best they would do in the first half of the season, as the offensive pall known as "the year of the pitcher" shut down the Orioles' bats. Baltimore lost its grip on the league's top spot to eventual AL champion Detroit and by the All-Star break had dropped to third place, 10½ games out with a 43–37 mark. Falling batting averages had been a trend in both leagues throughout the 1960s, but the Orioles seemed to be acutely affected in 1968, as evidenced by their lowly .218 team average at the break. With a drab won-lost record and scoring but 70 total runs in the 24 games prior to July 8, manager Hank Bauer sensed that change was imminent.[1]

Bauer's fate mirrored that of the Twins' Sam Mele—whose honeymoon lasted just a year and a half after the Twins' 1965 World Series appearance—and the Orioles skipper bitterly acknowledged that when the front office brought in new coaches against his will in 1967, an unmistakable message was being sent that the incumbent manager's job security was precarious.[2] Harry Dalton dismissed Bauer on July 10, as Bauer admitted, "Our pitching has been going good, but the hitting has been bad."[3] The following day, Orioles first-base coach Earl Weaver was introduced by Dalton as the team's new manager, thereby ushering in a new era in Baltimore Orioles history and putting in place the central figure who would guide the team to its greatest triumphs over the next fourteen years.

## *"He Wasn't Going to Hug Anybody"*

Earl Sidney Weaver's path to Baltimore was not unlike that of many Orioles currently on the club's roster. With fifteen former Oriole minor leaguers now calling Memorial Stadium home, Weaver became manager, as Dalton told the press, after he was "signed into, developed, trained and promoted through our own organization, rather than bringing in a man from the outside. We are happy about this and a little proud about it."[4] This latest assimilation of a minor leaguer, albeit a manager, was perhaps the most important call-up the Baltimore franchise ever made.

Standing a mere five feet, eight inches tall and of slightly chunky physique, Weaver scrapped and scraped his way as a second baseman through the St. Louis Cardinals system and attended spring training with the major league team in 1952, yet he was not good enough to clear the last hurdle to make the Cardinals roster. But his true baseball talent blossomed when, shortly before his 26th birthday, he was handed his first managing assignment in the Sally League, where he piloted the Knoxville team for the final part of the 1956 season. In his second full managerial season, he began an eleven-year run during which his teams never finished below .500, finishing in first place three times and in second place on five other occasions. Not content to lead only during the regular baseball season, Weaver also managed in the Orioles' instructional league and in the Puerto Rican Winter League.

Dalton knew his managerial prospect well when he stated, "[Weaver] has the knack of taking talent given to him and making championship teams or strong contending teams out of that talent."[5] Although Weaver developed this skill at the minor league level, his track record in Baltimore would also lend veracity to Dalton's comment. Weaver's personality could not have been more polar-opposite than that of former Orioles skipper Billy Hitchcock. Future Baltimore star Bobby Grich also noted years later that Weaver was very tough on rookies, even those whom he had once managed in the lower ranks of the farm system. "He didn't go to the Tommy Lasorda school, didn't coddle any young players.... He wasn't going to hug anybody," Grich recalled.[6] Players like the Robinsons and Boog Powell justified the reason why Weaver held more faith in his veterans, since the overall strength of the Orioles, even in their swoon of 1968, meant that for any new player aspiring to wear Baltimore's orange and black, "you had to be *outstanding* to impress him."[7]

The baseball philosophy that Earl Weaver would put into practice included implementation of a platoon system to allow him "to go with the best players that night," and the farm system had two "excellent" outfield prospects, Don Baylor and, in particular, Merv Rettenmund, who was raising speculation of a call-up to Baltimore.[8] Embracing the challenge of trying to overtake the Detroit Tigers in the second half of the 1968 season, Weaver believed that an invigorated Orioles squad could make a run at the pennant.

Just five weeks before his 38th birthday at the time of his appointment, Weaver's experience as a minor league manager had earned him the reputation of a competitor, a pilot who not only knew how to handle regular players and pitchers but also one capable of using every man on the roster for profit, an excellent thinker who was "always two innings ahead" during a game, and a disciplinarian who had "no doghouse."[9] Weaver proved himself a worthy protégé of Paul Richards for the attention he gave to the pitching staff, but his comportment was less aloof than Richards. Off the diamond, the manager's office was Weaver's domain, as his generally loose hand over the Orioles clubhouse fostered a relaxed atmosphere for the players because of Weaver's respect for the sanctity of their space.

In taking on Weaver as the new manager, however, the Orioles also assumed the burden of his volcanic temper. Weaver's profanity-laced tirades — directed mostly at umpires, but his frequent use of the "f-word" seemingly knew no bounds — and on-field histrionics when arguing calls would become the stuff of legend and lead to scores of ejections over the course of his years in Baltimore. Barely two months into his managerial career with the Orioles, Weaver already had gone toe-to-toe with eighteen-year veteran umpire Larry Napp, who predictably labeled the rookie manager "bush."[10] Often punctuated with a full repertoire of scornful gestures, Weaver's protests contained such classic moves as turning his hat around in order to get face-to-face with a wayward — in his opinion — umpire, or motioning to throw the umpire out of the game. His yelling was made all the more acerbic by a voice rendered raspy by the cigarettes he consumed. Weaver became notorious for sneaking smokes during tense games.

What did benefit the Orioles, according to scout Jim Russo, was Weaver's penchant for making his teams "win with execution," and as the victories accumulated, the aura of a championship team began to re-emerge from the wilderness of 1967 and early 1968.[11] Grich thought that the Kangaroo Court facilitated the "good social interaction" so vital to the camaraderie among the players, a quality further proven by the lack of racial issues in a clubhouse lorded over by Frank Robinson, a future Hall of Famer who after arriving from Cincinnati dispelled the notion that he could be a malcontent.[12]

Following many an Oriole win, the team's Kangaroo Court was in session, with Judge Frank Robinson presiding with a mop on his head.

The upbeat morale of the players, combined with Weaver's knack for getting his team to produce, generated a synergy that moved Baltimore to the top of major league baseball.

## Success from the Start

The 10½ game deficit Weaver inherited in July 1968 forced him to immediately put his spurs to the Orioles. He encouraged more aggressiveness on the bases and saw the team steal 53 bases of its season total of 78 after he became manager. Because an ankle injury nagged Paul Blair (Weaver suspected that it may have been the cause of the outfielder's .196

average in the first half of the season), Weaver began to play Don Buford in Blair's place. Already one of the few bright spots in the lineup, Buford ignited a six-game winning streak by hitting safely (9-for-25) in each victory.[13] Baltimore continued to nip at the Tigers' lead but could do no better than maintain its hold on second place for much of the last eleven weeks of the campaign, finishing 48–34 under Weaver, 91–71 for the season, and a distant twelve games behind eventual World Series champion Detroit. Dave McNally won 22 games and posted a 1.95 ERA, Jim Hardin assumed a starting role and logged 18 victories, and, in a season where only one player in the American League batted over .300, Buford finished as the Orioles' top hitter at a respectable .282.

Signed only until the end of the season but having solidified his position with what Dalton described as the "exciting brand of baseball" played under him, Weaver was awarded a one-year contract for 1969.[14] Although Baltimore's batting downturn required attention, the Orioles were hardly the only team to suffer a decline in offensive production during 1968. Some small measure of comfort was taken in most AL cities because the Yankees had clearly lost the hold on their dynasty that ended in 1964, as an interesting pattern had developed in the four ensuing seasons since New York last appeared in the World Series. From 1965 to 1968, there were no repeat pennant winners, with the Twins coming closest in 1967 to capturing a second title. The ostensible parity among the contenders would be further aided by a new format to be implemented in 1969 that created two divisions in each league, resulting in twice the number of pennant races than otherwise would have taken place. A Baltimore resurgence under Weaver could put the Orioles atop the new American League East division.

The expansion of the American League and its split into two divisions put the Orioles in the AL East with five existing franchises: Boston, Detroit, Cleveland, New York, and Washington. This collective and geographically rational alignment meant that Baltimore's road to a divisional title would be more difficult because of the quality of most of its divisional foes at that time. Although the Senators were the worst of the lot, the Orioles' immediate competition would come from the defending World Series champion Tigers; the Red Sox, who were only one year removed from their miracle season of 1967; the Indians, winners of a respectable 86 games in 1968; and even the Yankees, with manager Ralph Houk breathing new life into the Bronx Bombers.

Ironically, Baltimore chose to focus on strengthening its pitching in the offseason by trading Curt Blefary, whose stock had fallen precipitously. Only three years beyond his great rookie season, Blefary struggled at the plate while he was shifted between left field, right field, first base, and catching duties. When Weaver assumed command, Elrod Hendricks was handed the backstop chores while Blefary, troubled also at the time by his failing marriage, began to press and bottomed out with a poor .200 average. During the winter meetings of 1968, the Orioles and the Houston Astros completed a trade in which Blefary and the Astros' Mike Cuellar were the principal subjects. Blefary was "mortified" by the trade, but Cuellar, a Cuban-born southpaw barely six feet tall who threw a devastating screwball, happily found a niche in the Baltimore rotation after establishing himself as one of the better hurlers for the Astros in the mid–1960s.[15]

Aside from the addition of Cuellar, the Orioles began 1969 with a roster similar to that of the prior year. In the Paul Richards tradition, Baltimore in 1969 continued to build on the strength of its pitching staff, while the rules changes enacted to put more offense into the game could only help the Orioles, whose league-best .258 average in the title year of 1966 had plummeted in two seasons to third-worst at .225.

The challenge now for Earl Weaver was to build on the stable groundwork he had laid in the second half of 1968. His first full year as a manager in 1969 proved to be one of the most successful ever enjoyed by a major league skipper despite four crushing losses the Orioles would suffer later that autumn.

## An Unsettled Spring

Three weeks into the new year of 1969, Harry Dalton informed the Orioles players that he expected them to report to spring training "in acceptable physical condition" so that the team could prepare for its inaugural season "in a very strong division."[16] The vice president for player personnel expressed his satisfaction with the performance of the pitchers the prior season and was optimistic of George Bamberger's ability to guide the staff once more to fulfill its potential.

But spring training was a contentious time since many players refused to report to their respective camps due to a concerted action by the Major League Baseball Players Association to secure more revenue from the club owners for the benefit of the players' pension fund. Struggles between players and owners over salaries were nothing new, but the players — very few of whom were signed for the upcoming season — were mobilized by their union's executive director, Marvin Miller, in early 1969 to hold out in a collective move to exact a better contribution from the leagues to their pension plan. Since four expansion teams and a new round of playoffs were now part of the major league landscape, the players felt, not without reason, that they were entitled to a portion of the higher income to be generated from the sale of broadcast rights to additional regular-season and postseason games. At the time, the pension contribution was a huge consideration for the many players whose minimum salaries were less than $10,000 per season.[17]

After lengthy negotiations and haggling over the winter months, a settlement was reached between the players and the club owners on February 25, about one week after the date when training camps would have normally opened. The players succeeded in gaining a total of nearly $5.5 million for their pension fund, which by today's standards appears minuscule, but in the context of the era, this gain by the players was hardly trivial.

Miller's endeavor to secure the confidence of the players in taking a firm stand during the protracted negotiations was no small accomplishment. As the former leader of the steelworkers' union, Miller's past association with this group falsely led some players into believing that Miller would possibly advocate the use of violence to attain better benefits for the players' union. "Players were conservative guys who were anti-union," explained one former player, so the image of "picket lines, goons, and [the use of] bicycle chains" to augment the union's negotiating tactics was abhorrent to those leery of casting their support for Miller.[18] But Miller's visits to the spring training camps enabled players to meet the union leader face-to-face and see him for the patient, circumspect man that he was. Impressing the union members as "more like a college professor than a firebrand," Miller gained the faith of the players, and this first victory for them served to embolden their union for far bigger battles against ownership that lay in the not-so-distant future.[19]

## *Making It Look Easy*

Weaver began spring training in 1969 by laying down strict rules for all players, which the *Baltimore Morning Sun* reported included a special proviso that forbade pitchers from swimming in the ocean, bays, or pools of Florida.[20] As coaches were handed assignments for putting players through their paces, Dalton was hardly a passive observer once camp opened. In late March he questioned Weaver on what was being done to improve some of the finer points of the Orioles' game plan. Shortstop Mark Belanger was the subject of several queries, as Dalton asked, "How much work is Belanger doing on bunting?" and "Are we continuing to work regularly with Belanger and [second baseman] Johnson on double plays?"[21] The hope for the front office was that Boog Powell would report to camp at a svelte — for him — 240 pounds; while Boog was never light on his feet, Dalton demanded to know,

Just as his cigarettes were close to his heart — notice the outline of the pack under his jersey next to the uniform number — fiery manager Earl Weaver had a way of making a point with an umpire.

"Are we continuing to work on Powell on [his] footwork at first base?"[22] Nor did Dalton shy away from mildly venting some frustration over the streak-hitting, strikeout-prone Johnson, who "continues to be a puzzle to me ... [because] it is hard to know what to expect from him."[23] Addressing those issues showed the organization's attention to detail and made winners of the Orioles from the very beginning of exhibition play as they dominated their opponents en route to a 19–5 record, easily the best in either spring training circuit.

With the exception of Buford in left field and Belanger at shortstop, the everyday lineup was populated by the same faces that had graced the 1966 championship squad, as expectations were that Weaver would continue to employ the men on his bench in appropriate situations. "My philosophy on making substitutions, either pitching, hitting, or defensive," the manager stated early in his tenure with Baltimore, "is that I'd rather lose a ball game by making a move than by just sitting on the bench and watching us blow it."[24]

The starting rotation welcomed back Jim Palmer, who had spent 1967 and 1968 disabled by shoulder and back miseries after winning 15 games in 1966. No guarantees accompanied Palmer's return, however, and his status was so tenuous that during the expansion draft to stock the new Seattle Pilots and Kansas City Royals, the future Hall of Famer was left unprotected by the Orioles in the first two rounds. Less conspicuous by his presence but nonetheless influential was Charlie Lau, the former catcher whose mentoring as the new hitting coach was especially important to several key Orioles.

Taking a cue from their outstanding spring exhibition play and letting little of that nascent momentum escape, Baltimore opened the regular season on April 8 and reached first place in the AL East eight days later, never to relinquish their perch atop the division. In a year of superlatives, Weaver had the Orioles at the top of their game, the likes of which had seldom been seen in major league baseball.

Through the end of April and again through the end of May, Baltimore won at a pace in which they were victorious, on average, two out of every three games. The lead they held in the AL East was slender, just a handful of games separating the Orioles and a Boston club that refused to quit as it unleashed a powerful offense in an attempt to recapture their miraculous spirit of 1967. But during the month of June, Baltimore stifled any chance of being overtaken when they won 21 of 27 contests and padded their lead to a full eleven games. A modest three-game losing streak entering the All-Star break dropped the Orioles to 65–31, but their eleven-game margin was difficult for any rival to surmount.

Several factors worked in favor of the Orioles as their win column grew in the season's first half. Inclement weather had plagued many teams and forced some games to be rescheduled as doubleheaders later in the season, but Baltimore was so affected just twice in the first two months. This meant that the Orioles pitching staff was less fatigued by makeup games that took a toll on the opposition as the hot summer wore on. Baltimore sported an AL-best team ERA of 2.90, with starters Palmer (9–2, 1.96 ERA), Cuellar (10–9, 2.51), and McNally (12–0, 2.88) among the best pitchers. Palmer was subjected to more back trouble in June after his fiery start, but McNally proved literally unbeatable, and Cuellar put to rest any concern over the sore arm that impacted him in his final year with the Astros. Cuellar used his specialty pitch to fine effect and through July he had pitched better than his record indicated, while Tom Phoebus rounded out the rotation with a 9–3 record and 3.59 ERA. The bullpen supplied starters to fill in for Palmer and collectively chalked up nearly two dozen victories. It seemed that the only big loss suffered by Baltimore was its inability to come to terms with its 40th round pick in the June amateur draft, a lanky kid from Central High School in St. Paul, Minnesota, by the name of Dave Winfield.

On offense, the Orioles' run-scoring capability was relentless. Buford and Blair set the pace in the top two slots of the batting order, as Blair was having an immense impact with his superb all-around performance, hitting .312 with 19 home runs, stealing 14 bases, and playing a near-flawless center field. Following this duo was Powell and his .308 average, 24 home runs, and 86 RBIs with the remainder of Baltimore's own Murderer's Row, Frank Robinson (.328, 22, 64) and Brooks Robinson (.237, 15, 54) in tow. Frank's double vision seemed to have subsided, and Dalton speculated that Brooks' ostensibly low average would have been higher had some of his hard-hit balls found a hole. Generous in his praise for the Orioles' new batting coach was Powell, who said, "Charlie Lau still keeps reminding me not to lunge.... He's really been a help."[25] Also heeding Lau's advice was Belanger, who was drastically reducing his strikeout total while significantly raising his average.[26]

Directing the whole operation was Weaver, who was still learning his job at the major league level but, in the eyes of his predecessor, appeared to be "a push-button manager."[27] So groused Hank Bauer, now managing in Oakland, who complained, "The only difference between my Orioles of last year and [Weaver's] this year was that all of the sick players got well the minute I left."[28] Bauer's statement was not exactly true, but unmistakable was the degree of confidence that Weaver had instilled in his players, a trait that had its roots from the moment of his appointment as manager the previous summer and was manifest in the growing trove of Oriole victories.

All of the winning enjoyed by Baltimore moved the hijinks of the Kangaroo Court to another plane. From his position as the supreme justice, Frank Robinson levied a fine against himself on two occasions, with infractions now including being under-dressed when visiting the post-game buffet, basketball-style shooting (and missing) dirty laundry into the clubhouse hamper, and even booting a ball during pregame fielding practice. Weaver himself failed to escape punishment when he inserted Belanger as a late-inning defensive replacement only to have the usually sure-fielding shortstop commit a pair of miscues in a win over the Indians in late June. Such revelry drew players and non-players into the fray, as the japes to which all comers were subjected became an invaluable bonding agent that held the clubhouse together. Besides possessing a talent for playing baseball, any Oriole who wanted to make the most of his experience in Baltimore needed a thick skin to brace himself against the jibes of the clubhouse humor.

The Orioles paused for the All-Star Game, which featured the naming of Blair, Johnson, McNally, Powell, and both Robinsons to the AL squad, and then picked up where they left off by winning 21 of their next 25 games. With a lead of 17 games on August 19, little was left to accomplish other than finishing out the season and staying focused for the postseason, as Baltimore barreled past their divisional foes and won another 10 of 11 contests, including the division-clinching game on September 13.

A five-game losing skid at season's end did not dim Baltimore's anticipation of playing the Minnesota Twins in the first-ever American League Championship Series, but some irony accompanied the Orioles through the course of the campaign. For all the dominance on display as they amassed win after win, Baltimore was hard-pressed to draw fans to Memorial Stadium. Only on the last day of the season did their attendance eclipse the one million mark, and barely at that with a total of just 1,000,811.[29] Winning, it appeared, had become so commonplace that Orioles fans favored tracking the team's progress via the media rather than watching them play in person.

But the grandeur of a 109–53 won-lost record hardly went unnoticed in baseball circles, and salient in the final statistics was the damage that the Orioles had inflicted upon the rest of the league. In a season replete with outstanding performances, Baltimore out-paced many of its American League rivals in most major categories of offense and defense, foremost among them the best team ERA at 2.83 — a full half-run better than runner-up New York — and allowed the fewest runs (517), walks (498), hits (1,194), and home runs (117) in 1,473 innings of work. Backing up the hurlers was a defense that rarely let itself be beaten, committing the fewest errors (101) for a league-best .984 fielding average, with the batteries combined for the least amount of wild pitches and passed balls (48). Four Orioles — Brooks

Robinson, Belanger, Johnson, and Blair — earned a Gold Glove for their prowess in the field. At the plate, the Orioles at .265 joined Minnesota (.268) as the only two AL teams to compile a team batting average above .260, and Baltimore's .414 slugging percentage was runner-up by one point to that of Boston. Total production of 779 runs put the Orioles a close second to the Twins' 790. The lethal combination of stellar outings on the mound, smooth glove work in the field, and clutch hitting facilitated 44 victories that came after the seventh inning.

By individual performance, Baltimore was well-represented in the upper tiers of the league statistics as well. On offense, Frank Robinson (.308) and Powell (.304) placed fourth and fifth, respectively, for best batting average, Frank's 111 runs scored were second, Powell was runner-up with 121 RBIs, and Blair came in third by rapping 178 hits. Most impressive about the lineup was the balance among the regulars, most of whom were a threat to reach base via a hit or walk, hit for power, steal a base, or spark the offense in some combination thereof. Belanger, Blair, and Buford each stole at least 14 bases; Blair, Powell, and the Robinsons belted a minimum of 23 home runs with at least 76 RBIs; and excepting Brooks Robinson, who hit only .234, this group, along with Dave Johnson, all hit .280 or better. Even the catching trio of Andy Etchebarren, Elrod Hendricks, and Clay Dalrymple contributed a composite .245 average with 18 home runs and 70 RBIs. Weaver employed his bench with fine results coming from Dave May (.242), Curt Motton (.303), Merv Rettenmund (.247), and Chico Salmon (.297), a solid group of reserves that emerged, with the exception of Salmon, from the Baltimore farm system.

The pitching mound, however, was where the Orioles dominated in the late 1960s and early 1970s. After tying Cleveland for the best team earned-run average in 1968, Baltimore again led the American League in ERA and would continue to do so each year through 1973. The effects of pitching coach George Bamberger's tutelage had taken a firm hold among the hurlers. In spite of Bamberger's own modest assessment of his mission — "My job is to find the best things a guy has going and help him use them to his best advantage," he stated in the spring of 1969 — his keen focus was essential to drawing out those qualities that placed Orioles pitchers at the top of the league.[30] Whether a pitcher needed assistance with the mechanics of his delivery or a bit of psychological consultation to help him relax on the mound by removing self-induced pressure, Bamberger appeared to have the answer for every pitching-related issue. "It's plain that mainly through the efforts of Bamberger, Baltimore has been transformed from the sore arm capital of the solar system to the home of one of the best and healthiest gang of slingers around," observed *The Sporting News*.[31] This proved to be bad news for Orioles opponents for most of the decade in which Bamberger served as Baltimore's pitching coach, as Weaver felt that his decisions regarding pitchers were made easier with Bamberger's input. "It's not guesswork because he knew how well a pitcher did against a certain batter," said the manager, who also reviewed the statistical performance of batter-pitcher match-ups to optimize his chances of winning.[32]

The harvest reaped from Bamberger's 1969 crop was the envy of the league. Mike Cuellar, a man possessed of numerous superstitions and eccentricities, soldiered on as the workhorse and won 23 games against 11 losses with a 2.38 ERA. Cuellar's dominance was also reflected in his strikeouts-to-walks ratio (182 to 79), and he surrendered only 213 hits in his team-best 291 innings of work. Avoiding stepping on the foul lines and insisting that Dalrymple serve as his warm-up catcher somehow worked into the magic of the season for

Cuellar, who earned honors as the co-winner, with Detroit's Denny McLain, of the AL Cy Young Award. McNally reached the 20-win level and was also stingy with opposing batters, yielding just 232 hits and 84 walks over 269 innings, while Phoebus was victorious 14 times and, like McNally, lost but seven games. Palmer led the league with an .800 winning percentage on the strength of a 16–4 record and 2.34 ERA. Palmer's effort followed nearly two full years on the shelf with arm and back woes, the latter of which again forced him to the sidelines for six weeks in the early summer of 1969. In his second start after returning from the disabled list, Palmer shut down the Oakland Athletics with a no-hitter, 8–0, on August 13, a momentous event that still occasioned the awarding of a baseball shoe to Palmer by Judge Frank Robinson for sloppy running on the bases. During Palmer's stint on the DL, Jim Hardin filled the gap in the Orioles rotation by starting 20 games and in ten other appearances fashioned a 6–7 mark. Working exclusively out of the bullpen, the

Following his acquisition from the Astros, Mike Cuellar returned an instant dividend when he won the 1969 AL Cy Young Award, which he shared with Denny McLain of Detroit.

trio of Dick Hall (5–2 record, 1.91 ERA, and six saves), Pete Richert (7–4, 2.21, 12 saves), and Eddie Watt (5–2, 1.65, 16 saves) gave Weaver every confidence to make changes on the mound when necessary.

Following a regular season in which nearly everything seemed to go right, Baltimore prepared to face the formidable Minnesota Twins in the first-ever American League Championship Series, with the winner advancing to the World Series. Curiously, divisional titles earned neither Weaver nor Billy Martin, his rookie managerial counterpart in Minnesota, honors as the AL Manager of the Year. That distinction went to Ted Williams, the former Red Sox and Hall of Fame slugger who, also as a first-year pilot, led the Washington Senators to fourth place in the AL East with a surprising record of 86–76.

## A Sweet Sweep in the First ALCS

During the regular season, the Orioles matched up well against their playoff foes, splitting the six games in Minnesota and taking five of six at home. Most of these dozen tilts were closely contested — half were decided by a single run — with McNally's 5–0 shutout over Jim Kaat in mid–May the largest winning margin. With 97 victories of their own, the offensive-minded Twins were led by league MVP Harmon Killebrew and had taken the AL West title by nine games over Oakland.

Weaver expressed concern about McNally's relatively poor showing in August and September, because after opening the season with fifteen consecutive wins the left-hander went 5–7 until the end of September, as well as Palmer's chronic back ailments and susceptibility to run his pitch counts high. Faced with having to select three starters for the short set against the Twins, Weaver opted to leave Phoebus, also slump-ridden in the campaign's latter half, as the odd man out. Because the Twins lineup was heavily laden with dangerous left-handed hitting, Weaver selected Cuellar, who pitched very well in the second half, as his Game 1 starter to confront Jim Perry. The series opener in Baltimore did not lack for drama. Taking a 2–1 lead entering the seventh inning—home runs by Frank Robinson and Belanger doing the damage—Cuellar served up a two-run homer to Tony Oliva, but Boog Powell evened the score with a solo shot in the bottom of the ninth off Ron Perranoski, who led the league with 31 saves. Minnesota's relief ace persisted through the tenth and eleventh innings and held the Orioles at bay, but a suicide squeeze by Blair with two out scored Belanger in the twelfth for the Baltimore win. "It was a wild, completely unexpected ending to a game that had produced four home runs," the Orioles press guide later reported, "yet was decided by a base hit that traveled only 22 feet."[33]

Using his second southpaw starter in Game 2, Weaver sent McNally to square off against Dave Boswell, a 20-game winner in his own right. Both starters traded zeroes through ten innings, and after McNally silenced the Twins in the eleventh, Curt Motton's pinch-hit single with two down in the bottom half of that inning scored Powell from second base with the game's only run.

Shifting to Minneapolis for Game 3, the series could reasonably have been expected to shift in the Twins' favor. But instead of starting Jim Kaat, manager Billy Martin handed the ball to Bob Miller, who was victimized by a crucial error by Oliva and did not survive the second inning as the Orioles scored three times and cruised to an eventual 11–2 romp. Palmer was sharp enough in hurling a complete game to capture the first ALCS for a Baltimore team that was left with but one last hurdle to clear in order to stake a claim outright as one of the best teams of the 1960s.

Celebrating their victory in a scene described as "merely properly festive, not hilarious" and aware of who their opponents in the upcoming World Series would be, the Orioles immediately convened the Kangaroo Court, as Judge Frank bellowed, "Bring on Rod Gaspar!" to the delight of his teammates.[34] Robinson's taunt at the spare New York Mets outfielder was a clear indication that after having conquered a tough Twins club, Baltimore stood ready to dispatch an upstart and upset-minded Mets squad whose patchwork lineup appeared—on paper, at least—to be no match for the Orioles.

But Robinson's memory of Baltimore's fabled 1966 run at the World Series eluded him in 1969. Just as the Dodgers underestimated the drive, focus, and will of those 1966 Orioles, so too did Robinson put himself at peril by ignoring the determination of a foe managed by Gil Hodges. The Mets skipper quietly commanded the respect of his players and made believers of those who doubted his team's ability to achieve the unthinkable by riding a wave of wins and emotion that purged the blight of the Mets' 120-loss inaugural season of 1962. Weak offensively, the Mets focused on strong pitching and a defense that was among the NL's best to win 100 games en route to the NL East title and a sweep of the Atlanta Braves in the NLCS for the National League crown. The Mets too were prepared for the showdown against Baltimore in the hope of victoriously capping their own magical year.

## "We Still Don't Know If They're for Real"

Earl Weaver was not as derisive about the Mets as Frank Robinson. Deeming them "as worthy an adversary as anyone in the National League," Weaver relied on scouts Jim Russo and Al Kubski to inform him as to how best to confront a Mets team whose specialty seemed to be overachieving.[35] The biggest names to play at Shea Stadium were three All-Stars, pitchers Tom Seaver and Jerry Koosman and outfielder Cleon Jones. The remainder of a roster filled out by the likes of J.C. Martin, Wayne Garrett, and Don Cardwell, among others, raised more curiosity than fear among the Orioles. For the most part, the New York Mets were a mystery to many of the Orioles, as typified when Boog Powell remarked a few days before the Series opener, "We still don't know if they're for real, but we'll find out."[36]

The Mets confounded the experts, however, as they entered the playoffs batting only .242 as a team yet averaged nine runs per game in dismantling the Braves, thus raising trepidation among the Orioles about whether the Mets would lose any of the precious momentum they had built. Cuellar was entrusted to start Game 1 in Baltimore against Seaver, the youthful Met ace and soon-to-be-named Cy Young Award recipient, and the Oriole southpaw prevailed, 4–1, in a six-hit complete game. In the bottom of the first inning, Orioles leadoff man Buford parked a Seaver pitch over the fence in right field to give Baltimore an early lead, which was padded in the fourth by a two-out, none-on flurry of three runs. Years later, catcher Elrod Hendricks admitted that winning the division in a cakewalk during the regular season, breezing through the ALCS, and then beating Seaver in the Series opener may have inflated the Orioles' confidence a bit too much.[37]

Game 2 featured a pitching duel between left-handers Koosman and McNally, as the Mets hurler stopped Baltimore, 2–1, coming within one out of a complete game. The Orioles managed only a pair of singles off Koosman, who observed the free-swinging manner with which Baltimore batters came to the plate in the first game and used his control to hold the Orioles hitless through six innings. Entering the ninth with the score 1–1, the Mets used three singles off McNally to drive in the go-ahead run; in the bottom half of the inning, Koosman retired the first two batters before encountering trouble. Hodges employed a four-man outfield when Frank Robinson came to the plate, the better to keep the slugger from taking an extra base on a hit down the line or in the outfield gaps, but Robinson drew a walk, as did Powell, and Hodges brought in Ron Taylor, who induced Brooks Robinson to ground out to third. The threat was stifled, and the Series, tied at one game each, shifted to New York, with Baltimore now having lost the home-field advantage. Weaver later opined that Koosman did not exhibit "the stuff" displayed by Seaver in the opener and that "over-anxiousness" on the Orioles' part was the real culprit that derailed them in the remaining games.[38]

Moving into the gaping maw of Shea Stadium for the next three games, the Orioles would be exposed to what *New York Times* columnist Arthur Daley termed "Metsomania," a phenomenon in which "wild-eyed, vociferous, partisan rooters" of the home team would turn each game into a living hell for the visiting club.[39] Palmer answered Weaver's call to start Game 3, while Hodges sent rookie Gary Gentry to the mound, but the star of the game was Tommie Agee, the Mets center fielder. Leading off the bottom of the first with a solo home run for a lead that the Mets never relinquished, Agee made spectacular catches to end both the fourth and seventh innings, potentially saving five runs and keeping the

Orioles off the scoreboard. Gentry helped his own cause with a two-run double in the second, while Palmer, who saw the young Met pitch in the minor leagues in 1968 and felt that Gentry looked even better than Koosman, took exception to his team's scouting reports that rated Gentry's fastball as simply "fair to average."[40] Gentry was pulled with two out in the seventh when he walked the bases full, but Agee's dramatic catch bailed out reliever Nolan Ryan, and the Orioles did not deliver in the ninth inning, again with the bases loaded, as the Mets closed out a 5–0 win.

Down two games to one, Baltimore was truly in a predicament. The thrill of their Game 1 victory now only a memory, the Orioles had scored but a single run since the fourth inning of that win. Pressure was on Cuellar to square the Series in a rematch with Seaver. While the final score of 2–1 was befitting of a game pitched by the eventual 1969 Cy Young Award winners, the result was not what Baltimore had hoped for. In one of the most controversial World Series games ever played, the Mets outlasted the Orioles in a ten-inning affair that featured several singular moments. Donn Clendenon opened the scoring with a solo home run in the bottom of the second inning, but Baltimore tried to answer quickly when Belanger singled to lead off the top of the third. Following this base hit, home plate umpire Shag Crawford strode toward the visitors' dugout on the third-base side and motioned as if to warn the Orioles about abuse coming from their bench. When Weaver went to see what Crawford's issue was, the umpire's short fuse expired and Weaver was ejected from the game, the first managerial ejection in a World Series since 1935.[41] When play resumed, Cuellar singled to add to the rally, but the next three batters failed to hit the ball out of the infield, and the Orioles remained scoreless as Seaver retired all but one of the next 16 batters.

Nursing a 1–0 lead in the ninth inning, Seaver allowed one-out singles to Frank Robinson and Powell. But when Brooks Robinson belted a line drive to the gap in right field, Ron Swoboda, instead of playing it safe and chasing after what would likely have been a double, attempted to make the grab. Even the Orioles tipped their caps to Swoboda's effort, noting that the Mets outfielder "made a miraculous headlong back-handed diving catch inches off the grass that must rank among the best of all the great World Series defensive plays."[42] Frank Robinson tagged up and scored for the Orioles, but that would be the only run Baltimore could muster. After Eddie Watt held the Mets at bay in the ninth and Seaver pitched out of a jam in the top of the tenth, the Mets clinched the game with the assistance of a questionable call.

Orioles reliever Dick Hall yielded a bloop, lead-off double to Jerry Grote, a hit that was misplayed by Buford in left. With Rod Gaspar running for Grote, Al Weis was intentionally walked, and Seaver was lifted for pinch-hitter J.C. Martin. Pete Richert was called in from the Orioles bullpen, and when Martin laid down a sacrifice to the first-base side, the noise level was such that Richert did not hear catcher Elrod Hendricks call for the ball and fielded the bunt himself.[43] As Martin ran to first, he did so on the infield grass in fair territory rather than in the running lane of the basepath, so when Richert attempted to put Martin out, his throw struck Martin on his left wrist and caromed toward right field. As the ball rolled away, Gaspar sprinted home with the winning run, which withstood the Orioles' protest because Crawford exercised his judgment — incredulously so — in ruling that Martin had been touching the foul line on his way to first base. Despite photographic evidence to the contrary, there was no appeal of the play, the Mets had won 2–1, Weaver was not around to start a new argument with Crawford, and the vaunted Orioles were now on the brink of elimination.

In Game 5, with McNally and Koosman again paired off, the Baltimore starter equaled his team's run output of the previous three games combined when he socked a two-run home run in the third inning, which was followed later that inning by Frank Robinson's solo shot. Another potential rally was snuffed out when Robinson was hit by a pitch in the sixth, but home plate umpire Lou DiMuro claimed the ball hit his bat first, not Robinson's right thigh, and he struck out when his at-bat resumed after Weaver unsuccessfully pleaded the Orioles' case. McNally kept the Mets off the scoreboard until the sixth when controversy erupted once more, again over another hit-by-pitch ruling. Leading off for New York, Cleon Jones was struck in the foot by a McNally pitch, an occurrence that somehow eluded DiMuro as the ball bounced into the Mets dugout. Jones protested that he had been hit, but the umpire refused to believe him. Only when Gil Hodges emerged from his bench and showed DiMuro the baseball smudged with a spot of shoe polish did the umpire agree that Jones indeed had been hit.

Not understanding why it took DiMuro so long to make a ruling on Jones, Weaver said after the game, "The ball hit him. Everyone in the park knew it."[44] The delay of several minutes to sort out the Jones affair upset McNally's rhythm, for when play resumed, Clendenon stepped up to bat and sent a McNally offering into the left-field stands for a two-run homer that cut the Orioles' lead to 3–2. In the bottom of the seventh, Mets second baseman Al Weis, who had never before hit a home run at Shea Stadium, tied the game at 3–3 with a solo blast as Koosman continued to keep Baltimore in check. Moving to the bottom of the eighth inning, the Mets scored two runs off reliever Watt, with a pair of doubles and a pair of infield errors allowing New York to take a 5–3 lead. Frank Robinson walked to start the ninth, but Koosman retired the side thereafter, and Shea Stadium exploded in a scene of sheer bedlam when Dave Johnson's fly ball settled into Jones's glove for the final out.

Rather than revel in the glory of a second World Series title, Baltimore took its place next to the 1954 Cleveland Indians, winners of 111 regular season contests, as one of the best teams to lose a Fall Classic. Tipping his cap to the Mets, Johnson soberly spoke at length about the stunning defeat the Orioles had suffered. He cited the momentum enjoyed by New York, faulted the Orioles for "not doing what we were supposed to do," and believed that a palpable sense of urgency arose as his team pressed to win more than one game in the Series.[45] Reactions from some of Johnson's teammates ranged from bitter — Frank Robinson said, "We were better, but so what? [New York] got the big hits" — to sheer disbelief, with which Paul Blair was still smitten decades after the defeat.[46] The Mets had just made patently clear that "pitching is going to dominate any short series," as Weaver confirmed years later. "We had no excuses in '69, we were healthy, we were strong, we were well-rested."[47]

For the second time in nine months, a New York sports underdog enjoyed an upset of seismic proportions at the expense of its Baltimore opponent. In football in January, Super Bowl III saw the heavily favored Colts fall to the Jets, and the Orioles' loss to the Mets was an ironic echo of their win over the Dodgers three years earlier. Baltimore's loss meant no World Series rings, but shares of $14,904 per player, coach, and manager did soften the blow of defeat. The derisive challenge to "bring on Rod Gaspar" had been met by Gaspar and his teammates, especially the New York pitching staff, which allowed only nine runs in 45 innings against the Orioles. The Kangaroo Court did not convene in the Shea Stadium clubhouse and not until a new season began would there be a revival, with good reason as it turned out, of Baltimore's trademark antics.

## One Small Step Toward Free Agency

A prima facie look at the 1969 season would indicate that the state of major league baseball was a sport enjoying good health with the positive effects of the overall offensive rebound fostered by rules changes and diluted pitching strength due to league expansions. Fan reaction was positive as attendance in the American League set a new record, the commissioner's office announced that fans would be allowed to cast ballots to select the starting players for the following year's All-Star teams, and the Macmillan Publishing Company introduced the first edition of its famed *Baseball Encyclopedia*, a hefty tome that was a groundbreaking attempt to provide statistical information on every player ever to step on a big league diamond. Exciting races in both National League divisions, climaxed by the Mets' "amazin'" achievement, as Casey Stengel would have called it, all pointed to a successful season for Bowie Kuhn as he completed his first year as commissioner.

Beneath the veneer of this ostensible glory, however, were several rumblings of trouble. After bringing major league baseball to Seattle, the Pilots quickly became orphans and found their way to Milwaukee before the 1970 season began. Pro football, building on its own surge in popularity, was in the process of uniting the upstart American Football League with the entrenched National Football League. Baseball's labor troubles of early 1969 signaled another ominous cloud later that year.

St. Louis center fielder Curt Flood, who, like Frank Robinson, was a former pupil of Bay Area high school coaching legend George Powles, had completed his twelfth year in a Cardinals uniform, during which he won his seventh straight Gold Glove award, hit .285 with 31 doubles, and scored 80 runs, all very good numbers for a 31-year-old player now approaching the latter stage of his career. Exactly one week after the 1969 regular season ended, Flood learned in an "emotionless" phone call from a functionary in the St. Louis front office that he had been traded to the Philadelphia Phillies in a multi-player deal that included, among others, Richie Allen and Tim McCarver.[48] Flood's time in the Midwest had allowed him to establish a home not only for his baseball career but also in support of his life beyond the game, which he underpinned with his business ventures as a portrait artist and photographer.[49]

Flood's attitude was influenced greatly by the civil rights movement and its champions of equality. Having personally suffered the indignities of racial discrimination, Flood believed that he was entitled to more than a passing interest in how his employer chose to treat him. Steeled by his successful fight after the 1964 World Series to purchase a home in the white Oakland suburb of Alamo, California, Flood espoused the message inherent in the "I Am a Man" placards carried by so many black protesters striving to be treated on a par with their Caucasian peers. When Flood was traded to Philadelphia with what he viewed as abject disrespect by the Cardinals for a player of his stature, it was too much for the outfielder to bear, but the ironclad effects of the reserve clause held sway over any opinion that Flood had on the matter. As a fixture in all player contracts, the reserve clause, in effect, bound a player to remain with his team until it saw fit to assign the player to another club — via a trade, for instance — or otherwise release the player from any further obligation. The few previous challenges to the reserve clause, in 1947 by New York Giants outfielder Danny Gardella and three years later by pitcher George Toolson of the New York Yankees, had come to grief for the plaintiffs, irrespective of the faults with which some court decisions, including those of the nation's highest court, were reached. Baseball was not subject to the Sherman Antitrust Act of 1890 in spite of the disputes that had been directed at it in the American legal system. Even in the early 1950s the national pastime, which had conducted business across state lines for decades, was deemed by the United States Supreme Court in the Toolson case as *not* being engaged in interstate commerce.[50]

Flood's choices were few. He could report to the Phillies in accordance with the trade, or he could walk away from the game by retiring. But on the suggestion of Marian Jorgensen, a close friend and confidante, and Allan Zerman, his attorney, Flood instead chose to file a lawsuit against major league baseball to challenge the validity of the reserve clause.[51] After consulting with Marvin Miller, the head of the players' union whose probing questions supplied Flood with much food for thought as to the value of what Flood hoped to gain from a lawsuit, Flood elected to press forward with legal action despite Miller's cautionary advice that he was not likely to win his case and that the time required for the suit to wend its way through the court system might outlast Flood's playing career. Miller later wrote of Flood's determination — some labeled it obstinacy — that the player "wasn't betting on his chances to win; he had just made up his mind he was going to take a stand."[52] In essence, Flood would be sacrificing the remainder of his playing career not in pursuit of his freedom to move from one team to another in pursuit of monetary rewards, as players who became free agents after the 1976 season were able to do, but rather to preclude his assignment to a city where he did not desire to go.

To better his chances of victory in court, Flood addressed a meeting of over two dozen player representatives in mid–December 1969 in the hope of securing the players' union's backing to underwrite his legal expenses. Flood stressed that the trials he endured as a black player in a game dominated by whites did not enter into his decision to sue because the reserve clause was colorblind and harmful to all players regardless of race. The player representatives, however, still had fresh in their minds the unsuccessful bid to modify the reserve clause during bargaining sessions for the players' working agreement with the owners for the upcoming season, but they nonetheless voted unanimously to fund Flood's battle, with the caveat that they be allowed to pick the attorney to handle the case. Flood assented to the stipulation, and on January 16, 1970, *Curtis C. Flood v. Bowie K. Kuhn, et al.* was entered in U.S. District Court in New York as Flood began his one-man fight and prepared to sit out the 1970 baseball season in protest.

Representing Flood was former Supreme Court justice Arthur Goldberg, who was chosen on Miller's recommendation. Goldberg and Miller had served together with the steelworkers' union in the 1950s, and following a stint as President John Kennedy's secretary of labor, Goldberg was appointed by JFK to the Supreme Court. By 1969 Goldberg had returned to private law practice after serving briefly as the U.S. ambassador to the United Nations. When Goldberg took on the Flood case, his presence raised hope that Flood might be more successful than others who had fought the reserve system, since Goldberg was familiar with the machinations of the federal court system. Unfortunately, the former justice was less focused on Miller and his client when he decided to test his political ambitions by announcing in March 1970 his candidacy to run against New York's incumbent governor, Nelson Rockefeller. Another lawyer, Jay Topkis, was tasked with much of the work on Flood's suit. The trial in the late spring of 1970 returned a verdict in favor of major league baseball, as did a subsequent appeal in April 1971, whereupon later that fall, the Supreme Court consented to hear another appeal to ultimately decide the case.

For the plaintiff, whose personal finances had for several years been a smoking ruin due to back taxes owed the federal government, alimony payments, and shortcomings in his artistic enterprises, Flood found that his only ticket to a semblance of solvency was by doing what he did best. In late 1970, negotiations between the Phillies, who still owned the rights to Flood, the Washington Senators, and the commissioner's office finally resulted in a deal that gave Flood a $110,000 contract and put him in a Senators uniform for a comeback attempt in 1971. But after sitting out the prior season, Flood discovered that his nearly one and one-half years away from the game had eroded his skills too greatly. Flood aborted his return just a few weeks into the 1971 season, and after sending team owner Bob Short a farewell telegram, he departed for Europe and a self-imposed exile, absconding with half of the salary of his contract in return for less than one month's work.

When oral arguments finally went before the Supreme Court on March 20, 1972, reliance was placed on Goldberg to competently argue the case against baseball, but unfortunately for Flood, Goldberg failed miserably during the thirty minutes he was allotted. In his detailed book on the Flood case, attorney and law professor Brad Snyder tells in stark language the ineptitude of Goldberg's performance, from his mangling of simple facts regarding Flood's life and baseball career to the embarrassing, ham-fisted manner in which he made his presentation before the court. Fully and immediately aware of his egregious bungling, Goldberg admitted upon leaving the court, "That was the worst argument I've ever made in my life," and with his submission now entered into the record against a crisp defense by Lou Hoynes, major league baseball's attorney, the decision rested with the nine justices to render a verdict.[53]

Nearly three months later on June 19, the Supreme Court announced its decision in favor of Kuhn, et al., five to three with one abstention. The judgment was lambasted in a host of major newspapers while "backers of the baseball establishment," including *The Sporting News* and Hall of Famers Ted Williams and Joe DiMaggio, "applauded the ruling."[54] The reserve clause had repelled its latest challenge as the resilient system of baseball bureaucracy claimed another victim. More circumspect about the outcome, Kuhn later wrote in his autobiography, "Far from claiming victory, I was espousing collective bargaining as the road for change in the reserve system."[55]

As painful an endeavor as this was for Flood — "It was David fighting Goliath without a stone," as one former Oriole characterized the scenario — his action was at the forefront of the modern players' labor movement.[56] The case emboldened Marvin Miller to seek, successfully so, arbitration as a means for settling salary disputes, which was included in the 1970 basic agreement between the players and the owners. Flood once told a story about a salary negotiating session he had in the 1960s, a meeting in which the only participants were himself, St. Louis owner Gussie Busch, and Stan Musial, the great former Cardinal.[57] With no lawyers or agents present, this scenario was emblematic of a simpler time that was soon to pass forever. The game of baseball, and sports in general, was always a form of business, but the labor force of the national pastime was growing increasingly restless in its disputes with club owners who clung tenaciously to the sacred wording of the reserve clause.

In a memoir recounting his experience in baseball, Marvin Miller wistfully reflected on a man whom he hoped would succeed in court for the sake of all players. "Curt Flood didn't actually change the game," Miller wrote in 1991, "though he was a positive force and an example for others who did."[58]

## *Déjà Vu, 1970*

Carbon copies in baseball are few and far between, yet the Orioles' blueprint served as an uncanny template that produced nearly the same outcome in 1970 is it did a year earlier. Few changes were evident in Baltimore's personnel as the familiar names assumed their accustomed roles, but smarting from their World Series loss to the Mets placed one salient aspect ahead of all other considerations. "We played the entire 1970 season with one thought in mind — redemption," said Earl Weaver.[59] Regardless of how well the Orioles might play in the regular season, they would have to be in top form to remain victorious come October. Baltimore was determined not to suffer a repeat of 1969's galling disappointment.

Bolting once more from the starting gate of a new season, the Orioles opened with five straight wins, dipped into second place for a week in mid–April, and then climbed back atop the AL East where they remained for the balance of the season. Churning steadily through the month of May while increasing their lead to 7½ games, Baltimore joined the ranks of the more fallible teams by winning only 21 of 39 games in the six weeks leading up to the All-Star break, yet holding first place with a 54–33 record and six-game margin over Detroit, seven over the Yankees.

The tepid won-lost mark during that stretch was attributed to a shaky bullpen, whose members had let nine games slip away when the Orioles had a lead in the fifth inning or later. But overall in the first half of the season, the rotation triumvirate of Cuellar, McNally, and Palmer pitched so well that there was speculation that each of them could win 20 games, as their performances earned them spots on the AL All-Star team. On offense, Buford overcame his typically slow start to raise his average to .296, and Rettenmund, filling in for Blair after he was hit in the face by a pitch in a game at the end of May, went on a .407 tear in the month of June. Carrying a big share of the load were the bats of Johnson, Powell, and the Robinsons, all of whom also were named All-Stars for the midsummer classic to be played at Cincinnati's newly christened Riverfront Stadium. Powell and Frank Robinson were voted as starters by the fans, and Weaver, in his debut as the manager of the AL squad, picked Palmer as the starting pitcher.

This was the first year in over a decade that fans, using ballots fashioned from modified computer punch cards, were able to vote for each league's starting lineups. The process was not without faults. Because the ballots had to be printed in February in order to be made available around the country, the early submission of candidates for the eight non-pitching positions caused a furor when deserving players not envisioned to be originally worthy of inclusion on the ballot did not appear. Nonetheless, the benefit of fan interest outweighed the inherent glitches in the system, so the re-institution of fan voting has remained a staple for four decades.

Also in June the Orioles brought up one of their top prospects, Bobby Grich, a six-foot, two-inch Michigander who grew up in Long Beach, California, and was batting .383 at the Triple-A level. Living a dream which he vividly remembered years after his career ended — "You're playing in Rochester with plywood and chain link fences, and then you're in a huge stadium ... right away you're kind of in awe," he recalled — the infielder was immediately installed at second base by Weaver.[60] A right-handed batter, Grich received good ratings from Cal Ripken, Sr., his minor league manager, for his playing skills and the best grades possible for "desire, competitor, temperament, [and] aptitude."[61]

In the second half of the 1970 season, Baltimore won 54 of 75 contests and avoided slumps by losing two consecutive games only four times after the All-Star break. This group of Orioles suffered no swoon, no matter how brief, in the final two weeks of September and swept into the postseason determined to make good on Weaver's redemptive goal. After clinching the AL East on September 17, Baltimore continued to tear into the opposition and won twelve of its last thirteen games as Cuellar, Palmer, and McNally were complete-game winners in their final decisions and achieved the distinction of giving the Orioles three 20-game winners. Falling one game short of their mark in 1969, Baltimore compiled an equally impressive record of 108–54 and was determined to avenge their loss to the Mets.

The repeat banner year for the Orioles did not manifest itself in a trove of individual awards, although Boog Powell won the American League MVP honors. But in a crowded field of 24-game winners, Jim Perry of the Twins prevailed over Cuellar and McNally for the Cy Young Award. Weaver, with 108 wins, may have been bemused at losing once more in Manager of the Year balloting, although he brushed aside the snub by observing, "The idea is to come in first and that's what we've done the last couple of years."[62] At least the defense, fronted by Dave Johnson, Brooks Robinson, and Paul Blair, won the admiration of the managers and coaches who voted Gold Gloves for the trio of Orioles.

A bear of a man at six feet, four inches, and weighing 250 pounds, Boog Powell furnished power hitting and anchored first base during the Orioles' dynasty.

Among the non-award winners, there was ample reason to see why the Orioles had become an envious juggernaut, topping the AL in runs scored (792) and allowing the fewest runs (574). Billed as "the league's best leadoff man," Don Buford maintained his ability to spur the offense with his .406 on-base percentage, helped by his .272 average, 17 home runs, 109 walks, and 16 stolen bases.[63] In total, eight Orioles hit at least 12 homers, led by Powell's 35, Frank Robinson with 25, and the slugging threesome of Brooks Robinson, Blair, and Rettenmund at 18 each, the last of that group finding increased playing time as his average climbed to a robust .322. The best run producers were Powell (114), Brooks and Frank Robinson (94 and 78, respectively), Buford (66), Blair (65), and Rettenmund (58), while the catching corps of Etchebarren and Hendricks accounted for 17 home runs and 72 runs batted in. Belanger's .218 average was the only apparent weak spot on offense. In addition to Grich making his Baltimore debut, Minor League Player of the Year Don Baylor powered his way to a mid–September recall from Rochester after posting a .327 average with 34 doubles, 15 triples, 22 home runs, 107 RBIs, and 26 stolen bases.

On the mound, Cuellar and McNally, with 24 wins, and Palmer with 20 victories, met the expectations of the midseason diviners. The fourth spot in the rotation was filled by the tandem of Phoebus and Hardin, who totaled, relatively speaking, a disappointing eleven wins. The majority of the slack was picked up by relievers Hall, Richert, and Watt, who amassed 24 wins, and Moe Drabowsky, reacquired in mid–June, who won four games.

By virtue of their own repeat pennant in the AL West, Minnesota was paired with the Orioles in a rematch of the 1969 American League Championship Series. But with Baltimore tenaciously sustaining its late–September momentum, the Twins put up a weak front against the Orioles and again were quickly swept out of the ALCS in three games. Game 1 became a curiosity when the anticipated duel between Cuellar and the Twins' Jim Perry fell flat on a cool, wind-blown afternoon at Metropolitan Stadium. Perry was knocked out by a seven-run outburst in the fourth inning, highlighted by Cuellar's grand slam home run, the flight of which began as a sure foul ball but was twisted by the winds into a hit that made its way past the right-field foul pole. Cuellar, however, was also victimized by the Twins' bats and was gone by the fifth, so Hall finished with 4⅔ innings of relief in the 10–6 win. The following day, McNally clung to a 4–3 lead until his teammates erupted for another seven-run deluge in the ninth to seal the 11–3 victory. Back in Baltimore for Game 3, the Orioles administered the final blow to vanquish the Twins when Palmer hurled a seven-hit, twelve-strikeout gem, in Baltimore's 6–1 victory to cop the American League flag for a second straight year. The size of the crowds at all of the 1970 ALCS games may have been an indication that the outcome of the series was a foregone conclusion, as barely 54,000 fans combined to see the pair of games in Minnesota, and only 27,608 fans witnessed the final contest, which was played on a Monday afternoon at Memorial Stadium.

## Brooks at His Best

Having won 14 consecutive games since September 20, the Orioles were ready to square off in the World Series against Sparky Anderson's powerful Cincinnati Reds, who won the National League pennant with 102 wins, the only NL club to win more than 90 games. This Reds team was the forerunner of the Big Red Machine and would undergo a number of key changes before becoming the best major league team of the mid–1970s, but in Anderson's first year at Cincinnati's helm, the lineup featured key personnel such as Pete Rose, Johnny Bench, Tony Perez, and Dave Concepcion.

With an outfield of three .300 hitters and a trio of power hitters around the corners of the infield — catcher and NL MVP Bench belted 45 home runs, third baseman Perez hit 40, and first baseman Lee May clouted 34 — the Reds' 1970 offense was radically different from the 1969 Mets. Their league-leading team home run total and slugging percentage struck fear in opposing hurlers, while Cincinnati's pitching, not as dominant as had been New York's, was fourth in the NL in ERA and first in saves. Settling down from jitters he experienced in his first World Series the previous year, Weaver admitted to being more relaxed about his second trip to the Fall Classic, although he confessed that because of Cincinnati's formidable run-scoring ability, the Orioles "were more afraid of the Reds as a team" than they had been of the Mets because "against the Reds you had to worry about every man in the lineup except one — the pitcher."[64]

Cincinnati's road to the World Series ran through Pittsburgh, but the Reds swept the Pirates in the National League Championship Series in three close games, 3–0, 3–1, and 3–2, all of which were played in brand new stadiums that both teams opened partway through the season. This World Series was the first to have some of its games played on AstroTurf, the artificial surface on which only a few Orioles had played during that year's All-Star Game, but Weaver was confident that his superb infielders would be able to handle faster groundballs coming their way. He also used a bit of psychology in downplaying the impact the ersatz turf might have on the games by claiming that his fielders would adapt more easily to the carpet than the Reds batters would be able to adjust to the poor hitting background at Memorial Stadium caused by the presence of white houses in the local neighborhood beyond the center field fence.[65] Weaver felt the Orioles' chances of taking the Series were further enhanced by the ills suffered by Cincinnati's pitching, which had three of its starters — former Twin and 20-game winner Jim Merritt, 18-game winner Gary Nolan, and Jim McGlothlin — in various states of discomfort at the end of the season.

Cincinnati opened Game 1 by building a 3–0 lead against Palmer, but Baltimore chipped away with a two-run homer by Powell in the fourth inning and a solo home run by Hendricks the next inning to tie the game. The home half of the sixth was the most notable of the game for its stellar moments and controversy. Lee May of the Reds led off with a drive down the third-base line for what appeared to be a sure double, but Brooks Robinson speared the ball while lunging into foul territory and "threw almost blindly without really turning his body. His throw took *a perfect astro turf hop* right into the stretching Powell's glove and nailed May by a step."[66] A walk to Bernie Carbo and a single by Tommy Helms put runners at the corners. When Ty Cline's chopper in front of the plate traveled only a few feet, Hendricks stepped out to snare the ball. Following Hendricks was home plate umpire Ken Burkhart, who tried to position himself to make a fair-or-foul call on the hit, but when Carbo raced home in an attempt to score, the umpire became sandwiched between catcher and runner. As Hendricks wheeled around the trapped Burkhart to make a tag on Carbo, he did so with his glove, but the ball was in his bare hand. The umpire, his back to the plate and not able to see behind Hendricks, thrust his fist up and called "out" as Carbo slid past the plate without touching it. *Sports Illustrated* captured the essence of the play perfectly by declaring, "Three misses make an out when umpire misses catcher missing the runner missing home."[67] In any event, the call stood despite Anderson's protest, although the Reds manager conceded, "If Ken hadn't been in the way, Carbo would have been out by a mile."[68] Then Brooks unloaded another home run off Nolan in the top of the seventh to break the tie as the Orioles hung on for a 4–3 win.

Entrusted with the start for Baltimore in Game 2 was Cuellar, who as a warm-weather pitcher was finding the cooler autumn temperatures less favorable. Hampered by some slipshod fielding on the part Belanger and Blair, Cuellar fell behind 3–0 in the first inning and departed in the third after being tagged for a home run by the Reds' Bobby Tolan. But Powell's homer put the Orioles on the scoreboard in the fourth, and then they batted around in a five-run explosion that vaulted them to an eventual 6–5 win. Dick Hall pitched over two innings of hitless relief and was aided by a spectacular catch in center field by Blair to close out the game.

Shifting to Baltimore with a two-game lead in the Series instilled much confidence in the Orioles. After thumping the Reds, 9–3, in Game 3 behind McNally's complete game, Weaver envisioned yet another sweep to conclude the postseason. Brooks Robinson continued his spectacular play in the field and at the plate, his first-inning, two-run double giving Baltimore a lead they never relinquished, followed by a hit-robbing, diving stab of a Bench line drive in the sixth. However, with the Orioles' winning streak having reached seventeen, they experienced a letdown in Game 4 that snapped the victory skein and caused a mild degree of angst among the home team. Palmer started and, though not as dominant as he had been in the Series opener, entered the eighth inning ahead, 5–3, Brooks again excelling and already 3-for-3 with a pair of RBIs.

The lead slipped away when Palmer allowed the first two Reds batters to reach base, before Weaver brought in Watt to halt the rally. But Watt's first pitch to May, who had given the Orioles fits the whole series, was deposited over the wall in left field to put Cincinnati in front, 6–5. Clay Carroll finished a lengthy relief outing to earn the win and stave off the Reds' elimination.

The Orioles had their fingers crossed that the weather for Game 5 would be conducive to Cuellar. The high humidity with temperatures in the low seventy-degree range worked very much to the southpaw's advantage despite a thrashing he took in the opening frame. Four hits, all but one for extra bases, quickly put Baltimore down, 3–0, but after venting his frustration in the dugout when the inning was over, Cuellar was virtually untouchable, allowing only three runners over the last eight frames. Meanwhile, his teammates scored two runs in each of the first three innings to retake the lead, then added three more over the last four innings. Six Cincinnati pitchers could not stay the Orioles from achieving the redemption that Weaver chose as the theme for the 1970 season. The fitting conclusion came in the top of the ninth when Brooks again stole a hit away from Bench for the first out and, another out later, fielded a routine grounder and threw to Powell to seal the 9–3 triumph and Baltimore's World Series title. Brooks and Belanger led Baltimore with 14 assists each in the Series, affirming the third baseman's prescience — "I knew we were going to be busy," Brooks said later — that the tough right-handed bats of the Reds would send many balls to the left side of the infield.[69]

As Moe Drabowsky reveled by administering a hot-foot to commissioner Bowie Kuhn in the winner's clubhouse, Weaver's first priority before partaking in the raucous post-game celebration was to excuse himself from the crush of the media and personally thank every one of his players for the work they had put into making the team such a success since his appointment as manager. The ghosts of 1969 had been exorcised with alacrity by Baltimore as a team, but the World Series belonged to Brooks Robinson, who hit .429, drove in a team-high six runs, put on a clinic at third base with at least six fielding gems, and copped the award as most valuable player of the Series.

Harry Dalton, recipient of the Major League Executive of the Year award presented by *The Sporting News*, saw the strength of the 1969 Orioles as a trait that barely required fine-tuning, and with most players remaining healthy and having productive years, they vindicated Dalton's decision to play a nearly pat hand in 1970. Baltimore recovered a bit of their past with the June addition of Drabowsky, and the Orioles also glimpsed their future with the recall of Grich in June and Baylor in September. This was the finest season in Orioles history, and they still had the opportunity to build on Joel Chaseman's past advice to "keep the dynasty coming."

## *"It Was the Same Old Story"*

Repeating as American League pennant winners, which Baltimore did in 1970, was one matter, but repeating as World Series champions was quite another. The last team to perform that feat was the 1962 New York Yankees, but the 1971 Orioles were most capable of defending their Series crown given that they had every aspect of the game working in their favor. "The best damn team in baseball," in sportswriter Frank Deford's term had "the best players, the best manager, the best system, the best front office, the best morale, and, definitely, the best chances."[70]

Indeed, after 1970, the only area Harry Dalton addressed was finding a reliable fourth starting pitcher to replace Tom Phoebus. Dalton took his chances at the winter meetings by including Phoebus in a multi-player trade with the San Diego Padres, in which Dalton's main quarry was a tall right-handed pitcher who led the Padres with 14 wins, Pat Dobson. The acquisition of Dobson was the only move of significance made by the Baltimore front office in preparation for the 1971 season. So laden with talent were the Orioles that with no open spots on the 25-man roster, they found it in their best interests to send Baylor, the minor league player of the year, and Grich, back to Rochester to play every day rather than let them molder on Weaver's bench. The twenty-year-old Baylor, who hailed from Austin, Texas, had been ticketed for Triple-A in 1971 by Cal Ripken, Sr., even before his first call-up, while the extra time in Rochester enabled Grich to remain sharp and eventually win honors as the International League player of the year in 1971.[71]

As Dobson settled into the rotation, Baltimore opened the 1971 season in typical fashion by jumping into first place right from day one, but then played tepidly for a four-week stretch beginning at the end of April. After spending the entire month of May in second place a handful of games behind the Red Sox, the Orioles were awakened from their lethargy during a donnybrook in Chicago later that month. When White Sox pitcher Bart Johnson threw behind Don Buford after the latter had hit several home runs, a fracas ensued in which Buford said that "fans threw seat slats and rocks [at me], one attacked me near the dugout."[72] The incident elicited a call to arms for the Orioles, who won that game and the next nine as well to launch them into first place, never again to be overtaken in 1971. Thereafter the worst Baltimore streaks were a pair of four-game losing skeins and a week in mid–September when they lost six of seven contests. The Robinsons, Buford, Palmer, and Cuellar were all accorded All-Star honors for that season's game at Tiger Stadium. Overall the Orioles finished with a slightly less impressive 101–57 record, and became only the third team in baseball history to win 100 or more games in three straight seasons. The Orioles were primed to take on a new foe in the American League Championship Series. Baltimore may have drawn inspiration from the all-orange uniforms they occasionally wore in September, a sartorial display which reminded one player of beer-league softball rather than big-league baseball.[73]

Baltimore's ending figures for 1971 showed a remarkable consistency with previous Weaver-led clubs. The Orioles had the most potent offense in the league with 742 runs scored and a team batting average of .261, while their pitching was the stingiest in the league with a 3.00 ERA and allowed but 530 runs in total. No hitter eclipsed the 30-homer or 100-RBI barrier, but there was a balance among the regular lineup matched by few others in the American League. Power continued to be supplied by Frank Robinson (28 home runs, including the 500th of his career in mid–September), Powell (22), Brooks Robinson (20), Buford (19), Johnson (18), and the backstop duo of Hendricks and Etchebarren (9 each), while the best run producers were Frank (99), Powell and Brooks (92), Rettenmund (75), Johnson (72), and the backstop consortium of Hendricks and Etchebarren (71).

The defense was again among the leaders in the AL, tied with three other teams for second-best fielding average at .981, as Blair, Brooks, Belanger, and Johnson again won Gold Gloves. As if the starting rotation could not be better than featuring the three 20-game winners of 1970, Dalton's move to shore up the fourth spot returned another windfall and made a prophet of pitching coach George Bamberger. Pat Dobson, who in June and July had reeled off twelve straight wins, became the latest hurler to benefit from the treatment he received from the coach he nicknamed "the Great Madula." Bamberger's methodology in developing this historic quartet was easily explained by the vast amount of physical conditioning he demanded of his pitchers: "First you get the legs in shape," he intoned. "Once they're in shape ... that's where the arm comes in."[74] All the running and throwing yielded 20 wins for each of the Baltimore starters, the first quartet to accomplish the feat since the 1921 White Sox, thus achieving Bamberger's February prediction. McNally (21–5), Cuellar and Palmer (both 20–9), and Dobson (20–8) may have scrambled for the Cy Young Award, but Oakland's Vida Blue trumped the whole league, taking both the Cy Young and Most Valuable Player awards in 1971. The Baltimore bullpen was led by Eddie Watt's eleven saves and 1.80 ERA.

Blue and his Athletics teammates, however, proved to be as futile as the Twins had been in trying to wrest the American League pennant from the Orioles. Under their new manager, Dick Williams, Oakland was on the cusp of making its own imprint on the league, but the Athletics fell prey to yet another Baltimore sweep of the ALCS. In Game 1, Blue affirmed his reputation and seemed to be in control with a 3–1 lead going into the bottom of the seventh inning before the Orioles scored four more runs for a 5–3 win for McNally. Oakland starter Catfish Hunter was tagged four times for home runs in his Game 2 loss to Cuellar, 5–1. When the series moved to Oakland, Palmer choked off the Athletics' late rally in Game 3 and posted a 5–3 win to clinch Baltimore's third consecutive AL title.

In blasé fashion, a later Orioles publication called the sweep "the same old story," but awaiting Baltimore in the World Series were the Pittsburgh Pirates, who had slugged nine home runs in their three wins to take the National League pennant over the San Francisco

Giants.[75] Although weaker starting pitching forced the Pirates to be more reliant on their bullpen, they nonetheless had the NL's best offense, but ironically the Series outcome proved to be the same old story for Baltimore.

## Pulling Up Short Again

On the leading edge of a winning streak now at fourteen games — eleven wins to close out the regular season and three more in the ALCS — Baltimore was poised to repeat as World Series champion. Precious momentum was clearly on the Orioles' side, as the strength of their rotation bode well for them. After the Pirates made some noise in the Series opener at Baltimore by scoring three unearned runs in the second inning — two infield errors and a wild pitch causing the damage — the Orioles' bats came to life and struck sore-armed Pirates starter Doc Ellis for a pair of home runs and reliever Bob Moose for another to build a 5–3 lead that McNally made stand. Following a shaky start to the Pirates' third, McNally settled down and retired all but one of the final 22 Pittsburgh batters.

Palmer started for Baltimore in Game 2 and pitched his way out of trouble over the first three frames, then received a ten-run torrent in the middle three innings en route to an 11–3 whipping of the Pirates. Everyone in the Baltimore lineup save reliever Dick Hall either hit safely or drove in at least one run, as the Orioles' confidence was bolstered by a sporting press that had written off any chance for Pittsburgh to right themselves from a two-game deficit.

Scheduled to start for the Pirates in Game 3 at Three Rivers Stadium was Steve Blass, who had been raked by the Giants in his two appearances in the NLCS and had surrendered fourteen hits in just seven innings of work. Worrying about how he would try to contain Baltimore, Blass was sleepless the night before his assignment but pitched more like the fifteen-game winner he was that season. And although he had two hits in each of the Pirate losses, Roberto Clemente persevered through a bout of food poisoning and kept a positive attitude through Pittsburgh's early trials. The aging Bucs' star led by example and was the showpiece during the seventh inning in what Weaver aptly described as "the most memorable play of the series" that became the pivot point of the Fall Classic.[76]

Blass and the Pirates were clinging to a 2–1 lead when Clemente opened the home half of the seventh by hitting a high bouncer off the Three Rivers carpet back to pitcher Mike Cuellar. As Clemente was churning down the first base line while Cuellar nonchalantly waited to field the falling ball, the pitcher, rattled by the sight of the hustling Pirate, threw wide of first base for an error. Now knocked off his stride, Cuellar then walked Willie Stargell before serving up a three-run homer to Bob Robertson — who had missed a bunt sign — to salt away Blass's three-hit gem, 5–1.

Down two games to one rather than being on the precipice of another Orioles sweep, the Pirates exhibited little encouragement from their reprieve in the history-making fourth Series game, which was the first to be played as a night game.[77] Pittsburgh starter Luke Walker never made it out of the first inning and spotted Baltimore three quick runs before giving way to Bruce Kison. As the youthful Kison stymied the Orioles with one-hit pitching through the seventh inning, the Pirates climbed out of the hole dug by Walker. After Pittsburgh rebounded against Dobson and scored twice in the first, Clemente, who flustered opponents with his ability to hit all types of pitching, appeared to homer to give the Bucs a lead in the third inning. But when his drive down the right-field line was ruled foul, he eventually settled for a single to keep alive a game-tying rally. Pittsburgh ultimately edged the Orioles and reliever Eddie Watt, 4–3, by pushing a run across in the seventh to knot the Series at two games apiece. Frank Robinson lamented the Orioles' failure to hold the early lead, while Weaver, faulting his batters' impatience for the loss, said, "We swung at some bad pitches against the kid [Kison] and never recovered."[78]

Suddenly deficient in base hits, Baltimore could not solve Bucs' Game 5 starter Nelson Briles, whose acclimation to the pitching mound lowered by the 1969 rules change forced him to adjust his throws and resulted in the hurler occasionally landing face-first in the dirt at the conclusion of a delivery. Baltimore managed just two singles and two walks. The lack of support hurt McNally as much as the four runs he gave up in the 4–0 whitewashing as Pittsburgh forged a three-games-to-two lead.

Faced with elimination, the Orioles returned home for Game 6 and appeared headed to another loss as Clemente resumed his hitting clinic—he tripled and homered in his first two at-bats against Palmer—while Baltimore's batters were still stymied. Down 2–0 and with just two walks and two hits after five innings, Buford broke a 22-inning Orioles scoring drought with a solo home run in the sixth. Baltimore tied the contest in the next inning on Dave Johnson's two-out single and nearly won the game in the bottom of the ninth when Buford doubled to right field with two out and Belanger aboard. But third-base coach Billy Hunter exercised caution and held Belanger rather than test the rifle arm of Clemente, so the inning ended on Johnson's grounder to short. Pulling out all the stops, Weaver employed Dobson and McNally in relief roles in the tenth, when the Orioles escaped a Pirates' threat after several anxious moments that included a single, a stolen base, and two walks, one of these an intentional pass to Clemente. In the bottom of the inning, Frank Robinson, who was hitless for the day, drew a walk, scampered on a gimpy right Achilles tendon to third on Rettenmund's single—while pulling a thigh muscle in the process—and scored the third and winning run on Brooks Robinson's sacrifice fly on a 1–2 pitch to shallow center field. The Orioles had evened the Series at three games each, but they wondered which version of Blass—the ace of Game 3 or the flop of the NLCS—would be on the mound against them in the Series finale.

Frank Robinson's heroics were a dramatic prelude to Game 7, and the Blass-Cuellar rematch of Game 3 did not disappoint. Cuellar retired the first eleven Pirates he faced, until Clemente—"who seemed to be waiting for an off-speed pitch," according to Weaver—hit a slow curve for a home run.[79] Blass was as sharp this day as he was in his previous start, as he and Cuellar resumed trading shutout innings until Pittsburgh struck again in the eighth when Stargell singled to left field on a ball just beyond the reach of Belanger and scored on a double to left-center field by Jose Pagan. Second-guessing himself later, the Orioles skipper mused whether Paul Blair could have caught Pagan's drive, but in any event, Rettenmund was playing center field that day and did not get a jump on the ball in the way Blair would have.[80] The Orioles recovered one run in their half of the eighth but stranded a man on third. With the score 2–1 they averted another Pirates' threat in the ninth when the Dobson-McNally relief duo again kept Pittsburgh off the scoreboard. Blass, his nerves at the fraying point the entire game but whose change-up did not betray him, set down the heart of the Baltimore lineup in order without allowing a ball out of the infield, as the Pirates followed in the footsteps of the 1969 Mets to capture the World Series from another 100-win group of Orioles.

The manager of the now former World Series champions had boasted after defeating the Athletics a few weeks before that Baltimore was "the greatest club in the history of baseball," but with his bias now tempered by Pittsburgh's triumph, Weaver succinctly tipped his cap to the Pirates — and emphasized the prominence of pitching — by stating, "Clemente was great, Kison turned the Series around, but Blass was Mr. World Series."[81] Acknowledged by the Orioles as a "superstar," Clemente won Series MVP honors for his .414 average, .759 slugging percentage, and fine defensive work, yet they also credited Blass as being "equally valuable to the Pittsburgh effort."[82] Ironically, and in spite of the success enjoyed by Blass, Weaver assessed Pirates' pitcher Bob Johnson as "the only man on their staff I feared" because he "had faced us twice [in 1970 with Kansas City] and had made us look bad both times."[83] Blass, however, halted the Orioles' winning streak in Game 3 and administered the decisive blow in Game 7, thereby becoming the pitcher whom Weaver really should have feared the most.

## The Reign Comes to an End

For the Baltimore Orioles, their three-year reign as the most dominant team in the American League came to an end in 1972. The crescendo of the 1970 World Series title was framed by the AL pennants of 1969 and 1971, which were won by peerless teams that fell short of immortality against National League opponents whose pitching rose to the occasion at inopportune times for the Orioles.

Baltimore's demise in its two Series losses prompted some snide remarks in the press about "the Orioles' dynasty disappear[ing] from the planet quicker than Hitler's thousand-year Reich," but such unfair evaluations turn a blind eye to the singular accomplishments of baseball's strongest club from 1969 to 1971.[84] Pejoratives aside, no team in either league came close to equaling the three-year run enjoyed by the Orioles, who, in addition to far outpacing their divisional rivals in the regular season, were undefeated in three American League Championship Series. The 1969 Mets, the 1970 Reds, and the 1971 Athletics were the only other teams to win at least 100 games — each of them doing so only once during this period — while Baltimore was victorious a total of 318 times.

Four future members of the Hall of Fame, representing the infield (Brooks Robinson), outfield (Frank Robinson), pitching staff (Jim Palmer), and management (Earl Weaver), not only graced the Orioles roster but were the most integral of its uniformed personnel. And some of those who did not pass muster for Cooperstown, such as Boog Powell, Paul Blair, Dave Johnson, and Dave McNally, were nevertheless among the American League's best at their respective positions. These players, together with the other mainstays, reserves, and pitchers whose performance was orchestrated by Weaver, constituted the most formidable team of its day.

Following Baltimore's defeat at the hands of Pittsburgh in 1971, sportswriter Joe Falls asked a rhetorical yet circumspect question that put the Orioles' standing in the clearest light: "Does a dynasty topple because it loses the seventh game of the World Series and loses it by a run?"[85] In Baltimore's case, the Orioles were entitled to their share of the glory for which they worked so diligently, as no other team over those three grand years surpassed their many accomplishments. This was a club well-credentialed to stake a claim to being the first true post–Yankees dynasty.

Yet the winds beneath the Orioles' wings were shifting, as the task of repeating as American League champions would become the mission of a Baltimore team about to undergo personnel changes in the front office and on the field. The mighty prosperity which stamped the Orioles as a great team was about wane, and as this modest decline took hold, Baltimore regressed into a very good team. Granted, this would still be a team better than most, but one that was shy of the lofty standard it had set during the height of its reign.

# 7

## Very Good, but Not the Best

Three days after the conclusion of the 1971 World Series, Baltimore fulfilled its commitment to play an exhibition series of 18 games over the next month in Japan. Perhaps in an attempt to atone for their loss to Pittsburgh, the Orioles racked up a dozen wins against two losses, with four contests ending in ties. Baltimore's 1971 season concluded in late November with all hands finally getting the chance to take a well-deserved rest.

### Breaking Up That Old Gang

Conspicuous by his absence from that trip, however, was Harry Dalton, who, rather than accompany the Orioles to the Far East, traveled instead to Los Angeles to meet with Gene Autry, owner of the California Angels. After building and shaping Baltimore into the champion that it became, Dalton sought a new venue in which to ply his trade, and being infatuated with the Angels ballpark in Anaheim, he charted his course to restructure the Angels into a contending team. Departing with Dalton was an indefatigable work ethic that served both him and the Baltimore organization well for so many years. A document among his personal papers serves as a paean to his accomplishments, noting his extensive travel, ability to network with officials on the major and minor league levels, and his prescience in "surveying and analyzing present situations and what effect they have on [the] future of [the] Orioles."[1]

A mere two days after the Series loss to the Pirates, and immediately before departing for California and his interview with Autry, Dalton wrote a confidential note to his boss, executive vice president Frank Cashen, regarding what he believed to be the next steps necessary to ward off the sclerotic effect of complacency and to address the issue of advancing age by some notable Orioles such as the two Robinsons. The Orioles' status as runners-up in the World Series showed that there was room for improvement, so Dalton furnished Cashen with a series of recommendations to consider as the winter meetings and their attendant trading season approached.

Content to keep Dave Leonhard and Grant Jackson in the bullpen, Dalton felt all of the other relievers could be used as trade bait. He also insisted that most of the current reserves be removed in order to make room for a clutch of newcomers: Johnny Oates, a top-rated catching prospect; Roric Harrison, a journeyman minor league pitcher who was now the top winner at Rochester; and both Don Baylor and Bobby Grich, Baltimore's best overall

136

minor league players who had nothing left to prove at the Triple-A level. Besides looking for a backup first baseman to help Powell, Dalton advised caution in trading Dave Johnson because he believed that swapping the second baseman was wise only "if it was [in] a major trade that brought us an immediate improvement for our 1972 club."[2] Dalton was willing to see Grich assume a full-time role, but if Johnson remained aboard, a "sales job will be necessary on Grich to make him a willing utility man starting the season."[3]

But the most profound comment Dalton made to Cashen concerned the aging veteran whose presence had catalyzed the Orioles dynasty: "I really feel we should trade Frank [Robinson] if we could and would not expect a lot in return."[4] Dalton simply affirmed the reality of his superstar's status. With Robinson now 36 years of age and drawing near the end of a spectacular career, Merv Rettenmund with his .318 batting average was deemed a very acceptable replacement. There seemed to be little to fear with some combination of Baylor, Buford, Blair, and Rettenmund patrolling the Orioles outfield. Dalton was fully cognizant of the diminished market value of Robinson but hoped that a new address to the future Hall of Famer's liking — a team in New York or Los Angeles was preferred — would soothe Robinson's angst of being traded.[5]

Upon his arrival in Baltimore, Robinson had resoundingly proved to Bill Dewitt and the rest of the baseball world that he was not an "old 30." But six years later, with viable candidates poised to replace him, the Frank Robinson era came to a close. On December 2, 1971, Cashen, now in charge of personnel, shipped Robinson and Pete Richert to the Los Angeles Dodgers for four players, only one of whom — pitcher Doyle Alexander — made any significant future contribution to the Orioles.[6]

## Strike One

Even before Dalton's or Robinson's departure were set in stone, Earl Weaver had already set a goal for 1972 of winning 100 games, a rational expectation considering the general strength of the Baltimore roster and the infusion of youth that was presumed to move the dynasty further into the 1970s.

The reality of the transformation, however, proved to be more challenging than the Orioles expected. This difficulty may have been presaged by the cover of their 1972 media guide, which featured the Orioles' cartoon mascot perched under a rain-spattered umbrella. Stormy times lay ahead for the defending three-time AL champions and, indeed, all of major league baseball.

Faced with a renewal of their agreement with the Players' Association and trouble expected over issues of the players' pension fund and health insurance coverage, the owners in late 1971 had been forced to provide data to the union related to their television revenues that were channeled to the pension reserve. Upon receipt of these records and the revelation of how small a percentage of the revenue was actually credited to the fund, the union and its leader, Marvin Miller, became emboldened to take action via a strike unless a new pact called for a substantial increase in pension contributions.[7] Miller noted that the baseball owners had recently inked a $70 million dollar deal with NBC for a host of broadcast rights, so he felt that the union's requests of an additional $700,000 for the pension fund and a $500,000 supplement for health coverage were reasonable.[8]

When Miller learned in early March 1972 that the owners intended to leave the pension contribution untouched and proposed a reduction in the health care funding, he recognized the tactic as "an unmistakable signal: Management was baiting [the Players' Association] into a strike."[9] In this respect, the owners succeed in getting what they asked for. Miller toured the spring training camps across Florida and the Southwest, canvassing the players as to what course of action they desired to take as they endeavored to enhance their benefit package, while the owners collectively remained virtually intractable with their offer. Despite an ostensibly united facade, some owners, Baltimore's Hoffberger among them, realized that the players' requests were warranted, while others, like Walter O'Malley of the Dodgers, smugly wanted the players to retain an obsequious status and be grateful for the largesse handed them. Although the owners were optimistic of a settlement, the ballots cast by the players overwhelmingly favored a strike; the tally, according to Miller, was 663–10, with two abstentions.[10]

A strike was called and carried out, much to the anguish and indignation of the sporting press, owners, and fans who expected that the players would submit to their employers. While Hoffberger was a minority voice among his brethren of hardline owners, Weaver stated that most of his players preferred to be on the field rather than a picket line, but baseball operations nonetheless ceased on April 1. The opening of the season was delayed as the owners' Player Relations Committee and union representatives wrangled their way to an accord nearly two weeks later. The unlikely figure of Charles Finley, owner of the Oakland Athletics, emerged as the integral character in convincing the group of owners that a compromise pointed the most logical way to a settlement, in which the players exacted an extra half-million dollars in supplemental health care benefits to go along with their pension gains — for a total annual contribution of $5.94 million by the owners — but received no back pay for the 86 games cancelled in both leagues due to the brief stoppage in play.

Commissioner Bowie Kuhn, who was not completely oblivious to the consequences of the strike, came away from the work stoppage with a fair degree of respect for the head of the players' union. "I think the players should have a players association and a capable leader of that association," Kuhn intoned at a news conference following the announcement of a settlement. "I think Marvin Miller has done many beneficial things for the players — and I have told him so."[11] Although Kuhn ultimately reported to the club owners, who collectively were in essence his real boss, the commissioner straddled a fine line between management and labor, and he later admitted that "the image of the players in the eyes of the fans was our most important asset."[12] At least he recognized that it was the fan base who purchased tickets, since without that revenue stream, baseball would be a virtual nonentity.

The baseball strike was the first such sport-wide job action in the nation's history. As ugly as it had been perceived in many public quarters, it turned out, from a historical perspective, to be a minor event. At the time that it occurred, however, the strike was an affront to the masses who took for granted that the sanctity of a major league baseball season was not to be disturbed by the quibbling factions of labor and management.

## A "Mysterious Lack of Hitting"

When the Orioles' schedule finally commenced in earnest on April 16, a gathering of just over 13,000 fans attended the home opener against the Yankees. Although they were victorious, Baltimore embarked on what transpired as a very strange trip. From that date until the beginning of September, the Orioles were in first, second, or third place and no worse than four games out — and even that was only for one day, on June 6. In what became a replay of 1967's frenzied pennant race, so tightly bunched was the American League East that when Baltimore lost to the Yankees on September 5, they fell from a tie for first into fourth place. After their victory against Boston on September 18, the Orioles were still in third place yet only one game out. When they won just three of their last eleven contests, Baltimore limped to the finish line at 80–74, in third place, five games behind the Tigers, 4½ behind Boston, and 1½ ahead of New York.

Pitching and defense, the chief assets that had carried the Orioles for so many years, spearheaded their charge. Baltimore hurlers led the league in team ERA with a 2.53 average and the stingiest on-base percentage at .282. The mainstays of the

Jim Palmer hit his stride at the close of the 1960s and went on to win three Cy Young Awards in the 1970s.

rotation all produced yeomanly: Palmer (21–10, 2.07 ERA) was at the head of the group, followed by Cuellar (18–12, 2.57), Dobson (16–18, 2.65, his loss total being the highest in the league), and McNally (13–17, 2.95). But the lack of run support, the Orioles' most nettlesome bugbear of 1972, struck McNally most acutely as the southpaw received no runs on five occasions and a mere single run nine other times. In his first year as an Oriole, Alexander worked mostly out of the bullpen and went 6–8 with a 2.46 ERA, while Eddie Watt, Grant Jackson, and rookie Roric Harrison combined to post 19 of the team's 21 saves.

The fielders committed only 100 errors as the defense finished second with a .983 average — Paul Blair and Brooks Robinson earning Gold Gloves in the process — but the dearth of offense was what handicapped Baltimore most seriously. "The mysterious lack of hitting … touched not just one or two [players], but seemed to overcome nearly all the hitters," lamented the Orioles' own recap of the 1972 season.[13] This statement needed a qualification to emphasize that the *veteran* hitters were those most at peril. Two long-time Orioles had barely passable years, even by their standards: Boog Powell hit .252 with club-highs in home runs (21) and RBIs (81), Blair (.233, eight homers, 49 RBIs) scored only 47 times, down from 75 in 1971; and Brooks Robinson, now in the twilight of his illustrious career, hit .250 but with only eight homers and 64 RBIs. The rest of the old guard's production ranged from poor to simply awful. Don Buford had his worst season (.206, 46 runs scored, 83 strikeouts); Dave Johnson, still smarting from a shoulder injury incurred the year before, became expendable with his 61-point drop in average and power outage (.221, down from .282, 5 home runs, 32 RBIs); Merv Rettenmund plummeted from 1971's .318 and 75 RBIs to .233 and 21; and Belanger's .186 mark put him on the bench. The reputation of the catching corps of Andy Etchebarren (.202) and Elrod Hendricks (.155) was salvaged somewhat by rookie Johnny Oates (.261, four home runs, 21 RBIs in 82 games).

Premature in his rash critique of the team but nonetheless frustrated by the Orioles' inability to push runs across the plate, Weaver by the end of June ranted that his team was in need of a major shakeup. All told, Baltimore was 38–51 in games decided by two runs or less, and their final .229 team batting average (second worst in the AL) and 519 runs scored (fifth worst) were woefully lacking from a team that had scored no less than 742 runs in each of the previous three years. The recently-departed Frank Robinson could not have made up such an enormous deficit by himself, but it can only be left to speculation as to the positive difference he would have made had he still been wearing an Orioles uniform.

This swoon of the immediate post–Frank Robinson era was shot through with the interesting paradox that the newest arrivals in Baltimore outperformed the returning veterans, who struggled mightily. Oates was a pleasant surprise as a backstop and left-handed bat in the lineup to replace Hendricks, who was eventually traded to the Cubs in mid–August for outfielder Tommy Davis. As an outfielder, Baylor was not impressive defensively, but his six-foot, one-inch frame of muscle and speed were honed during his outstanding 1971 season

One of the highest-rated prospects to emerge from the Baltimore minor league system, Bobby Grich lived up to the billing as a solid, all-around player.

in Triple-A that made the decision of the front office to trade Robinson an easier one. Baylor had trepidations about filling the large shoes of the former Triple Crown winner, admitting, "I wasn't ready to be the next Frank Robinson.... In my mind the trade took the heart out of the team. Besides, I wanted to play alongside Frank, not replace him."[14] As Baylor's playing time increased through 1972, his statistics cemented his place in the lineup. In his 102 games — most of them stationed in right and left field — he finished the season at .253 with 11 home runs, 38 RBIs, and 24 stolen bases. In the Orioles' outfield sweepstakes, the odd-man-out became the 35-year-old Buford. As the last new player to carve a niche for himself, Grich fulfilled Dalton's prophecy by playing all around the infield, primarily at shortstop. Earning appearances in 133 games, Grich in his first full season led Baltimore with a .278 average, added 12 home runs, drove in 50 runs, and stole 13 bases. A second baseman by trade, Grich took on the demands of playing on the other side of the keystone — "If you can play shortstop, you can play anywhere," he said later — and proved his readiness for a full-time role while at the same time landing the starting assignment at shortstop on the American League All-Star team.[15]

This infusion of youth boded well for the future of the Orioles. Oates was 26 years old, Baylor turned 23 at midseason, and Grich was also 23. That three products of the Baltimore farm system found significant playing time *and* had the top batting averages on the team seemed to point to a return of the Orioles to the top of the American League East. Augmenting the trio was yet another young prospect, Terry Crowley, an outfielder-first baseman who hit .231 with 11 homers and 29 RBIs, although he was destined to serve in a reserve capacity.

Weaver continued to press his case for a shakeup after the end of the 1972 campaign. Of that disappointing year, he wrote, "I made it clear to everyone that any time we were losing as a result of individuals performing beneath their capabilities, I wasn't going to be easy to live with."[16] The time had come for another trade of the Frank Robinson variety, circa 1965, a deal that would deliver an impact player in his prime or about to hit his stride who could be counted on for at least five productive seasons in an Orioles uniform. The irascible manager knew the pitching staff was generally sound, and he appreciated the potential of Baylor and Grich, especially the latter's ability to take Dave Johnson's place. Less than thrilled with Belanger's play but realizing his value as a fielder, Weaver was exasperated by Johnson's performance and weight gains in his effort to transform into a power hitter. When Weaver vowed that the Orioles would reclaim the AL East if he had a catcher able to hit twenty home runs, scout Jim Russo had just the man for him. If a trade could be worked out that eased the crowding in the middle infield and put a slugging backstop in the lineup, Baltimore's manager was confident that the Orioles would be a cinch to resume its domination.

## The Second Earl of Baltimore

Russo had explored the availability of Atlanta's 24-year-old catcher, Earl Williams, a strapping six-foot, three-inch, 220-pound native of Newark, New Jersey, and sold Weaver on the idea that if the Orioles could engineer a trade to bring Williams to Baltimore, the manager should be up to the task of dealing with the "little problem" that Williams would surely bring with him.[17]

Williams, the 1971 National League Rookie of the Year, hit 33 and 28 home runs in his first two full seasons with the Braves and was a nimble, gifted athlete despite his size. Yet the baggage accompanying him was the fact that he was a first baseman/third baseman who was less than enthusiastic about his assignment behind the plate in Atlanta; his posture would not change regardless of the uniform he wore. Nonetheless, the Orioles moved forward with the acquisition on December 1, 1972, sending Pat Dobson, Dave Johnson, Johnny Oates, and Roric Harrison to the Braves in return for Williams and a minor leaguer. Baltimore's front office was optimistic of Weaver's ability to get the best measure of virtually any player under his command, and Weaver thought it worth the inconvenience of Williams's attitude so long as he could expect at least twenty home runs in return.[18]

From the onset of spring training in 1973, Williams did nothing to endear himself to his new team or those associated with it. He proved to be a problem child who carped about the catching fundamentals in which the Orioles were attempting to tutor him, moaned when he had to warm up the starting pitcher, was habitually tardy for every item on the club's itinerary, and feuded with management, teammates, and anyone else whom he felt offended him. Since fans were quick to hurl racial epithets at Williams for his chronic failure to hustle or run out routine groundballs, the catcher's penchant for slugging a baseball with authority was soon outweighed by the pandering and coddling lavished upon him by the Orioles in an effort to get him to perform as they had hoped.

## A New Batter in the American League Lineup

Proposed for several years but not officially incorporated into major league baseball until mid–January of 1973, the creation of the designated hitter became an new attempt to rekindle offenses that continued to flag, especially in the American League, despite the rule changes of 1969 that were intended to give batters the upper hand. The following tables illustrate the trend in both leagues for the 1960s through 1972 and emphasize the acuteness of the AL's predicament:

### American League

|       | # of Teams | Batting Average | Hits/Hits per Team | Runs/Runs per Team | ERA |
|-------|------------|-----------------|--------------------|--------------------|-----|
| 1960* | 8  | .255 | 10,689 — 1,336 | 5,414 — 677 | 3.87 |
| 1961  | 10 | .256 | 14,037 — 1,404 | 7,342 — 734 | 4.02 |
| 1962  | 10 | .255 | 14,068 — 1,407 | 7,183 — 718 | 3.97 |
| 1963  | 10 | .247 | 13,609 — 1,361 | 6,599 — 660 | 3.63 |
| 1964  | 10 | .247 | 13,637 — 1,364 | 6,607 — 661 | 3.63 |
| 1965  | 10 | .242 | 13,158 — 1,316 | 6,388 — 639 | 3.46 |
| 1966  | 10 | .240 | 13,005 — 1,301 | 6,276 — 628 | 3.44 |
| 1967  | 10 | .236 | 12,766 — 1,277 | 5,992 — 599 | 3.23 |
| 1968  | 10 | .230 | 12,359 — 1,236 | 5,532 — 553 | 2.98 |
| 1969  | 12 | .246 | 16,120 — 1,343 | 7,960 — 663 | 3.62 |
| 1970  | 12 | .250 | 16,404 — 1,367 | 8,109 — 676 | 3.71 |
| 1971  | 12 | .247 | 15,957 — 1,330 | 7,472 — 623 | 3.46 |
| 1972  | 12 | .239 | 14,751 — 1,229 | 6,441 — 537 | 3.06 |

### National League

|       | # of Teams | Batting Average | Hits/Hits per Team | Runs/Runs per Team | ERA |
|-------|------------|-----------------|--------------------|--------------------|-----|
| 1961  | 8  | .262 | 11,029 — 1,379 | 5,600 — 700 | 4.03 |
| 1962  | 10 | .261 | 14,453 — 1,445 | 7,278 — 728 | 3.94 |
| 1963  | 10 | .245 | 13,434 — 1,343 | 6,181 — 618 | 3.29 |
| 1964  | 10 | .254 | 14,032 — 1,403 | 6,517 — 652 | 3.54 |
| 1965  | 10 | .249 | 13,794 — 1,379 | 6,558 — 656 | 3.54 |
| 1966  | 10 | .256 | 14,202 — 1,420 | 6,624 — 662 | 3.61 |
| 1967  | 10 | .249 | 13,698 — 1,370 | 6,218 — 622 | 3.38 |
| 1968  | 10 | .243 | 13,351 — 1,335 | 5,577 — 558 | 2.99 |
| 1969  | 12 | .250 | 16,461 — 1,372 | 7,890 — 658 | 3.59 |
| 1970  | 12 | .258 | 17,151 — 1,429 | 8,771 — 731 | 4.05 |
| 1971  | 12 | .252 | 16,590 — 1,383 | 7,601 — 633 | 3.47 |
| 1972  | 12 | .248 | 15,683 — 1,307 | 7,265 — 605 | 3.45 |

*Source: Gary Gillette and Pete Palmer,* The ESPN Baseball Encyclopedia

The effects of 1968's "year of the pitcher" at last forced baseball's rules committee to take the drastic measures that it did, but the respite in the AL was for too brief a period. Coincidentally, in 1969 the Triple-A International League experimented with allowing a pinch-hitter to bat for the pitcher, a trial that produced a welcome result: "Batting averages rose 10 per cent, the number of runs scored rose 6 per cent, and games took six minutes less time to play on average."[19] As the American League's decline in hits and runs scored reached alarming lows, implementation of a bold, offensive catalyst was given a high priority.

For the time being, the NL declined to follow the AL in employing the designated hitter, preferring to retain the customary role of having the pitcher bat for himself and reserving judgment for a later date whether to adopt the DH rule. (To this day, the DH is not employed in National League parks nor does it appear that it will be in the near future.) *The Sporting News* viewed the American League's break with tradition in a favorable light so that the circuit could address "its sagging fortunes," but players and managers around the league gave mixed reviews to the change.[20] Texas Rangers skipper Whitey Herzog said that his candidate to fill the role, Rico Carty, who was afflicted with bad knees, was "the perfect DH."[21] But Carty and others such as Boog Powell, who worked ardently to improve his glove work at first base and relished the reputation of being a complete player, took umbrage at the prospect of being relegated to a part-time position.

In the Orioles' case, Williams's disinclination to catch did not coerce Weaver to move him into the designated hitter's spot. Acquired to be the primary backstop, Williams caught 95 games and also spelled Powell at first base 42 times. Tailor-made to be Baltimore's DH was Tommy Davis, the former two-time National League batting champion acquired in August 1972 but who was hampered in recent years by ankle and knee problems. Davis adapted well to his new role and posted impressive numbers (.306, seven home runs, 89 RBIs), as did other renowned hitters such as Tony Oliva (.291, 16, 92) and Orlando Cepeda (.287, 20, 86), whose playing days defensively were curtailed by injuries but who could still swing the bat with authority. The designated hitter added more offense to the American League and helped extend the careers of good batters who were beset by medical issues or may have lacked defensive skills.

## Blazing Their Way Back

Reflecting on the Orioles' 1972 season, it may seem hard to believe that the singular absence of Frank Robinson would have such a debilitating effect on Baltimore's ability to score runs. The remaining cast of regulars changed little, yet the offensive collapse was a stunning group effort. Help was on the way again from the farm system, so a palpable transformation was evident in the Orioles lineup for 1973. Power production from Powell and especially Brooks Robinson was waning, and neither Grich nor Baylor had reached their potential to hit for distance, so the burden of supplying the long ball fell to Williams. Thanks to a duo of swift rookies, Al Bumbry and Rich Coggins, the element of speed now became an integral weapon, as Weaver "almost wore out the steal sign" in moving Baltimore back atop the American League East.[22]

With the pains of labor negotiations over the 1973 basic agreement between the players and owners concluded only slightly less painfully but in a more timely manner than the year before, the new contract most importantly gave players the right to have their salaries determined by "an impartial arbitrator whose decisions were binding."[23] There was no delay to the opening of the regular season, and the retooled Oriole lineup, lacking the power of their World Series predecessors, embarked on the new campaign with the hope that the transformation to a speed-oriented attack would be fruitful.

Bumbry and Coggins — short of stature, both were listed at five feet, eight inches tall — made their Oriole debuts late in 1972 after each had hit well over .300 at Rochester, the former winning honors as the International League's best player. By late May, the pair of left-handed batters had found their way to the top two spots in the Baltimore batting order and made Buford only a memory, with Bumbry — the "fastest runner in [the] O's organization," according to the team's media guide — leading off.[24] Weaver was prudent in not rushing either of the rookies into a full-time role and used them in part to offset slumps endured by Baylor and Rettenmund in the first half of the year. By season's end, the deep outfield of Baylor, Blair, Bumbry, Coggins, and Rettenmund had well over 300 at-bats each, and the first four members of that group combined to steal 90 bases. Grich added 17 steals, Belanger had 13, and Davis and Rettenmund swiped 11 each as the Orioles were the first club to feature eight players with ten or more stolen bases en route to a club record of 146. Baltimore also employed the element of surprise by laying down 52 bunts that went for base hits, the bulk of these executed by Blair (14), Bumbry (8), Belanger (8), and Baylor (6).[25]

The running game eventually brought a fine dividend, but not until mid-summer did Baltimore exhibit the dominance akin to the later halcyon days of the Frank Robinson era. Likening his club's difficulty in gaining traction to "a Latin American dance," general manager Frank Cashen opined, "Two steps forward, two steps back."[26] Up until the All-Star break, the overall team performance and many of the batting averages served as unpleasant reminders of the frustrating shortfall of 1972. Baylor, Belanger, Etchebarren, Grich, Robinson, and Williams were all hitting .229 or less, and many fine pitching efforts had been wasted in games that ended as low-scoring losses. At 51–41 for the season's first half, the Orioles lost 29 games by two runs or less yet were in second place, merely 1½ games behind the front-running Yankees. Powell had finally come around after suffering early-season shoulder trouble, and Williams powered 12 home runs and led the team with 44 RBIs. But at .319 with 42 RBIs, newly-minted designated hitter Tommy Davis headed off disaster when one considers what the Orioles' record might have been had their pitchers been forced to take their turns at bat.

Following the All-Star Game, Weaver looked forward to series against the Texas Rangers and Cleveland Indians, two of the worst clubs in the league, in order to build enough momentum to move to the top of the AL East. Successful in this endeavor, the Orioles also went on a 14-game tear beginning August 12 against the Royals and bolted to a six-game lead by September 1. Palmer, Cuellar, McNally, and Alexander formed the bulwark of the starting rotation and were assisted by rookie right-hander Jesse Jefferson.

Meanwhile, the inert bats of some who struggled earlier came to life in support of the second-half drive. Foremost among those taking charge was Baylor, whose .364 average, seven homers, and 29 RBIs made him "[feel] like I was helping to fill the void caused by the Frank Robinson trade."[27] Grich (.282), Powell (.294), and Brooks Robinson (.295) helped lead the resurgence, while Bumbry (.376) continued his torrid hitting with Coggins (.352) close behind. When the Orioles won at Milwaukee on September 22, they clinched the AL East for the fourth time in five years. Generous in expressing gratitude to his staff for their hard-fought success, Weaver treated his coaches to "a celebratory drink and to thank them for bearing up under the duress created by Earl Williams."[28]

Baltimore ended a bit short of their previous 100-win standard, but they still posted the best record in the American League, 97–65. Had they scored five more times, they would have led the league in that category, tallying 754 runs while allowing the fewest (561). As the best baserunning team in the AL, the Orioles had the most triples (48) and stolen bases (146), and the club's 3.07 ERA was the league's best.

By year-end, individual statistics, the outfield quintet of Baylor (.286, 11 home runs, 51 RBIs), Blair (.280, 10, 64), Bumbry (.337, 7, 34), Coggins (.319, 7, 41), and Rettenmund (.262, 9, 44) provided Weaver insurance and depth, while Davis (.306, 7, 89) was one of the best designated hitters in the AL.[29] Bumbry won laurels as AL Rookie of the Year, while Coggins finished second, offering further proof of the profusion of talent rising from Baltimore's minor league system. Brooks Robinson, now 36 years old, held forth with respectable numbers (.257, 9, 72), Belanger (.226, 0, 27) contributed more with his glove than his bat, and although Powell raised his second-half average, overall figures (.265, 11, 54) for the former MVP were nearly on a par with Grich's (.251, 12, 50). Leading the Orioles in home runs and making true Weaver's proclamation that given a power-hitting catcher Baltimore would win the division, the enigmatic Williams (.237, 22, 83) also placed second on the team in RBIs.

In the pitching department, Palmer continued on his path to the Hall of Fame by winning 22 games with nine losses, posting a league-best 2.40 ERA in 296 innings, to capture his first Cy Young Award. The best pitcher in the AL later noted, "All of Earl [Weaver's] determined, demented, demonic drive to win-win-win, all of the yelling and fighting and arguing ... seemed worth it when they said the Cy Young Award was going to a guy named Palmer."[30] Hurt by the 29 home runs he served up as well as the 23 unearned runs surrendered in his appearances, Cuellar (18–13, 3.27) fell short of the 20-win circle, while McNally (17–17, 3.21) soldiered on despite being hit in the head by a line drive in late July. Easing further into the rotation as the fourth starter was Alexander (12–8, 3.86), but when he was sidelined for most of July and early August, Jefferson (6–5, 4.11) stepped in, albeit with mixed results. The stars of the bullpen were Grant Jackson (8–0, nine saves, 1.90) and right-hander

Even in his later years, Brooks Robinson could still dazzle with his glove at third base, diving for hits to the shortstop hole.

Bob Reynolds (7–5, nine saves, 1.95), with Eddie Watt (3–4, five saves, 3.30) still contributing in what was his final year for Baltimore.

The Orioles defense was back to its usual stellar standard, with Gold Gloves for Blair, Robinson, Belanger, and Grich, but it was the second baseman that drew special attention in 1973. Committing but five errors in 162 games, Grich had one of the best defensive seasons ever turned in by a second baseman, leading all players at that position in putouts, assists, double plays, total chances per game, and fielding average, not to mention participating in a pair of around-the-horn triple plays.

At last receiving his due as American League Manager of the Year was Earl Weaver, who delivered a division crown with a team whose character was very different from the 1969–1971 version. After suffering the trials brought on by his reluctant catcher — to say nothing of the hate mail he received for letting Dave Johnson, who was busy hitting 43 home runs for the Braves, get away in exchange for Williams — and sparring with the ace of the staff, Weaver was reticent about his personal achievement because the Orioles' postseason appearance was too short in his estimation: "It was nice to finally win [the Manager-of-the-Year award], but I would rather have won the pennant."[31]

## A Bittersweet October

The 1973 American League Championship Series pitted Baltimore against the defending World Series champion Oakland Athletics. Many members of the 1971 Athletics team that had been swept by the Orioles in that year's ALCS had matured and become battle-tested in winning the 1972 World Series and repeating as champions of the 1973 AL Western division.

Initially, Baltimore kept intact its ALCS winning streak with a 6–0 whitewashing of Oakland at Memorial Stadium behind Palmer's five-hit shutout. Vida Blue did not last the first inning, as Davis, who lit up the Athletics pitching for a .513 average in the regular season, Williams, and Belanger all drove in runs to chase Blue. Oakland made history in Game 2 by handing the Orioles their first-ever defeat in ALCS competition, as starter Catfish Hunter and relief ace Rollie Fingers combined to even the series with a 6–3 win, as most of the Athletics' scoring resulted from four home runs.

In the third game at Oakland, a pitchers' duel between Cuellar and Ken Holtzman lasted for eleven innings, as the home team prevailed, 2–1, with a run in the eighth on two "cheap" hits — by Weaver's account — and Bert Campaneris's lead-off homer in the bottom of the eleventh.[32] Palmer, undefeated in four ALCS decisions, faltered early in Game 4 and was lifted in the second inning, down 3–0. Oakland tacked on another run in the sixth, but the Orioles rallied in the top of the seventh, capped by Etchebarren's three-run homer, and won the game 5–4 on Grich's solo shot off Fingers in the eighth.

The climactic Game 5 was another masterful outing by Hunter, who tamed the Orioles with a five-hit shutout. When Alexander fell behind 3–0 with two out in the fourth, he was relieved by Palmer, who held the Athletics scoreless the rest of the game, but Baltimore failed to generate any offense against Hunter. Baylor was confounded upon seeing Catfish drinking at the bar in the Orioles' hotel the night before the finale, but the copious spirits seemed only to invigorate the pitcher. What constituted Hunter's way of "getting ready" worked for him, much to Baltimore's chagrin.[33] Oakland deservedly advanced to the World Series, but the final line totals show that both clubs scored 15 runs each, the team batting averages were .200 for the Athletics and .211 for the Orioles, and the team ERAs were Oakland's 2.74 to Baltimore's 2.80.

Baltimore again had won the American League East, yet the weakness of the fourth spot in the rotation needed to be addressed. It was clear that Pat Dobson was missed, and a pitcher capable of producing like the erstwhile Oriole was needed to solidify the starting corps. At the December 1973 winter meetings, Cashen brokered a multi-player trade with Cincinnati, the central figures being Rettenmund, part of the Orioles outfield surplus, and 23-year-old Ross Grimsley, a left-handed starter whose specialty pitch was a change-up. Except for the departure of Rettenmund and the addition of Grimsley, Baltimore carried a relatively static roster heading into 1974, which became the most trying season for Weaver to that point in his managerial career.

## The Coup That Worked

Although the final standings of the American League East for 1974 showed the Orioles on top by two games over an improved Yankees team, one needs to look a bit deeper at Baltimore's furious drive over the last five weeks of the season to appreciate the outcome of the three-way dogfight involving the Baltimore, New York, and Boston.

Throughout the spring and most of the summer, the Orioles were as listless as they had ever been with Weaver at the helm. While suffering only one losing streak of consequence, a five-game skid one month into the season, the Orioles could not establish themselves with any authority. They plodded along in third place for much of the year as Palmer landed on the disabled list in mid-summer and Alexander seemed challenged to pick up the slack. But despite these travails, Baltimore remained only a handful of games out of first place. When they began a slide that dragged them to a season-worst position of an eight-game deficit, Brooks Robinson and Paul Blair called a players-only meeting and led a palace revolt that salvaged the Orioles' fortunes.

Interpreting Weaver's managing style as one in which the skipper continued to "[wait] for three-run home runs that no longer came," the veteran players took matters into their own hands.[34] They elected to forego signals and instructions from Weaver or the coaches if any player believed he had a better chance of getting a hit or advancing a runner by doing other than what he had been advised. Palmer confirmed that the players devised their own signs so as to "squeeze every hit and every base and every run you can out of every play."[35] In his autobiographical account of this period, Weaver did not mention the players' usurping of his authority, and even though the manager finally caught on to what was happening, Baylor believed that Weaver turned a blind eye to the mutinous behavior so long as the victories continued to accumulate.[36]

At roughly the same time the division-leading Red Sox hit a losing streak in early September, both the Yankees and Orioles moved ahead of Boston. As a Baltimore team publication later noted, "[While] the public and press marvelled [*sic*] at the upstart Yankees, the Orioles in the midst of a ten-game winning streak had moved quietly back into contention, just two games off the pace."[37] Because so many players were a part of the "insurrection" and the team was performing so well, Baltimore's clubhouse took on the same aura and solidarity that had enveloped the 1965 Twins, namely, "Our motto became, 'Who's the hero today?'"[38] With the wind now at their backs, the Orioles catapulted themselves to 28 wins, including the last nine in a row, against just six losses from August 28 until October 2. The sprint was at once wearying and exhilarating, and by vaulting from a 63–65 record to 91–71, Baltimore secured its fifth divisional title in six years as they edged the Yankees by two games in the final AL East standings.

## A Second Chance Against Oakland

The momentum of Baltimore's intrepid stretch drive carried for only one game of the 1974 ALCS, in a rematch against the Athletics. Cuellar hurled the series opener on the West Coast and rode the home-run support of Blair, Robinson, and Grich to defeat Catfish Hunter and the Athletics, 6–3. Grimsley entered in the ninth inning and finished for the tired Cuellar, as the Orioles captured the home-field advantage, beating Hunter after falling to him in seven previous starts.

However, in an ill-timed rerun reminiscent of the 1969 World Series, Baltimore's offense suddenly went flat in the remaining contests. The Orioles defeated Ken Holtzman three times in the regular season but could not solve him in Game 2. Trailing just 2–0 in the eighth, Oakland salted the game away when Ray Fosse launched a three-run homer off Grant Jackson in the 5–0 win, with McNally taking the loss.

Moving to Baltimore for the remaining games brought no change of luck for the Orioles. Palmer received only two hits of support in Game 3 while Vida Blue, a two-time playoff loser to Baltimore in 1971 and 1973, made Sal Bando's solo homer stand up in the agonizing 1–0 Oakland victory. Now charged with heading off elimination in Game 4, Cuellar again took the mound and combined with Grimsley — once more pitching in relief — to limit Oakland to one hit. But Cuellar was extremely wild, issuing nine bases on balls, including one that drove in the first Athletic tally with a bases-loaded walk. Another pass to Bando in the seventh was followed by a Reggie Jackson double for the second Oakland run. Hunter resumed his dominance over the Orioles and held them in check for seven innings before yielding to Rollie Fingers, who closed out the Orioles, 2–1, despite surrendering a run in the bottom of the ninth. The Athletics had defended their AL pennant at the Orioles' expense and thus forced Baltimore to re-evaluate the speed-oriented strategy that had been employed over the last few seasons.

In the three losses, Baltimore scored but two runs. Although pleased with the efforts of the pitching staff, Weaver had seen enough of what fleetness could do to help a club win. Clinching the AL East by playing extremely well at the tail-end of the season could not mask or modify the underlying problems that beset Baltimore for the majority of the season. Weaver sought a return to the days of three-run home runs, a remedy he believed that could only be applied with "an extended visit by Dr. Longball."[39]

Hardly a failure by any stretch of the imagination, the Oriole pitching staff's 3.27 ERA in 1974 was the American League's second best, and their team fielding was also tops at .980. Stealing almost as many bases (145) as they did in 1973, Baltimore scored only 47 more runs than they allowed (659 to 612), a curious — and low — surplus for a division titlist. Offensively, the Orioles' chief producers were Davis (.289, 11 home runs, 89 RBIs), Grich (.263, 19, 82), Blair (.261, 17, 62), and Baylor (.272, 10, 59). Brooks Robinson (.288, 7, 59) had his highest average since 1965, but his dwindling home run output reflected the sunset into which his career was fading. Accompanying Brooks was Powell on his decline (.265, 12, 45), lending more credence to Weaver's desire to restore power to the corners of the infield. Earl Williams (.254, 14, 52) proved the manager wrong in one sense by showing that the Orioles could win the division even without benefit of 20 homers from the catcher. But the rookie sensations of 1973 had a hard landing in their sophomore year. Neither Bumbry (.233, 1, 19) nor Coggins (.243, 4, 32) approached their first-year levels, which impacted the top two slots of Baltimore's batting order. Belanger had a typical season at the plate (.266, 3, 27) but was steady in the field, winning a Gold Glove as did Grich, Blair, and Robinson.

The pitchers were fronted by the trio of Cuellar (22–10, 3.11 ERA), Grimsley (18–13, 3.07), and McNally (16–10, 3.58), but Palmer (7–12, 3.27) was smitten by chronic arm pain for most of the season. Alexander (6–9, 4.03) was less than effective, but George Bamberger's latest pupil, right-handed rookie Wayne Garland (5–5, 2.97) pitched very well at times after his recall from Rochester in late May. As was the case the previous year, Bob Reynolds (7–5, 2.74, 7 saves) and Grant Jackson (6–4, 2.55, 12 saves) were the best coming out of the Orioles bullpen.

## A Power Search

Looking to the immediate future, Baltimore was confronted with several exigencies if they were not only to retain their supremacy in the AL East but also find a way to return to the World Series. Issues persisted at three corners of the infield: Brooks Robinson's inexorable march toward retirement, the incessant headache of Earl Williams's presence on the roster, and the downturn in Boog Powell's production.

Not surprisingly, the Orioles front office had given due attention to the coming day when Robinson would no longer man the position he played so well. Robinson's heir apparent, Doug DeCinces, had apprenticed well in the minor leagues by playing at various positions around the infield, but his focus at Rochester had been directed to third base to prepare him to take Robinson's place. By moving DeCinces into a temporary utility role with the big club, he would be handled in the same manner as was Grich; if successful in that transition, third base would become his full-time position. As difficult as it might be for a player as great as Robinson to segue to a reduced role, Baltimore handled this period as best they could by grooming a replacement who was a two-time International League all-star.

Removal of Williams from the Orioles organization was a case of addition by subtraction. When the trade that brought him to Baltimore proved to be one of the rare mistakes committed by the front office, owner Jerry Hoffberger demanded that Cashen not even bring the malcontented catcher to spring training in 1975.[40] Despite attempts to put roots down in a city where he was no longer wanted — Williams bought a home in Baltimore and played for the Orioles' basketball squad — he remained an Oriole until mid–April when he was at last sent back to Atlanta for a minor league pitcher and $75,000.

The alarming drop in Powell's home run and RBI statistics, attributed to a bad right shoulder, prompted Cashen to use Enos Cabell, another prospect with experience at first base, in a trade to acquire Lee May from the Houston Astros during the 1974 winter meetings. May's home run totals, which had been in the mid–30s during his best years in Cincinnati, dipped to the upper 20s as a result of playing in the cavernous Astrodome for three years when he was traded to Houston in 1972. Yet his ability to hit for distance was exactly what Weaver sought for his revamped lineup. Powell remained an Oriole until early 1975, when just as spring training camps were opening, the Orioles traded Boog and pitcher Don Hood to Cleveland for veteran catcher Dave Duncan and a minor leaguer. Boog's departure was painful to many, not least to Hoffberger, who bade farewell in an emotional phone call to Powell, although the burly first baseman was now reunited with Frank Robinson, the Indians DH who was named baseball's first black manager.[41] Williams had been marginalized until he could be disposed of, and Duncan was now charged with primary catching duties.

Baltimore's hallmark of strong pitching had been flagging in the fourth starter's spot for two years, and there was no small degree of trepidation about the miserable year that Palmer had just endured. Now having just three proven, frontline starters in Cuellar, McNally, and Grimsley — and the first two of this group were getting on in years — the Orioles sought to upgrade their rotation. Prior to the 1974 winter meetings, Baltimore scout Jim Russo trained his sights north of the border and found much to like about Montreal

Expos' 15-game winner Mike Torrez. In negotiations with the National League club, a potential deal expanded to include the Expos' switch-hitting right fielder Ken Singleton, praised by Russo as a player who "could hit blindfolded."[42] Montreal wanted an outfielder with more speed than the tall, lumbering Singleton, and two pitchers to replace Torrez, so a deal was struck in which Torrez and Singleton were traded to the Orioles for McNally, who had spent twelve full seasons in Baltimore, Rich Coggins, whose youth and 26 stolen bases piqued Montreal's interest, and a minor league pitcher. Now past his prime, McNally was destined to play a role later in 1975 that had a far greater impact on the national pastime than his performance on the mound with the Expos.

This overhaul of the Orioles for 1975 was emblematic of a team more to Weaver's liking. Baltimore would be less dependent on speed, the Orioles no longer had to hope that players like Jim Fuller — who demonstrated a great

**A twenty-game winner four times for the Orioles, Dave McNally later became a trailblazer for players' free agency.**

home-run stroke in early 1974 but flamed out quickly — would fill the power void now that May and Singleton were on board. And with 28-year-old Torrez in essence now taking the place of the 32-year-old McNally, Baltimore held its breath that Palmer would recover to pitch like the Cy Young Award winner he had been. DeCinces's place on the roster made him a work-in-progress, but learning from Brooks Robinson, the master of his craft, would help him in the long run. As these new players adjusted, Eddie Murray, Dennis Martinez, and Mike Flanagan were still working their way through the farm system to be just a few years away from adding to the Orioles' tradition of power-hitting and fine pitching.

## Just Second Best

An interesting phenomenon occurred in 1975 when Baltimore's roster underwent its radical makeover. The Orioles slipped from first place to runner-up behind the Boston Red Sox with a 90–69 record, 4½ games out, as the anticipated power surge did not materialize. Since the change in output from 1974 to 1975 was minimal at best, the major acquisitions appeared to have been in vain. A decrease in doubles (from 226 to 224) and slight rise in triples (27 to 33) and home runs (116 to 124) yielded a barely perceptible increase in runs scored (659 to 682).

False hopes had been stirred in spring training when Baltimore went 18–9 in the Grapefruit League. When the regular season commenced, the Orioles played inconsistently and faltered so badly during the last two weeks of May that they lost eleven of twelve contests and tumbled into the basement of the AL East. Grimsley opened with a record of 1–8, yet the *Official 1976 Baseball Guide* later reported, "Most of the problems centered around the bullpen, which had a 1–9 record (with no saves) and a 5.25 ERA nearly two months into the campaign."[43] When Dyar Miller, who had pitched in parts of four seasons at Rochester, was finally recalled to the Orioles in early June, the rookie became the most reliable reliever to stanch the poor showings of the bullpen.

Attempting valiantly to correct the early damage, the Orioles' attack was enhanced by May's productive adjustment to American League pitching and Baylor's home run stroke, which Weaver and coach Jim Frey urged the outfielder to use to pull the ball for power. However, another feverish and remedial second-half rush was not enough to allow Baltimore to defend their AL East title, with a 49–25 record in the last 74 games still leaving the Orioles nearly five games short of catching the Red Sox. May put up Powell-type numbers (.262, 20 home runs, 99 RBIs), and Baylor (.276, 25, 76) continued to mature as a hitter. The newly-acquired Singleton (.300, 15, 55) hit well, but his run production was short of expectations, and the same held true with Davis (.283, 6, 57) and Grich (.260, 13, 57). New catcher Duncan (.205, 12, 41) provided power as well as RBI totals nearly on a par with the departed Earl Williams, and when combined with Hendricks (.215, 8, 38) gave the backstop contingent a solid total for the year.[44] Bumbry (.269, 2, 32, 16 stolen bases) raised his figures closer to but still short of those in his rookie season, while DeCinces (.251, 4, 23) was respectable in his utility role, which was an asset to the Orioles because Brooks Robinson's output (.201, 6, 53) continued to diminish. Belanger (.226, 3, 27) was relied upon for his defense, but also falling into this category of one-dimensional play was Blair (.218, 5, 31), whose free-swinging style was wreaking havoc with his average. Blair and Robinson, along with Grich and Belanger, again received Gold Gloves, the fourth consecutive year the quartet was so honored.

Upholding the Orioles' rotation was Palmer, now recovered from his 1974 arm trouble and winner of his second Cy Young Award thanks to his 23–11 mark and 2.09 ERA. Torrez (20–9, 3.06) tied for third in victories in the AL, Cuellar (14–10, 3.66) had what proved to be his last good season, Grimsley rebounded from his dreadful start and finished 10–13 with a 4.07 ERA, and Alexander (8–8, 3.04) continued as a starter and reliever. Reynolds, so effective in his two seasons with Baltimore, was completely lost in seven outings and was traded to Detroit in late May, leaving Miller (6–3, eight saves, 2.72) and Jackson (4–3, seven saves, 3.35) as the main relievers.

## Jacksonian Era

It must be pointed out that 1975 was hardly the end of the road for the Orioles as contenders. Under the front office guidance of Hank Peters, who assumed the duties of the departed Frank Cashen following the 1975 season, Baltimore continued to be active on the trading front and remained very competitive on the field.

Several notable events took place in this regard. The March 1976 transaction sending Torrez, Baylor, and pitcher Paul Mitchell to Oakland for Ken Holtzman, Reggie Jackson, and a minor league pitcher, was a blockbuster deal in its time. Because of the change in the rules regarding free agency (which will be reviewed later in this book) teams in the position of losing a player to the open market often chose to take on another player, especially of star quality, in the hope of taking advantage of his impending status as a free agent. Any potential free agent wanted to have the best season possible to maximize his bargaining leverage for a new contract. Already satisfied with having Singleton in the fold, Baltimore wished to balance its offensive power of the right-handed-hitting May with a left-handed bat. With Jackson and Baylor among those eligible to offer their services to the highest bidder upon completion of the 1976 season, the Orioles risked acquiring Jackson, even though their chances of signing him beyond 1976 seemed remote. The trade devastated Baylor, who knew no organization other than the Orioles, but Jackson was a hired gun who had envisioned further fame and fortune if given the opportunity to play for a team in a big-city venue, not a small-market franchise like Baltimore. When he finally reported to Baltimore, Jackson performed as expected—the 1973 AL MVP hit 27 homers and drove in 91 runs in his only year as an Oriole—but thereafter quickly fled to the Yankees.

Midway through 1976, the Orioles used Holtzman, Alexander, Hendricks, Grant Jackson, and a minor leaguer in a trade with the Yankees to secure five players, three of whom would fortify Baltimore for years to come. Arriving in Baltimore were southpaw starters Rudy May and Scott McGregor, catcher Rick Dempsey, left-handed reliever Tippy Martinez, and pitcher Dave Pagan. Dempsey would spend his best years behind the plate in Baltimore, McGregor played his entire major league career in an Orioles uniform and won 138 games over 13 seasons, and Martinez became a most dependable relief ace in his ten years with Baltimore. In its long-term effect, this trade was as valuable to the Orioles as was the Frank Robinson deal and certainly more than the one involving Reggie Jackson. In turn, Rudy May won eleven games for Baltimore in 1976, 18 more in 1977, and was subsequently shipped to Montreal as the main player in a trade for pitchers Don Stanhouse and Joe Kerrigan and outfielder Gary Roenicke, who became a fixture in the Orioles outfield until the mid–1980s.

Other notable personnel continued on their courses, with Palmer lasting his entire Hall of Fame career in Baltimore, Brooks Robinson bowing out as he ceded his post to DeCinces, and Grich, like Reggie, testing the free agent market in 1976 to depart for Southern California to join the Angels despite Hank Peters's "strong offer" of a five-year contract to stay with the Orioles.[45]

Although Baltimore lost the cachet of lording over the American League and its East Division as it had from 1969 to 1971, through the maneuvering of personnel and the managerial guidance of Earl Weaver, the Orioles contended nearly every year for the entirety of Weaver's first tenure at the Baltimore helm.[46] His teams finished second in 1976, 1977, 1980, and 1982, and reached the World Series in 1979, a testament to the ethic and mindset of a man who was nurtured in the Paul Richards school of the late 1950s and pursued pennants with a diligence that few other franchises could match.

In the summer of 1973, Weaver anticipated that the Orioles could win six pennants in the next ten years.[47] He was not correct in the literal sense, but had the breaks gone the Orioles' way in the years of those second-place finishes, he would have come very close to realizing his prophecy. Not without his foibles, detractors, and enemies, especially a clutch of select umpires, Weaver nonetheless delivered results where they most counted. He was recognized for his accomplishments in 1996 when he was voted into the Baseball Hall of Fame. His best years spanned from the era of Frank Robinson to that of Cal Ripken, Jr., as he was the prime factor in Baltimore's long-term success as the best overall team in the American League from 1965 to 1975.

# 8

## A Tale of Three Cities

The ascent of the Oakland Athletics to the apex of the baseball world in the early 1970s is a most entertaining tale, owing much to the actions of Charles O. Finley, the team's bombastic and often outrageous owner. Rooted in the old Philadelphia Athletics franchise of the great Connie Mack, this charter member of the American League that was born in 1901 had become, a half-century later, subjected to the forces of economic transition that would eventually sweep several other teams to western destinations. The Athletics' trek to the West Coast was a tale of three cities: Philadelphia, an eastern city that by the early 1950s was no longer capable of sustaining two major league teams; Kansas City, a Midwestern way station that hosted a fourteen-year visit by the Mackmen; and Oakland, a western city by the Bay, which the Athletics have now called home for over four decades.

### Point of Departure

Throughout the first half of the twentieth century, the Philadelphia Athletics' topography contained peaks and valleys under its longtime owner-manager, Connie Mack. The five-time World Series champions had enjoyed little glory since 1930 when they captured the Fall Classic and successfully defended the American League pennant in 1931. For most of the twenty-three years following their last AL title, Philadelphia finished at or near the bottom of the league, and by 1954 attendance at Connie Mack Stadium had dropped to a bleak 304,666.

After commencing a transfer of ownership within his own family in the years immediately following the end of World War II, an aged Mack sought to distance himself from the team's operation. There were disputes among Mack's three sons as to whether the Athletics should be sold to a party that was likely to move the team to a new city or to one that would keep it in Philadelphia, but during the 1954 season Chicago business mogul Arnold Johnson emerged as the club's new owner. Approval for Johnson's purchase was given by American League club owners in the full knowledge that the Athletics were to be relocated to Kansas City, a minor league outpost where Johnson had negotiated with civic leaders to refurbish Blues Stadium in preparation for the arrival of major league baseball.

The $3,375,000 paid by a consortium of investors fronted by Johnson was leveraged in such a way that his own out-of-pocket cost was minimal, since his ulterior motives involved not the creation of a well-established team in Kansas City but rather a pair of scenarios working in his favor.[1] The first had Johnson devoting just enough time and spending a minimal amount of money to build the Athletics into a club whose attractive short-term return on investment would serve as a springboard to allow a resale of the team for a handsome gain. Johnson's second scheme would allow him to take advantage of his short-term lease in Kansas City by invoking an attendance-based escape clause that would enable him to leave the Midwest for brighter prospects presumably somewhere in California. But when Johnson unexpectedly passed away in early 1960 at the age of 53, his death opened the door for new ownership of the team.

During Johnson's years of control over the Athletics, the club showed few signs of escaping the American League's second division, placing no better than sixth in its first season in its new venue. Consistently poor performance on the field overshadowed the glimmer of hope raised in 1958 when the Athletics finished a respectable 73–81 and hinted at being a competitive team. Also in the Johnson era, Kansas City acquired the reputation of being a quasi–farm team of the New York Yankees, who profited immensely from the trades that delivered Roger Maris, Clete Boyer, and other players so integral to the perpetuation of the Bronx Bombers' dynasty in the late 1950s and early 1960s. Although author John E. Peterson has carefully analyzed the trades executed between Kansas City and the Yankees and concluded that the Athletics actually benefited from the transactions more than they are given credit for, the club gained little traction in the AL standings and averaged just 62 wins per year from 1955 through 1960, the season in which the Athletics ownership was in limbo following Johnson's death.[2] Yet to be determined was whether control of the team would remain with the owner's widow, Carmen Johnson, or another member of the Athletics' limited partnership, or if the team would be sold to an outside interest.

## Charlie Finley Comes to Town

The lone bright spot of the 1960 season was Kansas City's hosting of that year's first All-Star Game, as the forlorn Athletics flirted with the hundred-loss mark and landed in the AL basement with a 58–96 record. Ownership of the club became a struggle between two widows, Carmen Johnson, who inherited controlling interest of 52 percent of the club from her late husband, and Margaret McGillicuddy, Roy Mack's widow who now owned the biggest portion of minority stock at 20 percent.[3] Ultimately, the team was put up for sale in the summer of 1960 by the executors of Arnold Johnson's estate with the wish to have the Athletics remain in Kansas City, when two suitors were drawn to the bargaining table. The first was a local syndicate, led by attorney Byron Spencer, and the second a group based in St. Louis, but the ultimate victor who emerged with the title was an insurance broker from Chicago whose earlier failed attempts to purchase the Athletics, Tigers, and White Sox only whetted his appetite for spending whatever he deemed necessary to become the owner of a major league franchise.

A native Alabaman, Charles Oscar Finley had made his financial fortune in a post–World War II insurance business that sold group insurance to physicians. His own life nearly lost to the affects of pneumonic tuberculosis, Finley persevered with his sales career, exploited the niche market he had discovered, and by the mid–1950s had attained the wealth of a multimillionaire. In 1954 he failed in his attempt to purchase the Athletics in a collaborative effort with drugstore entrepreneur Harry Sylk. Two years later, Finley tried to buy the Tigers, and then White Sox in 1958, all in vain. By late 1960, with an American League expansion franchise available in Los Angeles, Finley was determined not to be denied again. Crisscrossing the country by airplane to cobble a consortium together, Finley came a cropper while endeavoring to impress AL moguls that he was ready to lead a pioneering trail into Southern California. But when the Athletics club became available once more, the indefatigable Finley at last broke through with a winning bid of nearly $2 million to secure the team's ownership. Thus, barely two weeks had elapsed in December 1960 from the time Finley lost out in his effort to acquire the Los Angeles franchise until he triumphed in his bid to purchase control of the Athletics from Arnold Johnson's estate.

However, as Finley was entering the fray in Kansas City, trepidation was quickly building among Kansas City residents who feared that he would promptly begin shopping for a new venue for the Athletics if he were to succeed in his bid for the team. Shifting to a different location, such as Calvin Griffith's maneuvering from Washington to Minneapolis, opened the possibility of playing in a new or recently built stadium, which was an obvious lure to any club owner. The expansion Angels would be using old Wrigley Field in Los Angeles but only for 1961, thereafter becoming co-tenants with the Dodgers in their sleek, new Dodger Stadium. But Finley adamantly rejected accusations of having a wandering eye in search of a better deal, stating in mid–December, "Moving the Athletics from Kansas City is the farthest thing from my mind. My only interest is putting a winning baseball club in Kansas City … I am not in this for a quick buck."[4]

Understandably skeptical after hearing the rumors of a possible transfer, the sports editor of the *Kansas City Times* cautioned that Finley "will need to furnish some proof he is not in this venture for speculative reasons."[5] To that end, Finley did exhibit sincere intentions to build a solid organization. During his most recent failure to acquire the AL's Los Angeles franchise, Finley had courted the deposed Yankees tandem of general manager George Weiss and field manager Casey Stengel, both of whom had been jettisoned by New York's ownership following the Yankees' loss to Pittsburgh in the 1960 World Series. Finley's overtures fell flat here, but he had demonstrated his willingness to hire the general manager who had been integral to the most dominant baseball team ever.

Finley's quest for a baseball team having been attained, a major flaw in Finley's personality was about to come to the fore quickly. Possessed of a meddlesome nature and a penchant to micromanage his organization, Finley's approach to running the Athletics was diametrically opposed to that of Baltimore's Jerry Hoffberger, who preferred to let his front office staff handle the Orioles baseball operations. Strong commitment by ownership toward the viability of a business is a most valuable asset to any enterprise, but from the onset of Finley's tenure as the head of the Athletics, he seldom failed to inject a cult of personality into his dealings. Finley could be praised for his actions one minute and reviled the next, a man who took credit for successes but quickly looked for scapegoats when things went awry. His foray into baseball ownership could be best described as an egocentric enterprise.

To be sure, benefits could reaped by Finley's employees, many of whom received instant rewards for a job well done, although Finley made certain that everyone knew that he was the wellspring of that generosity. But beneath Finley's bombast ran an ugly undercurrent of vindictiveness and avarice that hurt and insulted many who served him, as Finley at times gave an impression as baseball's version of Lionel Barrymore's Henry Potter. Unquestionably Finley contributed mightily to the success of the Athletics, yet by the end of 1976 the storied championship teams he had built evolved into the very cornerstones of the Pyrrhic victory he himself had engineered.

## Finley Takes Control

In early January 1961 Finley signed veteran general manager Frank Lane to run the Athletics baseball operations. Lane's forte was aggressive pursuit of new talent via player trades in order to revitalize flagging teams, which he had done previously for the Chicago White Sox, the Cleveland Indians, and the St. Louis Cardinals. Finley was confident that when Lane applied his methodology in Kansas City, a rebuilt and winning club was sure to follow. Assessing the state of his latest club, Lane declared the Athletics to "[look] like champions compared to the White Sox I took over in 1948," as the first media guide of the Finley regime informed readers that Lane had been "credited with getting [the White Sox] out of the second division."[6]

Furthering his commitment to the stability of the Athletics, Finley constantly pledged to infuse the franchise with the cash necessary to upgrade Municipal Stadium, improve the minor league system, and put a halt to the incessant trades with the New York Yankees that appeared at the same time to milk the team of the best players Kansas City had nurtured and fortify the Yankees at the height of their power in the late 1950s.[7] Oaths of fidelity notwithstanding, all this toil could not overcome the fact that the Athletics simply were not close to mounting any sort of a challenge to gain substantial ground in the American League standings. As Lane endeavored to retool the club, his judgment was called into question by Finley, and the bickering that began early in the season finally prompted Finley to fire Lane in mid–August. The riot of colors in which Municipal Stadium was decorated at Finley's behest — *Sports Illustrated* reported that seats and a variety of stadium structures had been painted yellow, turquoise, orange, and pink — could not gloss over the drab performance of the team on the field, as Kansas City fans' "baseball fare ... [had] been reduced to starvation rations."[8]

In fact, while Lane was maneuvering player personnel, Finley was intent on employing several modes of gimmickry to lure fans to Athletics games despite his assertions that attendance — as well as the

Bombastic and irascible, Charles O. Finley in his twenty-year reign as owner of the Athletics rarely lacked for excitement or controversy.

possible invoking of an escape clause in his stadium lease should the turnstile count fall below 850,000—was not of the owner's concern. Drawing inspiration from some of Bill Veeck's contrivances, Finley appropriated for his own purposes stadium trappings such as a mechanical ball lift near home plate that supplied baseballs to the umpire and a "Fan-A-Gram" message board, as well as implementing more practical measures like rest room improvements and the creation of picnic areas. A menagerie holding monkeys and sheep on the ballpark grounds was augmented by the later introduction of a new team mascot, a Missouri mule dubbed "Charlie O," that by some accounts was better cared for than some of Finley's players and employees.

From the inception of the Finley regime, a cloud of suspicion seemed to hover over the franchise that indicated the Athletics were destined to be short-term residents in Kansas City. Almost immediately upon his dismissal, former general manager Lane exacted a bit of revenge on his erstwhile employer by confirming that Finley was actively browsing for a new location for his team. Just eight months after Finley's purchase of the Athletics, a lead story in the *Kansas City Star* reported that Dallas, Texas, was looked upon as a potential new venue for the club, with Lane claiming that such a transfer "has been in Finley's mind for some time."[9] Finley contradicted himself by his own actions, on the one hand playing the role of huckster to draw fans to the Athletics' home games while also courting other cities as sites for his team. While Finley staged a tacky bus burning to prove that the shuttling of Athletics players—ostensibly via motor coach—to the Yankees was finished and also burned an alleged copy of his stadium lease to show his lack of regard for its escape clause, he remained smitten with the notion that he could reap better profits in another city.

In addition to Dallas, Finley investigated transferring to San Francisco in 1963 but was blocked by the Giants' refusal to allow the Athletics to become co-tenants at Candlestick Park. The city of Milwaukee offered a possible home, with Finley deeming his team to be a good replacement for a Braves team that was in a legal battle to depart for Atlanta. Finley's search for a new home then moved apace at the close of that year, when the city of Oakland first drew attention as a feasible venue for the Athletics because the American League desired a West Coast companion club for the Los Angeles Angels. In early January 1964, Finley believed that he had succeeded in brokering a deal to shift to Louisville, Kentucky, an attempt that was quashed by AL owners so offended by Finley's actions—he had contracted to move without their approval—that they threatened to expel him from the league. When his Louisville endeavor failed, Finley barely broke stride by consummating a deal with Oakland officials three weeks later to play in Youell Field for 1964 and 1965 pending the completion of the Oakland–Alameda County Coliseum, then under construction. Meantime, Finley's fellow owners had vetted a new, four-year lease proposal that would keep the Athletics in Kansas City through 1967; finding its terms to *their* satisfaction, the other owners issued an ultimatum to Finley: sign the lease or face expulsion from the American League.

Under duress, Finley endorsed the contract but not without recognizing that the brethren of owners coerced his signature in order to force him to operate his club under terms he thought so unfavorable that he would sell the team. "They tarred and feathered me," whined Finley. "It's one of the greatest injustices in baseball history."[10] With the wound of this bullying fresh in his mind, Finley sought legal redress but was denied by the courts late in 1964.

Finley viewed green pastures everywhere but in Kansas City. As he alienated municipal and baseball officials over his proposed transfers and the stadium lease, Finley exacerbated his problems by expecting fans to support a product on the field that remained poor by any standard. Animal attractions and a portfolio of zany promotions such as cow-milking contests increasingly failed to hold the audience that Finley needed to maintain a respectable revenue stream. Paying customers grew distrustful of an owner whose top priority was finding a new city to which he could relocate the club, despite the knowledge that the Athletics would remain in Kansas City for at least another four seasons. After applying his signature to the lease in early 1964, Finley saw the team flounder through consecutive 100-loss seasons as attendance plummeted to a Kansas City record low of 528,344 in 1965.

A bad baseball club whose owner was repulsed by his fellow owners and the team's fans begat an internecine and irreparable relationship. Followers of the Athletics may have loved their players but had lost all stomach for the self-absorbed Finley, who was also offended when fans did not respond positively to innovations that he thought they would — or should — like. The novelty of stunts such as using a hay wagon to bring in a pitcher or Farmer's Night promotions — featuring prizes such as ducks, hogs, rabbits, riding mowers, tractors, and even a distant cousin of Charlie O, "one genuine Missouri mule" — may have catered to those with short attention spans but did little to increase the totals of the win column or move the Athletics out of the second division, as the stunts certainly lacked staying power at the box office.[11]

Regarding winning games, which was the supposed mission of the team, Finley could not resist the impulse to dispense advice to his field personnel on how to play the game. If his team was performing poorly, Finley reasoned that it could do no worse by implementing changes that he himself had recommended. The owner briefly took over as minor league director in 1961, meddled in decisions affecting players to be called up from or sent to the minor leagues, forced managers to move pitchers in and out of the starting rotation, demanded audiences with his managers at any hour of the day, and eroded the dignity of his players in 1963 by cladding them in gaudy gold-green-and-white uniforms. Finley incurred the wrath of umpires when he installed a clock, visible to the fans, that was meant to remind the arbiters of the often-ignored rule that gave the pitcher 20 seconds to make his delivery. No phase of the game escaped Finley's purview, much to the chagrin of his employees, players, and many others with whom he dealt. While he became noted for his proclivity to hand out spot awards — such as the presentation of three hundred silver dollars to Rocky Colavito to commemorate his 300th career home run — the tight-fisted Finley was a skilled titan at the bargaining table who overwhelmed his players when it came to contract and salary negotiations.[12]

The misery of the last-place finishes was briefly abated in 1966 when Alvin Dark was named manager. After a horrible 3–14 start, the soft-spoken, religious Dark righted the team and brought the Athletics to a seventh-place finish ahead of Washington, Boston, and, having bottomed-out completely, the Yankees. The following season brought a relapse of gloom with a return of the Athletics to the AL basement. By this time, Finley had scant return on his investment, but in 1965 the franchise turned a corner, even if ever so slowly, when he decided to take on the responsibilities of general manager, thus assuming dual roles in the fashion of Minnesota's Calvin Griffith. That Finley lacked a baseball lineage similar to Griffith's mattered not at all to him, as Finley was willing to employ his tireless work ethic of "sweat plus sacrifice equals success" to achieve his ends.[13] The addition of general manager to Finley's workload had no immediate impact on the fate of the club, but the pendulum of fortune began to swing in a positive direction at the same time Finley realized a goal which he had sought for over six, long years: permission to move the Athletics out of Kansas City.

The year 1967 devolved into another wretched season that could not even be enhanced by Finley's introduction of sartorially radical white baseball spikes made from albino kangaroo pelts, gold helmets to adorn the batters when they stepped to the plate, and green-and-gold stockings "designed by an Army captain now serving in Korea."[14] The newest gear did nothing to stem the tide of 99 losses the team would suffer. On September 27, the Athletics played their final home contests — in the role of spoilers, their doubleheader sweep of the White Sox all but dashed Chicago's pennant hopes — before a crowd 5,325. The following day, the *Kansas City Star* reported that a good portion of the fans "finally accepted that the Kansas City Athletics were playing their last game as Kansas City Athletics."[15] During 1967, Finley had shopped his team to Seattle, a city whose voters were expected to approve construction of a domed stadium; New Orleans, also soon to commence work on what became the Superdome; and Milwaukee, whose Braves had fled for Atlanta after the 1965 season. But Finley opted for northern California as the new domicile for the Athletics, since, in his view, four advantages would instantly accrue to the franchise as a result of the move. The Athletics would be tenants in the newly-built Oakland–Alameda County Coliseum, the climate in the eastern end of the Bay Area was "second to none," the rapid population growth of the region foretold of a broad fan base of roughly six million people ready to be tapped, and "the enthusiasm for sports in the area is overwhelming."[16]

Shortly after the close of that frenzied season, the American League granted Finley the freedom to relocate to Oakland while simultaneously promising that Kansas City would be awarded an expansion franchise in 1969. High-level politicians, such as city mayor Ilus Davis and Missouri senator Stuart Symington, had threatened to stop the move and open an inquiry into baseball's anti-trust exemption, but the assurance of a new replacement team placated jilted officials and fans.[17] For Finley's part, much to his delight, he visited Oakland shortly after the transfer was sanctioned and was greeted by an adoring throng as "Oakland's No. 1 Citizen," all this coming amid rumors that either former Twins' skipper Sam Mele or possibly Billy Martin would be named the next Athletics manager.[18]

The Athletics' departure from Kansas City ended what author John E. Peterson called "a bad marriage," but the move west was bittersweet for those left behind.[19] "[The] people of Kansas City were not thrilled with losing a ball club," noted one player, "but they were thrilled to see Charlie leaving."[20] Hanged in effigy by disaffected Kansas City followers upon his departure from the Midwest, Finley had yet to wear out his welcome on the West Coast. Just days after the move to Oakland was announced, he acted quickly to endear himself to new fans by signing former Yankees great Joe DiMaggio as an executive for the Oakland front office. One player later recalled that Joltin' Joe, who was born in nearby Martinez, California, and now lived less than thirty minutes from the Coliseum, cast an unequivocal and inspiring aura over the Oakland franchise.[21] More than just a Hall of Famer in the front office was needed to help the Athletics escape from the American League cellar, but as the team settled into its new home, positive changes soon appeared on the horizon of Oakland's brightening future.

## *Planting the Seeds*

As is the case with the formation of any contending club, years may pass before attempts to improve a moribund team produce tangible results, and the Athletics' journey to the prosperity they enjoyed in the early 1970s was representative of such undertakings. Throughout their later years in Kansas City, Charlie Finley and his group of scouts discovered, drafted, and signed prospects who formed the nucleus of what became a team that would capture three consecutive World Series. Although Finley's overarching demeanor captured most of the attention directed at the team, a growing stream of solid players slowly sprouted from the farm system by the time the Athletics fled Kansas City. A group of select bonus players, such as pitchers Lew Krausse and Jim Nash, accompanied the Athletics to Oakland but did not fulfill the promise that justified their substantial payouts.[22] Other players around Finley's diamond, however, endured and contributed greatly toward future Oakland contenders.

In 1963, Finley earmarked a $65,000 bonus for a strapping catcher named Dave Duncan, a high school star from California who struggled in his early minor league career but suddenly developed a power stroke in 1966 when he hit 46 home runs for Modesto and won Most Valuable Player honors in the Class A California League. The right-handed-hitting backstop still needed further time on the Athletic farm through 1968 but finally reached the major leagues in earnest in 1969.

Two of the longest-serving players under Finley formed the core of the Athletics infield. Dick Green, whose chunky physique facilitated his tendency to swing for the fences, debuted in 1963 and in his twelve years with the team became perhaps one of the finest fielders at second base never to win a Gold Glove. His shortstop partner, Bert Campaneris, joined Green the following year and by 1965 the native of Cuba had supplanted team captain Wayne Causey as the club's shortstop. Before settling in at short, Campaneris demonstrated his versatility not only with some playing time in left field but also on the occasion of his appearance at every position during a game in September 1965. Since speed was Campy's biggest asset, he combined this gift with an ability to reach base to become the vital catalyst at the top of the batting order. In his first full year at the major league level, Campaneris captured the stolen base crown from perennial league leader Luis Aparicio, topping the AL in five of the next seven years. Although Campaneris was labeled a "whiz" at shortstop by one manager, that same skipper also credited Green with helping Campaneris hone his defensive play.[23]

Coming to the Athletics in 1964 was outfield prospect Joe Rudi, whom the Athletics traded to Cleveland in early 1965 in a swap "designed to protect Rudi and ... an Indian farmhand from the first-year bonus draft rules then in effect."[24] This bit of bureaucratic legerdemain later returned a fine dividend when Rudi was sent back to Kansas City after the 1965 season to resume his employment with Finley. A tall, lean right-handed batter with some power, Rudi also played at first and third base but would not become a fixture on the Athletics roster until after the team moved to Oakland.

Dominant pitching was to become a trademark of the great Athletic teams, and the signing of two Southern high school stars provided two enduring right-handers for the rotation. A prospect from Georgia, Johnny Lee "Blue Moon" Odom, posted a superb 42–2 record for his Macon high school and upon his graduation in 1964 was given a $75,000 bonus by Finley, who had personally recruited Odom. Although Odom did little to distinguish himself while the Athletics remained in Kansas City and spent time perfecting his craft in the minor leagues, he flourished after the club's move to Oakland and was twice named an All-Star, in 1968 and 1969.

Taking his own place among the Kansas City starters in 1965 was a North Carolina native whose rural upbringing, relaxed persona, and a penchant for hijinks served him very well during his years under Charlie Finley. James Augustus Hunter excelled in his high school career in Hertford, North Carolina, and attracted the attention of many scouts until an untimely mishap — his brother's shotgun accidentally discharged dozens of buckshot pellets into Hunter's right foot as they returned from a hunting venture — imperiled his athletic aspirations. Kansas City birddog Clyde Kluttz was one of the few not scared away by the injury, and when Hunter stoically completed his senior year, during which he pitched a perfect game and a no-hitter, he solidified his reputation as a formidable competitor. When Finley personally visited Hunter and saw the extent of the wound, the owner was aghast but nonetheless "fell in love with him" and arranged for Hunter to be treated at the Mayo Clinic after meeting his demand for the same $75,000 that Odom had received.[25] Barely one month past his 19th birthday, Hunter began his career in Kansas City with the moniker of "Catfish" bestowed on him by Finley, who insisted that his pitcher have some sort of nickname.[26] After minimal time in the Florida Instructional League in late 1964, Hunter joined the Athletics in 1965 without having spent any time in the minor leagues.

Several notable hurlers who began as starters early in their Athletics career went on to be valuable in relief roles. One of the few southpaws to be developed by the Kansas City farm system was Paul Lindblad, a gifted athlete whose batting ability prompted his manager to use him occasionally as a pinch-hitter. A spot starter in his early years with the Athletics, Lindblad was used almost exclusively as a reliever during his extended career in Oakland. Yet to make his debut in an Athletics uniform at the time of the club's transfer was a lanky Ohioan signed in 1965 out of Chaffey Junior College in California. Six-foot, four-inch Rollie Fingers impressed the Kansas City front office with an earned-run average that was never above 3.00 and a fine ratio of hits allowed to innings pitched, all of which was enhanced by his recovery from several facial fractures he sustained when hit by a line drive during a minor league game in 1967. Signed for about $20,000, Fingers started and worked in relief, with the latter role ultimately becoming his forte as he evolved into the ace of the Athletics bullpen.

The above players came to Kansas City prior to the inaugural amateur draft in June 1965, when the Athletics scouts became diligent in vetting the prospects who would be available on draft day. Several vital cornerstones of the future championship Athletics clubs were drafted prior to the team's move to Oakland, and maturation in the farm system prepared the best of those players for the rewards that were to follow. Although outfielder Rick Monday, whose premier selection was covered in Chapter 3, did not play for any of Oakland's World Series teams, his market value as a talented player facilitated a later trade to the Cubs which delivered left-handed starter Ken Holtzman to the Athletics.

Supplementing the collection of Athletics already in Finley's fold were several other notable draftees of 1965. Monday's fellow teammate at Arizona State, third baseman Sal Bando, was picked by Kansas City five rounds after Monday. Talented, intelligent, and durable, Bando was quick to earn the respect of so many teammates on the various levels at which he played that he was a natural to someday become the captain of the Athletics. The last 1965 draftee to eventually make a huge impact on the team's fortunes was Fury Gene Tenace, a shortstop in high school who was fated to play every position except shortstop during his major league career.

When the 1965 Athletics repeated their dismal last-place finish of the prior season, they were again entitled to be the first American League team to pick in the 1966 draft. Possessing the second overall choice — the Mets had the first selection and chose Steve Chilcott — Kansas City opted for yet another Arizona State product, who, like Rick Monday, was a left-handed-hitting outfielder. A standout high school running back from Wyncote, Pennsylvania, Reggie Jackson developed into a solid all-around baseball player at ASU who was especially noted for his powerhitting. With Athletics farm director Eddie Robinson, scouting director Ray Swallow, and scout Bob Zuk in fervid pursuit of Jackson during the 1966

The first pick of the inaugural amateur draft in 1965, Rick Monday became an All-Star outfielder but missed out on Oakland's best years when he was later traded to the Cubs for Ken Holtzman.

collegiate season, Jackson displayed the potential to step into the Kansas City lineup with minimal time in the minor leagues. After the amateur draft, Finley held forth in the bargaining sessions to bring Jackson to terms. Although the youngster landed short of his goal of signing for $100,000 — the amount that Monday had received — Finley secured Jackson's services for $84,000 plus a new car.[27]

As the Athletics lumbered through the summer of 1967, Swallow trained his sights on another two-sport star, this one from Louisiana, who, in addition to dreaming of throwing fastballs past big league sluggers also envisioned himself as a future quarterback for his favorite football team, the Baltimore Colts. Torn by the decision of which sport to pursue, southpaw Vida Blue was selected by the Athletics in the regular phase of the June amateur draft and passed on the chance to play football at the University of Houston. Because Blue's father had recently passed away, Vida's mother Sallie, fearing for her son's safety on the gridiron as well as being wary about the "prevailing prejudice against black quarterbacks," implored him to accept Finley's "fat bonus offer" of $25,000 that would help to restore the financial health of their relatively poor household.[28]

A clutch of farmhands, the most prominent of which were Duncan, Jackson, Rudi, and Fingers, vaulted the Double-A franchise in Birmingham, Alabama, to the Southern League pennant in 1967. This was a team appropriately cited by baseball maven Bill James as one of the best minor league clubs of the 1960s, as the success enjoyed by this group foreshadowed the championships they would celebrate at the big league level.[29] Jackson recalled the peril of a black athlete playing in the Deep South at that time, yet while he was working his way through the Kansas City minor league system, he and his future Oakland mates "had no way of knowing ... this was the start of something that would be so big in the early '70s."[30]

By claiming during the summer of 1965 that "[I] can see my team growing into something good," Finley over-indulged his optimism with a roster so devoid of promise at that time.[31] Finley viewed players such as Ken Harrelson and Rene Lachemann as keys to lifting the Athletics out of the American League basement, but the maturing process that would eventually bring the Mondays, Bandos, and Jacksons to the big league lineup had barely begun. By 1967, however, the farm system had been stocked and more talent was being assembled as the team shifted to California, as readers of the first Oakland Athletics yearbook were told, "The A's Farm System is one of the most proficient and productive in the Major Leagues today."[32] Eddie Robinson had been replaced by Art Parrack as the farm director by the time the Athletics moved west, but Ray Swallow retained his position as scouting director. They, along with chief scout Tom Ferrick and his staff of birddogs, were lauded by the team publication for their "hard and diligent efforts ... not to mention the considerable amount of time and money put in by Owner Charles O. Finley."[33] That diligence practiced by the Athletics unearthed another pair of players who, following short stints in Oakland, were sent to other organizations where they forged lengthy, eventful careers. George Hendrick was the first selection in the January 1968 draft and broke in briefly with the Athletics in 1972, while Manny Trillo, drafted from the Philadelphia Phillies minor league system in late 1969, was developed by the Athletics farm system before being traded to the Chicago Cubs after the 1974 season.

The production of the Athletics minor league system was as vital to Oakland's success as it was to the Baltimore Orioles and Minnesota Twins. Through the negotiation of some shrewd trades, the Orioles were able to coalesce their dynasty, and the Athletics also found it necessary to explore the marketplace to acquire players that filled critical voids on the bench and on the pitching staff. Nevertheless, the bedrock of Oakland's foundation consisted of men scouted and signed by the Athletics. By the dawn of the 1970s, Duncan, Bando, Campaneris, Green, Rudi, Jackson, Hunter, Odom, Fingers, and their supporting cast were nearly ready to cross the fine line between contender and champion.

## An Ugly Ending

In the wake of the Kansas City Athletics' departure to Oakland, Finley left behind hard feelings from his feud with municipal officials over protracted stadium lease issues, the controversy of his unending quest to find a new home for his club, and the ill will of his cult of personality.

Amid this putrid atmosphere was a paternity suit that nagged at Bert Campaneris during the closing phase of the Athletics' time in the Midwest and the furor stemming from an incident on an airplane flight in early August 1967 that raised the hackles of owner and players. Returning to Kansas City from an eastern road trip, several players allegedly took advantage of the flight attendants' generous offering of alcoholic beverages and were said to have become intoxicated and unruly. But there were few passengers on the plane other than the team, so the number of witnesses was scant and apparently not offended by — or aware of — any of the players' antics. At the time, little was made of the episode, so no action was taken as the affair appeared to have amounted to nothing more than a benign display of poor judgment and bad behavior.

Two weeks passed with no fallout evident, when suddenly Finley demanded that manager Alvin Dark fine and suspend pitcher Lew Krausse, supposedly the most culpable of the miscreants, and reliever Jack Aker, who was the team representative for the players' union. Players quickly denied that any indecent actions had occurred on the flight, and they instigated a palace revolt against Finley upon the release of a statement they drafted that denounced Finley's disciplinary measures. Dark, who refused to support Finley, was fired with forty games left on the schedule, and first baseman Ken Harrelson, formerly viewed by Finley as a hope for the Athletics' future, was summarily given his release after refusing to retract his own statement in which he publicly castigated the owner for making "a fool of himself, a scapegoat of Krausse, alleged drunks out of us all, and an apparently ineffectual manager out of Dark."[34]

Luke Appling was given the unenviable job of interim manager — his 10–30 record ensured his dismissal after the season, too — and the sordid drinking incident lingered until the end of the season as Finley sought to mete out punishment while at once privately threatening to expose dalliances and misdeeds in some of his players' personal lives.[35] When the players took their complaint of Finley's intimidation to the Major League Baseball Players Association, union director Marvin Miller in turn filed a grievance with the National Labor Relations Board. The conflict with "Hurricane Charlie," as Miller referred to Finley, was resolved without federal intervention.[36]

As owner, Finley had a right to expect professional conduct at all times from everyone in his organization, but with so many players in their early and mid-twenties still possessed of youthful exuberance, their judgment could have been easily clouded by the use of alcohol. Yet in an era when men of exactly that age were aware of the rebellious attitudes expressed with increasing volume by those protesting the Vietnam War, there can be little wonder that players who felt they had been wrongly accused would revolt against *their* establishment, in this case, Charlie Finley. The same young prospects — Bando, Jackson, Duncan, Hunter, et al — who held the keys to the Athletics' success on the diamond became galvanized by this confrontation with Finley and carried with them a grudge against the owner's demeaning subjugation. As history showed by the middle of the 1970s, an epic flight of many of these same players took place with the advent of true free agency.

## A New Beginning by the Bay

As the rancor of the final season in Kansas City grew more distant in Finley's rearview mirror, the promise of the Athletics' new beginning in Oakland became a much anticipated event. To better advertise the crop of budding stars on the Athletics roster, the banal, understated thumbnail sketches of the players which appeared in the Kansas City media guides — date and place of birth, height, weight, bats/throws, and the signing scout (or means of acquisition) had been all the information provided — now blossomed into short biographies that included educational background, marital status, career highlights, and in some cases, ethnicity, such as Dick Green's Norwegian-Dutch heritage and Mike Hershberger's French-Polish-German roots. Curiously omitted from these vignettes, *The Sporting News* noted, was the traditional bottom line summing up the total big league statistics for each player. "Charlie the censor" had been fingered as the culprit whose "selective deletions" kept Oakland fans in the dark about how little his players had accomplished in their careers, at least to that point.[37]

The team's media guide enthused over the Athletics' new ballpark, the Oakland–Alameda County Coliseum, which featured "individual plastic contoured seats of the utmost in comfort for the fans, … the World's most educated and advanced scoreboard, a Charles O. Finley innovation," and the stadium's open, circular, cantilevered tiers that meant the facility was "without a bad seat in the 'house.'"[38] Like its recent predecessors Shea Stadium, Houston Astrodome, Atlanta–Fulton County Stadium, and Busch Stadium in St. Louis, the Oakland Coliseum was the latest in a series of circular, multi-purpose stadiums that catered to baseball and football. The stadium configuration, which dictated that the field be adequately wide to enable the gridiron to be laid out across the infield from third base to first base rather than from home plate toward center field, guaranteed a gigantic amount of foul territory that favored all pitchers.

Receiving a special citation in the media guide were the men charged with bringing so many Athletics into their minor league system as well as the special instructors who would endeavor to develop raw, young talent into major-league-quality players. Bill Posedel, a roving minor league pitching instructor, was named pitching coach in Oakland, joining fellow coaches John McNamara and Sherm Lollar in support of new manager Bob Kennedy. Mickey Vernon and Gus Niarhos complemented management of a farm system which the Athletics touted as one of the best in baseball. Adding an air of dignity — even royalty — to the mix was Joe DiMaggio. Sal Bando later observed that he very much appreciated the diligence employed by the coaching staff to groom and shepherd the prospects through the lower ranks of the organization, and he claimed that more than a superficial public relations ploy was behind the hiring of DiMaggio, whose presence as club vice president added luster to the Athletics executive branch and whose instruction as coach was respected and valued by many players.[39] Crediting DiMaggio with inculcating the finer points of playing defense, Joe Rudi recalled the Yankee Hall of Famer "hitting fly ball after fly ball directly over my head" to teach the outfielder how to react and move when the ball came off the bat.[40] According to Catfish Hunter, members of the pitching staff were handled "perfectly" by Posedel, who endeared himself to his pitchers by letting them learn from their mistakes and "offer[ing] suggestions on mechanics, not lectures" when a hurler suffered a bad outing.[41]

For all the on-the-job training still taking place for many on the Oakland roster during the team's initial transition period of the late 1960s, what took place on the field was a harbinger of noteworthy proportions. During 1968's famous dearth of offensive production known as "the year of the pitcher," DiMaggio's tutelage nonetheless sparked a rise in the Athletics' team batting average from .233 in 1967 to a league-best .240 as several Oakland players found their names at or near the top of statistical leaders in several categories. Again leading the American League in stolen bases with 62, Campaneris also topped the circuit with 177 base hits, Monday and Jackson were fourth in on-base percentage (.371) and home runs (29), respectively, and Danny Cater, acquired in 1966 from the White Sox, trailed only Carl Yastrzemski in the batting race with a .290 average. Establishing himself in right field was Jackson, while Bando, tepid at the plate with just nine homers and a .251 average, quickly established the durability that became his trademark by playing in every game during his first full year in the majors. On the mound, Hunter flashed the greatness still to come in his career when he pitched a perfect game in May against the Twins and finished with 13 wins, a victory total equaled by Jim Nash, while Blue Moon Odom led the staff with 16 victories.

Leaping from the AL basement to sixth place with an astounding 82–80 record, Oakland had reached third place as late as the end of June but faltered thereafter. However, the twenty additional wins over their 1967 total that fueled the players' *esprit de corps* failed to lure fans into those comfortable seats at the Coliseum, as the Athletics actually played before more fans on the road (931,967) than they did at home (837,466). Yet the die of a new era in Athletics' history had been cast, as the products of the old Kansas City farm system prompted teams across the American League to take notice of the development of these young men, nearly all of whom were in their mid-twenties and were later described by Monday as players who "didn't get their baptism in the minor leagues, they got it in the major leagues."[42] It can be left only to speculation as to the extent to which Harrelson may have helped Oakland's cause had he not been so irrationally discharged by Finley in the summer of 1967. Leading the AL in RBIs with 109 and finishing third with 35 home runs for Boston, Harrelson and his .275 average would have been most welcome had he remained an Athletic.

Since a bright future appeared close at hand, the split of the American League into two divisions brought a heightened anticipation to Oakland. The Twins, who had finished three games behind the Athletics in 1968, also looked to rebound in an AL West division into which was placed the two new expansion teams, the Kansas City Royals and the Seattle Pilots. In the final 1968 AL standings, Oakland and Minnesota were followed by California and Chicago, so even if the holdover franchises performed in 1969 at a level similar to that of the season just ended, the Athletics had a very good chance to compete for their first division title.

## Boggling the Mind

Manager Bob Kennedy had accomplished a minor miracle by leading Oakland to the middle of the American League pack, as he had earned the distinction of being the first winning manager in the employ of Charlie Finley. But job security is a tenuous asset, and Finley proved this in a most stunning way

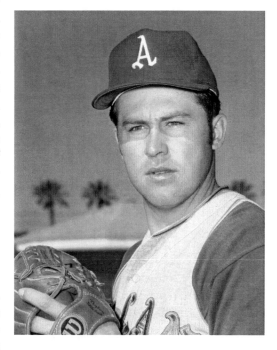

A young Catfish Hunter showed the greatness that lie ahead for him when he pitched a perfect game against the Twins in May 1968.

when he rewarded Kennedy for the team's illustrious performance in 1968 by firing him. Contemporaneous accounts in the media reported that "Finley was not in agreement with moves Kennedy made on the field," as the startling news of Kennedy's removal came after Finley had refused to even speak with his manager for the last two months of the season.[43] With such a spectacular improvement in Oakland's record, it is difficult to imagine what discord Finley perceived, but *The Sporting News* shrugged, "The ways of Finley are strange indeed and boggle the mind."[44] Trying to make sense of the affair, which was another in a series of bewildering incidents between the owner and the players and managers at his command, became an exercise in futility.

Next in the manager's hot seat was Hank Bauer, late of the Baltimore Orioles and the man who had been Charlie Finley's first manager in Kansas City during 1961 and 1962. Reunited with former Yankee teammate DiMaggio, Bauer exuded optimism in the Athletics' ability to capture a divisional title in the realigned AL, as the club noted that Bauer "has the tools at hand to make and back up such a statement."[45] Stiff doses of discipline that Bauer learned in the Marine Corps were to be doled out to the young upstarts. Two other bright spots could be seen on Oakland's horizon, Rollie Fingers and Vida Blue, both of whom were coming off fine seasons in the farm system.

As a minor leaguer, Fingers was a member of the starting rotation, but, according to Hunter, he was discomfited by the time off between starts, as Fingers's "lack of stamina" translated into outings that were not on a par with those expected of a starter.[46] Posedel realized that channeling Fingers's energy and edginess into the role of reliever would maximize the right-hander's potential. Blue, meantime, had stifled batters in the Midwest League by leading that circuit in strikeouts and was methodically working his way up the farm system ladder.

Bauer was also to face an interesting challenge in 1969, one which pitted him against the Twins' rookie manager — and another former Yankee teammate of Bauer's — Billy Martin. Compared to the Athletics, the Twins were a seasoned club featuring many veterans who had been through pennant races and knew well the rigors of performing at a championship level. But pressure was nonetheless on Bauer to bring home a pennant because, as one preseason forecast opined, "The Twins and the Athletics are the only decent teams in the division."[47]

In a shrewd move that was a seminal event in Oakland's history, Bauer selected Bando as the team captain at the end of May, claiming that the third baseman had been already serving unofficially in that capacity. Leading by his own fine example on the field at various levels of competition — he was captain of his high school basketball and football squads and was about to become captain of the Arizona State baseball team when he was drafted by Kansas City in 1965 — Bando's durability, work ethic, and calm demeanor in the face of strife earned him the trust and respect of his manager and fellow players. "I wasn't afraid to communicate with other players or with my manager," Bando said after his career had ended, as this bulwark of confidence enabled him to act as a conduit to present suggestions to the manager, whoever he may have been at the time.[48] Bando devoted time and energy to dispense advice to teammates who counseled him, extended praise for deeds well done, and offered a helping hand to those who were struggling. Commanding such a level of respect spoke volumes about the maturity of Bando, who, at the age of 25 and in only his second full year in the major leagues, accepted the honor of the team captaincy and its attendant responsibility with a commitment to excellence that guided the Athletics through their upcoming and most turbulent years. Bando's policy was to refuse to second-guess his manager or otherwise usurp his authority, thus earning the confidence of his skipper, while he also enhanced the trust of his teammates through the tact he exhibited even in the face of harsh — and often unfair — criticism from Finley.

The summer of 1969 evolved into the predicted duel between Minnesota and Oakland. Although the excitement of the competition was somehow lost on Oakland fans — attendance for the year totaled 778,232, down more than 59,000 from 1968 — the Athletics traded first and second place with the Twins during the first three months of the season. Taking advantage of the newly-implemented rules intended to restore some offense to the national pastime, Oakland saw Reggie Jackson build on the power output of his first full season by belting 37 home runs by the All-Star break, while Bando, heeding advice from DiMaggio to alter his stance, also developed into a long-ball threat worthy of his cleanup slot in the batting order. Various injuries kept nipping at the roster, the most serious of which were a broken right finger sustained by Campaneris, a shoulder ailment that plagued Nash, and a pair of injuries that put Green out of action for a total of 26 games. But Bauer cobbled a lineup together to keep Oakland in the hunt, so that when August came to a close, the Athletics were still just a handful of games behind Minnesota. Drawing on their previous experience with pennant pressure, the Twins sent Oakland reeling in two crucial head-to-head series in September, taking three of four contests — including a 16–4 drubbing in the finale — at the Coliseum just after Labor Day weekend and then sweeping a pair of games in Minnesota to drop Oakland ten games out.

Outraged by the unfortunate collapse, Finley sacked Bauer shortly after the Twin Cities debacle and touched off a chain of finger-pointing as to the causes of how this hopeful season had gone amok. Bauer blamed Finley for recalling several players from the minor leagues without consulting him about the roster moves, some players took complaints against the manager directly to Finley, Finley resented Bauer's comment that his players gave up after the key September losses to the Twins, and the injuries, with special emphasis placed on Nash's bad shoulder and the subsequent void it created in the rotation, literally became a sore subject for all concerned. Stepping into the breach was John McNamara, the third-base coach who, as the interim skipper, coaxed eight wins from the club in their last 13 games and merited the opportunity to manage the Athletics for the following season.

Shortfall of 1969 notwithstanding, there were some stellar efforts put forth that yielded an 88–74 record and more solid building blocks for Oakland's future. Although the pitchers around the circuit caught up with Jackson — he clubbed only ten home runs in the second half of the season — he finished with 47 homers and 118 RBIs, while Bando had his own breakthrough campaign with 31 home runs and 113 RBIs. Three other Athletics reached double-digits in homers — Cater (10), Green (12), and Monday (12) — and Campaneris was second in the league with 62 stolen bases. The rest of the supporting cast was weak, however, with various left fielders supplying little run production and a catching corps of four backstops who struggled to make contact at the plate. On the mound, Odom and Chuck Dobson registered 15 wins apiece, Hunter added 12 more; among the relievers, Fingers saved 12 games and Lindblad nine.

The latest Oakland skipper, even-tempered McNamara, had several advantages in his new role. He had managed a fair number of the current Athletics as they progressed through the Kansas City minor league system and had worked with them further in his role as a coach during the Athletics' two seasons in Oakland. Also, McNamara would have some new faces at his disposal as a result of a makeover Finley gave the roster in the offseason. Yet the rookie manager still stood to incur the wrath of the tempestuous owner if he could not collect the victories needed to overtake the defending AL West champion Twins.

## More Managerial Musical Chairs

The growth of the Athletics' win column from 1967 to 1969 offered hope that they could build upon their momentum and remain in contention for the divisional title. Perhaps sensing that an infusion of veteran help would indeed enable his young team to vault Oakland into first place in 1970, Finley went on a binge at the December 1969 winter meetings, bringing in a number of seasoned players to augment those developed by his franchise.

To address the weakness in left field, where Rudi had difficulty reaching the level of success against major league pitching that he had enjoyed in the minors, Felipe Alou was acquired from the Atlanta Braves for Nash, whose unfortunate injury curtailed his effectiveness. Infielder Ted Kubiak and a once-promising pitcher named George Lauzerique were dealt to the Seattle Pilots for shortstop Ray Oyler, a pathetic-hitting shortstop whose fielding ability was his only asset, and Diego Segui, a former Athletic pitcher who had been taken by the Pilots in the expansion draft after the 1968 season. Pitcher Mudcat Grant was purchased from St. Louis, and Finley sent spare infielder Ossie Chavarria and first baseman Danny Cater to the Yankees in exchange for southpaw Al Downing and catcher Frank Fernandez, whose arrival in Oakland was necessitated by Duncan's inability to hit major league pitching.

After a brief respite, Finley continued his personnel revisions in January 1970 by packaging another former bonus baby, Krausse, along with pitcher Ken Sanders, the light-hitting journeyman catcher Phil Roof, and outfielder Mike Hershberger in a trade to the Pilots for infielder Ron Clark and Cater's replacement, first baseman Don Mincher. Reggie Jackson's apparent coming of age rendered Hershberger expendable, while Mincher would give Oakland another power-hitting, left-handed bat.

These wholesale changes yielded another second-place finish in 1970 for a team that lacked the intrigue of 1969, when Oakland spent much time within hailing distance of the Twins. In 1970, the Athletics' only appearance in the division lead came after their Opening Day win in Kansas City against the Royals, thereafter becoming entrenched in third place while playing .500 baseball through the month of May. A one-game improvement over 1969 gave the Athletics an 89–63 record, but the trials and tribulations of their brightest star kept the team from making a serious run at unseating Minnesota.

Trouble began well before Opening Day as Jackson, seeking to capitalize on his banner season just concluded, staged a holdout in spring training while trying to exact from Finley a $60,000 salary he thought equitable. Finley demurred, citing his contract with the team's best pitcher, Catfish Hunter, for $40,000, and although the owner and Jackson ultimately settled at $45,000, the outfielder confessed to "play[ing] the season like a man who hadn't had any spring training."[49]

In fact, Jackson blundered so badly that two months into the 1970 campaign he and his .194 batting average had been demoted to pinch-running and fill-in work as a defensive replacement. Finley wanted to send Jackson to the Triple-A Iowa Oaks to help him regain his touch — an offended Jackson bristled at the notion — but the outfielder eventually reclaimed his place in the lineup and missed only 13 games for the whole season. However, his season-ending .237 average with 23 home runs, 66 RBIs, and 26 stolen bases, totals which would have been respectable for many players, were far short of what was expected from someone who vied for AL MVP honors the year before. Other obstacles to Oakland's pennant quest stemmed from Dick Green's uncharacteristically poor fielding and arm trouble suffered by Blue Moon Odom.

Jackson's misfortunes, when combined with military-related absences of Monday and Duncan, prompted manager John McNamara to adjust the lineup, with favorable results. Provided with an opportunity to enjoy his own break-out season, Rudi heeded the lessons of new hitting coach Charlie Lau and batted .309 while assuming Jackson's spot in the batting order and patrolling left field, while Alou (.271, eight homers, 55 RBIs) shifted between left and right field, and Jackson spelled Monday (.290, 10, 37) in center. Raising eyebrows around the league was Campaneris, who led the AL with 42 steals and nearly out-produced Jackson by slugging 22 home runs and driving in 66 runs in addition to hitting .279. Campy was one of eight Athletics who hit at least ten homers, joining Jackson, Monday (10), Duncan (10), Rudi (11), Fernandez (15), Bando (20), and Mincher, who led the team with 27. The composite totals for the catcher's position was a source of solid support, as Duncan, Fernan-dez, and Gene Tenace, who shuttled between Iowa and Oakland to substitute for Duncan when the Marine Reserves beckoned, hit a combined 32 home runs and drove in 93 runs.

Oakland's league-best 131 stolen bases and improving pitching showed that the Athletics were hardly a one-dimensional threat. Hunter's 18 victories led the staff, and returnee Segui split his 20 decisions but posted the best ERA in the AL at 2.56. Working solely out of the bullpen for the first time in his career and relishing his new role as relief ace, Mudcat Grant converted all but one of his 25 save opportunities, went 6–2, and logged an ERA of 1.82 before being sent to Pittsburgh in mid–Septem-

Bert "Campy" Campaneris was the mainstay at short-stop and a sparkplug at the top of the Athletics batting order.

ber for the Pirates' successful stretch drive. The staff ERA dropped from 3.71 in 1969 to 3.30 in 1970, yet the offense produced fewer runs (from 740 to 678, some of which could be ascribed to Jackson's miserable first half of the season), as the Athletics foundered in their attempt to oust the Twins. Attendance at the Coliseum was drab, as 778,355 fans clicked through the Coliseum's turnstiles, a paltry increase of 123 over the previous year. It appeared that the only fireworks in Oakland would have been the sparklers Finley wanted his players to carry to home plate to greet a teammate who had hit a home run.[50]

An examination of Finley's player transactions shows that the addition of Alou, Fernandez, Grant, Segui, and Mincher proved invaluable to Oakland in spite of the repeat second-place finish, for without their efforts the club may have slipped below .500. A series of other transactions in June, in which the Athletics purchased outfielder Tommy Davis from Houston and pitcher Bob Locker from Milwaukee and also traded Al Downing and Tito Francona to the Brewers for outfielder Steve Hovley, were of marginal utility. Years later, Bando stated that Finley was able to facilitate any transaction he desired because, as the team owner, he didn't need to counsel any opinions as to the value of a particular deal.[51] The man who signed the checks always had the last word, so nobody in the organization was positioned to overrule Charlie Finley.

Regardless of how all the roster pieces fit and with little attention paid to the slight improvement in the victory total over the prior year, at the conclusion of the 1970 season Finley reverted to form by firing McNamara. One controversial account in the press claimed that Duncan, who was sharing an apartment with coach Charlie Lau, accused Finley of meddling as the de facto manager, which Duncan viewed as the root cause of McNamara's ostensible failure to capture the AL West. "Because of the atmosphere [Finley] creates, there's no spirit, no feeling of harmony," fumed Duncan. "We should be close like a family, but it's not here."[52] Finley had expected his manager to deny "any front-office interference," but if the owner had paid attention to statements that McNamara gave to the press, he would have found that the manager was supportive of him.[53] For better or worse, such was employment under Charlie Finley. Years later, Mudcat Grant somberly recalled that Finley "got a kick from stepping on people's dream[s]" because he seldom let common sense supercede his megalomaniac tendencies.[54]

## Another Bad Marriage

In his 1987 autobiography, Bowie Kuhn made abundantly clear his dislike of Charlie Finley even before he personally met the Athletics owner. While in American League president Joe Cronin's office before being named baseball commissioner in 1969, Kuhn could easily hear Finley's obscene-laced tirade as Cronin spoke with Finley over the telephone. This rant left a sour impression on Kuhn and further reinforced his belief that Finley's baseball interests resembled "a Three Stooges look" rather than professional conduct.[55]

Establishing himself as a far more dynamic figure than his predecessor, William Eckert, Kuhn realized that in so doing he was sure to upset some club owners. Kuhn was bestowed with authority shortly after his appointment that allowed him "dictatorial power" to restructure the executive management of his office as well as those of the American and National leagues, thus permitting baseball to project "a forceful and vigorous image" as the sport

Kuhn now led faced the challenges posed by its decline in popularity during the 1960s.[56] Early in his administration, and for the sake of baseball's integrity, Kuhn forced Finley and Atlanta Braves owner Bill Bartholomay to divest themselves of minority interests that each held in several Las Vegas casinos, so conscious was the new commissioner of even the slightest connection of baseball to gambling. In 1970, Kuhn also chastised Finley during his controversy with Reggie Jackson, labeling the owner's attempts to farm out the slumping outfielder an "abuse of the reserve system" that could ultimately undermine the credibility of the game.[57] The contentious relationship between Kuhn and Finley took form early and quickly, with other more serious episodes of disputation to follow as the 1970s unfolded.

Another wrinkle in baseball's labor situation emerged in early 1969 when Yankees pitcher Al Downing, whose effectiveness was constrained by a shoulder problem the previous season, engaged his club in a salary dispute. He refused to sign a new contract for the upcoming year, claiming that his 1968 contract had already been renewed by the club because of its inclusion of the reserve clause. Baseball rules stipulated that unsigned players could not suit up, but when Downing asserted that New York had already renewed his contract in an *ex post facto* manner because of the reserve clause, he felt entitled to join the team with no further restrictions. Downing ultimately signed an official contract on April 20, 1969 — and was traded to the Athletics during the 1969 winter meetings — but the case revealed another interpretation of the machinations of the reserve clause, now coming under increased scrutiny by Marvin Miller and the Players' Association. Curt Flood's outright legal challenge of the reserve system was soon to occupy the center stage of baseball's labor theater. Although that drama played out to Flood's dissatisfaction, other players would ultimately follow Downing's pioneering path by beginning a season playing under what was seen as a renewed contract. In the era before true free agency commenced following the 1976 season, 22 other major league players from 1972 to 1975 opted to use the leverage of renewal to keep playing rather than suffer the idleness of a contract holdout.[58] Although the right to salary arbitration won by the players in their 1973 basic agreement with major league baseball was a huge advance in its own right, contract renewal also became a factor that contributed to the erosion of the power of baseball's heretofore sacrosanct reserve clause.

The reserve clause was especially vital to the cohesion of the Athletics at this critical juncture in their history because this provision yoked the players to an owner whose overbearing demeanor made him increasingly unpopular. But Finley held the key to their fate — as did all owners over their respective clubs — and Oakland's best talent could not escape his clutches without his permission. The next manager to lead the Athletics' run at the Twins had the unenviable task of suffering Finley's hectoring while also continuing to extract more wins from the team. The players that Finley refused to part with were the same players who formed the core of this incipient dynasty; however flawed the owner was, he wisely kept nearly intact the nucleus that would power the forthcoming three-time World Series champions.

## "A Crisp Military Presence"

Once again in the market for a new manager, Finley wasted little time in tracking down a replacement, selecting a man who had tasted success as the pilot of the Boston Red

Sox "Impossible Dream" team in 1967. Dick Williams, according to Catfish Hunter, gave Oakland "a crisp military presence" that would saturate the Athletics with the "*baseball* discipline" vital to winning the elusive divisional crown.[59] After being fired late in 1969 by Boston, Williams found a new position as the Montreal Expos third-base coach the next season, where he learned the nuances of managing while serving under pilot Gene Mauch. "I had refined my skills under a master," Williams admiringly wrote in his autobiography. "I'd learned how to work [a game] two or three innings ahead."[60] Such lessons culled from as prodigious a tactician as Mauch, regardless of the former Phillies manager's lack of post-season appearances, informed Williams's baseball wisdom in handling a game and dealing with his players as he accepted the challenge of working in Finley's managerial maelstrom.

Quickly recognizing that a triumvirate of Athletics were its team leaders — Jackson, Bando, and Hunter — Williams chose to let them run the clubhouse, with the caveat that the manager had the final word with all players regarding all matters on the field and, when appropriate, off the field. Williams later admitted that his job was actually made easier by the presence of Finley because "the players were upset with the owner instead of the manager," which created an animosity that further galvanized a bond that brought Williams closer to his Oakland players than any team he had ever managed.[61]

The cross-country journey of the Athletics franchise had brought it to a third city, the glory of the Philadelphia Mackmen a long-faded memory, with the ineptness of the club's years in Kansas City now about to be expunged by a renaissance of triumph in Oakland that no doubt would have won Cornelius McGillicuddy's approval. Stocked with maturing, quality players commensurate with those of his 1967 Red Sox, Dick Williams brought his stern guidance and freshly-learned lessons to the West Coast and set to work in 1971, under Finley's gaze, to bridge Oakland's gap between contender and champion.

# 9

## Straight A's, Williams's Way

Late in the Oakland Athletics' 1970 season, a harbinger of greatness appeared in dramatic fashion. In consecutive mid–September starts, southpaw Vida Blue hurled a one-hit shutout in Kansas City and then followed that with a no-hitter against Minnesota, which was hoping to clinch the AL West title in Oakland on the night Blue worked his magic to stymie the Twins. Charlie Finley handed Blue an instant bonus of $2,000, and catcher Gene Tenace received $1,000. Yet the dominance with which Blue, who allowed only one baserunner, set down the eventual division champions drew the attention of many baseball observers.

By the conclusion of spring training in 1971, at a time when Blue "was just trying to protect a place for himself on the big team's roster," he had vaulted to the front of the Athletics starting rotation.[1] After falling to the Senators in the last American League season opener in the nation's capital, Blue set upon the opposition with a lengthy winning streak, a skein that presaged the long-anticipated arrival of Oakland at the top of the American League West.

### A Blue Summer

The unfolding of the Dick Williams era in Oakland could not have had a more inauspicious start. A trio of season-opening losses in which the staff surrendered 26 runs caused the manager to grumble, "The name of the game is pitching, and we haven't had it yet," as the early returns were more reminiscent of the bad days of Kansas City rather than a sign of imminent pennant contention by the Athletics.[2] Finley was already conferring with Williams and pitching coach Bill Posedel to determine what remedies could be applied to the quickly faltering team.

As Williams's attitude soured because of his club's poor early showing, he was further enraged when a megaphone went missing from a jetliner, which had just delivered the Athletics to Milwaukee for the team's second road game of the year. Detained by ground personnel until the item, which belonged to the airline, was returned, the manager exploded at his players and demanded the megaphone's return (Catfish Hunter was later unmasked as the thief). Whatever role the incident played in shaking the team from its season-opening slump, Oakland then embarked on a 12–1 tear. By April 20, and on the strength of Hunter's 4–0 shutout over the Angels in Anaheim, the Athletics reached first place in the American

League West and never relinquished its lead, finishing the month at 17–8. When asked about Williams's ability to control his players, Reggie Jackson said, "Even though he has that easy-going air about him, you know he can get tough in an instant…. His personality and leadership create respect."[3] It was by Williams's command of the players' respect that he was able to mold his men into the best baseball team of its era.

Surging to the divisional lead, however, came with perils that challenged Williams's ability to maintain his team's edge. Starters Chuck Dobson and Blue Moon Odom were hampered by bone-chip-plagued elbows — the latter recovering from corrective surgery — which forced the manager to insert Rollie Fingers into the rotation to join Hunter, Blue, and Diego Segui. Yet the emergent story above all others was that of Blue, who repeatedly flashed the brilliance he exhibited in his two outstanding performances of September 1970 and gave his manager every reason to believe that he, like Denny McLain just three years before, would win thirty games in a season. As his ERA dwindled and the strikeouts he recorded soared, Blue amassed seventeen victories — against three losses — by the All-Star break, where he was the winning pitcher in the All-Star Game held in Detroit. Blue struggled in the All-Star Game, giving up three runs on a pair of homers to Johnny Bench and Hank Aaron. But Reggie Jackson bailed him out with his own home run, a titanic shot that nearly went out of Tiger Stadium to give the American League a 4–3 lead in the eventual 6–4 win. Following the All-Star break, Blue resumed his mastery over the league, as even three of his five losses during that time (by scores of 1–0, 1–0, and 2–1) were attributable to a lack of run support. For the entire season, AL batters could only muster a collective .189 batting average against him.

Although he began to flag as the summer wore on, Blue was the unparalleled attraction at ballparks round the league, as Finley, ever the opportunist, tried to bribe his star to change his legal name to True Blue, an antic that the pitcher dismissed as "selfish" on Finley's part.[4] The sensation of Blue's domineering year fueled his teammates' confidence, which in turn led to more wins. In August the Athletics played to a 23–8 record and pulled ahead of their AL West rivals by seventeen games by the beginning of September. Finley sought to capitalize on the windfall of noticeable spikes in attendance whenever Blue took the mound and implored Williams to adjust the starting rotation so that Blue would pitch more frequently at home as the season came to a close. But such a disruption bred ill feelings among the remaining starters, notably Hunter, who followed Blue in the rotation and thus had his own starts pushed back. Williams later stated, because the Ath-

Dick Williams's stern approach set Oakland on the road to playoff and World Series championships.

letics had bolted to so great a lead, "Nobody came to watch us that last month, even when Blue was pitching."[5]

Correct as Williams's observation may have been, Athletics' author Tom Clark noted that Blue's impact across the league in 1971 was invaluable: "One out of every twelve tickets purchased for an American League game [was] bought to see Vida Blue pitch," and those who came to the park witnessed Blue's "dexterity of an acrobat.... His motion is all fluid power and grace" that had batters "connecting with nothing but oxygen."[6] Finley's interloping aside, Oakland drew 914,993 at home and another 1,222,741 on the road. At the age of twenty-two, the southpaw's season of superlatives prompted the Coliseum message board to remind attendees that the team colors were "Kelly Green, California Gold, Wedding Gown White, and Vida Blue."[7] Besieged with autograph requests and offers of advertising endorsements, Blue tried hard to be faithful to his humble roots. "I thought I would get the Most Valuable Player [Award] and Mickey Lolich would get the Cy Young," commented Blue upon his being named the AL's best pitcher.[8] But the 24–8 record, league-best 1.82 ERA, eight shutouts, and 301 strikeouts made him the youngest Cy Young Award recipient as well as the circuit's Most Valuable Player, which placed on Blue the onus to continue to live up to the exceedingly high standard he had set for himself.

A batter's-eye view of Vida Blue, who dominated the American League in 1971 when he was voted both the MVP and Cy Young Award.

## "The Season Was Fun"

Although Dick Williams's cross–Bay managerial counterpart, Charlie Fox of the San Francisco Giants, upstaged the Oakland skipper for Manager of the Year honors in 1971, Williams burnished his growing reputation as a leader capable of molding a team of young talent into a winner. "The season was fun," wrote Williams, reflecting on the 101–60 season in his autobiography, as he had the good fortune to step into the Athletics dugout at the right time to make the most of his new opportunity.[9] When Vida Blue burst onto the scene, the budding star's arrival as perhaps a "black Sandy Koufax"—another label Blue disliked but could not avoid—seemed to ensure both the current and future success of the Oakland franchise.[10]

Slightly less obvious but equally important to the Athletics' achievements in 1971 were the accomplishments of the players continuing to mature at the major league level. Hunter won twenty games for the first time in his career, posting a 21–11 log with a 2.96 ERA. Bando led the club with 94 RBIs and was second in home runs (24) and batting (.271) among the regular players, while Jackson led the power hitters with 32 homers, drove home 80 runs, and hit .277. Now entrenched in left field, Rudi batted .267 with ten home runs and 52 RBIs, as Monday's average slipped to .245 — attributed to difficulties against left-handed pitchers and a tendency to be a strikeout-prone, streak hitter — but he hit 18 home runs and drove in 56 runs. Fingers segued into a primary relief role after several early-season starting assignments to lead the club with 17 saves in 20 chances. Still serving in a reserve role but showing a muscular stroke, Tenace batted .274 with seven homers and 25 RBIs in only 179 at-bats. Meanwhile, another pair of right-handed-hitting rookies, George Hendrick and Angel Mangual, found their way into the Oakland outfield and hit respectably, Hendrick at .237 and .286 for Mangual, although the latter raised concern because of his weak fielding.[11]

Other veterans contributed in various ways, such as Campaneris (.251, 5 home runs, 47 RBIs) with his customary team-leading 34 stolen bases, although his league-worst 26 errors at shortstop caused other concerns. Coaxed out of retirement, Green hit .244, belted 12 homers, and drove in 49 runs, Duncan increased his playing time profitably with a .253 average, 15 home runs, and 40 RBIs, and Tommy Davis was still proficient at the bat, as evidenced by his .324 average with 42 runs driven in. On the mound, Segui, now 34 years old, continued to produce in his 21 starts and five relief outings (10–8, 3.14 ERA), while Odom (10–12, 4.28) and Chuck Dobson (15–5, 3.81) returned from arm troubles and pitched well until their injuries again flared up late in the season. Working exclusively out of the bullpen, Bob Locker went 7–2 with a 2.88 ERA and six saves.

During the course of the 1971 season, Finley consummated several transactions that fortified the roster with help at first base, the bullpen, and the outfield, each addition providing key support and strengthening the depth of the Oakland bench. At first base, Finley swapped the underperforming Don Mincher, who was hitting just .239 with two home runs and eight RBIs after one month of play, to the Senators for *their* underperforming first baseman, Mike Epstein. Five years Mincher's junior, the left-handed Epstein batted only .234 for his new team and carried with him what Hunter described as the baggage of being a reputed "clubhouse lawyer," but he also brought to Oakland the muscle that powered 18 home runs and drove in 51 runs for the Athletics.[12] Departing Oakland in that same trade — one local scribe termed the transaction "daring" — were catcher Frank Fernandez and reliever Paul Lindblad, while accompanying Epstein to the Athletics was southpaw Darold Knowles, who won five games, lost two, saved seven others, and posted a 3.59 ERA.[13] Knowles and Lindblad had each fallen out of favor with their respective previous management, and although Hunter preferred that Lindblad had remained his teammate, he admired the way in which Knowles took on the left-handed relief role when he joined Oakland.[14]

Several other minor transactions helped the Athletics throughout the 1971 season. In April, Finley shipped outfielder Felipe Alou to the Yankees for pitcher Ron Klimkowski, who won two games that month when the Athletics were struggling, and hurler Rob Gardner, who was all but ignored in Oakland and then sent back to the Bronx in exchange for Curt Blefary, the 1965 AL Rookie of the Year. In a utility role, Blefary mainly caught but also filled in at every position except center field and shortstop. Lastly, as a defensive complement to the weak-fielding Epstein, Finley purchased from the Milwaukee Brewers the fine-fielding first baseman Mike Hegan. Commenting on the direct approach with which Williams handled his players, Hegan was appreciative of the manager's forthright explanation that he could expect to be used almost exclusively for late-inning defensive purposes.[15] This communicative trait of Williams's management technique enhanced his reputation among his players because it allowed them to better prepare for the roles they were expected to fill.

Capturing their first divisional title was a tremendous accomplishment for the Athletics, even though, according to Dobson, the clinching itself was "anticlimatic" [*sic*] because of the large lead Oakland held for so much of the season.[16] The Athletics struck a fine balance with pitching (second in the American League in team earned-run average, saves, and strike-outs), defense (tied for second in fielding percentage), and offense (fourth-best run production). Williams, who understood the sharp contrast between the ease with which Oakland won the AL West in 1971 and the tortuous route to the AL pennant taken by his 1967 Red Sox, was adept at orchestrating pitchers to fill in for the injured Odom and Dobson, while Finley's moves to acquire a pair of first basemen whose tasks were suited to their respective fortes enabled Williams to alternately employ power and defense at appropriate times. And the quality of Oakland's young veterans continued to be as vital an attribute for the team as was Williams's guidance.

Absent a long-time veteran leader of the caliber of Frank Robinson, Brooks Robinson, or Harmon Killebrew — all of whom had substantial service time at the major league level when they led Baltimore and Minnesota into postseason play in the 1960s — many key Athletics under Williams had barely five years of big league experience. The nucleus of the Athletics had matured together with no elder statesman to guide them. As the team captain, Bando became the cohesive element who led by example. With another youthful phenomenon in the person of Vida Blue in the fold, Oakland appeared to be well-positioned for a serious run at the fearsome defending AL champion Baltimore Orioles.

## No Luck in the "Tournament"

In their first taste of postseason competition, the Athletics fell victim to Baltimore, which was fronted by a quartet of twenty-game winners and, as history showed, at the height of its dynasty. In a late–September column in the *Oakland Tribune*, Ed Levitt attempted to give his hometown team an advantage by proposing that the teams with the best record in each league should be declared the World Series participants. "After a long, tedious 162-game schedule," Levitt asked, "why should there be a need for an additional five-game tournament?"[17] On the day in which Levitt's opinion was published, the Athletics were conveniently one victory ahead of Baltimore, but the American League Championship Series had been inexorably woven into the fabric of major league baseball. To make matters worse for Levitt and those interested in Oakland baseball, the Orioles juggernaut wrapped up the regular campaign riding an eleven-game winning streak, as the Athletics, with their pitching rotation thinned by injuries to Odom and Dobson, would have no more luck against the Orioles than had the Twins in each of the first two ALCS "tournaments."

Since the 1971 playoffs were scheduled to begin on October 2, Williams had planned to use Vida Blue and Catfish Hunter in the two games at Baltimore, then take advantage of a travel day back to Oakland to pitch Blue on short rest in Game 3. However, rains from

Hurricane Ginger soaked the Eastern Seaboard, forced postponement of Game 1, and eliminated the day off since Game 2 was moved back to what would have been the travel day.

But Blue was still being counted upon to hold the streaking Orioles at bay, and the young hurler was also doing his best to fend off the media, now looking for an extra story to file because of the delay. A tense Blue became aloof with reporters and their questions, but when the weather broke and the players finally took the field, the Athletics' star was in midseason form, holding Baltimore to three hits and a single run over the first six innings as his teammates scored three times against Dave McNally. The post-storm humidity, however, began to fatigue Blue, when in the bottom of the seventh he was roughed up for four runs. Williams later admitted that he struggled with the decision whether to leave Blue in the game or bring in Rollie Fingers, who to that point in his career had yet to impress his manager as being mature enough to handle the pressure of Oakland's most important game of the season.[18] Blue soldiered on but lost the game when Paul Blair, 0-for-11 lifetime against Blue, pulled a double down the third-base line to drive in the final two runs in the 5–3 Baltimore win.

In the final contest at Memorial Stadium, Hunter answered Williams's call as the Game 2 starter but told the press after the game, "What bothers us more than losing is that we've let Dick Williams down.... We let a guy down who loved us."[19] The reason for Hunter's despair was the pair of home runs he served up to Boog Powell, as well as others to Elrod Hendricks and Brooks Robinson, in the Orioles' 5–1 triumph. Hunter also blamed the lengthy rest he had had since his previous start — "Six days is too much for me," he said — and his failure to spot his pitches forced him, at inopportune times, to throw four fastballs, all of which were sent over the Memorial Stadium fence.[20]

To stave off elimination in Game 3 and yet another Baltimore ALCS sweep as the series moved to Oakland, Williams elected to use Diego Segui as his starting pitcher — the manager later called him "overmatched"—because of the unavailability of Odom, who had been dropped from the postseason roster, and Dobson, whose elbow failed to hold up at the end of the regular campaign.[21] The manager's fears were realized when Segui, 3–10 in his career against the Orioles and loser of his last four starts against them, failed to last five innings and departed down by a score of 3–1, while several personnel changes intended to breath life into the lineup also fell short of expectations. While Bando homered and Jackson, showcasing his emerging penchant for delivering big hits in playoff action that would earn him the title of "Mr. October," belted a pair of solo home runs, the efforts were in vain as Jim Palmer tamed Oakland, 5–3, to earn the Orioles their third straight trip to the World Series.

In the Athletics clubhouse, the mood was naturally downcast, with Jackson in particular almost inconsolable. Although they had lost all three playoff games, Oakland had been within hailing distance in each one; with a break or two at a crucial moment, the results could have swung in their favor. Reasons for the Athletics' shortfall were plentiful and varied. Mike Hegan noted the vast disparity between Baltimore's playoff experience and Oakland's lack thereof, several critics blamed Williams for employing the bunt too often, and the starting pitching corps, already diminished for a short playoff schedule, found itself with only two dependable pitchers, Blue and Hunter. Relied on to catalyze the Athletics' offense, the speedy Campaneris hit only .167 on a 2-for-12 performance at the plate and never scored in the entire series. With Games 1 and 3 decided by just two runs, Campy's absence on the basepaths grew more conspicuous. Perhaps sensing an imminent victory by the Orioles in the third contest, Bay Area fans failed to take advantage of blocks of tickets priced between three and seven dollars, as only 33,176 of the Coliseum's roughly 50,000 seats were occupied.

The first trip to championship play was bitter for the Athletics, yet the ages of their mainstays, having endured their own postseason initiation, pointed to more prosperity if they could demonstrate that their performance as a team in 1971 was not a fluke. Among the regular players at the close of that season, the oldest was Green (30), while Rudi (25), Monday (26), Jackson (25), Bando (27), Campaneris (29), Epstein (28), Duncan (26), Mangual (24), and Tenace (25) were entering the prime years of their careers. On the pitching staff, Blue (22), Hunter (25), and Odom (26) — if he could overcome his arm ailment — had lasting star potential, while Fingers (25) and Knowles (30) comprised a tough right-left combination out of the bullpen.

The aftermath of the ALCS loss resulted in one move *not* made by Charlie Finley. Some rumblings indicated that Williams would be sacrificed in the latest of his string of managerial firings, but luckily those rumors proved false. Immediately following the loss in Game 3, Williams told his players that they need not "hang their heads in shame" and apologized to Finley for the team's poor playoff showing.[22] But the owner was upbeat and already anticipating better days ahead. Shaking hands with Williams, Finley acknowledged the need to make some trades to address some weak spots, but he also exuded optimism that Oakland would be hosting the World Series in 1972.

## A Blue Winter

Recognizing that one pair of frontline starters, Blue and Hunter, was inadequate to the task of carrying on in the immediate future — to say nothing of another postseason — while another pair, Odom and Dobson, each had injuries that could jeopardize their careers, Finley acted to find another quality pitcher for the Oakland rotation. At the opening of the 1971 winter meetings, Finley sent Rick Monday to the Chicago Cubs for a lanky, 26-year-old left-handed starter named Ken Holtzman, who had logged seventeen wins in 1969 and 1970 (plus had thrown two no-hitters) but had fallen to 9–15 in 1971 and was also not on good terms with his manager, Leo Durocher. The trade was prompted by a necessity for another starter but also by a surplus in the Athletics outfield. Jackson and Rudi had taken root in the lineup, and Oakland believed it saw the future in Angel Mangual, who finished second in voting for the 1971 Rookie of the Year award; George Hendrick appeared headed for a backup role in the outfield.

Holtzman's presence in Oakland over the next four seasons would prove just how valuable an addition he was and reinforce the opinions of those who believed that Finley was truly possessed of a keen eye in knowing what roster adjustments would work best. Speaking of his owner, Jackson enthused, "He had this innate sense about people and chemistry and the kind of nucleus he needed to have a winner," as Holtzman's record on the mound delivered for Oakland in a manner not unlike that of Mike Cuellar when he arrived in Baltimore in 1969.[23]

The Holtzman trade lent an air of heightened anticipation to the Oakland offseason, but the success enjoyed by Vida Blue in his double award-winning campaign forecast an inevitable salary dispute when contract negotiations between him and Finley began. Paid a reported $14,750 for his services and given a Cadillac in 1971, Blue was destined — and deserved — to cash in handsomely on his next contract, so a salary of $100,000 seemed to be within reason given his meteoric rise as a pitcher and his box office appeal, which translated into revenue for Oakland and any team he pitched against.[24]

Blue spent a very busy winter making television appearances, touring military installations in Vietnam and other Asian ports of call with entertainer Bob Hope, endorsing products — milk, after-shave lotion, and batteries, to name a few — and reviewing offers to star in several motion pictures. The fast-moving world of Vida Blue also included ever-increasing contact with attorney Bob Gerst, who was now charged with representing the hottest sports client in America. When Blue's salary negotiations commenced in early January, Gerst opened the bidding at $115,000 and left enough room to settle for perhaps at least $100,000. But Finley stubbornly countered with $45,000, a figure he raised to $50,000 but then vowed would be his best offer.

As the bargaining quickly reached an impasse, Blue's position was strengthened when misfortune befell two other starting pitchers. Dobson, nagged by elbow trouble in 1971, was recovering from surgery and hoped to regain his effectiveness. Odom, who was vexed by his own elbow problems, was nearly killed when he was shot while attempting to thwart a burglary near his mother's Macon, Georgia, home. Hit in the neck and chest from fifteen feet away, Odom healed in time for spring training, but considering the potentially fatal gunshots that might have been inflicted, he was extremely lucky to escape with relatively minor wounds.

With Dobson and Odom recuperating, negotiations between Gerst and Finley continued, but there was speculation in the press that Blue might have to be content with the owner's proposal because of restrictions established by President Richard Nixon's wage-freeze board, a federal bureaucracy established to stem the tide of spiraling inflation in the late 1960s and early 1970s.[25] After the initial bargaining session in January 1972, Blue returned to Oakland to fulfill his monthly duty for the Army Reserves, but as spring training approached, the salary figure discrepancy between owner and player remained vast. Acrimony between the sides escalated, as Finley cried to the media about the outrageousness of the contract demand, while Gerst retorted with his own charges that "Finley tried to blackmail Vida."[26] At this time, Gerst also unearthed a technicality that he believed could lead to Blue's immediate free agency.

Gerst noted that Blue had signed with the Athletics in late August 1967 just one month after he had turned 18, so that contract was thought by Gerst to be invalid because Blue had not reached the age of majority. But the true wrinkle in the case, claimed Gerst, was lingering doubt as to whether Finley had made good on the last of several small bonuses payable to Blue upon reaching the major league roster.[27] Blue's initial contract called for him to receive $1,000, $1,500, and $2,500 for 90-day stays at the Double-A, Triple-A, and major league levels, respectively, so Gerst's contention was that Blue's "contract will be rescinded if the club does not live up to any part of the agreement."[28] However, this argument gained no traction for Gerst, as spring camp opened without Blue, who officially became a holdout. Unable to keep a straight face at the preposterous turn he was allowing his career to take, Blue announced that he was leaving baseball to become a public relations executive for Dura Steel, a Los Angeles–based steel products company.

Fearing a total depletion of his starting rotation should Blue really turn his back on the game, Finley in early March engineered a trade with the Texas Rangers to acquire Denny McLain, the 1968 Cy Young winner and AL MVP, by sending pitchers Jim Panther and Don Stanhouse to the club that had relocated from Washington, D.C. at the end of the 1971 season. In a more sober moment, Gerst asked Finley for a $50,000 contract that did *not* contain a reserve clause — a request containing more than a dose of ironic and prescient overtones. The Blue controversy roiled for weeks on end, as some of his teammates chided him for an excessive salary demand despite his very limited seniority as a major leaguer. Yet others in the sporting press laid the blame at Finley's doorstep for an inability to swallow his pride and compensate Blue for his proven — and prodigious — athleticism as well as his box office allure, which according to one estimate generated ticket revenue of $1.5 million in Oakland during the 1971 season.[29]

Preoccupied as many were with the Blue-Finley dispute, another confrontation between players and owners, the beginnings of which smoldered for weeks, flared up into the first full-scale battle between labor and management over the contributions made by owners to the players' pension fund. At Oakland's training camp in Mesa, Arizona, as Odom worked his way back into form and Blefary fought for a roster spot as an all-purpose utility man, players in both leagues took the lead of their union's director, Marvin Miller, to draw a line in the sand and dare the owners *not* to increase their contribution to the players' pension fund. The result of this show of player solidarity was the first concerted work stoppage by players on all teams in the history of major league baseball.

## "The Players Aren't Being Greedy"

While the main aspects of baseball's 1972 strike were related in Chapter 7, there remain a few salient details from the Oakland perspective. Calling for a strike was a bold step on the part of the players, but the galvanization of the union inherent in such a move demonstrated, according to Sal Bando, that the players desired to have a direct impact on their future by forcing alterations in baseball ownership's mores.[30] At this time much attention had been devoted to Blue's contract dispute, yet the plight of the young pitcher was but one example in the age-old battle between players and owners at the negotiating table. As a union of more than 600 players collectively locked horns with 24 club owners, it was the latter group who blinked first during the infamous stare-down in the spring of 1972.

After the exhibition games of March 31 were played and with the opening of the regular season just days away, the players walked out over the pension and health care issues, yet they were accorded first-class air travel to their homes, with the clubs picking up the tab. Reggie Jackson said that the timing of the walkout was important to the unity of the players, because if the season had opened and any teams had started playing exceptionally well, players on those clubs may have felt less compelled to interrupt their early success. Dobson, the Athletics player representative, affirmed that the stand made by the union had less to do with money than with the poor way in which he believed the owners had treated the players.

But Jackson's and Dobson's ultimate boss felt otherwise. "I can't help but feel sorry for the players," lamented Finley over the union's decision to follow Marvin Miller's advice.

"They've been misled. Once the players have all the facts and figures, they'll be a little ashamed."[31] Some trepidation was expressed that obstinacy on the part of either side in the dispute might force the entire season to be scrapped. One Oakland sportswriter, siding with the owners and speaking for the overwhelming majority of fans who supported the owners' position, urged the players to "count your blessings" rather than "trade [your pension] for what the milkman or policeman or fireman has at the present time."[32]

Toward the end of the first week of the strike, Finley fretted over the logistics of what city his team's new Italian-made uniforms should be sent to, pending the anticipated opening of the season, and griped about Miller's bargaining tactics that he feared would force some owners to drastically increase ticket and concession prices as a result of a strike settlement or otherwise drive teams into receivership. However much Finley felt obligated to chide the players for their stance, he also began to reveal himself as a defector from the owners' camp. Dobson disclosed that Finley had contacted him on April 6 to divulge a proposal that the owner believed might lead to a settlement. The pitcher told the *Oakland Tribune*, "It sounded promising. Mr. Finley always has been friendly through this whole thing."[33]

Finley's cordiality may have been influenced by the fact that the strike had begun to eat into the Athletics' home schedule and was now causing a genuine loss of revenue. But several other owners—the Twins' Calvin Griffith, John Allyn of the White Sox, Francis Dale of the Cincinnati Reds, and Bob Short, who had moved the expansion Senators to Arlington, Texas, to become the new Texas Rangers—urged an accelerated pace toward a settlement and implored Commissioner Bowie Kuhn to intervene. On April 10, a *Tribune* headline blared, "Finley Calls for Compromise," as readers were informed that Finley, after consulting with "actuarial experts" in Chicago for several days, concluded that "this strike never should have occurred in the first place."[34] Unearthed by the actuaries was a surplus in the players' pension fund, an increase derived from a better-than-expected rate of return on investments that put the financial health of the fund in a new light. "The players aren't being greedy," Finley pleaded, a statement made all the more curious when one considers that his own ace, Blue, remained unsigned.[35] Although efforts to convince the majority of owners in both leagues of the veracity of this finding remained a difficult battle, Finley's softened stance played a key role in brokering a deal with the union. Finley's stunning change in attitude was also driven by a desire to keep the federal government, which was now being looked upon as a mediator, from intervening in the strike.

Now brimming with optimism, Finley permitted his team to use the Coliseum for their own workouts—Dick Williams and his staff, in street clothes, observed but did not direct these sessions—and encouraged an expedited settlement by imploring other owners not to "split hairs" over the issue of back pay for cancelled games.[36] Finally, on April 13, as club owners gathered in Chicago—they were joined by Kuhn, who was reportedly assisting in the settlement away from the spotlight—and Miller and the player representatives assembled in New York, the agreement was ratified. Nearly $6 million was to be given annually by the clubs toward the players' retirement and health benefits fund.

On its April 29 cover, *The Sporting News* heralded the arrival of "spring ... a little late this year," as fans, thirsting for games and box scores but instead subjected to a diet of reports from the bargaining sessions, could again follow the national pastime in their accustomed way. Nonetheless, the power structure of the game was forever altered by this divisive and tortuous episode in sports labor. In this same issue of *TSN*, Oscar Kahan noted that issues of labor-management relations would be viewed no differently than those between the steelworkers' union and U.S. Steel, although Miller hoped that "lingering bitterness" between the players and owners would not be a factor in future contract negotiations.[37] Kahan further observed that from the viewpoint of labor and management, "there seems to be agreement on both sides, based on their bad experience, that *there will never be another strike.*"[38] Unfortunately, any lessons learned in 1972 were not only forgotten but seemed instead to embolden labor and management for far worse confrontations in the years ahead. As the stakes and vested interests of players and owners grew, so too did the intransigence to hold fast to their respective demands during negotiations over future basic agreements.

For now, peace had been reached, and on the eve of the season opener, the *Oakland Tribune* hopefully and presciently mused that the Athletics might not only repeat as defending AL West champions but added, "In fact, there's good reason to believe the World Series might be played here next year [*sic*]."[39] While it remained to be seen if these scenarios would come true, the Athletics showcased newcomer Ken Holtzman to start what became their best season yet in Oakland.

## Play Ball, at Last

The return of players to work did not guarantee that all of them would be pleased about the commencement of the 1972 season. After batting .360 during spring training and fully expecting to be Oakland's opening-day catcher, Blefary complained about being relegated to utility status when he discovered that he was the apparent odd-man-out among Oakland backstops, with Gene Tenace and Dave Duncan considered the front-runners. Meantime, Blue continued his work with Dura Steel, much to the consternation of fellow players who, at Finley's behest, paid personal visits to the reigning AL MVP attempting to persuade him to abandon his self-imposed exile.

Having lost seven contests to the strike — all of them against intra-division rivals Chicago, Texas, and Minnesota — the Athletics opened the season at home on April 15 with a 4–3 victory over the Twins before a crowd of just 9,912 fans. Oakland did not keep its grip on the top of the American League West for long, slipping to second place yet no worse than a few games out. After Catfish Hunter beat the White Sox in late May, the Athletics reached first place, where they remained for nearly the rest of the 1972 season.

The jousting between Finley and Blue came to a merciful end three weeks after the season began when the pitcher inked a $63,000 contract, although the agreement came only after the intervention of Bowie Kuhn. The commissioner was reluctant to inject himself into a fracas between player and owner, yet the thought of a young pitcher who had scaled the heights of stardom so quickly remaining on the sidelines seemed incomprehensible as the stalemate continued. At Kuhn's request, Finley, Blue, and Blue's attorney met the commissioner in Chicago for a marathon negotiating session, which was punctuated not only by hostility between player and owner but also an air of distrust of both Blue and Finley toward Kuhn. Trying to assume an impartial stance during the impasse, the commissioner nonetheless believed that the warring factions "suspected that I favored the other side," thereby winning points with neither.[40] An accord was tentatively agreed upon but no signatures were forthcoming to close the deal because a dispute arose over how the terms were to be described, Finley claiming them to be a $50,000 contract plus bonuses for a total of $63,000, while Blue interpreted the entire package as a $63,000 contract. When Kuhn demanded that the offer remain in effect until Blue signed, lest the commissioner unilaterally declare Blue a free agent, Finley exploded at the imposition of Kuhn's gunboat diplomacy. Finley relented, however, and on May 2 in Boston, the parties reconvened and Blue at last signed his 1972 contract.

With the strife now behind him, Blue occasionally exhibited his domination upon his return, only to be hurt by a lack of run support; at other times he pitched more like a public relations executive than a Cy Young Award winner. It became obvious that Blue's holdout and lack of spring training affected his performance not unlike the doldrums into which Reggie Jackson sank in 1970 due to his own contract dispute with Finley.

## Mustache Mania and the Kaleidoscopic Roster

One of baseball's signal events of 1972 took place during the summer. While it was several weeks in the making, this landmark became emblematic of the stamp that the Oakland Athletics in particular left upon major league baseball. Conservative styles of dress in the mid– to late 1960s were inexorably yielding to style and fashion trends that called for longer hair, brighter colors, and polyester fabric as part of one's personal appearance, especially with the younger crowd. The denizens of Oakland's clubhouse were no exception to the latest modes. Given Finley's proven tendencies toward garish baseball attire and gimmickry, it should come as no surprise that he chose to move the appearance of his players to another dimension.

When Reggie Jackson sported a mustache to begin the 1972 season, he became the first major leaguer in nearly 60 years to do so. Never passing up an opportunity to add to his repertoire of antics, Finley offered a $300 bonus to any player or coach if he grew a mustache by Father's Day. Sal Bando, who had been sporting longer hair even before spring training began, and his teammates also liked Dick Williams's policy of not making players wear neck ties on road trips, as fashions in general became more influenced by clothes worn by black players. No longer were players being "laughed out of the clubhouse" for the attire they chose.[41]

The financial incentive that Finley offered his team to make a hairy statement simply added to the aura of idiosyncrasies that were the Athletics' stock in trade. Come June 18, the entire roster of active Oakland players and coaches each received checks for $300 as well as special Finley-commissioned, gold mustache spoons. It was a red-letter day at the Coliseum as Vida Blue, who prior to the game ironically had shaved his mustache, won his first game of the year, a 9–0 shutout of the Indians.[42]

Amid the sprouting of so much hair, a good portion of the Athletics roster seemed to resemble the waiting area of a barber shop. For the most part, the mainline position players and pitchers remained fixtures in the lineup, but those on the bench or deep in the bullpen shuffled in and out of Oakland during most of the 65 moves involving 41 players who bided their time in anticipation of the call of "next." The Athletics "traded, they bought, they sold, they waived, they released, they disabled, they activated, they sent down, they brought up, they did everything but pull players out of a hat," summarized beat writer Ron Bergman of the plethora of transactions that kept the Athletics lineup in a state of perpetual flux.[43] Finley's micromanagement seemed intent on adjusting personnel to meet the smallest of needs or trying to breath life into his latest brainstorm that he felt would give the Athletics an edge.

An example of a perceived edge was the place on the roster occupied by Allan Lewis, a lithe Latino dubbed "The Panamanian Express," whose primary duty was to serve as a pinch-runner. Enamored with Lewis's fleetness, Finley ensured the speedster's availability by foisting him on several Athletics managers despite Lewis's limited baseball instincts. Upon seeing Lewis for the first time, Williams thought he was a batboy, and though the manager admired Lewis for his speed, he blanched at his overall lack of skills. Bando later remarked that the employment of such a running specialist impressed more as a ploy for the owner to satisfy his ego than to provide a long-term practical benefit for the team.[44]

Other players with more baseball-worthy talent did arrive for varying lengths of stay. In the month of May alone, pitcher Mike Kilkenny was purchased from Detroit but just a week later was shipped with Blefary to the San Diego Padres for right-handed power hitter Ollie Brown. Reliever Don Shaw was acquired for infielder Dwain Anderson. When Dick Green was disabled by back surgery, Larry Brown took over second base, but then spare outfielder Brant Alyea was traded to the Cardinals for infielder Marty Martinez to serve as a back-up.

Whether because of or in spite of these changes, Williams coaxed eighteen wins from his troops during May while losing but eight games, and with Blue back in Oakland's rotation, the Athletics went 18–11 in June. The core of frontline players changed little, as Jackson, Rudi, Campaneris, Bando, Hunter, and Holtzman, played well enough to earn spots on the American League All-Star team. Yet the supporting cast continued to change like the images of a kaleidoscope. In early June, Diego Segui was sold to St. Louis, and toward the end of the month, outfielder Bill Voss arrived from Milwaukee in exchange for Ron Clark, first baseman Art Shamsky was purchased from the Cubs, Ollie Brown was sold to Milwaukee, and McLain (trying to rehabilitate his shoulder with Oakland's Double-A franchise in Birmingham), was traded to the Braves for Orlando Cepeda.

No abatement of the blizzard of transactions was in sight in July as the Athletics labored toward a slow extension of their lead, reaching a season-high nine games after beating Milwaukee on July 19. When Shamsky was released and Epstein was sidelined with an eye injury, Finley sent Martinez and infielder Vic Harris to the Rangers for infielder Ted Kubiak and first baseman Don Mincher, now in his second tour of duty with Oakland.

After barely breaking even with a 16–15 record in July, Rudi, who was vying for the AL batting title, was holding up the Athletics outfield when Jackson went on the disabled list. The Athletics' lead in the AL West shrank to such an extent that they clung to no better than a 1½-game edge and dipped to second place in their duel with the White Sox late in the month. Jackson's injury during a brawl at home with the Kansas City Royals on August 2 forced him to miss three weeks of action while George Hendrick, Voss, and Alyea (who had returned to Oakland in late July) were barely hitting their weight. So Finley again reached into the marketplace and dealt Voss and a minor leaguer to the Cardinals for standout hitter and former National League batting champion Matty Alou. By the end of August, infielder Dal Maxvill was acquired from St. Louis in time to be placed on the postseason playoff roster. When Jackson returned from the disabled list, he was repositioned in center field while Alou was installed in right field.

The preponderance of extra infielders that appeared throughout the season may seem odd, considering that Bando and Campaneris anchored the left side of the infield and hardly missed any playing time. But with Green and Larry Brown sidelined with back problems and missing a significant amount of games, the innovative realm of Charlie Finley had concocted a new strategy, which was naturally passed on to Dick Williams, calling for the second baseman to be lifted in favor of a pinch-hitter, in some cases nearly every time that middle infielder was to take his turn at bat. Years later, Williams admitted that the "rotating second baseman maneuver [was] Charlie's only in-game order that I felt compelled to carry out," as Williams bristled at the edict of having to deplete his bench in order to placate Finley's meddlesome whim.[45] Although the position often was manned by a truly qualified infielder like Kubiak, Brown, or Tim Cullen, who played the most games at second in 1972, in some cases second base fell into the hands of a player like Gene Tenace or Larry Haney, both of whom were catchers by trade and were obviously playing out of position. As was the case with pinch-runner Lewis — and later Herb Washington — Finley was desperate to put his own signature on the team even though he was not in charge of handling the daily lineup card.

Perhaps the most durable Athletic was team captain Sal Bando, who anchored the infield at third base.

Locked in a tight race as the summer wore on, the Athletics experienced tension and turbulence that took a toll on Dick Williams, who became the subject of rumors that his job was in peril when his club entertained Chicago for a crucial mid–August series. Although Finley silenced the gossip by signing Williams to a contract extension through the 1974 season, Oakland was unable to shake the White Sox until early September when they gradually pulled away and clinched their second consecutive AL West title in their last home game on September 28. The return trip to the ALCS prompted Finley, vindicated by the Athletics' defense of their divisional title, to heap praise on his manager for recognizing that "the talent is here, and Dick Williams has put it all together the right way."[46]

The Athletics finished with a record of 93–62 and drew 921,323 fans to the Coliseum in what was hardly a season free of turmoil. At a time when Oakland was still establishing itself as the new frontline team of the American League, the Athletics evinced a trait that confounded any theory espousing the notion that camaraderie, such as that enjoyed by the 1965 Twins or the Orioles of the late 1960s, was synonymous with success on the field. Winning can foster an élan in many a clubhouse, but in Oakland, discord seemed to carry the day more often than not.

It is fair to say that among any group of 25 people, some degree of friction, however minor, will exist at any given time. In the case of the Athletics' clubhouse, which was inhabited by a core of long-term regulars such as Hunter, Jackson, Odom, Bando, Green, and Duncan, a comment later made by Fingers perhaps best describes the potential for conflicts among personalities. "We had all played ball together for so long, it was like being married. You're going to have disagreements now and then," observed the future Hall-of-Fame reliever, who also was of the opinion that "the press blew [the fighting] out of proportion a little bit."[47] In his retirement, Bando believed that there was no more conflict in the Oakland clubhouse than in others around the majors — including that of the Brewers, for whom he also played — and he further thought that as Oakland's amassing of pennants grew more impressive, it also drew the attention of media that otherwise may have been indifferent to the Athletics had they not been contenders.[48] By the summer of 1972, with long hair, mustaches, and restyled green-and-gold uniforms — to say nothing about the antics of a brash owner — already having drawn an expanding audience to the Oakland scene, the embellishment of angry shouting, a shoving match, or a punch-up of some sort between teammates only added to the team's character. Creating the Athletics' version of Baltimore's Kangaroo Court, Hunter admitted that he conspired with Bando to select likely targets among their teammates in order to rib them for misdeeds committed on the field, but Fingers conceded that those players possessed of "short fuses" were likely to take umbrage at such treatment.[49]

Although McLain observed the manager for only a few months and felt that Williams was as much of a carouser as some of his players, the answer to the question of how the Athletics were able to put the strife behind them when the game began may have been answered best by Don Mincher, who believed that Williams's managerial style was the key factor in his ability to earn the respect of his players and extract the best measure of performance from them. Thus, a noteworthy fracas between Jackson and Epstein over the use of complimentary tickets, the assorted verbal jousts between players (including one between Blue and Odom following a playoff game), gambling that McLain alleged was going on between players who partook in recreational golf, bowling, or card games, all could be written off as collateral damage when the wins ultimately translated to pennants. "We didn't think of ourselves as being controversial or different," said Jackson in his 1984 autobiography, but his own out-sized ego was a contributing factor to some of the team's malaise.[50] Although the Oakland brand of *esprit de corps* was not necessarily a model to be emulated by other sports franchises, it nonetheless was undeniably a salient element in the team's chemistry.

## Taming the Tigers

The Athletics embarked on their second voyage to the American League Championship Series with an impressive cast whose combined offensive efforts resulted in the most home runs (140) and second-most runs scored (604) in the AL behind Boston, while their pitching staff led in shutouts and saves and trailed only Baltimore in runs allowed and ERA. Oakland's power at the plate was well-distributed among a group of regulars, although no Oakland batter even reached the 80-RBI mark. The left-handed muscle of Epstein (.270, 26 homers, 70 RBIs) and Jackson (.265, 25, 75) was complemented on the right by Rudi (.305, 19, 75), Bando (.236, 15, 77), and Duncan (.218, 19, 59). Although Bando confessed toward the end of the regular season that his prolonged slump had caused him no small amount of anguish, Jackson bluntly stated that the team's pitchers made the difference because "our offense collapsed after the All-Star break."[51] Campaneris was atop the AL stolen base leaders with 52. Other outfielders who concluded the season in Oakland did so with a wide range of success, as Mangual (.246, 5, 32) and Hendrick (.182, 1, 15) spent more time on the bench as Alou (.281, 1, 16) patrolled right field from late August until the close of the year. Tenace (.225, 5, 32) was still a part-time catcher and filled in at spots around the infield and in right field. Meanwhile at second base, Tim Cullen (.261, 0, 15) ended up with the most playing time — 72 games — as Campaneris's keystone partner.

But it was Rudi, having enjoyed a season uninterrupted by military obligations, who blossomed as the club's best player. No longer encumbered by reserve duty, which earlier had removed him from the team for uncomfortable lengths of time, Rudi played solidly in left field, committing but two errors in 147 games, yet it was at the plate where he excelled. Finishing fifth in the AL batting race with a .305 average, Rudi was first in hits (181), third in total bases (288), second in runs scored (92) and doubles (32), and tied for the league lead (with the lumbering Carlton Fisk of the Red Sox) in triples (9).

On the mound, Hunter became entrenched as the stalwart of the rotation, his 21 victories in 28 decisions giving him a league-leading .750 winning percentage, which was embellished by a tidy 2.04 ERA. But the value of Holtzman's arrival from the Cubs cannot be underestimated. At a time when the Vida Blue holdout could have crippled the pitching staff, Holtzman (19–11, 2.51 ERA) looked more like the 17-game winner he had once been, as he capably filled Blue's void by winning 13 times before the All-Star break, a victory total that was nearly one-fourth of the Athletics' 56 wins. The southpaw was also credited by Williams for indoctrinating quick-witted Rollie Fingers with "street smarts" that helped mature the reliever and strengthen his role as the ace of the bullpen.[52] Serving as a counterweight to the raucousness that otherwise pervaded the Athletics, this type of mentoring between some players was an indispensable asset, which in Fingers's case transitioned him from Oakland's best fireman into becoming one of the most formidable relievers in baseball.

When he finally returned to the pitching staff, Blue, his career still in front of him, brought back some but not nearly as much of the domination he held over the league's batters in 1971, logging six wins — four by shutout — and ten losses with a 2.80 ERA in his abbreviated season. Odom fell one win short of equaling his career-high, posting a 15–6 mark with a 2.50 ERA, and Oakland benefited from the pitching of rookie left-hander Dave Hamilton (6–6, 2.93 ERA), whose four wins in a three-week period beginning in late May helped keep the rival White Sox at bay. Williams boasted, and with good reason, that he had the league's premier relief corps at his disposal and was not reluctant to use it. The Athletics bullpen was anchored by Fingers (11–9, 21 saves, 2.51 ERA), who was now employing his "rubber arm" exclusively as a reliever; also contributing were fellow right-handers Bob Locker (6–1, 10 saves, 2.65 ERA) and Joel Horlen (3–4, 1 save, 3.00 ERA).[53] Darold Knowles (5–1, 11 saves, 1.36 ERA) provided valuable late-inning help from the left side, but his season was cut short by a broken thumb he sustained on his pitching hand with one week left on the schedule. The injury forced Williams, who planned to use only three starters for the ALCS, to switch Blue from starter to temporary reliever lest the Oakland bullpen be completely lacking a left-hander for the postseason, even though the move wounded Blue's pride.

Blocking Oakland's path to the World Series were the Tigers, led by fiery Billy Martin, who guided Detroit to the AL East pennant by one-half game over Boston. The strange margin of victory was a consequence of the contests lost to the spring strike, and making the situation more agonizing for the Red Sox was the fact that four of their seven cancellations were games against the Tigers, including three at Fenway Park. Detroit advanced to the ALCS with an 86–70 record and masked a relatively weak and elderly offense with standout pitching from Mickey Lolich and Joe Coleman and a fundamentally sound defense that was the best in the circuit with only 96 errors committed.

The 1972 ALCS was one infused by ill will between the contestants, as the Tigers and Athletics had engaged in a donnybrook at the end of August. The melee, which the *Oakland Tribune*'s John Porter described as "15 minutes of anarchy on Tiger Stadium's infield," was a big factor in the enmity, as was a mud-slinging campaign waged in the press between Martin and Charlie Finley.[54] When the series opened in Oakland on October 7, Hunter and Lolich locked up in a classic duel as each allowed only one run through eight innings. Blue relieved in the ninth but yielded to Fingers, who pitched three full innings and survived Al Kaline's go-ahead solo home run when Oakland scored two runs in the bottom of the eleventh to win, 3–2, as Gonzalo Marquez, a late-season roster addition who carved a welcome niche through his pinch-hitting heroics, delivered the tying run. Game 2 pitted the Tigers' Woody Fryman, who was chased by a four-run outburst in the fifth inning, against Odom, who masterfully shut out Detroit on three hits, 5–0, with the indelible moment of this game occurring in the home half of the seventh inning.

Taking offense with several close pitches during the contest and still smarting from being decked by a Tiger pitch that contributed to the August tussle, Campaneris could bear it no longer when reliever Lerrin LaGrow felled him with a pitch to the left ankle. After righting himself, the enraged Campy, 3-for-3 with two runs scored in the game, sought immediate revenge by hurling his bat at LaGrow, who ducked just in time to avoid being skulled, as both teams' benches emptied onto the field. Martin, equally enraged by Campy's action, unsuccessfully sought his own revenge against the bat-thrower but was restrained. Ejected from the game were Campaneris for his actions and LaGrow, who was banished by home plate umpire Nestor Chylak "just to keep peace" and remove the potential for any other explosion of fury.[55] Campaneris's misdeed cried out for a suspension, and justice was meted out by American League President Joe Cronin, who expelled the Athletic for ten games beginning with Game 3 of the ALCS.[56]

In Game 3 at Detroit, Holtzman started for Oakland but was on the short end of Coleman's 3–0 shutout, the Tiger hurler striking out 14 batters to ward off an Oakland sweep. Overconfident of a quick end to the series, the Athletics had checked out of their hotel prior to the third game, but they sheepishly returned after Coleman derailed their aspirations. Electing to use his best pitcher in Game 4, Williams sent Hunter to face Lolich while shunning Blue. The skipper's decision caused an eruption by the former Cy Young Award winner, who lambasted Williams for failing to communicate his intentions of how to use him in the ALCS and charged that Finley wanted him withheld from a starting assignment for fear that he "might pitch a no-hitter now and that'd give me a good bargaining point for next year's contract."[57] When the game was played, the Hunter-Lolich tilt did not disappoint, even though neither starter was around for the final out.

Tied 1–1 after nine innings, the balance of the game rested with each team's bullpen. The Athletics struck in their half of the tenth, scoring a pair of runs and raising hopes for the franchise's first American League pennant in over forty years. Since Williams had ushered Fingers and Blue to the mound in the eighth and ninth innings, the latter being replaced by a pinch-hitter in the tenth, the manager went deeper into his bullpen in the hope of shutting down Detroit. In a most critical failure, Locker, Horlen, and Hamilton let the final inning slip through their hands as the Tigers rallied to score three runs to edge Oakland, 4–3, and send the series to a fifth and final game. The defeat was particularly galling for catcher Gene Tenace, who, according to an *Oakland Tribune* columnist, "played second base ... just long enough to drop a throw and cause hell to break loose."[58] On the play in question, Bando fielded a grounder with the bases loaded and none out and elected to go to second to start a double play, but Tenace bobbled his throw, allowing the first Tigers run of the inning to score.

Odom and Fryman faced off in the finale on a cold day at Tiger Stadium, as the Athletics rode the combined five-hit pitching of Odom and Blue to capture the ALCS. Spotting Detroit a quick one-run lead after the opening frame, the Athletics knotted the game in the top of the second when Jackson scored on the front end of a double-steal, but the outfielder tore his hamstring on his way to the plate and was lost for the remainder of the postseason. Heroically redeeming himself, Tenace got his only hit of the series to drive in Hendrick in the fourth for a 2–1 margin, as Blue relieved with four scoreless innings to seal the Tigers' fate. Champagne flowed in the victor's clubhouse, but the celebration became tinged with anger when Odom, who had grown nauseous from the game's tension, charged at Blue for mocking his inability to pitch more than five innings.

Nonetheless, Oakland had earned its trip to the 1972 World Series. The Athletics served as an interesting counterpoint to their opponents, the Cincinnati Reds, whose clean-shaven faces, stodgy black spikes — club policy demanded that the trademark of the shoe manu-facturer's striping be painted over — white home uniforms, and gray road uniforms reflected a conservative appearance that was diametrically opposed to Oakland's abundant hair and colorful field attire. The Reds' own journey to the Series was facilitated when they won Game 5 of the National League Championship Series in the bottom of the ninth on a wild pitch. With a solid roster featuring players with experience in the 1970 World Series, the Reds were the oddsmakers' choice to beat an Oakland club now hobbled by the absence of Jackson.

## "Anyone for Tenace?"

The Athletics could feel pride in their achievement of winning the American League pennant, but few observers would have found fault if they were not brimming with optimism as they opened the Fall Classic at Cincinnati's Riverfront Stadium. Jackson was out of the lineup, but at least Campaneris had been re-instated by the grace of Commissioner Bowie

Kuhn's thoughtful ruling in the matter of the shortstop's suspension. Drawing on his legal experience, Kuhn invoked *stare decisis* when he learned that in late 1942 Frank Crosetti of the Yankees had been banished for thirty games as the result of a run-in with an umpire but was allowed to play in the World Series, his suspension postponed until the beginning of the next regular season. In like fashion, Kuhn permitted Campaneris to return to the Athletics for the Series, with the seven-game balance of his punishment to be carried over to the beginning of the 1973 season.[59] Thus, Dick Williams would not be handicapped by having to employ a consortium of infielders — Ted Kubiak, Dal Maxvill, and Tim Cullen took over for the rest of the ALCS — to fill Campy's spot in the lineup.

Holtzman was tabbed to start Game 1 and bested the Reds' Gary Nolan, 3–2, although the Oakland southpaw was lifted after surrendering a lead-off double to Johnny Bench in the sixth inning. Fingers and Blue combined to close out Cincinnati on one hit and one walk each, the latter earning a save. But Gene Tenace was the star of the game, setting a record by socking home runs in his first two World Series at-bats to drive in all the Athletics runs. Tenace, the starting catcher who thankfully remained behind the plate for the entire contest, was awarded a $5,000 salary increase courtesy of an instant bonus by Finley, who had rushed to the visitor's clubhouse after the final out to bestow the windfall on his back-

stop. Before the game, Blue raised eyebrows with his comment saying that he was pitching for himself and no one else in the Oakland organization, yet with dispatch he logged his second straight save in the postseason and relished seeing Tenace drive in the winning runs in each of Oakland's last two games.

Game 2 was Catfish Hunter's turn to shine on the mound as he nearly pitched a complete game and drove in the first of the Athletics' two runs in his 2–1 win over Cincinnati's Ross Grimsley. Hunter was aided by the heroics of Joe Rudi, who hit a solo homer in the third and made a dramatic grab against the left-field wall in the bottom of the ninth to save a run. (In another fit of generosity, Finley lavished Rudi with a $5,000 bonus and on the return flight to the West Coast he renewed Williams's two-month-old contract for even more money.[60]) When Hunter flagged and yielded the Reds' only tally in the ninth, Fingers relieved to get the last out to send the Series to Oakland with the Athletics ahead two games to none. The trip back home, however, was not all joy for

**Catcher Gene Tenace became an instant hero when he belted home runs in his first two World Series at-bats in 1972.**

Williams despite Finley's unexpected generosity. Mike Epstein, who committed an error in the fifth inning, was lifted by Williams after the first baseman walked in the sixth, when Allan Lewis was sent in to pinch-run. Mike Hegan was installed at first base for the remainder of the game, a move that paid off handsomely in the bottom of the ninth when he made a diving stop of a line drive and recorded the crucial second out. Still irked at being taken out so early in the game, Epstein aired out Williams in mid-flight, and the manager instantly retaliated with his own choice words. No blows were struck, but the incident branded Epstein as disgruntled. Happier moments were luckily just ahead — when the Athletics landed at Oakland International Airport, they were greeted by an enthusiastic crowd of 8,000 fans, as well as "Charlie O" the mule.

Game 3 was postponed one day by the worst rains in the Bay Area in more than eight decades, but the break in the action gave Vida Blue a bit too much time to speak to the press. Blue furnished the Reds with some incentive to climb back into contention when he claimed that Oakland was "handling the Cincinnati Reds easier than we did the Texas Rangers," an affront that Sparky Anderson's players, Jack Billingham in particular, answered with a narrow 1–0 win over the Athletics when play resumed.[61] Billingham allowed only three hits, two of them in the infield, over eight-plus innings, beating Blue Moon Odom, who over seven strong innings gave up only four hits, one of which was Cesar Geronimo's single that drove in the lone run of the game. Both teams combined for a mere seven hits, with the sluggish offense attributed to the 5:15 P.M. West Coast starting time, which put most of the game's pitches in the glow of the early evening twilight.

The top of the eighth inning featured some interesting moments, the first occurring when reliever Blue was chased off the mound by the Reds, who took a measure of revenge for his deprecating "Rangers" comment. Blue retired leadoff batter Pete Rose but allowed a walk to Joe Morgan and a single to Bobby Tolan that moved Morgan to third base. To face the next several right-handed Cincinnati batters, Fingers was summoned. After Tolan stole second, Johnny Bench worked a full count and appeared to be headed to first on an intentional walk when Williams hastily conferred with Fingers, Bando, and Tenace, who was catching that day. Bench, already having been called out on strikes twice, stood in the batter's box as Tenace, his right arm extended to signal for an outside pitch, awaited the delivery. But instead of a slow lob to the plate, Fingers broke off a slider — Williams later said the pitch had to be a breaking ball for the maneuver to work — for another called strike three, as the stunned Bench unwittingly became the second out.[62] Bench was the Reds' most dangerous hitter — he would later be named the National League's 1972 MVP — so the gamble paid off in helping to keep the Reds off the scoreboard.

Hitters on both teams resumed somewhat normal output in Game 4, tallying a total of 17 hits in the contest, yet runs were in short supply. After seven innings Holtzman held Cincinnati scoreless, and the only mistake Cincinnati's Don Gullett made was serving up a solo home run to Tenace. In the eighth, the Reds seemed poised to even the series at two wins each when they struck for two runs, one off Holtzman, the other off Blue, to take the lead. But the Athletics rallied with their own pair of runs in the bottom of the ninth to capture the pivotal fourth game. Showing a deftness for using his bench, Williams used three pinch-hitters and two pinch-runners to engineer the comeback, as Gonzalo Marquez once more ignited the outburst with a one-out, pinch single, and Angel Mangual, batting for Fingers, drove in the winning run.

Now on the brink of a World Series championship with a commanding three-games-to-one advantage, the Athletics looked to clinch the title in their final game at the Coliseum, but the Reds, far from quitting, were driven by professional pride and an anger prompted by the taunting of unruly fans who heaped verbal abuse on some players and threw eggs and oranges at others. For Game 5, Williams sent Catfish Hunter to the mound against Lynn McGlothlin, the fifth different starter used by the Reds. Although Hunter was staked to a 4–2 lead — Tenace connecting for a three-run homer — he did not survive the fifth inning. Fingers came out of the bullpen for a long stint and held Cincinnati in check through the seventh inning, but surrendered single runs in the eight and ninth. Down 5–4, Oakland threatened in their half of the ninth but the magic of the previous day's rally failed to return. The Athletics managed to put runners on the corners with one out, but Campaneris fouled out behind first base to Morgan, who then threw out pinch-runner Blue Moon Odom at the plate for a game-ending double play. Reds skipper Sparky Anderson, upholding his reputation for quick use of his bullpen, employed five relievers to squelch Oakland for the last half of the game.

Returning to Cincinnati, the Athletics were menaced by a fan who was arrested for carrying a loaded gun outside Riverfront Stadium — Tenace was said to be his intended target — and extra security was provided for protection of the team. Oakland's rotation had become a jumble, with the best-rested among the trio of starters used thus far in the series being Odom, who would have been pitching on two days rest. Williams turned to Vida Blue, who had hurled less than one total inning of relief since Game 1 and presciently said before Game 6 that if he could get three or four runs from his teammates, the Athletics would win.[63] Had that offensive support materialized, Oakland may well have been victorious, as Blue kept the Reds close and was down 2–1 going into the bottom of the sixth. Cincinnati was determined to end its World Series losing streak of seven home games, however, and after Blue was relieved with two down in the sixth, the bullpen — Dave Hamilton in particular — was roughed up for five more runs in the 8–1 drubbing. Blue felt that he pitched well, but the Big Red Machine employed its traditional weaponry of power, speed, and deep bullpen — Anderson's quick hook removed starter Gary Nolan with two out in the fifth — to even the Series at three games apiece.

Resorting to gallows humor after the Reds stole three more bases for a total of eleven in the first six games, one Oakland columnist suggested that Finley might do well to shoot Tenace if the catcher proved unable to stop the speedy Cincinnati baserunners.[64] Williams adjusted his lineup by inserting Dave Duncan behind the plate and kept Tenace's hot bat available by moving him to first base. Kept uninformed about the death threat until after the final game, Tenace again delivered a pair of clutch hits, a run-scoring single in the first inning and a double to drive in another run in the sixth. Odom started and held Cincinnati scoreless through four innings before encountering trouble in the fifth. Odom and reliever Catfish Hunter — all pitchers were available to throw in the finale — were charged with single runs in the fifth and eighth innings, respectively, and after Holtzman spelled Hunter and allowed a hit to the only batter he faced, Williams, in one of the last of his sixteen trips to the mound that day, summoned Fingers once more. Sporting the most famous of the mustaches grown by the Athletics, a perfectly waxed handlebar, Fingers held Cincinnati scoreless in his two full innings of work, albeit with the drama of escaping a bases-loaded jam in the eighth. When Rose flied out to Rudi in left-center field for the third out in the bottom of the ninth, Oakland's 3–2 win had earned the Athletics an arduous but most satisfying World Series title.

Early in the series, the Oakland catcher's power surge became a source of inspiration to fans and punsters — "Anyone for Tenace?" went the line — and Tenace's just reward for his .348 average, four home runs, and nine RBIs was being named the Most Valuable Player of the World Series. The accolades continued on October 23 when the *Oakland Tribune* took the occasion of the freshly-minted championship to proudly lionize the Athletics with a front-page editorial that placed the team in the pantheon of heroes — Frank Robinson, basketball star Bill Russell, and Olympic swimmer Mark Spitz, to name a few — whose pasts were rooted in Oakland. An "outpouring of sheer joy" from thousands of fans greeted the Athletics at the airport upon their return from Cincinnati and in a spectacular parade through the streets of Oakland.[65]

In contrast to the great Orioles dynasty immediately preceding Oakland's own ascension, the Athletics did not run roughshod over the league and in fact had to rebound in late August to outlast the White Sox just to win the AL West. They struggled mightily with injuries at inopportune times, including the losses of Knowles and Jackson at season's end. After sprinting to a quick two-game lead in the ALCS, Oakland lost Campaneris for the three games in Detroit but persevered to edge the Tigers. Upon reaching the World Series, Dick Williams's troops again took a quick two-game lead over the Reds and nearly let a three-games-to-one advantage slip away before outlasting Cincinnati. This Athletics club was battle-tested, the margin of victory in all four of their Series wins — and two of their losses — was a single run. Although Williams's lineup could sometimes appear to be held together with tape and bandages, in reality it was secured by the underpinnings of firm timber like Bando, Rudi, Campaneris, Jackson, Hunter, and Holtzman. With pressure on them to win games and placate their irascible owner, the Athletics of 1972 reached baseball's summit with enough grit and guile to convince many baseball observers that the "A" on their uniforms could easily have stood for assiduousness.

One final laurel was awarded at the conclusion of 1972, and its recipient was none other than that irascible owner. Despite the vexation that Charlie Finley caused for many of his fellow major league club owners, front office staff, manager, coaches, and players, to say nothing of the commissioner, the results produced by dint of Finley's efforts through the years leading up to the World Series title gained further currency when he was named Sportsman of the Year by *The Sporting News*. Finley could be excused for "still walking on air" when he predicted a successful defense of Oakland's crown in 1973, since the penchant for success which he developed in the business world had now decisively crossed into the sports world.[66] Aware of the exigencies that the Athletics had to address, Finley quickly set to shoring up weaknesses on the roster during the winter while hoping that Reggie Jackson's leg would heal. Finley again donned his general manager's hat and began the process of personnel adjustments so that the repeat performance he anticipated would indeed happen.

## Title Defense Number One

In one respect, the Athletics were preparing for a new season before they had even clinched the AL West in 1972. Pitching coach Bill Posedel, who was so instrumental in molding the staff that made Oakland's one of the best in baseball, was returning to minor league instruction within the organization, while Wes Stock, late of the Milwaukee Brewers, was named in early September to succeed Posedel. Shortly after the Athletics' World Series victory, a restive Charlie Finley continued activity in the trading market with as much gusto as he had displayed during the regular campaign.

Beginning in late October, Finley re-acquired southpaw reliever Paul Lindblad from the Rangers and in a separate deal sent first baseman Mike Epstein to the Rangers for another reliever, Horacio Piña, a transaction that raised eyebrows since Epstein had led Oakland in home runs. But Finley was impressed with the fifteen saves recorded by Piña to lead Texas in that category, and he was confident that World Series star Tenace could transition from catcher, where his defensive liabilities — attributed to a supposedly sore shoulder — were grossly exposed in the World Series, to a safer haven at first base.[67] Tenace's power hitting was forecast to replace that of the departed Epstein, and under Mike Hegan's tutelage, Tenace learned the finer points of playing defense at first base. Oakland's center field position had not become the jumble that existed at second base, but the earlier trade of Rick Monday and the failure of both George Hendrick and Angel Mangual to stabilize that spot in the lineup led Finley to reach out, ironically, to the same team to which he had sent Monday. Although Monday was not Finley's intended quarry, the owner nevertheless catered to his penchant for speed by acquiring the Cubs' fleet outfield prospect Billy North in exchange for reliever Bob Locker. Three days after North's arrival, outfielder Matty Alou, who had become a liability because of his high salary, was dispatched to the Yankees for infielder Rich McKinney and pitcher Rob Gardner, who, like Lindblad, would be on his second tour of duty with the Athletics.

When 1973 spring training again brought the players together, Oakland counted on a recuperated Reggie Jackson to pick up where he had left off in 1972, as he was driven by a desire to eclipse the $100,000 salary level. It was hoped that Dick Green had recovered sufficiently from his back surgery to fortify second base and perhaps put an end to the revolving door at that position. And in the bullpen, Darold Knowles was ready to return, his broken thumb now healed. Originally intended to be acquired as part of the Ollie Brown trade, Billy Conigliaro blanched at reporting to Oakland in the summer of 1972 but was officially brought aboard to contend for an outfield job.

The Athletics training camp was disrupted by Dave Duncan's holdout and a potential walkout by Vida Blue, but Finley settled both cases by renewing Duncan's contract and coercively signing Blue after threatening to trade him to the lowly Rangers. When Duncan refused to sign his renewal pact, Finley dealt him and Hendrick to the Indians in late March for infielder Jack Heidemann and catcher Ray Fosse, the latter a *wunderkind* and potential backstop star with the Tribe whose progress was stalled by several injuries, not least of which was a horrific collision at home plate with Pete Rose on the ending play of the 1970 All-Star Game.

Shortly after the Fosse transaction, Finley was granted his wish to use orange baseballs in an exhibition game, an innovation he had long pressed the league to at least try as an experiment. However, the non-standard color received a tepid reception when many batters had difficulty picking up the rotation of the ball — the red seams were blurred by the orange cover — so further pursuit of this latest Finley novelty was scrapped.

Revamping of lineups for all American League teams in 1973 featured the inclusion of the new designated hitter, but Oakland had unwittingly let several good candidates for that role slip away. Tommy Davis and Orlando Cepeda, both afflicted with chronically poor knees, had been briefly with the Athletics for part of 1972 but had been released. After drawing an unenthusiastic contract offer from Finley at the end of the season, Don Mincher opted for retirement. Despite the crowding in the outfield, Matty Alou would have also served well as a DH as he appeared to be still capable of swinging a productive bat.[68] But when the season opened, Dick Williams initially used North as DH in the leadoff spot and put Conigliaro in center field, although North was soon to take over in center and drop to number two in the order behind Campaneris.

As determined as Finley was to address weaknesses on the roster, his efforts initially appeared to be in vain. Opening defense of their championship at home, the Athletics — without the services of Campaneris, who was completing his suspension imposed during the ALCS — were swept three straight by the Twins and quickly plunged into the AL West basement. Advancing to fifth place in mid–April but unable to sustain any kind of momentum, a listless Oakland club seemed vulnerable to being overtaken by almost any of its division rivals, save the Rangers. The silver lining of this bleak cloud rested in the fact that the Athletics were only a handful of games out of first place, so any sudden outburst of a modest winning streak would vault them back into the divisional lead. Aiding the offense was burly Deron Johnson, brought over from Philadelphia in exchange for a minor leaguer in early May. Johnson's muscle from the right side of the plate gave Oakland a solid designated hitter who could also fill in at first base. Hitting safely in his first seven games in an Athletics uniform, Johnson gave Oakland some traction as the Athletics tried to climb out of fifth place.

Still Oakland ended the month of May hampered by Joe Rudi's lengthy, popup-filled slump — his .217 average was the third-worst on the team — while Odom (1–8, 6.79 ERA) and Blue (3–2, 4.97) floundered on the hill. Blue, now using more breaking pitches and relying less on his fastball, was the subject of debate as to whether he could ever recapture his glory of 1971, yet he won two key games in late June that kept the Athletics in or near the divisional lead. In sartorial displays meant to help their fortunes, Oakland tried all-green and all-yellow uniforms at this time with mixed results, but of greater import were the five straight wins earned by sophomore left-hander Dave Hamilton and Hunter's own nine-game victory streak. Line drives again flew off Rudi's bat, and as June drew to an end, the Athletics' team hitting and pitching statistics were near the top of the American League.

Befitting of Oakland's milieu, controversy was always close at hand, with the latest episode occurring over the Fourth of July holiday. Fireworks of a different kind were ignited in the clubhouse over comments made by Jackson in a pique of frustration following a loss to the Angels. Whining about management's "constructive criticism" — a term used by Williams — intended not only for Jackson but teammates Fosse and Green as well, the outfielder fumed, "I can't play here and be happy. Make a mistake, and the manager and coaches are on you," to which coach Jerry Adair, in rapping Jackson's recent defensive lapses, fired back, "I'm tired of seeing him play half the time."[69] In his report on this latest spat, writer Ron Bergman presciently reported that Finley, unwilling to brook an attack on his coaching staff even by one of his best players, was not likely to remain idle for long. Three days after Jackson's complaint, Finley gave the coaches a resounding vote of confidence by renewing their individual contracts for the 1974 season and extended Williams's contract through

1975. At the same time Finley was defending his staff—the owner also denounced rumors emanating from New Orleans that had the Athletics moving there upon completion of the Superdome in 1974—Jackson expressed fear that he might be traded, thereby joining Duncan and Epstein as former Oakland malcontents.

As the All-Star break approached, Williams was sidelined by an emergency appendectomy on July 19, but a miraculous recovery allowed him to tend to his managerial assignment at the All-Star Game in Kansas City. Jackson, who was among the league leaders in most major batting categories, earned honors as a starter in the AL outfield, while Williams added Bando, Campaneris, Holtzman, Hunter, and Fingers as reserves to the squad. At 56–42, the Athletics began the second half of the campaign hoping to expand their 2½-game edge over the Kansas City Royals, but they would do so without the AL's best pitcher. Having sustained a hairline fracture to his pitching thumb in the second inning of the All-Star Game, Hunter and his 15–3 record were sidelined until the third week of August.

The Athletics continued to labor when Rudi also missed significant playing time due to an injured thumb and was hospitalized with strep throat along with other viral afflictions, creating a cause for concern as the bench consistently failed to deliver in the clutch. After the Athletics were victims of a no-hitter by Jim Bibby of the Rangers on July 30, Finley resumed his role of roster adjuster and acquired three new players. Purchased from Pittsburgh was Vic Davalillo, a pint-sized outfielder and former Gold Glove winner who contributed several timely pinch-hits and fine plays in the field; another outfielder, Jesus Alou, was purchased from Houston and became the last of the Alou brothers to wear an Oakland uniform; and infielder Mike Andrews, a member of Williams's 1967 miracle Red Sox, was signed after being released by the White Sox.

As Oakland's frail lead evaporated in early August, Finley's health stole headlines when he suffered a mild heart attack, the effects of which relegated him to a wheelchair for several weeks. But a nine-game cloudburst of wins during several series against American League East teams catapulted the Athletics into the lead, highlighted by Vida Blue's August 16 victory, after which the Athletics were never surpassed in the AL West. A significant change—by way of a minor adjustment, really—to the Oakland batting order occurred when Williams elevated North, whose pluckiness had become a source of irritation to both teammates and foes, from the number two spot to leadoff and demoted Campaneris from leadoff to second.[70] Since the shortstop's average and on-base percentage had been dropping, Williams sought to capitalize further on North's speed and emerging talent.

A torn tendon in Deron Johnson's right hand, incurred in mid–August, led to a late-season slump, which Finley tried to address by purchasing standout hitter Rico Carty from the Cubs with barely three weeks left in the season. Fortunately for the Athletics, Hunter's fracture healed well enough that he went 6–2 after missing four weeks of action, Blue was victorious in his last five decisions, including the division-clinching game on September 23, and Holtzman rounded out Oakland's trio of top starters by continuing on a 20-win pace. The Athletics' winning of their third straight AL West pennant came fortuitously and coincidentally in Chicago, where Finley spent most of his time handling his insurance business. Although he attended the contest at Comiskey Park, Finley was on doctors' orders to stay out of his team's celebratory clubhouse so as not to upset his coronary-related recovery.

Once again haunted by late-season injuries, however, the Athletics lost the services of

Jackson on an intermittent basis due to recurring hamstring problems, but the team's chances for a second AL pennant suffered a most unfavorable setback when North severely sprained an ankle on September 20 and was forced out for the remainder of the season. Mangual was called upon to fill North's place in center field, Campaneris was raised to the top of the order, and Davalillo filled in for Jackson in right. After a flurry of nine wins in ten mid-September contests, the Athletics won only four of their last eleven games and limped across the finish line at 94–68, drawing 1,000,761 fans to the Coliseum for the 1973 season.

Overall, the final statistics of Oakland's primary regulars were solid and well-balanced. Despite being absent for one-quarter of the season, Rudi still hit .270 with a dozen home runs and 66 RBIs, North helped ignite the upper part of the order with his .285 average, 78 walks, and 53 stolen bases, while Jackson continued apace and led the American League in runs (99), homers (32), RBIs (117), and slugging percentage (.531), batted .293, and stole 22 bases on his way to a unanimous selection as the AL's Most Valuable Player. Around the infield, Bando (.287, 29 home runs, 98 RBIs) played in all 162 games and topped the league with 32 doubles in one of his best seasons, Campaneris (.250, 4, 46) continued to be a bell-

Ken Holtzman enjoyed his best year in Oakland during 1973 when he won 21 games in the regular season and three more in postseason play.

wether at shortstop and stole 34 bases, Green (.262, 3, 42) returned for a full season with his steady glove work afield, and Tenace (.259, 24, 84) not only found a home at first base but demonstrated that the power stroke which earned him so much attention in the 1972 World Series was not an aberration. Behind the plate, Fosse (.256, 7, 52) shouldered the catching burden for 141 games, and Johnson (.246, 19, 81) as the Athletics designated hitter put up some of the better run production numbers at the newly-created position.

Not quite matching the redoubtable Oriole rotation of 1971, Oakland nevertheless finished with a trio of twenty-game winners, with some grudging admiration given to new pitching coach Wes Stock. With a style of communication bordering at times on sarcastic, Stock's temperament differed from that of his predecessor, but he was able to slowly convince Blue (20–9, 3.38 ERA) to use a hard-thrown breaking ball for profit, and the result was vast improvement over his lost season of 1972.[71] Hunter (21–5, 3.34) posted the best winning percentage in the AL at .808, and Holtzman (21–13, 2.97) yielded only two walks per nine innings pitched, one of the best such ratios in the AL, in becoming the Athletics' third 20-game winner. The fourth main starter, Odom (5–12, 4.49), overcame a horrendous first half but pitched less than 90 innings over the last three months of the season and was rumored to be trade bait for another outfielder for the September stretch run. The patented depth of the Athletics bullpen was fronted by its ace Fingers (7–8, 22 saves, 1.92 ERA) and backed up by Knowles (6–8, nine saves, 3.09), Piña (6–3, eight saves, 2.76), and Lindblad (1–5, two saves, 3.69). Hamilton (6–4, no saves, 4.39) served as starter and also worked in relief for a staff that as a whole had the second-best rankings in team ERA and saves.

Playoff-bound for the third year running, Oakland was paired against pitching-rich Baltimore in a rematch of the 1971 American League Championship Series. Dick Williams fretted over having to continue using the erratic Mangual in center field as North's replacement, and the manager's angst was worsened by Mangual's demand to be traded just days before the ALCS began. Also handicapping Oakland was Finley's trade of reserve catcher Jose Morales to Montreal *after* the September 1 deadline for determining postseason rosters, which meant that the Athletics could add a replacement only with the approval of the Orioles. Williams groused about the permission Baltimore granted allowing Allan Lewis's addition to the roster when the manager and several players would have preferred to have the bat of Rico Carty, who was denied a postseason spot, coming off the bench. Substituting for the injured North was a young infielder, Manny Trillo, who was soon to become a pawn in a controversial episode after the league championship series. Already bewildered by the owner's trade of a playoff-eligible player, many on the team had their moods soured further upon learning that well-regarded front office assistant Bill Rigney, who had been scouting the Orioles in preparation for the playoffs, was fired by Finley for leaving his duties to tend to his ailing wife without having first notified the owner of his intentions. Such was the bristly milieu of the Athletics as they headed into the postseason.

## Finally Beating Baltimore

Williams hoped for a smoother playoff run than that of the contentious 1972 series against Detroit, and his team also had the home-field advantage, which would turn out to provide Oakland with a precious edge in a hard-fought ALCS. Picked to open the series for the Athletics, Vida Blue was enthusiastic — too enthusiastic, perhaps — about his Game 1 assignment in Baltimore and never made it out of the first inning. The Orioles struck quickly and chased Blue, who was charged with four runs, as Jim Palmer tamed the Athletics bats with a five-hit, 6–0, shutout, but Oakland evened the series with a 6–3 victory in Game 2, as Catfish Hunter received the support of four home runs. Campaneris hit a leadoff homer in the first, and heading into the sixth tied at 1–1, Rudi and Bando connected off Dave McNally to open a lead. Bando then added a two-run shot in the eighth to give reliever Fingers some insurance.

Shifting to Oakland, Game 3 was postponed by a torrential October rain. When play resumed, left-handers Mike Cuellar of the Orioles and Ken Holtzman locked up in a pitchers' duel, both starters surrendering just one run on three hits each into the eleventh inning. Campaneris led off the bottom of the eleventh and broke the deadlock with a fly ball to left field that just cleared the fence and the outstretched glove of Don Baylor, giving the Athletics a 2–1 win and a two games to one lead in the best-of-five series. Game 4 featured another Blue-Palmer tilt, as Blue limited Baltimore to four hits in the first six innings, but his 4–0 lead vanished in the seventh thanks mostly to Andy Etchebarren's three-run, game-tying homer. Blue gave way to Fingers to stanch the flow of Baltimore runs, but the ace of the Oakland bullpen served up a solo home run to Bobby Grich in the top of the eighth, and Grant Jackson shut out the Athletics over three innings to win, 5–4, and square the series at two games each. Afterward in the Oakland clubhouse, Odom took exception to a comment by Fingers regarding the blown lead, and when Odom interpreted the remark as a slight against Blue's collapse rather than Fingers' undoing, he barked back at Fingers and lay the blame for the loss with the relief ace's home run offering to Grich. A modicum of calm was restored before punches were thrown, but the outburst was emblematic of Team Turmoil, which now would have just one last chance to defend its AL pennant.

In the Game 5 finale, Hunter added to his reputation as a money pitcher — "This was special, a game I *wanted* to pitch," he later told readers of his autobiography — and dominated Baltimore, shutting out the Orioles on five hits in the 3–0 clincher, as Rudi, Davalillo, and Alou drove in the Oakland runs.[72] For many Athletics, a return to the World Series brought heightened anticipation, especially so for Reggie Jackson, who after missing out the previous October would be playing in his first Fall Classic. Oakland veterans were braced for a tussle with the New York Mets, whose clash in the National League Championship Series against the Cincinnati Reds also went five games.

## Title Number 2 and "l'Affaire Andrews"

The Athletics faced a Mets squad whose core was similar to New York's miracle team of 1969, with the strong, effective pitching of Tom Seaver and Jerry Koosman supplemented by that of Jon Matlack, another promising left-hander. As a spiritual leader, 42-year-old Willie Mays, late of the San Francisco Giants, was finishing his illustrious career in a New York uniform. The Mets had found dependability with new blood at three other positions. First base was manned by young, power-hitting John Milner, Felix Millan handled second base, and steady-hitting Rusty Staub patrolled right field. New York's tenacity belied their unimpressive 82–79 regular-season record because they barreled through the campaign's last few weeks by winning 20 of 28 games and drew motivation from their ebullient relief ace Tug McGraw, whose exhortations of "You gotta believe!" became a mantra for the Mets. Reggie Jackson warned that the Mets were "the underdogs who always win ... if you underrate them as a team, they can beat you," as the Athletics were soon to discover that their hands would be just as full against New York as they had been a year earlier against the Reds.[73]

While the Mets were looking to reprise their championship of four years prior, Oakland's concern was defending their World Series crown with a roster now shorthanded due to a technicality. Although the Orioles allowed the Athletics to substitute Lewis and Trillo for North and Morales in the ALCS, New York was under no such obligation to extend the same courtesy and only allowed Lewis as a replacement for North, thereby rendering Trillo ineligible. Desperate to have a full complement of players for the World Series, Dick Williams brokered a deal that would have returned Morales from the Expos, but such a move required that Montreal first place him on waivers, thus exposing him to the potential of being claimed by another National League team. The transaction came undone when the Expos withdrew Morales from the waiver wire and compelled Oakland to carry on with 24 players.

Game 1 resulted in a victory at Oakland as Ken Holtzman was a hero on the mound and at the bat. Holtzman allowed one run on four hits over five innings, and, with the designated hitter not in effect for the Series, hit a double and scored in the third inning as the Athletics edged the Mets, 2–1. Fingers pitched 3⅓ innings of relief, as Knowles retired the last two batters to preserve the victory.

In a dramatic contest that lasted over four hours, Game 2 was a tooth-and-nail struggle in which the Mets were ultimately victorious, 10–7. Starters Vida Blue and Jerry Koosman were not at their sharpest, as Oakland led 3–2 after chasing the New York left-hander in the third inning. Blue faltered in the Mets' half of the sixth, and relievers Piña and Knowles were ineffective — the latter committing a costly miscue to allow a pair of runs — in halting a four-run New York rally. But the Athletics rallied and scored a run in the seventh and two more in the ninth with two out to knot the score at 6–6. Fingers shut out the Mets in the tenth and eleventh, while McGraw — New York's bullpen ace would work over six innings this game — did the same. In the fateful twelfth inning, the Mets' Bud Harrelson and McGraw reached safely to lead off, Mays drove in Harrelson with a single, and two outs later it appeared that Oakland would escape down 7–6 when Milner hit a grounder to second base. However, the ball went through the legs of Mike Andrews, the third second baseman of the game for Oakland, allowing two runs to score. On the very next play, Jerry Grote hit another grounder to Andrews, who threw high to first base for his second error to let in a third run, although Williams felt that the miscue should have been charged to Tenace because he had not properly positioned himself at the bag.[74] The Athletics tried to come back in the bottom of the twelfth and scored once but left the bases loaded in the 10–7 loss. Oakland committed five errors that were charged to four different players in a contest played with nearly 3,400 seats vacant at the Coliseum, yet another thorn in the side of Athletics players who could not understand why such an important game was not sold out.

Controversy ensued immediately after the game's last out was recorded. While there were complaints from Oakland fielders about poor visibility caused by an optic jumble of sun and haze that remained stagnant due to a lack of wind — "The seeing [*sic*] out there is terrible — in the field, at bat, all over," complained Joe Rudi — the gloaming of the later innings should not have impacted a simple ground ball.[75] Yet Andrews, offering no excuses, utterly failed to make the play on either of his chances in the last inning. Ushered to a hastily arranged meeting with Finley and Dr. Harry Walker, the club's orthopedist, Andrews was quickly diagnosed to be suffering from an ailment to his right shoulder, bicep groove tencosynovitis, a condition which Finley determined would disable the infielder for the remainder of the Series and, in Finley's mind, facilitate the addition of a substitute — namely Trillo — to the roster.[76] Coerced into signing a statement in which he agreed with the diagnosis and its preposterous recommendation that he be "disabled for the rest of the year," Andrews was in essence fired from the team and tearfully departed for his home in Massachusetts while the rest of the Athletics headed to New York for the third game.[77] The largesse of Finley's spot awards and instant bonuses for jobs well done had cruelly devolved, in Andrews's case, into a summary dismissal with no apparent recourse for the player.

When the Oakland players learned the fate of their teammate — Andrews was not allowed on the team flight back east — a mutiny nearly ensued. When Bowie Kuhn was petitioned by Finley to allow Trillo to assume Andrews's place on the club, the commissioner swiftly denied the request. To deal with the "clumsy deceit on Finley's part," Kuhn issued a directive to soothe the "unfair embarrassment" heaped upon Andrews by restoring him as "a full-fledged member of the Oakland World Series squad."[78] Finley had a right to be "dissatisfied" with Andrews, but the owner was the only person who believed that "Andrews' signature [on the doctor's statement] just adds credence," despite the patent duress under which that signature was obtained.[79] Andrews rejoined his mates at Shea Stadium for the fourth Series game, but the bizarre incident pushed Dick Williams to an intractable tipping point in his career at Oakland's helm.

For nearly the entire three years he had managed the Athletics, Williams had endured Finley's incessant interference, haranguing, and constant pestering by telephone — calls that could come at any hour — that had long been the owner's trademark. But the manner in which Andrews had been punished for his unfortunate misplays was more than he could abide and he thus took the only action available to remove himself from the fiasco. Williams, who felt that by the middle of the 1973 season he was starting to break down mentally and physically, announced to his stunned players that he was resigning as manager at the conclusion of the Series, regardless of its outcome.[80] Rumors already had Williams moving to the Yankees, as speculation of possible tampering on that team's part also surfaced, but this phase of the drama had yet to play out.

When the teams at last returned to playing baseball, the hazy sun of the East Bay had given way to the mid–October chill of Flushing Meadow with temperatures more suitable for football. The starting match-up featured the aces of the respective staffs, Tom Seaver for the Mets and Catfish Hunter for Oakland. With the focus back on the game at least temporarily, New York struck quickly for a pair of runs their first time at bat. Seaver held the Athletics off the board until the sixth when they cut the lead to 2–1, and then tied the score on a Rudi single that scored Campaneris in the eighth. With Hunter pulled after six innings, the Oakland bullpen held the Mets scoreless as the game moved into extra innings. In the top of the eleventh, the Athletics, assisted by a crucial passed ball by Mets catcher Jerry Grote, pushed a run across on a Campaneris single, as Fingers came on to relieve Lindblad in the bottom half to preserve an emotional 3–2 win that was tinged with more than a bit of tribute to Andrews, their banished teammate. The Athletics had channeled their anger into a positive force that spawned another victory, which led Blue Moon Odom to blurt out after the game, "Dissension did it again!"[81]

As if the acrid air that enveloped the team could not get any worse, the visiting Athletics players seethed when they learned that their wives had been given seats not near the visitor's dugout on the third-base side but instead behind home plate at the front of the third — and upper — deck. When some nearby Mets fans learned of the wives' location and became abusive toward them, some of the women escaped by cab — on their own dime — to the relative safety of their hotel. The seating debacle nearly prompted a strike among the Oakland players, but seating arrangements were amended for Game 4, when Williams and company received an emotional lift as Andrews, now reinstated, arrived in time to suit up for action.

The welter of distractions passed as the Series resumed with the fourth game, a rematch of the opener's Holtzman-Matlack tilt. On another cold night in Flushing Meadow, Matlack was superb, allowing just three hits and one unearned run over eight innings, as New York right fielder Rusty Staub put the game out of reach by driving in five runs, including three with his first-inning homer, in the Mets' 6–1 win to square the series at two wins apiece. Back in uniform for what turned out to be his last appearance in a major league game, Andrews drew a rousing and sincere standing ovation from the New York partisans when he stepped to the plate to open the eighth in a pinch-hitting role and then grounded out to third base. Throughout the cheering, Finley remained seated, although he was seen waving an Oakland pennant.

Game 5 featured a continuation of dominant Mets pitching as Koosman and McGraw teamed up to hold Oakland to just three hits, and although they combined to walk seven Athletics, none crossed the plate. Blue made his second start of the Series and pitched well until he faded in the sixth, but he was on the short end of the 2–0 loss. Happy as one New York sports columnist might have been to see his hometown team on the verge of capturing its first World Series since 1969, Dave Anderson of the *New York Times* noted that the departure of both teams from frigid Shea Stadium signaled a return to the ghastly sunshine in Oakland. Charlie Finley, kept warm in New York "with a blanket over his legs and lap," again reminiscent of Old Man Potter, had hoisted his own petard by promoting prime-time World Series games, Anderson observed, as the resumption of action at the Coliseum with the attendant late-afternoon starting times did not bode well for those playing the outfield in Oakland.[82] And as if another fit of agitation was needed, Finley, who also owned the California Golden Seals of the National Hockey League and the Memphis Tams of the American Basketball Association, announced after the game that because of his health considerations, he would be putting those non-baseball entities up for sale. Despite Finley's insistence that the Athletics would remain firmly under his control and stay in Oakland, the *Oakland Tribune* reported that a Bay Area group aptly named "A's Fans for Local Ownership," as contrasted with Finley's Chicago-based ownership, made known its interest in a possible acquisition should the team go on the market.

On the brink of elimination and having scored only one run in their last two games, the Athletics needed desperately to revive their struggling offense. Seaver was again lying in wait for them in Game 6, but this time around, Hunter got the better of the Mets ace, holding New York to four harmless singles and one walk over 7⅓ innings. Jackson, with three hits in four trips to the plate, supplied most of the scoring punch, driving in single runs in the first and third innings. Oakland answered a threat in the eighth — during which the Mets scored their only run — with another tally in their half of that inning. Fingers began his relief stint in the eighth to quell an uprising and retired all four batters he faced in saving the 3–1 win to knot the series at three games each.

Holtzman and Matlack were again paired for the Game 7 showdown. The Athletics' most productive outburst of the whole Series — four runs in the third chased the New York southpaw — featured two-run homers by Campaneris and Jackson. Oakland padded their lead to 5–0 as Holtzman allowed just four runners over his first five innings before waning in the sixth when back-to-back doubles prompted Williams to call in Fingers. The handle-bar-mustachioed bullpen ace once more thwarted New York over three innings before he, too, tired and surrendered a run in the ninth and yielded to Knowles. Making his seventh appearance in relief, Knowles coaxed Wayne Garrett to pop out to Campaneris and earn

the Athletics a 5–2 victory and their second straight World Series championship, which was a monumental
accomplishment when weighed against
the frenetic events that coursed through
the entire season.

Encumbered by a feeble postseason
offense, Finley's self-inflicted disgrace of
what the *Tribune*'s Ron Bergman called
"l'Affaire Andrews," and the controversy
of Williams's mid–Series announcement
of his intent to resign, Oakland conquered all the adversity to become the
first team to win consecutive World
Series in more than a decade.[83] Jackson's
MVP performance during the regular
season was followed by his winning of
World Series MVP accolades — he batted .310 and led the team with six
RBIs — despite the shadow of protection
granted by the FBI when a death threat
was lodged against him.

**Winner of both the 1973 American League and
World Series MVP awards, Reggie Jackson was the
primary source of the Athletics' power hitting.**

After making his resignation official, Williams announced his departure
by tactfully praising Finley for giving him the chance to manage again in the major leagues
following his firing from the Red Sox helm. Oakland won despite Finley's noxious shroud,
as the owner's actions formed what some players viewed as a climate that so revolted Williams
that he felt he had no choice other than to quit. With three consecutive AL West titles and
a pair of World Series victories now etched on his resume, however, Williams had earned
the respect of his players, a commodity lacking in their assessment of Finley. By the end of
the Game 7 victory, Jackson, fully appreciative of Williams's leadership ability and the
results it produced, achieved a renewed harmony with his now former manager and expressed
his regret at the departure of Williams.

Speculation in the press pointed to the naming of Dave Bristol or possibly Ted Williams
as the next Oakland manager, while Dick Williams was still rumored to be moving to the
Yankees. Somehow seeing the lights of New York on the distant horizon, Reggie Jackson
desired to have Dick Williams continue writing his name on the lineup card. But the reality
of the extant reserve clause did not favor the likelihood of such a reunion. "I'd love to go
with him," Jackson said wistfully. "But Mr. Finley told me I'll die in his green and gold."[84]

# 10

## *Dark Days and the Diaspora*

The roster of the Oakland Athletics in the spring of 1974 showed few major changes from that of the previous year save for the absence of Dick Williams, whose getaway from bombastic Charlie Finley came with an inconvenient string attached. In early February, a judge with the United States District Court in San Francisco issued a ruling that declared that Williams's contract extension of late 1972 and the subsequent extension he received and signed in the summer of 1973 were valid. Williams, who after his departure from Oakland agreed to manage the New York Yankees — thus confirming the rumors that were swirling about him during the World Series — found himself, as upheld by the legal system, still shackled to Finley. Willing to sit out the season rather than remain under Finley's employment, Williams resolved to stay away from the Athletics in order to force the owner's hand to quickly find a replacement as training camps were about to open.

Reaching to his list of managerial candidates, Finley recalled the name of Alvin Dark, the quiet and religious skipper who had led the Kansas City Athletics in 1966 and most of 1967 before being axed. Since moving to Cleveland, where he piloted the Indians from 1968 until he was relieved mid-way through the 1971 season, Dark had been out of baseball — and seemingly out of touch with the game — when Finley tabbed him on February 20, 1974, to fill the Athletics' vacancy. Addressing the media about Oakland's prospects in the upcoming season, Dark may not have elicited much confidence as he groped for words to describe his new situation. As the *Oakland Tribune* reported, "Dark began enumerating the reasons the A's should win again but he stumbled after mentioning six names, looked up and said, 'Really, I haven't even looked at the roster.... I'm going to have to see who the best reliever is, where players should hit, and so forth.'"[1] Since Dark was at a loss to understand that there were more than six vital and well-known cogs in the two-time World Series champions, or that Rollie Fingers had firmly established himself as the ace of the bullpen, it is little wonder that Dark failed to inspire confidence among his new charges.

Finley was vexed not just by the search for a new manager that spring. In the unending battles over salaries for his players, the owner found his better players now reaching and even eclipsing the $100,000 mark. Catfish Hunter signed for that figure, as did Sal Bando, while Reggie Jackson beat Finley in an arbitration hearing for $135,000, an amount that placed him in the elite class of the game's top stars. As the prying — and deserving —fingers of his players were loosening increasingly large sums of cash from Finley's treasury, the owner's wife of 32 years, Shirley, filed for divorce. Few people closely associated with the Finleys were at liberty to discuss details of the couple's falling out, but there was ample evidence that pointed to Charlie's abusive behavior toward his wife, including several incidents that required the intervention of the local police. Their split forced the owner to move away from the family's LaPorte, Indiana, farm and reside in Chicago.[2]

The divorcée was not alone in her ill feelings about how the spiteful Finley treated people. "You kind of come to the realization over the years that he doesn't care about you as an individual," Joe Rudi observed, and the outfielder believed that Finley's attitude had now become infected with the assumption that his team would be somehow destined to win the World Series every year.[3] Emboldened by this pretense and increasingly bitter toward his players and office staff alike, Finley continued to misanthropically lay the groundwork for the future departure of his employees. The dismissal of Mike Andrews during the 1973 World Series exposed the ugliest side of Finley and proved to be a watershed in Finley's tenure as club owner. Shirley Finley's escape from Charlie's clutches would be followed later in 1974 by the flight of another significant person in the owner's life, a star who became the first player to lead an exodus from Oakland.

## Title Defense Number Two

Pressured by Finley with the expectation of winning their third World Series in a row, the Athletics embarked on this undertaking during the 1974 season in less than convincing fashion. After splitting their first twenty games in April, there was grumbling among the second-place Athletics about Dark's handling of the players, who then held a private meeting intended to address issues of how to deal with the manager. "A lot of people thought [Dark] shouldn't have been hired in the first place," Reggie Jackson told his diary, but in the early stages of the 1974 season, the outfielder believed that Dark had to be given a chance to gain a foothold as the skipper rather than fall victim to a possible rash decision on the part of Finley to fire him due to poor team performance.[4]

Continuing to plod along at a .500 pace after briefly falling to fifth place in the AL West, Oakland began a road trip on May 16 with a visit to Finley's base of operations, Chicago. The owner decided to take in the third game against the White Sox but was disturbed by what he saw as the Athletics fell, 3–2. Irked about the team's lack of spirit, Finley unleashed an obscenity-laced tirade that spared few of his uniformed personnel. Targeting players, coaches, and the manager, Finley spread blame for the team's lethargy to all corners of the clubhouse but

Manager Alvin Dark's second tour of duty with Charlie Finley proved to be more profitable than was his first, by piloting the Athletics to the 1974 World Series title.

reserved most of his anger for Dark by reminding him during the twenty-minute tongue-lashing, "We won two World Series without you, and if you don't get your rear in gear, you're gone."[5] A pall — in which the players blamed the owner and the manager, the skipper was not on good terms with two of his coaches, and the owner sought scapegoats in everyone with whom he came in contact — settled over the Athletics that outpaced any such ill will under Dick Williams.

A new factor in the tempestuous Oakland environment was a ballplayer with no professional experience on the diamond but who was nonetheless signed by Finley — allegedly at Alvin Dark's behest — because of his belief that a runner with world-class speed was better than former pinch-runner Allan Lewis, who was released before the season began. Given a salary of over $40,000, an astounding sum considering what little baseball acumen he possessed, Herb Washington, a sprinter who set records in the fifty- and sixty-yard dash, assumed Lewis's role. Virtually devoid of any baseball instinct, Washington found himself being picked off base or thrown out trying to advance at times when he should not have made an attempt. Reluctant to use the error-prone Washington as he struggled through on-the-job training at the major league level, Dark incurred Finley's wrath for failing to use the speedster in close games where even a single run was especially crucial, including the recent loss to the White Sox. Believing that Washington's presence was just another ploy by an attention-hungry owner, Sal Bando later stated that the true professionals on the roster shouldered the burden of winning games, while Jackson admitted that many team members were trying to teach Washington the fundamentals of the game.[6]

The deeply religious Dark tried to rebuff Finley's rants by resorting to his patience and soft-spoken demeanor in answering his chief critic. However much one wants to use Finley's outburst as a benchmark, the unmistakable evidence shows that when the Athletics left Chicago on May 19, they regained a tie for first place in the AL West, assumed undisputed possession of the divisional lead the following day, and were never overtaken thereafter. The road ahead for the veterans who were shouldering the lion's share of the burden was nonetheless difficult, with one incident — self-inflicted at that — providing a particularly damaging blow as the Texas Rangers, resurgent under their new skipper Billy Martin, and the Kansas City Royals chased Oakland in the standings.

Another clubhouse fracas erupted when the Athletics moved to Detroit for a series in early June. Claiming that Reggie Jackson was an unwanted third party in his own relationship with a woman, Billy North ripped into Jackson with a profane, verbal assault that turned physical; a pair of brief fights between the two outfielders cost Jackson an injured shoulder. Even worse, however, was the injury suffered by catcher Ray Fosse, who was hurt while acting as peacemaker and ended up undergoing surgery in early July for a ruptured disk in his back, his recuperation shelving him until late August.[7] Disappointed by the outfielders' display of anger, Gene Tenace suggested that the team form a "boxing club ... or maybe a karate association" to indulge its pugnacity.[8]

With Fosse sidelined, Tenace, who after losing his salary fight in February vowed to play no position other than first base, was shifted from first base to catcher, until he went out with a pinched nerve in his neck and yielded to third-string catcher Larry Haney. Amid the lineup juggling, an odious undercurrent continue to course through the clubhouse regarding the team's respect — or lack thereof — for their manager. The griping concerned some of the game strategy Dark employed, such as not calling for a bunt when one seemed appropriate, or removing a prime player in favor of a pinch-hitter at an inopportune time. In a galling loss in mid–June, Dark could have called for a sacrifice to move a runner up in a key situation but instead the batter hit into a double play, prompting a frustrated Bando to complain that the manager "couldn't manage a flipping meat market."[9] While Bando vented, he was unaware that Dark was immediately behind him as the team filed into the clubhouse after the game, so the captain apologized to him immediately. But the incident became public knowledge because the press, which had also fallen out of favor with many associated with the team, duly reported the incident.[10] Some pitchers who were dissatisfied with their removal from a game showed their displeasure with Dark by tossing the ball to him rather than handing it over when he appeared at the mound to make a change. Even the mild-mannered Joe Rudi, who was the team's top run producer, carped about being lifted for pinch-runner Washington.

Departing this unsavory setting shortly after the Bando affair was Deron Johnson, who along with his .195 batting average was sold to Milwaukee. The scene gloomed further on July 8 when third-base coach Irv Noren, who got along much better with Dick Williams than he did with Dark, and bullpen coach Vern Hoscheit were both dismissed at Dark's urging. Questioned as to why new coaches were being brought on halfway through the season, Dark defended his turf by claiming, "Any manager likes to have his [own] coaches," but then strained his credibility by adding, "This is no reflection on [Noren and Hoscheit]."[11] Named as replacements were Bobby Hofman and Bobby Winkles, the latter having been fired recently as the Angels manager, who was claimed by an embittered Noren as having been brought on board "to stand by as manager any time Alvin screwed up."[12] Observing the wreckage of what the *Oakland Tribune* dubbed "The Tuesday Night Massacre" and coming at a time when rumors of a possible sale of the Athletics again made the news, Catfish Hunter sighed, "Nothing surprises me anymore on this team."[13]

Also introduced to the East Bay tumult in early July was Claudell Washington, a 19-year-old left-handed outfielder promoted from Double-A Birmingham. This newest Washington to wear an Athletics uniform quickly dazzled his teammates by hitting well in several key situations and contributing toward Oakland's slowly widening lead in the AL West, as their 55–41 record gave them a lead of five games at the All-Star break. At the All-Star Game, Jackson, the league's top vote recipient, and Bert Campaneris started for the American League and were joined by Rudi, Bando, Hunter, and Fingers on a squad managed by Dick Williams, who had returned from his self-imposed exile to accept an offer to pilot the California Angels in late June.[14]

Just prior to the All-Star Game recess, Dark finally let go with a rare emotional outburst in New York in an attempt to assert his authority, "putting aside his bible … and let[ting] some of his heroes have it between the eyes."[15] Through all the bickering, hirings, and firings, by late July the Athletics still had yet to be overtaken in the AL West; however much of this success could be ascribed to Dark's chastising, their lead had expanded to nine games. But a severe ankle sprain put Campaneris on the disabled list, and the club received a scare shortly thereafter when Vida Blue complained of chest pains which thankfully proved to be nothing of consequence. Campy returned on August 17 but was again quickly hobbled, much to the dismay of Finley, who was making a rare visit to Oakland and witnessed the shortstop re-injuring himself. In Finley's eyes, the scapegoat for the shortstop's latest problem was trainer Joe Romo, even though Finley himself had urged an early return for Campaneris so that he could help boost the Oakland attack. Despite the trials endured through mid–August, the Athletics, at 70–52, still had the best record in the American League.

An interesting trend developed as the summer wore on, namely as the Athletics' team batting average was mired near the bottom of the league, they remained one of the league's top-scoring teams. Patience at the plate, exemplified by Gene Tenace's ability to draw many bases on balls, helped Oakland maintain a respectable on-base percentage, as the power stroke of Tenace, Jackson, Bando, and Rudi made up for deficiencies in other areas, especially reserves coming off the bench. But as was the hallmark of the great Oakland teams, the pitching staff was its bedrock, and as the end of the season loomed ahead, the hurlers collectively whittled the team ERA — already the best in the AL, just above 3.00 — down even further.

Yet the home stretch to the Athletics' fourth consecutive American League West title was not without its anxious moments. During the month of September, Oakland dropped three home games to the Texas Rangers — one of the losses further tainted when Darold Knowles had an on-field argument with Dark when the manager came to the mound to take out the reliever — and Rollie Fingers, who had experienced a very strained relationship with his wife over the course of the year, took umbrage with jokes about his marital problems. An ostensibly safe lead of 8½ games early that month fell to just four less than two weeks later. Noticeably worried and perhaps recalling the ignominious collapse of the Philadelphia Phillies a decade earlier, Finley demanded that Dark reinstitute the merry-go-round at second base as a means of breathing life into the Athletics following two crucial losses to the Rangers in Texas. The keystone revival helped as Oakland finally salvaged one win against their divisional rival to hold off the charging Rangers, and the Athletics finally clinched the AL West — albeit on a night they lost — on September 27. "I think all of the players were proud of it, but they took pains not to show it," Jackson remarked of the unenthusiastic celebration marking their fourth straight AL West title. "Someone said our clubhouse looked like a church on Monday."[16]

The subdued revelry reflected the strains endured by the defending World Series champions in the regular season, as it seemed that no corner of the Oakland franchise had escaped the furor and fractiousness that pervaded the team. Posting a final record of 90–72, this Athletics club had its lowest win total since 1970. With the number of promotions, such as discounted ticket nights and the like, at the Coliseum drastically cut, attendance also suffered. Fans voted with their feet — and their wallets — as the gate for 1974 was only 837,150, a sixteen percent drop from 1973. Bando acknowledged that a team like Oakland should have had better box office appeal to Bay Area fans, but poor marketing and a failure on Finley's part to grow his baseball business made trips to the Coliseum a less attractive entertainment alternative.[17]

Glum as the environment may have been, Oakland still had another postseason to look forward to, and the anticipation of perhaps another World Series appearance did spur some excitement as the Athletics were again paired off against the American League East champion Baltimore Orioles in the ALCS. The Athletics would rely on the strength of its arms, most prominently that of Catfish Hunter, whose Cy Young Award–winning season was capped by a 25–12 record, a 2.49 ERA, and a stunning total of just 268 hits *and* 46 walks allowed in 318 innings pitched, an average of less than one runner per inning. Southpaw starters Vida Blue (17–15, 3.26) and Ken Holtzman (19–17, 3.07) took their regular turns in the rotation while the fourth slot was filled mostly by Dave Hamilton (7–4, 3.15) and a six-foot, six-inch, rookie right-hander, Glenn Abbott (5–7, 3.00). Longtime starter Blue Moon Odom (1–5, 3.83) was nearing the end of his career and was used primarily in relief. The bullpen, supported by the work of Paul Lindblad (4–4, 2.05, six saves) and Darold Knowles (3–3, 4.25, three saves), was still lorded over by Rollie Fingers (9–5, 2.65, 18 saves), who led the league's pitchers with 76 games. In total, all pitchers combined to lead the AL with a 2.95 ERA and in the process allowed the fewest opponent runs (551) and the fewest walks (430).

By the end of the season, a host of familiar names among the regular players had produced in somewhat typical fashion. Sparking the top of the order were Billy North (.260, four home runs, 33 RBIs, 54 stolen bases) and Bert Campaneris (.290, two homers, 41 RBIs, 34 steals), the duo finishing first and fourth, respectively, in the AL in steals. Reggie Jackson, who flirted with a .400 average early in the season, settled for .289 and 29 home runs with 93 RBIs; the captain, Sal Bando (.243, 22, 103) led in run production; Joe Rudi (.293, 22, 99) continued his fine all-around play and won his first Gold Glove; and although short on average, Gene Tenace (.211, 26, 73) let patience and a keen eye enable him to draw 110 bases on balls. In his half-season in Oakland, rookie Claudell Washington (.285, no home runs, 19 RBIs) came through in late August with clutch hits to help the Athletics widen their lead in the division. These contributions helped Oakland's cause immensely, but the bottom part of the order and the reserves proved to be the primary culprits in stalling the club's progress.

A fine all-around player and one of the quieter members of the Athletics, Joe Rudi won the first of his three Gold Gloves in 1974.

Undoubtedly the injury to Ray Fosse, who finished at .196 with four home runs and 23 RBIs, was the worst blow to the Athletics' run production, as his replacement, Larry Haney could not even hit his weight (.165, 2, 3). At second base, Dick Green (.213, 2, 22) was more valuable with his glove, but the same could not be said for Angel Mangual (.233, 9, 43), who continued to cause concern due to his fielding deficiencies and seemed destined not to fulfill the promise manifest in his rookie season. Except for Jesus Alou (.286, 2, 15) coming off the bench, the parade of substitutes inspired little confidence for manager Alvin Dark. Ted Kubiak (.209, 0, 18) and Pat Bourque (.229, 1, 16) were the only reserves with significant playing time who hit above .200, while eight others in lesser roles never came close to that mark. And the Athletic who never stepped outside the basepaths, Herb Washington, stole 29 bases and scored 29 runs, but he was also caught stealing 16 times. Had more production been forthcoming from the bench, a more balanced attack would have boosted the total in the team's win column and improved upon its 25–28 record in one-run games. But the deficit in these close games vanished in the postseason, much to the delight of the Athletics and much to the dismay of their playoff opponents.

## Besting the Birds

Waiting again to challenge Oakland for the American League pennant were the Baltimore Orioles, winners of the AL East for a second straight year. These teams were evenly matched, having split the twelve games they played against each other during the season. When the ALCS opened on October 5 in Oakland, Catfish Hunter disappointed his teammates with a sub-par outing when he surrendered three home runs in a 6–3 loss to Mike Cuellar. From that point on, the Athletics — or more precisely, their pitching — took control, yielding only one run in the remaining contests.

The next day Ken Holtzman spun a masterful five-hitter in shutting out Dave McNally and the Orioles, 5–0, as Ray Fosse iced an otherwise close game by launching a three-run homer in the bottom of the eighth to clinch the victory and square the series at one win apiece. Moving to Baltimore for Game 3, Vida Blue and Jim Palmer matched each other zero for zero in a splendid duel, but Palmer's only mistake was a fourth-inning pitch to Sal Bando that the captain hit for a home run and the sole tally of the game. Blue shook off a pair of miscues by the usually reliable Green and completed his 1–0 gem by allowing no walks and two hits. Tenace, though, refused to shed the anger enveloping him when Dark removed him in the seventh inning in favor of designated pinch-runner Herb Washington, who was cut down attempting to steal. Tenace was infuriated because he sensed that Dark used Washington simply to placate Finley; Jackson, who served mostly as DH in the series due to a hamstring injury of his right leg, felt that it would have made more sense for Washington to be used in *his* place rather than Tenace's.[18] The substitution could not be undone, but the Athletics nevertheless prevailed and set up another Hunter-Cuellar showdown in Game 4 with Oakland ahead two games to one.

Pitching more authoritatively than he did in the ALCS opener, Hunter was in command in the fourth game as he shut out Baltimore in his seven innings of work. Receiving but one hit of offensive support, Hunter was staked to a 2–0 lead thanks to Tenace's bases-loaded walk in the fifth and a run-scoring double by Jackson in the seventh. Cuellar was his own worst enemy, walking nine batters, yet according to Jackson, the Orioles starter did not have difficulty in finding the plate but rather was careful — perhaps overcautious — in not letting the heart of the Oakland order beat him as Rudi, Bando, and Jackson drew three walks apiece.[19] Ross Grimsley relieved Cuellar in the fifth and hurled the remainder of the game, while Fingers came on in the eighth in relief of Hunter. After some anxiety in the bottom of the ninth when the Orioles rallied for a run, Fingers struck out Don Baylor to end the threat to give Oakland a 2–1 win and its third straight American League pennant.

After another subdued clubhouse celebration, a very reserved Hunter apologized for the way Alvin Dark had been treated during the season and tried to atone for those misdeeds by dedicating the third consecutive AL pennant to the oft-times embattled manager. Dark, obviously finding the occasion a glorious achievement, fittingly blurted out, "Praise the Lord!"[20] The Athletics now prepared to face their in-state rival, the Los Angeles Dodgers, who, on the same day that Oakland clinched their pennant, had defeated the Pittsburgh Pirates to win the National League Championship Series to earn their trip to the World Series. Embracing what would be the first all–California Fall Classic, Bando gushed about the "showbiz" and "Hollywood" aspects of the Series, firmly believing "this will be the best Series."[21]

## Oakland's Trifecta

Team Turmoil entered the 1974 World Series with several off-field dramas in progress. Mike Andrews, Finley's scapegoat of a year earlier, announced that he was taking Charlie Finley to court to recover $2.5 million in damages he claimed as a result of the humiliation he suffered at the owner's hands, not the least of which was his inability to continue his playing career in the major leagues. Another subplot concerned Catfish Hunter, who was owed $50,000 by Finley as payment for a deferred annuity that was part of his contract. As the pitcher's request for said payment dragged on through the late summer and early fall, the consequences of the legal action Hunter initiated against Finley as a result of the annuity issue would eventually set him free from Oakland. As if these side stories failed to provide enough grist for the media mill, Blue Moon Odom and Rollie Fingers obliged the day before the World Series opened by engaging in a fight when the relief ace took exception to comments that Odom made about Fingers' marital issues. Odom came away with a twisted ankle, while Fingers suffered a cut to the back of his head, as it seemed like the atmosphere of the clubhouse was primed at just the right time for the Athletics.

With questions regarding Dark's future as the manager, the team embarked on their trip to Los Angeles for the Series opener, as Finley provided the players with a four-page scouting report as part of the in-flight entertainment. Rankled as some on the club were by Finley's handout, Jackson admitted that most of his teammates were very focused on the mission set before them. "One of the stewardesses later told a writer we were one of the best-behaved ball clubs she's ever had on a plane," remarked Jackson as a testament to the sobriety displayed by the Athletics.[22]

Commencing on October 12 at Dodger Stadium, the Series opener featured Ken Holtzman pitching against Dodgers ace Andy Messersmith. The Oakland southpaw was staked to a 2–0 lead going into the bottom of the fifth on Jackson's solo home run in the second and Campaneris's fifth-inning sacrifice squeeze that plated Holtzman, who in the designated-hitter-less Series had doubled in his first at-bat of the year. But Dark quickly pulled Holtzman, who was not sharp this day, in the home half of the fifth when the Dodgers rallied to cut the lead to 2–1. Summoned for an extended appearance, Fingers pitched 4⅓ innings before tiring with two out in the ninth and nursing a 3–1 advantage. After a Jim Wynn home run and Steve Garvey single, Dark brought in Catfish Hunter, who fanned Joe Ferguson to seal the 3–2 victory.

The second game also had a final score of 3–2, but this time the Dodgers prevailed on the strength of starter Don Sutton's eight strong innings of work. Los Angeles touched Vida Blue for a run in the second inning and then two more in the sixth on Ferguson's home run. Trailing 3–0, Oakland mounted a desperate comeback in the ninth but fell short. Joe Rudi's single off eventual NL Cy Young Award winner Mike Marshall, who came in after Sutton left in the ninth, drove in Bando and Jackson, but Marshall struck out Tenace and, employing a notorious pick-off move, nailed Herb Washington — who had replaced Rudi — before fanning Angel Mangual to end the game.

Knotted at one win each, the Series shifted to Oakland, where Dodgers left-hander Al Downing was victimized by catcher Joe Ferguson's error, which led to a pair of unearned runs in the third. The Athletics scored another run in the fourth, while Hunter held the Dodgers scoreless until Bill Buckner homered in the eighth and prompted Dark to bring in Fingers, who surrendered a base hit to Wynn but then was the beneficiary of Dick Green's fielding gem. Green snagged a drive by Garvey and then doubled Wynn off first base to end the threat, and then the second baseman started a 4–6–3 double play to end the ninth inning, giving Oakland a 3–2 victory and Fingers his first save of the Series. In the Dodgers clubhouse afterward, Buckner whined about what he viewed as Oakland's "luck" in gaining an edge in the Series and claimed that over the long haul of a full season, his Dodgers were far superior to the Athletics.[23]

The skein of 3–2 scores was broken in Game 4, as Oakland and Holtzman overcame a 2–1 deficit by erupting for four runs in their half of the sixth inning to beat the Dodgers, 5–2. In that key inning, nine Athletics came to the plate against Messersmith, who was undone by run-scoring singles from Bando and pinch-hitter Jim Holt, with Green also adding an RBI groundout. Fingers got the call to put out a fire in the eighth inning, and in the ninth, Green, who confessed to being "quite a bit out of position," again superbly thwarted a Dodgers rally with a diving stop to rob pinch-hitter Von Joshua of a hit and start a game-ending 4–6–3 double play.[24] There were fireworks following the game, not to honor the spectacular play of Green, but in the clubhouse afterward when Tenace, still smarting from being lifted for Herb Washington in Game 3, raged at being a last-minute scratch from the fourth game and hoped for a trade that would relieve him of his frustration.

Just one win away from a third World Series title, Dark sent Blue to

**Sporting the most famous mustache in Oakland, Rollie Fingers emerged as the team's uncontested bullpen ace.**

face Sutton in Game 5, as Oakland struck for single runs in the first inning on Bando's sacrifice fly and in the second on Fosse's solo home run. Blue made good on the 2–0 lead until the sixth, when Wynn and Garvey drove in runs to tie the score at 2–2. Tiring in the seventh, Blue was relieved by Odom, who pitched for one-third of an inning and was the good-luck winner when Rudi hit relief ace Mike Marshall's first pitch of the bottom of the seventh inning for a home run and a 3–2 lead. Fingers made his fourth appearance and earned another save, thanks in part to a great defensive play executed by Jackson, Green, and Bando, who collectively put out Bill Buckner as the Dodgers left fielder greedily tried to take third base after his eighth-inning leadoff single was misplayed by Billy North. Backing up North in the outfield, Jackson threw a strike to cutoff man Green, who in turn nailed Buckner as Bando made the putout. Fingers thereafter set down the Dodgers in order for the 3–2 victory and his third save that enabled the Athletics to win their third consecutive World Series. North regretted committing his error on Buckner's hit, but he savored the revenge exacted on the Dodgers outfielder for his overly aggressive running. "I'm glad it was Buckner who made the stupidest mistake of the Series," crowed North after the game, yet even in defeat, Buckner held fast to his belief that the Dodgers were the better team and only grudgingly offered his congratulations to the Athletics.[25]

In a departure from the tame celebrations that marked the AL West and ALCS clinchings, the Oakland clubhouse was a scene of bedlam as players doused their lair with champagne, some of which was specifically aimed at Commissioner Bowie Kuhn, who was on hand for the presentation of the World Series trophy. For his stellar work out of the bullpen, Fingers was named the Series MVP, but Green, who failed to get a hit in 13 at-bats, also garnered attention for his fielding prowess, notably the double plays he started in Games 3 and 4 as well as his crucial assist in the eighth inning of the deciding contest.

So ended the most contentious of seasons in Oakland's history. The Athletics cemented their place in the pantheon of dynasties with their third consecutive World Series crown, having survived bouts of dissension between players and the manager, the firing of two coaches at midseason, fights among the players themselves, the injuries that resulted from some of the fisticuffs, and — certainly not the least of the issues that plagued the team in 1974 — the bluster and interloping of Charlie Finley. Even as the summer was just heating up, one San Francisco Giants player observed of the Athletics, "They fight in the clubhouse, then go out on the field ... and win.... They fight with their owner, their manager, among themselves. It's a strange chemistry."[26] This dysfunction could hardly serve as a template for virtually any organization to emulate, but in Oakland's case, an exception had to be made because, as unorthodox or counterintuitive as that chemistry may have been, it was what worked for the Athletics. In its front-page editorial immediately after the Series, the *Oakland Tribune* lionized "our swinging baseball team," implored fans and readers to "write Finley, Dark, and your favorite ballplayers letters of congratulations," and pleaded with readers to "show better support at the box office next year."[27]

If there were any axiom about winning postseason games, the Athletics' performance was telling, especially in contests decided by a single run. Whether the pressure to come through with a clutch hit by the offense, a great outing by a starter or reliever, or a superb play in the field, Oakland had a knack for delivering when the stakes were highest during its three years of domination.

*Oakland's Record in One-Run Games*

| | |
|---|---|
| 1972 ALCS | 2–1 |
| 1972 World Series | 4–2 |
| 1973 ALCS | 1–1 |
| 1973 World Series | 2–0 |
| 1974 ALCS | 2–0 |
| 1974 World Series | 3–1 |
| Total | 14–5 |

Writing for *The Sporting News* just as Oakland was on the cusp of capturing its third World Series, sportswriter Herb Michelson rhetorically asked if Charlie Finley was "a genius or a jerk," and he came to the conclusion that Finley was neither: "He was merely a man who always worked very hard and very long hours, made a great deal of money, bought a baseball team and discovered the deliciousness of his own sense of power. Nothing more, nothing less, nothing unique."[28] That power which Finley invested in himself did translate into championships of the highest caliber in major league baseball, yet this legacy was to become a Pyrrhic victory.

Virtually friendless, at odds with the local press and the majority of his fellow major league club owners, unpopular among most of his playing and non-playing personnel, irked by the baseball commissioner, and with his marriage at a rocky end, Finley was even "roundly booed" at the team's post–Series parade.[29] He had become successful in the insurance business, but it had become apparent that the deeds of his prized baseball team could not bring him popularity nor compensate for his overbearing demeanor. As the World Series cheers — or, in some cases, jeers — faded with the autumn, Finley learned how anxious some of his best players were to leave the Athletics for a baseball life beyond Oakland.

One Oakland figurehead who was able to maintain tenure, despite rumors of his temptation to emulate Dick Williams's exit of 1973, was Alvin Dark. The skipper had also been thought to be managing "under an [*sic*] unique day-to-day contract," which offered incremental incentives for championships at the divisional, league, and World Series levels.[30] In spite of the successive — and successful — achievements gained by Dark and the Athletics in 1974, the manager's return for another season was not a foregone conclusion. It was not until the occasion of the team's victory parade that Finley announced "for the first time that [he] indicated he wanted Dark back," while Dark "prayed ... for guidance" in accepting Finley's offer, which included a hefty raise, on October 19 to manage for the 1975 season.[31]

The overall lineup was expected to be relatively static, so Dark figured to be playing a pat hand again. But a weeks-long drama surrounding Oakland's ace starter continued to unfold and resulted in the unplanned departure of one of the legends who had made the Athletics the champions they were.

## The One That Got Away

When Catfish Hunter inked his 1974 contract for $100,000, the Oakland ace's deal was structured so that half that amount would payable to Hunter as salary while the other half would be placed in an annuity — controlled by the Athletics — as a tax shelter. When Hunter realized the $50,000 owed to him for the annuity had not been paid, his attorney, Carlton Cherry, began dunning Finley for payment during the late summer. Finley had been "advised in writing of this failure, on September 16, at which time he had a 10-day grace period to make amends but failed to do so," according to Major League Baseball Players Association counsel Dick Moss.[32]

By early October, with the annuity payment still outstanding and Oakland in the midst of its postseason play, Hunter decided to file a grievance through the Players Association. Moss firmly believed that Finley had defaulted on the annuity payment, thus violating the terms of the contract and entitling Hunter to become an unrestricted free agent. On the same day as Game 3 of the ALCS against the Orioles, Hunter was hastily called to a meeting with Finley, league president Lee MacPhail, and Commissioner Bowie Kuhn. Wounded by the fact that his ace would resort to legal proceedings to recover money that he was entitled to, Finley at once became fawning and pompous, offering to pay the entire outstanding amount in full to Hunter rather than the legally designated third party, an insurance company. But Hunter, on Moss's recommendation, refused, noting that the remittance should have been made in accordance with his contract. Hunter claimed his stance could have been softened had Finley added perhaps an extra one or two thousand dollars to make up for lost interest that would have accrued had the initial payment been met in a timely fashion.[33]

Not surprisingly, Finley took offense at Hunter's obstinacy, yet with the Athletics fighting for another World Series championship, all parties, especially Hunter, kept as quiet as possible so as not to distract from the team's mission. When the World Series concluded, however, the grievance over the contract violation, which would make Hunter a free agent immediately, came to the fore, as a second grievance to recover the $50,000 annuity payment also was filed. Section 7A of the standard player's contract was the focal point of Hunter's argument, a portion of which clearly stated the conditions that Finley was legally bound to uphold, namely that "the Player may terminate this contract ... if the Club shall default in the payments to the Player provided for ... or if the Club shall fail to perform any other obligation agreed to be performed by the Club ... within [a grace period of] 10 days."[34]

In late November, a hearing was convened in New York before an arbitration panel whose members were Marvin Miller, the head of the players union; John Gaherin, who chaired the owners' Player Relations Committee; and a third, neutral arbitrator, Peter Seitz, whose position on the panel had been sanctioned by both the union and the owners. Since Miller and Gaherin always sided with the players and owners, respectively, in such hearings, it was up to Seitz to render the ultimate decision, which he did after weighing the evidence presented by Hunter and his representatives as well as the arguments put forth by Finley's side. Two weeks later, Seitz's announcement produced a minor tremor — Hunter was to receive the $50,000 lump sum, plus interest, offered by Finley, with the pitcher taking a hit in taxable income in the process — but of greater significance was the shockwave resulting from the arbitrator's ruling that allowed Hunter to become a free agent based on the pitcher's contention that he desired to "invoke the rights granted in the termination provisions in the player's contract. In contrast to enforcing that contract, [Hunter] asserted that the Club's actions resulted in there being no contract at all."[35] Concurrence by Seitz thereby granted Hunter his freedom, putting the pitcher at liberty to strike a deal with any team of his choosing.

Reaction to the ruling was swift and predictable. Finley, believed to be shopping his team for a new owner, sought a legal remedy to stop other teams from bidding for Hunter's services, while Hunter began entertaining offers from nearly every team in both leagues while not ruling out the possibility, however remote, that he might return to Oakland should the team's ownership change hands. Commissioner Kuhn, who was not on cordial terms with Finley, nonetheless felt that the owner was being treated too harshly for what he believed was an incident not of "serious wrongdoing."[36] Kuhn's standard of "serious" confounds when one takes into consideration that at issue was half a year's salary for one of the top pitchers in baseball and was not on a par with another grievance heard by Seitz at this same time in which the arbitrator ruled against a player who sought release from his contract when his team did not reimburse him for moving expenses of several hundred dollars.[37] In the players' camp, Miller claimed that "there was rejoicing at the Players Association," as the leader of the union applauded "Seitz's fairness" while also acknowledging that "Finley's arrogance" was a large factor in the dispute.[38]

Catfish Hunter became the first star to flee Oakland when arbitrator Peter Seitz ruled in his favor after a dispute with Charlie Finley in 1974.

As December drew to a close, the financial siren song of offers presented to Hunter dwindled to those from the San Diego Padres, the Kansas City Royals, the Cleveland Indians, and the New York Yankees. The contract proposals were astounding relative to the time, but on New Year's Eve, Hunter agreed to a five-year package with the Yankees worth approximately $3 million.[39] The 1974 AL Cy Young Award recipient confessed that scout Clyde Kluttz, who originally signed Hunter for the Athletics organization and was now serving as the Yankees' emissary in the negotiations, was a major influence in winning him over to New York. Refusing to go down without a fight, Finley filed suit in Alameda County Superior Court to keep Hunter from heading east, while Finley's attorney claimed that Seitz had "invaded and destroyed the reserve system" by ruling in favor of Hunter.[40] For his own part, Hunter beamed at the press conference announcing his defection from Oakland by saying, "I've always wanted to be a Yankee."[41]

## The Last Hurrah

If Catfish Hunter found his new life in New York richly rewarding, the teammates he left behind in Oakland were bitter as ever. Finley continued to be tight as possible with his payroll, especially in light of the drop in attendance over the past season, and served as his own representative in the numerous salary arbitration cases that went to a full hearing. A select group of Finley's top players who had earned World Series laurels for a third straight year already knew that they would not be approaching the same salary level as the departed

Hunter. When Reggie Jackson ($135,000), Sal Bando ($100,000), Ken Holtzman ($93,000), and Ray Fosse ($50,000) went to battle with Finley at the arbitration table, they each had to settle for 1975 salaries that contained no raises. Rollie Fingers was luckier and won an increase from $64,000 to $89,000, as Finley was busy signing Joe Rudi ($84,000), Vida Blue ($80,000), Billy North ($55,000), Gene Tenace ($51,000), and Paul Lindblad ($50,000) before their cases could be heard. Bert Campaneris staged a walkout in the spring and eventually signed for $100,000.[42]

Although he shied away from breaking up the core of his squad, Finley considered trading Jackson and possibly Bando if the return would yield him a host of young — and much lower-paid — prospects. All the while, the rigors of preparing for the many hearings became a drain on Finley, who was irritated by the main rule of arbitration that dictated that the mediator hearing any given case could only pick one salary figure, either the owner's offer or the one requested by the player. In Finley's eyes, virtually all player requests were exorbitant, and he learned to emphasize decreases and shortfalls in a player's performance during the past season so as to maximize the negative light in which he could cast the player during a hearing. Simply stated, the process was denigrating toward the player and enhanced not one bit by Finley's theatrics during his presentation before the arbitrator, such histrionics including dramatic pauses for effect and sneering comments such as "*Mister* Reggie Jackson and his representative maintain that he deserves a *princely* salary."[43] When Finley had successfully defended his position — often with snide and sarcasm in addition to his trove of well-assembled, negative statistics — and won a dispute, his demeanor could only foster more resentment for the humiliating treatment he had just administered to the player, to say nothing of his gloating to the press about how happy he was to have beaten a player at the bargaining table. Bitter in defeat yet smug when victorious, Finley intoned, "Give the players anything they want, but don't give them arbitration," which he viewed as a process that would only force salaries to escalate regardless of who prevailed before the arbitrator.[44]

After several attempts to walk away from the game, second baseman Dick Green finally made his retirement official, a move which would have opened up that position for the pawn in "l'Affaire Andrews," Manny Trillo. But a week after the World Series, Trillo had been bundled with relievers Darold Knowles and Bob Locker in a deal with Finley's favorite trading partner, the Cubs, for aging slugger Billy Williams, who was acquired to shore up the designated hitter role. A curious aspect to the addition of Williams was that for all of Finley's complaints about salaries, the owner was willing to make Williams the highest-paid Athletic at $150,000 even though he was slated to be a full-time DH. Trillo's place was quickly filled by Phil Garner, a scrappy player who had apprenticed as a third baseman in the Oakland minor league system.

Obviously, the biggest hole to be filled was the one created by Hunter's flight, which was ably filled by Vida Blue, while Holtzman also remained a fixture in the rotation. The remaining starting roles proved to be a challenge to fill, however. It was into this breach that a cast of Oakland holdovers — Glenn Abbott, Dave Hamilton, and Blue Moon Odom — was mixed with another group of veterans, all of whom were at least 30 years old and imported from various teams. New to the Oakland stable were Stan Bahnsen, Dick Bosman, Jim Perry, and Sonny Siebert, who performed adequately but were no longer able to pitch into the late innings.

The 1975 season was a success, yet in the final accounting it was on the level of Oakland's

1971 standard rather than the lofty mark set in each of the prior three years. To be sure, the 98 wins — against 64 losses — were the Athletics' best total since Dick Williams's first year at the helm, but the team may have had help from a higher authority. Rumors swirled of prayer meetings in the noticeably calmer clubhouse, as Jackie Dark, the manager's wife, claimed that the Bible had become a pleasant addition to the lives of several players.[45]

Oakland bolted from the gate by opening with five wins in the first six games, and a rookie right-hander barely twenty years old, Mike Norris from neighboring San Francisco, seemed to be a tailor-made replacement for Catfish Hunter. In his first start, Norris blanked the White Sox, 9–0, evoking memories of another Vida Blue in the making, and followed that outing with seven shutout innings against the Royals. But disaster struck on April 20 when Norris experienced extreme pain in his elbow while pitching to the Twins' leadoff hitter, Rod Carew. Bone chips were discovered in the joint and remedial surgery was performed, but Norris was effectively done for the year. Odom, Abbott, and Hamilton were ineffective and of little value as long-term pitching solutions.

Desperate for help for the rotation, Finley completed a pair of deals in mid–May which brought Siebert from the Padres in exchange for infielder Ted Kubiak, and Bosman and Perry from the Indians for Odom and $15,000 cash. A month later, Hamilton and an outfield prospect named Chet Lemon were sent to the White Sox for Bahnsen. Posting an 11–4 record and a 3.52 ERA, Bosman proved to be the best of the lot, while Bahnsen (6–7, 3.24), Siebert (4–4, 3.69), and Perry (3–4, 4.66) basically broke even. The absence of Hunter allowed Vida Blue the chance to move to the head of the rotation, which he admirably did thanks to his 22–11 mark and 3.01 ERA, while Ken Holtzman (18–14, 3.14) remained the Athletics other frontline starter.

Fortuitously in reserve was a right-handed, career minor league hurler named Jim Todd, whom Finley had acquired in early April from his reliable trading partner in Chicago. Finley sent spare outfielder Champ Summers to the Cubs for Todd, who went 8–3 with a 2.29 ERA and 12 saves working exclusively from the bullpen. Todd, Paul Lindblad (9–1, 2.73, seven saves), and the reliable Rollie Fingers (10–6, 2.98, 24 saves) gave Oakland its dependably solid relief corps. As a whole, the staff ERA of 3.29 for the year was tied with the Yankees for second best in the American League behind Baltimore, with its 44 saves tops in the AL.

On offense, the Athletics finished second in the league in runs scored (758), home runs (151), and stolen bases (183). Claudell Washington (.308, 10 homers, 77 RBIs, 40 stolen bases) blossomed in his first full season, mainly in left field; Billy North (.273, 1 home run, 43 RBIs, 30 steals) held down center field; and right fielder Reggie Jackson (.253, 36, 104, 17) was the team's top run producer. Around the infield, Sal Bando anchored third base for every game except two, hitting .230 with 15 homers and 78 RBIs; Bert Campaneris (.265, 4 home runs, 46 RBIs, 24 stolen bases) was solid at shortstop, but his new double play partner, Phil Garner (.246, 6 homers, 54 RBIs) struggled in the field and led the league in errors at second base with 26; and Joe Rudi (.278, 21 home runs, 75 RBIs), superb in left field in 1974, found himself stationed at first base for 91 games but also won his second Gold Glove as an outfielder. Gene Tenace (.255, 29 homers, 87 RBIs) handled most of the catching chores, while Billy Williams adjusted to the role of designated hitter by batting .244 with 23 home runs and 81 runs driven in. Relegated to back-up status, Ray Fosse hit a paltry .140 with no homers and 12 RBIs in only 136 at-bats. Campaneris, Jackson, and

Rudi were voted as starters to the American League All-Star team, with Tenace and Washington in reserve and Blue and Fingers earning places on the pitching staff.

The Herb Washington experiment came to a merciful conclusion — he appeared in 13 games before being released a month into the 1975 season — but Don Hopkins (21 stolen bases) and yet another Cub import, Matt Alexander (17 steals), continued the Finley tradition to focus on running. Oakland never ceded its lead in the AL West after gaining the division's top spot on June 4. The Athletics withstood an early September charge by the Royals when Oakland limited Kansas City to just four runs in their three-game sweep at the Coliseum to drop the Royals eights games off the pace. Oakland later clinched their division for the fifth straight year and capped the season with a combined no-hitter by Blue, Abbott, Lindblad, and Fingers in the finale against the Angels.

In an attendance rebound, over one million customers entered the turnstiles at the Coliseum — 1,075,518 to be exact — to make up for the drop of 1974. In his two appearances at Oakland in his new Yankee uniform, Catfish Hunter drew a total of 41,268 fans.[46] But any exuberance over Oakland's AL West title was quickly squelched in the postseason when the Athletics made a hasty exit in the American League Championship Series, putting an end to Finley's rallying cry to "Keep It Alive in '75."

Oakland was pitted against the Boston Red Sox, who were led by a pair of young outfielders, Rookie of the Year and AL MVP Fred Lynn in addition to another rookie sensation, Jim Rice. In a sloppily played opener in Boston, the Red Sox clung to a 2–1 lead over Holtzman entering the bottom of the seventh inning, when Boston rang up five runs to seal their victory as Luis Tiant completed a three-hitter. Spotted to a 3–0 lead in Game 2, Vida Blue failed to survive the fourth inning, and with the scored tied at 3–3, Fingers surrendered single runs in three of his four innings of work in the 6–3 loss to Sox starter Reggie Cleveland. A move back to Oakland was of little value in Game 3 when Rick Wise pitched seven strong innings and Dick Drago earned his second straight save in closing out the Athletics, 5–3, Holtzman once more on the losing end. The sweep by Boston prompted plenty of speculation by the Oakland sporting press and players as to how much better the Athletics would have been had Catfish Hunter still been pitching while wearing green, gold, and white.

If Finley had been a bit hesitant about Dark's return after winning the 1974 World Series, he was emphatic about firing his manager after the 1975 ALCS loss. Prior to the tilt against the Red Sox, Dark was proselytizing to the congregation at his church in Castro Valley, California, where he was quoted as saying that Charlie Finley was an insignificant soul in God's realm and "if he doesn't accept Jesus Christ as his personal savior, he's going to hell."[47] Unfortunately for Dark, his Bible-speak was truncated by the local newspaper as "Finley's Going to Hell," and although Finley initially sloughed off the comment, Dark's words had been festering in Finley's mind. When the Athletics were summarily dispatched in the playoffs, Dark, as the most visible fall-guy, was fired on October 16.

Always having the final word, Finley — rather than God, in this case — decided that the theme for the next season would be "We're Gonna Fix 'Em in '76," but the truth was that the Oakland dynasty over which he had reigned was at an end.[48] The departure of Catfish Hunter occurred because of an oversight that was nobody's fault other than Charlie Finley's, but another arbitration verdict, with Peter Seitz again occupying center stage, would shake the sport of major league baseball to its core in late December 1975. Barely one year after granting Hunter his freedom from Oakland, Seitz issued a ruling in a dramatic case that removed the shackles that had bound baseball players to the reserve system for nearly a century.

## Free at Last

Now removed from baseball for more than a generation, the reserve clause had long been part of baseball's legal landscape from the late 1870s until its demise in 1975. Created by ownership and inserted into the standard player's contract as a means to keep players from seeking employment with another ball club, the reserve clause obligated a player to remain in the employ of his current club until that club released or traded him, thereby ceasing its relationship with that player. The effect of this inviolable clause prevented a player from offering his services to any team who might be interested in him, thus limiting the potential for a financial gain or an attractive fringe benefit such as playing in a city closer to his home.

For decades players did not even enjoy legal representation when negotiating their contracts with team owners, whose tight-fisted maneuverings were designed to hold salaries as low as possible. The crux of Paragraph 10A of the Uniform Player's Contract held the key which forever bound a player to his employer: "If prior to the March 1 next succeeding said December 20, the Player and the Club have not agreed upon the terms of such contract, then on or before 10 days after said March 1, the Club shall have the right ... to renew this contract for the period of *one year*."[49] The lynchpin of this passage implied that should the two parties fail to agree on a new contract, the club could retain the player by simply renewing the contract for another season and continue such renewals with each succeeding contract until the club saw fit to release or trade the player. If a player *did* come to terms with his team, the clause remained in the new contract, so the cycle of the reserve clause was never to be broken. With little leverage available to him except for withholding his services from his team, a player had no choice but to capitulate to the owner's offer. This system of servitude had been in place since the reserve clause was put into practice in 1879.

Previously, the reserve clause had been upheld by the courts in the cases of the Giants' Danny Gardella, the Yankees' George Toolson, and the Cardinals' Curt Flood. The verdict in the Catfish Hunter case of 1974 had no bearing on the reserve clause *per se*— Hunter was freed due to breach of contract — but Hunter's resultant ability to offer his services to the highest bidder whetted the appetites of many players who saw huge salaries in their future if only they were allowed the chance at their own freedom.

The undoing of the reserve clause came in 1975, a year in which a handful of players — Dave McNally of the Expos, Andy Messersmith of the Dodgers, and Richie Zisk of the Pirates — labored under contracts that had been renewed by their respective teams. Zisk eventually signed late in the season, so he obviously was again subjected to the effects of the reserve clause, but McNally and Messersmith remained unsigned for the entire year. Messersmith was miffed over the Dodgers' reluctance to include a no-trade provision in his contract and was poised to file a grievance over this issue, while McNally, the former Orioles ace who had been traded to Montreal, opted for retirement in early June 1975. In McNally's case, if he had decided to return to the game, he still would have been the property of the

Expos. Montreal management tried to lure McNally back into uniform in order to salvage something positive from a trade that was a disaster from the Expos' perspective. "Even though he was no longer pitching, McNally, because he had begun the season on a renewed contract, would be eligible to claim free agency after one year" if he remained unsigned and if Paragraph 10A were interpreted as being in force for only a single season rather than renewed by the club in perpetuity.[50]

Although he was offered a lucrative deal to return to the Expos in 1976, McNally never signed, and neither did Messersmith. Since both players had in effect completed their option years — that is, played one season at the club's option and therefore ostensibly fulfilled the one-year obligation stipulated by the reserve clause — in October 1975 grievances for both were filed through the players' union. The case was slated to come before the major league arbitration panel of Marvin Miller, John Gaherin, and Peter Seitz, the same trio who had adjudicated the Catfish Hunter grievance. Although Seitz was cited by Miller as ruling more in favor of the owners in grievance hearings than for the players, the baseball owners' bargaining team, the Player Relations Committee, nonetheless felt uncomfortable about the presence of Seitz, whose ruling liberated Hunter from Oakland.[51] After the PRC voted to allow Seitz to continue on the panel, the grievance hearing convened over three days in late November and early December.[52]

As if seeking to avoid the controversy he knew would result from his decision, Seitz pressed Gaherin, Miller, and Commissioner Bowie Kuhn to find a resolution among themselves if at all possible through collective bargaining. Seitz's efforts were fruitless, so the hearing proceeded, filling over 800 pages of transcripts in the process, as both sides pleaded their cases, not least of which was testimony from the commissioner that foretold of the demise of baseball should the reserve clause be scrapped. Two days before Christmas, Seitz rendered his verdict in favor of the players, his deliberation leading to the conclusion that "the option clause covered a *single* renewal of the terms of the contract" rather than siding with "management's analysis [that] would make the option perpetual."[53] His judgment struck down a reserve system that for generations of players had been impervious to change.

Although McNally kept his retirement permanent, Messersmith, like Catfish Hunter a year before, was now at liberty to offer his services to any team he wished to play for. Just turned 30 years old in the summer of 1975, Messersmith had won 19 games, recorded an ERA of 2.29, and led the National League in innings pitched (322), starts (40), complete games (19), and shutouts (7). Atlanta Braves owner Ted Turner, whose media empire was on the rise at the time, lavished the pitcher with a three-year, $1 million contract that included a no-trade clause.

Former Oriole Bobby Grich noted years later that several factors made Messersmith's cause the success it became. First, Grich stressed the importance of the arbitration process, which gave players a stronger bargaining position as opposed to trying to "take the system to court only to be annihilated by the owners' lawyers." Second, a "maverick player" was needed as a test case, one who was willing to play an entire season without a signed contract, which is exactly what Messersmith did in 1975. Finally, "a maverick owner" in the person of Turner wooed Messersmith at very favorable terms, a point which also demonstrated that million-dollar deals could be struck with teams located in smaller markets as long as those owners were willing to spend.[54]

Peter Seitz claimed that the wording of the Uniform Player's Contract, including Paragraph 10A, spelled the demise of the reserve clause, so he was not in a position to decide the merits of the reserve system itself.[55] Nonetheless, as a reward for the resultant unleashing of players from the reserve system, Seitz was dismissed — with Bowie Kuhn's blessing — as baseball's impartial arbitrator by the owners' group. Kuhn justified the firing because retention of Seitz would have implied management's satisfaction with his decision, and he defended the action by later saying, "It is commonplace to dismiss an arbitrator who has slain one of the party's sacred cows," which is what Seitz had done to the reserve system.[56]

The view from the players' union was far different for patently obvious reasons. Although Marvin Miller's reaction was blasé — Seitz's decision "was no bombshell," he later wrote — the head of the union shrewdly negotiated a new collective bargaining agreement for the players that was finalized in the summer of 1976.[57] Instead of letting every player simultaneously enter a completely open labor market, Miller brokered a deal whereby players with at least six years of major league service time — or those who played the 1976 season unsigned no matter how much or how little service time they had accrued — could play out their option year and then declare for free agency. Such a tactic took full advantage of the laws of supply and demand, thus bidding up the salaries for those players entering baseball's new employment bazaar. Had too many players become suddenly available, teams looking to shore up weaknesses would be able pick and choose more selectively among the many players available, but the relatively limited number now on the market — many of whom were excellent players — ensured that a higher number of suitors would pursue the best talent and offer generous contracts. There followed in the winter of 1976-1977 an expenditure of money on newly-minted free agents that, in its time, boggled the imagination.

## The Diaspora

The Oakland Athletics prepared for the transitional season of 1976 by hiring former Chicago White Sox manager Chuck Tanner to replace Alvin Dark. Tanner had gained credibility for his ability to deal with talented players whose personalities could be difficult, such as Dick Allen, who had won the 1972 American League Most Valuable Player Award with Tanner at the helm. Charlie Finley found reason to adjust his approach to staffing the roster in light of the new atmosphere created by the Messersmith case, since he was troubled greatly by his fear of an inability to sign his premier players so that they would consequently leave Oakland without his receiving some sort of compensation.

Messersmith had opened an escape route for many of Oakland's best players, yet Finley had backed himself into a corner from which *he* could not escape. Loath to sign a player to a multi-year contract, Finley could have only one last laugh at renewing a contract under his own terms, which meant that many Athletics could suffer through that renewal but reap the potential bonanza of a rewarding contract with another team in 1977. Reggie Jackson informed Finley that he was willing to sign a contract for at least two years, but the miserly Finley demurred. Rather than see Jackson walk away with nothing in return, Finley packaged Jackson, unsigned pitcher Ken Holtzman, who had long been weary of Finley's boorishness, and a minor leaguer in a trade to the Baltimore Orioles for outfielder Don Baylor and two pitchers, Mike Torrez and Paul Mitchell. A fearsome hitter, Baylor lacked the overall power of Jackson but was a faster runner, and Tanner, realizing that the Athletics could use speed on the bases as their new weapon of choice, gave the green light to nearly every runner who thought he had a chance to steal a base.[58]

But while Oakland was running hard during 1976 — they would lead the major leagues with 341 stolen bases — Finley attempted to get anything he could for some of his best players before the end of the season would allow them to flee Oakland as Messersmith had fled Los Angeles. Finley's intended dismantling continued in mid–June when he sold Joe Rudi and Rollie Fingers to the Boston Red Sox for $1 million each, and completed the third part of this fire sale by dealing Vida Blue to the Yankees for $1.5 million.

Bowie Kuhn, however, saw the emasculation of the Oakland lineup for what it was — Finley's desperate grab for cash, with no players going to the Athletics in return — and refused to sanction the sales. Finley retaliated by forbidding his three players to suit up for his own team. Only when the Athletics voted unanimously to go on strike in late June did Finley concede and allow Tanner to pencil Rudi's name on the lineup card and put Blue and Fingers back on the pitching staff. Oakland chased the eventual AL West champion Kansas City Royals through the summer, but the Athletics settled for a second place finish, 2½ games back. At the end of the final game of 1976, there was a small celebration in the Athletics clubhouse, complete with champagne, to commemorate the "liberation of the Oakland Seven," the septet of players who endured a hurtful season and were eager to become part of the first crop of free agents in the post–Messersmith era.[59]

Ready to depart Oakland for a better life beyond Charlie Finley's grasp were the durable captain, Sal Bando; speedy, dependable shortstop Bert Campaneris; World Series hero Gene Tenace; left fielder extraordinaire — and 1976 Gold Glove recipient — Joe Rudi; Rollie Fingers, the best reliever to come out of the Oakland bullpen; and rising star Don Baylor, acquired in the Reggie Jackson trade. The seventh player eligible to leave Oakland was Willie McCovey, who was purchased from San Diego in late August for the stretch drive but saw little playing time. This constituted a grim finale for a team only two years removed from its dynastic heyday. The sweat and sacrifice that had yielded Charlie Finley so much success now brought him only misery — self-inflicted misery, for the most part.

Oakland players had witnessed Charlie Finley's public humiliation of Mike Andrews, were brow-beaten when fighting Finley for a pay increase, and were embarrassed by his crass behavior.... Can it be any surprise that when the chance to flee Finley's clutches finally arrived that so many of his players availed themselves of the opportunity to do so? In mid–November, the latest phase of the Athletic diaspora, which commenced when Catfish Hunter left the Athletics at the end of 1974 and continued with the trade of Ken Holtzman and Reggie Jackson in the spring of 1976, now carried away the remainder of the heart and soul of Oakland's lineup and left Finley empty-handed. During a four-day span in mid–November, Baylor and Rudi signed with the California Angels, Campaneris joined the Texas Rangers, and Bando found a new home with the Milwaukee Brewers. Less then four weeks later on December 14, 1976, Fingers and Tenace both signed with the San Diego Padres.

The new average annual salaries for these six Oakland expatriates was shocking in its day and opened an era in what became referred to as "checkbook baseball," whereby wealthy owners, such as Ray Kroc, Gene Autry, or George Steinbrenner, could simply write a check to buy a player to fill a need at the major league level rather than develop talent through his franchise's farm system or acquire a player via the waiver wire or a more traditional trade. Although the lengths of contracts given to the prime free agents varied, the Class of

1976 fared well financially with their new teams: Bando (new average annual salary of $300,000), Baylor ($266,000), Campaneris ($190,000), Fingers ($320,000), Rudi ($418,000), and Tenace ($363,000).[60] Relative to the time, this was no small accomplishment considering that only the very best players eclipsed the $150,000 barrier in 1976. A torrent of cash poured from the coffers of other teams as well, with reliever Bill Campbell moving from the Twins to the Red Sox for $250,000 and Bobby Grich joining Baylor and Rudi in Anaheim for $310,000, but the player truly hitting the jackpot was Reggie Jackson, who left Baltimore and signed a five-year deal with the Yankees for an average salary of $580,000 per season.[61] Players who followed the trail blazed by Andy Messersmith did so profitably. Over the ensuing years, the inflation of salaries was staggering as many team owners of the late 1970s and onward exercised fiscal restraint similar to that shown by their predecessors in the days before the amateur draft was instituted in 1965; that is to say, they rushed at the chance to sign players in the hope of improving a poor team or making a good team even better, fiscal restraint be damned.

In 1975 the Oakland dynasty concluded its five-year reign over the American League West, and when the Athletic cupboard went bare after the 1976 season, there were few quality players from the farm system who could fill the huge void in Oakland's threadbare roster. Unlike the bounty harvested from the amateur draft in its early years, the Athletics farm system in the early 1970s did not develop an impact player on the level of a Reggie Jackson or a Sal Bando. By February 1977, holdovers such as Vida Blue, Billy North, and Claudell Washington found themselves in spring training with the likes of Ron Fairly, Ken McMullen, Tommy Helms, and Manny Sanguillen, a host of imported retreads now charged with the task of coalescing into a team under new manager Jack McKeon.[62] Later in the 1977 season — and with Washington already having been sent packing to Texas before the season started — Dick Allen, Earl Williams, Mike Jorgensen and Dave Giusti would be thrown into the breach, all to no avail as Oakland plummeted to the basement of the AL West division, finishing one-half game behind the sixth-place expansion Seattle Mariners.

The Oakland franchise had fallen into a classic economic death spiral, Finley paring expenses wherever he could, while the fans, who seemingly had to be coaxed to the Coliseum in the halcyon days of the early 1970s, now stayed away in droves, their flight further crippling the team's cash flow. Only 495,412 tickets were sold to the Athletics' home games, but there were likely far fewer people than that who actually went to the stadium that was now living up to its pejorative nickname of "the Mausoleum." A renaissance of baseball in Oakland would not take place until Finley at last divested himself of the Athletics after the dreadful season of 1979, selling his club the following year to the Haas family, the wealthy entrepreneurs of Levi Strauss and Company.

Before his departure, however, Finley bequeathed some treasure that helped enormously the fortunes of the new ownership. His trade to acquire Rick Langford and Tony Armas from Pittsburgh in early 1977 later melded with the talent of several draftees — among them Mike Norris, Dwayne Murphy, and Steve McCatty — to lead the Athletics' resurgence. In particular, the 1979 debut of Finley's prize draftee and future Hall of Famer Rickey Henderson opened a new era in speed, as Henderson's development would be stoked by none other than manager Billy Martin, the Berkeley native and former pilot of the Twins, Tigers, Rangers, and most recently the Yankees, when Finley hired him in February 1980. Martin's fiery style of leadership gave birth to the slick, alliterative term "Billy Ball" that brought Oakland the 1981 AL West crown.

But the Oakland dynasty of the 1970s had proved to be one for the ages; not until the 1998–2000 New York Yankees of Joe Torre would a team win three consecutive World Series. As great as Cincinnati's "Big Red Machine" was in the 1970s, it did not match the Athletics trio of wins in the Fall Classic, nor did the powerful Baltimore Orioles of 1969–1971.

The Oakland Athletics won on the strengths of several factors. The presence of four future Hall of Famers — Rollie Fingers, Catfish Hunter, Reggie Jackson, and manager Dick Williams — fortified the team in every key area of bullpen, rotation, power-hitting, and leadership, respectively. Underpinning the rest of the solid foundation were three durable and reliable veterans who anchored the left side of the field, Sal Bando at third base, Bert Campaneris at shortstop, and Joe Rudi in left field; not a Cooperstown candidate among them but without whose clutch hitting, consistent fielding, and ability to reach base the team would have surely faltered. Gene Tenace, unnerved at times when moved between first base and catcher, also contributed much productivity, while Vida Blue's emergence and the arrival of Ken Holtzman — he was to the Athletics what Mike Cuellar was to the Orioles — added two workhorses to the rotation. The supporting cast of Paul Lindblad and Darold Knowles in the bullpen furnished depth and balance to complement Fingers. The overall strength of the core lineup even allowed for a weak hitter with a great glove like Dick Green, who served a total of 12 years under Finley, to lend his talent to the cause.

Whither Charlie Finley, the kingpin of Oakland and the maestro of so much mayhem, at the end of it all? Had he been able to keep his team intact, mainly by endearing himself more to his players rather than repulsing so many, it can only be left to speculation how many more pennants the Athletics might have won with Jackson, Hunter, et al, at the peak of their careers and still at Oakland's disposal. Finley drove away the best manager he ever had in Williams, and alienated so many others associated with the franchise that it became too easy for them, fans included, to walk away from the Athletics with nary a backward glance. While Finley could look with pride at the three World Series trophies his dynasty had garnered, the wounds he suffered in the wake of the Messersmith decision were self-inflicted, and his indignant treatment of players and team employees as so much chattel fostered resentment by those who deserved better. Toward the end of his tenure as owner, Finley was on the brink of selling the Athletics to a party in Denver, but the team by then was as powerless as the ten-watt college radio station that served as its broadcast outlet. Any dynastic aspirations attended by Finley's "sweat plus sacrifice" had been realized in the historical sense, but by 1977 the mighty had fallen, indeed.

## Dynastic Aspirations

For generations the term "dynasty" as applied to sports has pertained to those teams whose dominance in their game was sustained for a period of years, often those years running consecutively. Over the last half century, teams in various sports — football's Green Bay Packers of the 1960s, basketball's Boston Celtics of the 1960s and 1970s, or hockey's Montreal Canadiens of that same era — have rightfully staked their claim to being among the best of all time, while in baseball the New York Yankees' post–World War II record from 1947 to 1964 is perhaps never again to be equaled. Over this same half century, however, sports leagues have expanded and competition has reached a level of parity, thereby making it more challenging for teams to defend their respective championships, let alone build a dynasty.

When the Yankees fulfilled George Weiss's gloomy prophesy by imploding within five years of his departure from that storied franchise in 1960, the door was opened for a possible successor to New York's baseball dynasty. The Washington Senators, reborn as the Minnesota Twins, overcame fits and starts after their move west to capture the American League pennant in 1965, came excruciatingly close to winning again in 1967, and then became Western Division champions in the first two years of the American League's split into two divisions. The Twins' best players, Harmon Killebrew and Rod Carew, were enshrined in Cooperstown, to be later joined by Bert Blyleven in 2011 but not Tony Oliva. Had his knees permitted him a healthier career, Oliva would most likely also be with his old teammates. Granted that just one league title, two division titles, and another pennant lost on the final weekend of a season make for a thinner claim to dynasty, but Minnesota had the bumpiest ride among the better teams striving to maintain a level of play consistent with that of a champion. In the period of their greatest success, from 1965 through 1970, Calvin Griffith's Twins won 556 games, a total second only to the 575 wins amassed by the Baltimore Orioles.

When Minnesota sputtered in 1966, the Baltimore Orioles wasted no time in leveraging an invigorated Frank Robinson to take charge over the American League and soon thereafter, under Earl Weaver, forged the teams of 1969 to 1971 which on paper — that most cursed of phrases — were nonpareil. With but one World Series title to show for Weaver's first three full years, this Baltimore dynasty continued to hold sway over the American League East by winning that division five out of six years from 1969 to 1974. The Orioles adjusted to inevitable personnel changes during that time, but the great pitching exemplified by Jim Palmer, superb defense that was the forte of Brooks Robinson, and dangerous hitting from multiple sources were constantly used by Baltimore to remain a formidable contender. To no one's surprise, Weaver, Palmer, and the "Robinson Brothers" earned their rightful places in the Hall of Fame, with Frank Robinson's credentials further enhanced when he broke another color barrier by becoming baseball's first black manager in 1975 with the Cleveland Indians. In the years 1965 to 1975, the Orioles won 1,034 contests, 88 more than their nearest rival, the Twins, and from 1969 to 1975 Baltimore was still 23 wins better than Oakland (676 to 653). The Orioles of 1969 to 1971 were better than their brethren of 1972 to 1975, yet in the early 1970s this team's shrewd trades and use of players raised through the farm system facilitated its transition in the post–Frank Robinson era to enable Baltimore to remain a contender through the 1970s.

For the Oakland Athletics' part, their story fit a convenient chronological slot that picked up where the best of the Baltimore teams left off. The talent collected by Charlie Finley in the last years spent by the Athletics in Kansas City matured together in the early Oakland years and under Dick Williams's unbending gaze jelled into baseball's best team from 1972 to 1974. Often appearing to thrive on dysfunctional relationships, the Athletics won when it counted and did so playing for the most hubristic, pompous owner in baseball or perhaps any sport. Five consecutive AL West titles and three straight World Series championships marked Oakland as a dynasty with no qualifications necessary. Though debate may linger as to whether Finley really knew how to run his team — to say nothing of the ruin he drove it to — there can be no argument about the results he achieved in his role as owner and personnel director in the first half of the 1970s. Oakland's quartet of Williams, Hunter, Fingers, and Jackson formed the backbone of their dynasty, and their deeds in an Athletics uniform were among the first on their Cooperstown résumés. It can only be left to speculation how many more World Series wins would have accrued to Oakland had Finley's toxic personality not rotted the framework upon which the Athletics were built.

Toward the middle of the 1970s, one team long absent from postseason play re-emerged as a formidable contender. By 1976 the New York Yankees, who were short on talent developed in their farm system, nonetheless showcased a regular lineup fortified by solid players obtained via key trades. Graig Nettles, Chris Chambliss, Willie Randolph, Lou Piniella, and Mickey Rivers were all products of organizations outside the Bronx, and the same was true of their frontline pitchers such as Catfish Hunter, Ed Figueroa, and Sparky Lyle. After his firing by the Texas Rangers, Billy Martin, accompanied by both his successful track record and the baggage of his troublesome reputation, made his managerial debut in New York and led the Yankees to their first World Series since 1964, albeit a loss in four straight games to the Cincinnati Reds. To uphold the standard of this new-found glory and guard against failure in a future World Series, George Steinbrenner opened his checkbook to add Reggie Jackson to his roster, a move that was truly a coup in the batter's box and at the box office. But the capstone of the Yankees' personnel maneuvers came when club executive Gabe Paul traded for Bucky Dent of the White Sox to fill the void at shortstop. Once that infield gap was plugged, the Yankees again took flight and won the World Series in 1977 and 1978 as Jackson earned the title "Mr. October" with his prodigious display of power, and the Yankees marked a return to traditional dominance of the American League.

No team can set its sights on creating a dynasty, but once having secured the first championship, that team will at least have established a toehold to move forward to its next title, and perhaps others still to follow. The period of 1965 to 1975 was an interregnum between Yankee dynasties, the Bronx Bomber teams up to 1964 and those beginning in 1976 serving as unwitting bookends in the chronology of American League history, while three other clubs experienced varying degrees of success in asserting themselves as the league's premier team and understood well the difficulties of maintaining the lofty standards of a champion. The Minnesota Twins, Baltimore Orioles, and Oakland Athletics bore the marks — and scars — of the best of the American League as they pursued dynastic aspirations of their own.

# Chapter Notes

## Chapter 1

1. Peter Golenbock, *Dynasty: The New York Yankees, 1949–1964* (Englewood Cliffs, NJ: Prentice-Hall, 1975). This quote comes from the full subtitle of Golenbock's book.
2. Golenbock, *Dynasty*, 354.
3. Bouton quoted in Golenbock, *Dynasty*, 375.
4. David Halberstam, *October 1964* (New York: Villard, 1994), 316.
5. Flood quoted in Halberstam, *October 1964*, 316.
6. Halberstam, *October 1964*, 344.
7. "Yankees Walloped 'Good Fast Balls,' Gibson Notes at Victory Celebration," *New York Times*, October 16, 1964, 44.
8. Gerald Eskenazi, "Illness Plagued Gibson as Child; He Was 'Born Sick,' Mother Says," *New York Times*, October 16, 1964, 44.
9. Joseph Durso, "Cards Win World Series, Defeating Yankees, 7 to 5," *New York Times*, October 16, 1964, 1.
10. Halberstam, *October 1964*, 338.
11. Golenbock, *Dynasty*, 278.
12. Ibid.

## Chapter 2

1. The notable exception to this trend was the shift of the St. Louis Browns eastward to Baltimore in 1954.
2. Letter from Walter Shannon to Al Fleishman, July 28, 1960, Papers of Harry Dalton, 1960–1993, BAMSS40, National Baseball Hall of Fame Library, National Baseball Hall of Fame, Cooperstown, NY, Box 2, Series I, Folder 2.
3. William Gildea, "Leaving for the Last Time," *Washington Post*, October, 21, 1999, D3.
4. *1963 Minnesota Twins Press Radio TV Guide*, 19.
5. Ibid.
6. Jon Kerr, *Calvin: Baseball's Last Dinosaur—An Authorized Biography* (Dubuque, IA: Wm. C. Brown, 1990), 54.
7. Ibid.
8. In 1959, the Senators enjoyed a 29 percent surge in attendance when 140,000 more fans attended games in Washington over the previous year, but the gate of just over 615,000 was still far short of what Minnesota was offering. See J. G. Taylor Spink, "Nats Will Shift to Minneapolis," *The Sporting News*, October 7, 1959, 4. The *New York Times* of October 27, 1960, claimed that the team was assured of a gate of one million per season for its first five years rather than three years.
9. These attendance figures run contrary to the nostalgic offerings of later memorabilia and observations. In a 2002 interview, Harmon Killebrew cited poor attendance for Griffith's desire to relocate, and the 1991 Twins yearbook, an edition commemorating the team's thirty years in Minnesota, noted that Griffith was "beset by slumping attendance." But these comments do not stand up to scrutiny in view of the fact that in the four years prior to the Senators' move, the team posted the following home attendance: 1955—425,238; 1956—431,647; 1957—457,079; 1958—475,288; 1959—615,372; 1960–743,404. An increase of nearly 75 percent over this period hardly qualifies as a slump. See Harmon Killebrew, interview by Jon Pessah, compact disk recording, February 21, 2002, National Baseball Hall of Fame Archives, Cooperstown, NY; *1966 Minnesota Twins Press Radio TV Guide*, 6; Craig Cox, "The Way We Were," *1991 Twins Yearbook*, 6.
10. J. G. Taylor Spink, "Nats Will Shift to Minneapolis," *The Sporting News*, October 7, 1959, 1. Griffith faced a major league filing deadline of October 31, 1959, to propose to American League officials his desire to change locations. He was also infringing on territory that was presently occupied by the St. Paul franchise of the Triple-A American Association.
11. John Drebinger, "American League, in '61, to Add Minneapolis and Los Angeles," *New York Times*, October 27, 1960, in *The New York Times Book of Baseball History* (New York: Arno, 1975), 217. The headline of this article gives the awkward impression that Minneapolis would be an expansion team, when in actuality the new Washington team taking the place of the departed Senators held that title.

12. This photograph was featured in an article from the Twins 1991 yearbook. See Craig Cox, "The Way We Were," *1991 Twins Yearbook*, 6.

13. This catchphrase appeared on each such cover until the 1966 edition was issued and paid tribute to the Twins' 1965 American League championship.

14. *1965 Minnesota Twins Press Radio TV Guide*, 20.

15. Killebrew interview.

16. Bob Addie, "50 Homers? 'Can Do,' Chirps Killebrew," *The Sporting News*, July 1, 1959, 4.

17. Killebrew interview.

18. Shirley Povich, "'Ready' Label Put on Pair of Nats' Rookies," *The Sporting News*, April 1, 1959, 18.

19. Ibid.

20. Arno Goethel, "Jimmie Tempted Many Times to Quit and Work in Mills," *The Sporting News*, September 14, 1963, 10.

21. Arno Goethel, "'Oliva Ready,' Cal Claims; Allison May Shift to First," *The Sporting News*, November 23, 1963, 20; Max Nichols, "Twins Wishing Tony Were Triplets," *The Sporting News*, May 16, 1964, 3.

22. Bob Addie, "Bob Addie's Atoms," *The Sporting News*, April 1, 1959, 18. Addie's column was a potpourri of items rather than an article with a single theme.

23. Tom Briere, "Cookie Hunting Pegs to Plug Pair of Holes at Short and on Slab," *The Sporting News*, March 8, 1961, 28.

24. Max Nichols, "Timely Tips from Battling Billy Sharpen Zoilo's Shortstop Play," *The Sporting News*, March 28, 1962, 17. In a less politically-correct era, player quotes were printed verbatim or were altered phonetically to emphasize the speaker's accent, notably that of Latino players. "Hit" at times became "heet," and, in reference to a couple of homers he slugged in the spring of 1961, another Twins infielder, Jose Valdivielso, was quoted, "Wind blowing out. I think Zoilo Versalles play good shortstop for Twins. But he no ready, I play." See Tom Briere, "Twins Tying '61 Hopes to Biffer Battey," *The Sporting News*, April 5, 1961, 27.

25. Bob Addie, "Base Bandits Just Sitting Ducks to Senators' Rifle-Armed Battey," *The Sporting News*, August 17, 1960, 18.

26. Shirley Povich, "Nats Plug 2 Holes with Pair of Swaps," *The Sporting News*, April 13, 1960, 10.

27. Arno Goethel, "Hustler Allen's Hot Bat Kayoes Twin Timetable," *The Sporting News*, March 28, 1962, 17.

28. Biographical feature of Jerry Kindall, *1966 Minnesota Twins Press Radio TV Guide*, 33.

29. "Mele's Efforts Tighten Up Defense — Only Two Breakdowns in 57 Contests," *The Sporting News*, June 27, 1964, 17. No byline is listed for this brief article, but its author is likely Max Nichols, who contributed Twins stories to many editions of the publication.

30. Max Nichols, "Zoilo Swings Hot Twin Cleaver to Silence Glove-Butcher Rap," *The Sporting News*, September 19, 1964, 9.

31. Max Nichols, "September Mourn Hits Twins as Vaunted Power Goes Pop," *The Sporting News*, September 26, 1964, 9.

32. Shirley Povich, "Pascual Spurts on New Control — of His Temper," *The Sporting News*, July 22, 1959, 15.

33. Herb Heft, "Hats Off — Camilo Pascual," *The Sporting News*, July 15, 1959, 22. As the season progressed and Pascual gained more notoriety as a pitcher to be reckoned with, he was quoted as saying, "Married life is better for me." See Shirley Povich, "Camilo Plays It Cool as Nat Hill Hot Shot," *The Sporting News*, September 16, 1959, 20.

34. Shirley Povich, "Reds' Million Offer for Pair Nixed by Nats," *The Sporting News*, December 23, 1959, 22. Cincinnati was just two seasons away from winning their first National League pennant since 1940, and Killebrew would have been a fine addition to the Reds' own powerful offense.

35. Shirley Povich, "Ailing Flipper Halts Camilo's Feud with Cal," *The Sporting News*, November 2, 1960, 21. In less than two years, the Soviet Union would precipitate the Cuban Missile Crisis when Nikita Khrushchev sent military assistance to Castro in the form of long- and medium-range missiles capable of striking nearly the entire continental United States.

36. Shirley Povich, "Cookie Coos Over Classy Pitching by Rookie Kaat," *The Sporting News*, May 11, 1960, 13.

37. Arno Goethel, "Twins Toss Bouquets to Their Late-Blooming Curver Jim Kaat," *The Sporting News*, June 30, 1962, 6.

38. Arno Goethel, "Kaat Cat's Whiskers As Homerless Hurler," *The Sporting News*, July 18, 1964, 13.

39. Jim "Mudcat" Grant, interview by Joseph P. Keaney, Jr., compact disk recording, February 12, 1991, National Baseball Hall of Fame Archives, Cooperstown, NY.

40. Max Nichols, "Mudcat Flexing Old Muscle as Kingfish of Twin Mound," *The Sporting News*, July 25, 1964, 13.

41. Grant interview.

42. Max Nichols, "Worthington Gives Twins Rich Return on Stingy Hurling," *The Sporting News*, August 29, 1964, 4.

43. Allen Lewis, "Phils Use Reliable Klipper to Mow Down N.L. Rivals," *The Sporting News*, May 2, 1964, 10. By selling Klippstein to Minnesota, the Phillies spared him the agony of their heartbreaking collapse at the end of the season as they squandered their lead and lost the pennant to the St. Louis Cardinals. Klippstein did make it to the World Series the following year with the Twins.

44. Milton Jamail, *Full Count: Inside Cuban Baseball* (Carbondale, IL: Southern Illinois University Press, 2000), 29.

45. Tom Briere, "Cookie Hunting Pegs to Plug Pair of Holes at Short and on Slab," *The Sporting News*, March 8, 1961, 28.

46. Tom Briere, "New Pilot Mele to Stress Speed as Twins' Boss," *The Sporting News*, July 5, 1961, 13.

47. Tom Briere, "Twins Seek Hill Aid; Ramos and Lemon on Block," *The Sporting News*, October 11, 1961, 20.

48. Arno Goethel, "'Fluke' Label on Twins Burns Up Mele," *The Sporting News*, April 6, 1963, 1.

49. Arno Goethel, "Mele Shocked, but Inks Pact with Pay Cut," *The Sporting News*, October 12, 1963, 10.

50. Arno Goethel, "'Best Yet to Come — We Have Potential,' Says Skipper Mele," *The Sporting News*, February 8, 1964, 17.

51. "Scouting Reports," *Sports Illustrated*, April 13, 1964, 76. Emphasis added.

52. Max Nichols, "Mele Notifies 7 A.L. Hurlers — 'You'll Pay for Flattening Oliva,'" *The Sporting News*, June 6, 1964, 8. Barber was quoted in this same article as saying, incredulously, "I thought the three pitches I threw him in the first inning were closer than the one that hit him. I thought the one that hit him was belt high. He sort of ducked into it." How Oliva could have moved his head into a pitch viewed by Barber as roughly three feet off the ground shows how fatuous the pitcher's claim was.

53. Max Nichols, "Mele Prods Twins as They Droop on Heartbreak Trail," *The Sporting News*, August 8, 1964, 15.

54. Ibid.

55. Max Nichols, "Those Blankety-Blank Errors — They Shriveled Twin Win Total," *The Sporting News*, October 24, 1964, 12. Emphasis added.

56. Ibid.

## Chapter 3

1. Max Nichols, "Hot-Blooded Camilo Loves Ice, Snow," *The Sporting News*, January 9, 1965, 7.

2. "Common Sense Will Solve Race Problems," *The Sporting News*, April 5, 1961, 10.

3. In his fine book on the 1965 Twins, Jim Thielman cited an exchange between Grant and Cleveland coach Ted Wilks while both men were in the bullpen during an Indians' game. An infuriated Grant stalked out with the contest still in progress and was subsequently suspended by the team. See Thielman, *Cool of the Evening: The 1965 Minnesota Twins* (Minneapolis: Kirk House, 2005), 41–42.

4. Hal Butler, *The Bob Allison Story* (New York: Julian Messner, 1967), 154.

5. Gene Schoor, *Billy Martin* (Garden City, NY: Doubleday, 1980), 118.

6. "Minnesota Twins," *Sports Illustrated*, April 19, 1965, 88. This article was part of the magazine's annual preview of all major league teams.

7. Ibid.

8. "Few Yank Problems, Many Strengths," *Minneapolis Tribune*, April 3, 1965, 15. This column was listed as the "first in a series, sizing up the Twins' American League competition for 1965."

9. Johnny Klippstein, oral history, Society for American Baseball Research Archives, Cleveland, OH.

10. Max Nichols, "Confident Kaat — Even Miscues Fail to Ruffle Twins' Southpaw," *The Sporting News*, May 8, 1965, 11.

11. Jim Kaat with Phil Pepe, *Still Pitching: Musings from the Mound and the Microphone* (Chicago: Triumph, 2003), 48.

12. Thielman, *Cool of the Evening*, 94.

13. Max Nichols, "Tiny Sandy Superb as a Pinch-Swinger," *The Sporting News*, May 15, 1965, 11.

14. Ibid.

15. Max Nichols, "Twins Run, Ignore Base-Line Caution," *The Sporting News*, June 5, 1965, 9.

16. Max Nichols, "Zoilo Quits Z-z-zing on Field, Sparks Twins with Fresh Zip," *The Sporting News*, June 12, 1965, 10.

17. Ibid.

18. Butler, *Bob Allison Story*, 159. Emphasis in original text. The only player to come close to playing every game was Versalles, who appeared in 160 contests.

19. Ibid., 159.

20. Tom Briere, "Twins' Griffith Says: 'Infielder, Pitcher Needed for Flag,'" *Minneapolis Tribune*, June 2, 1965, 21. Years later, the Boston Red Sox reserved a roster spot for Roger LaFrancois, who in 1982 appeared in a mere eight games as a catcher and batted only ten times the entire season.

21. Ibid.

22. Tom Briere, "Twins Belt Red Sox," *Minneapolis Tribune*, June 3, 1965, 29.

23. Allan Simpson, ed., *The Baseball Draft: The First 25 Years* (Durham, NC: American Sports Publishing, 1990), 10.

24. Ibid., 14.

25. Clifford Kachline, "Frick Lauds 'Great Progress Program,'" *The Sporting News*, December 19, 1964, 1.

26. Simpson, *The Baseball Draft*, 18.

27. Ibid., 23.

28. Ibid., 13.

29. Sal Bando, telephone interview with author, September 28, 2008.

30. Sid Hartman, "Hartman's Roundup," *Minneapolis Tribune*, June 9, 1965, 26.

31. Dick Cullum, "Cullum's Column," *Minneapolis Tribune*, July 8, 1965, 21.

32. Sid Hartman, "Hartman's Roundup," *Minneapolis Tribune*, July 17, 1965, 12.

33. The managers of the previous year's World Series teams are accorded the honor of piloting their respective league's All-Star squad, but with the Cardinals' Johnny Keane having moved to the Yankees and ex–Yankee Yogi Berra coaching for the Mets, substitute skippers had to be named. NL chores were trusted to Gene Mauch, whose front-running Phillies had ignominiously collapsed and finished runners-up to St. Louis, while the AL chose Al Lopez, manager of the White Sox, who had guided his team to second place, just one game behind the Yankees.

34. David Sheridan, "Amateur Vendor Strikes Out," *Minneapolis Tribune*, July 14, 1965, 1.

35. Dick Cullum, "Cullum's Column," *Minneapolis Tribune*, July 26, 1965, 23. Shortly thereafter, Griffith credited Mele with recommending the soft-spoken Naragon, which may well have influenced the owner's final decision. See Sid Hartman, "Hartman's Roundup," *Minneapolis Tribune*, July 29, 1965, 18.

36. Butler, *Bob Allison Story*, 168.

37. *1966 Minnesota Twins Press Radio TV Guide*, 34.

38. Jerry Kindall, oral history, March 18, 2003, Society for American Baseball Research Archives, Cleveland, OH.

39. Andrew Hanssen, "The Cost of Discrimination: A Study of Major League Baseball," *Southern Economic Journal*, Vol. 64, No. 3 (January 1998), 603–627. Hanssen's detailed analysis covers the years 1950 to 1984 and explores many facets of the impact that black players had on the game during this period. For statistical purposes, he considers "black Latin" players to be on a par with their African-American peers, thus counting Battey, Tovar, Oliva, and Valdespino among the black position players and Grant the lone black pitcher.

40. Jerry Kindall, telephone interview with author, September 9, 2008. In an interview Grant gave in 1991, the pitcher, despite his easy-going demeanor, admitted, "From a psychological standpoint, I had a hard time dealing with [racial strife]" that had gripped the nation in the latter part of the 1960s.

41. "A Summer Carnival of Riot," *Los Angeles Times*, August 13, 1965, A4. This editorial was printed before the worst of the rioting ended, and two days later the *Times* pleaded on its front page, "Decent citizens everywhere, regardless of color, can only pray that this anarchy will soon end." See "A Time for Prayer," *Los Angeles Times*, August 15, 1965, 1.

42. Kindall interview.

43. Pete Bentovoja, "Murderers' Row — Minus 'the Killer,'" *Los Angeles Times*, August 21, 1965, A1. This edition of the *Times* refused to pin the low attendance for the Twins' series on any pall that may have been cast over the city by the mayhem. In his "Sportslook" column, Don Page cited on page B2 three other extenuating factors that drew attention away from the Twins-Angels series: "[The Angels'] game is televised locally on Channel 5; the Dodgers and Giants are on Channel 11; [and] Sandy Koufax is pitching against Juan Marichal." As if the horrors of the riots were not enough, the Dodgers-Giants game was marred by the horrific clubbing of Dodgers catcher John Roseboro by Marichal in the game played at San Francisco. The Giants ace pitcher took exception to the closeness of Roseboro's return throws to Koufax when he was at the plate in the bottom of the fourth inning, and Marichal expressed his displeasure by hitting the catcher at least twice in the skull with his bat, thus precipitating a fifteen-minute fracas that left both teams shaken.

44. Rigney quoted in "L.A. Forecasters See Twins–Braves Series," *Minneapolis Tribune*, August 21, 1965, 12; Cuccinello quoted in "Twins Can Do No Wrong, Tony Says," *The Sporting News*, August 28, 1965, 7.

45. Charles Johnson, "Premature Hysteria Over Series Could Harm Twins' Cause," *Minneapolis Tribune*, August 15, 1965, 2S.

46. "Praise Pours in on Mele After Win," *Minneapolis Tribune*, September 27, 1965, 1.

47. Rick Little and Bill Morlock, *Split Double Header: An Unauthorized History of the Minnesota Twins* (Minneapolis: Morick, 1979), 20.

48. "Hail to the Pennant-winning Twins!" *Minneapolis Tribune*, September 27, 1965, 6.

49. Kerr, *Calvin*, 70.

50. Ibid., 71. Also among Murphy's gripes was the team's lack of a true general manager who possessed detachment from Griffith in handling personnel matters. Murphy believed that Griffith was not equipped to tend to both franchise ownership and those duties usually discharged by a general manager.

51. Kindall interview.

52. Roger Angell, "West of the Bronx," in *Before the Dome: Baseball in Minnesota When the Grass Was Real*, ed. David Anderson (Minneapolis: Nodin, 1993), 101–102.

53. Butler, *Bob Allison Story*, 173.

54. Sam Mele, "Sam Mele Says," *Minneapolis Tribune*, October 7, 1965, 39. During the entire World Series, the *Tribune* featured a column under Mele's byline, in which the Twins skipper gave his views of each game.

55. Jim Murray, "A Game of Pinches," *Los Angeles Times*, October 10, 1965, H1.

56. Paul Zimmerman, "Dodgers Feel Twins Shook Up by Bunting, Running," *Los Angeles Times*, October 11, 1965, B4.

57. Sam Mele, "Sam Mele Says," *Minneapolis Tribune*, October 12, 1965, 17.

58. Sid Hartman, "Grant: 'Knew It Was Homer,'" *Minneapolis Tribune*, October 14, 1965, 31.

59. Sam Mele, "Sam Mele Says," *Minneapolis Tribune*, October 14, 1965, 31.

60. Paul Zimmerman, "Rain May Be Key to Alston's Choice," *Los Angeles Times*, October 15, 1965, B1.

61. Frank Finch, "Alston Tells Why Koufax Got the Call," *Los Angeles Times*, October 14, 1965, B4.

62. Jim Murray, "Worker of Art," *Los Angeles Times*, October 15, 1965, B1.

63. Sam Mele, "Sam Mele Says," *Minneapolis Tribune*, October 15, 1965, 21.

64. "Minnesota Twins Came Awfully Close!" *Minneapolis Tribune*, October 15, 1965, 4.

65. Charles Johnson, "Upper Midwest Does Itself Proud as Host for Series," *Minneapolis Tribune*, October 17, 1965, 2S.

66. Butler, *Bob Allison Story*, 173.

67. Kaat, *Still Pitching*, 51; Tony Oliva with Bob Fowler, *Tony O!: The Trials and Triumphs of Tony Oliva* (New York: Hawthorn, 1973), 95.

68. Kerr, *Calvin*, 71.

69. Schoor, *Billy Martin*, 119.

70. Kindall interview.

71. Ibid.

72. Jamie Wallace, "Bouton and Haynes Help Hail Sain in Hometown," *The Sporting News*, November 27, 1965, 6.

73. Cleveland Indians owner Bill Veeck captured the top executive award in 1948, and Haney won it 1962 while he was with the Los Angeles Angels. George Weiss (1950, 1951, 1952, 1960) and Dan Topping (1961) represented the Yankees well during their dynasty. National League front office chieftains won in the other years of this period.

74. Max Nichols, "Minnesota Miracle Worker — Veteran Trainer George Lentz," *The Sporting News*, September 25, 1965, 13.

75. Charles Johnson, "Owners Swinging to Baseball Man as New Commissioner," *Minneapolis Tribune*, July 4, 1965, 2S.

76. Claflin quoted in Oscar Kahn, "Exciting Feats? Koufax Most with Best," *The Sporting News*, January 8, 1966, 38.

77. Charles Johnson, "A.L. Will Prosper Even If Yankees Lose Fan Appeal," *Minneapolis Tribune*, July 18, 1965, 2S. This was a remarkable statement considering Johnson made his observation just three months into the season; history proved that he was absolutely correct.

78. Thielman, *Cool of the Evening*, 23.

## *Chapter 4*

1. Max Nichols, "At Zoilo's House, Everyone's Happy," *The Sporting News*, December 4, 1965, 15.

2. Mele quoted in "Scouting Reports — Minnesota Twins," *Sports Illustrated*, April 18, 1966, 77.

3. Max Nichols, "Valdespino Hero of Flag-Hoisting Day in Minnesota," *The Sporting News*, April 23, 1966, 15.

4. Max Nichols, "Rain Idles Twins Five Games — but It's Not Griffith Record," *The Sporting News*, May 14, 1966, 11.

5. Arno Goethel, "Wake Up, Sam! The Twins Need a Kick in Pants," *The Sporting News*, June 11, 1966, 14. *The Sporting News* byline credited the *St. Paul Pioneer Press* with carrying the original story.

6. Tom Briere, "Orioles Sweep 2 from Twins," *Minneapolis Tribune*, July 3, 1966, S1; Tom Briere, "'66 Orioles Mirror Twins of Year Ago," *Minneapolis Tribune*, July 3, 1966, S1.

7. Mele quoted in Tom Briere, "'66 Orioles Mirror Twins of Year Ago," *Minneapolis Tribune*, July 3, 1966, S1.

8. Max Nichols, "Twins Aim for Place Position with Worthington in Harness," *The Sporting News*, August 13, 1966, 15.

9. Little and Morlock, *Split Double Header*, 33. If Twins fans were dismayed by Hall's weak production, they had company with Red Sox fans, who in 1964 watched Felix Mantilla belt 30 home runs but drive in just 64 runs.

10. Butler, *Bob Allison Story*, 179.

11. Sid Hartman, "Twins' Coaches Naragon, Sain, Join Detroit's Staff," *Minneapolis Tribune*, October 5, 1966, 23.

12. Max Nichols, "Wynn Renews Ties with Cal Griffith as Twins' Hill Coach," *The Sporting News*, November 5, 1966, 31.

13. Max Nichols, "Sain's Exit Puts Mele on Win-or-Else Spot," *The Sporting News*, October 22, 1966, 15.

14. Max Nichols, "Finding Single Spot for Killer First on Twin Plans for 1967," *The Sporting News*, October 15, 1966, 15.

15. Max Nichols, "Battey to Build Up Weak Knee — Tough Exercises in Store," *The Sporting News*, November 26, 1966, 27.

16. Sid Hartman, "Chance Salary Doesn't Worry Cal," *Minneapolis Tribune*, December 3, 1966, 13.

17. Charles Johnson, "Lowdown on Sports," *Minneapolis Tribune*, December 4, 1966, S2.

18. Rod Carew with Ira Berkow, *Carew* (New York: Simon and Schuster, 1979), 62.

19. Ibid.

20. Joe Jares, "Poor Sam — What a Weird Week," *Sports Illustrated*, May 1, 1967, 26.

21. Rigney quoted in Dick Cullum, "Cullum's Column," *Minneapolis Tribune*, June 5, 1967, 27.

22. Mele quoted in Sid Hartman, "Hartman's Roundup," *Minneapolis Tribune*, June 10, 1967, 13.

23. Adcock quoted in Sid Hartman, "Hartman's Roundup," *Minneapolis Tribune*, September 17, 1967, S3.

24. Dick Williams and Bill Plachke, *No More Mr. Nice Guy: A Life of Hardball* (New York: Harcourt, Brace, Jovanovich, 1990), 99. Emphasis added.

25. "Boston Defeats Twins, 5 to 3, Wins A.L. Pennant," *Minneapolis Tribune*, October 3, 1967, 1.

26. Sid Hartman, "Fair Share Assured Mele in Series Split," *Minneapolis Tribune*, October 4, 1967, 27; William Leggett, "A Wild Finale — and It's Boston!" *Sports Illustrated*, October 9, 1967, 40.

27. Kerr, *Calvin*, 76.

28. *1968 Minnesota Twins Press Radio TV Guide*, 20.

29. Rex Lardner, "The Pitchers Are Ruining the Game," *New York Times*, June 16, 1968, VI, 12.

30. Dwayne Netland, "Carew Incident Makes Twins One Big, Happy Family," *Minneapolis Tribune*, July 4, 1968, 22.

31. Dave Mona, "Griffith Releases Ermer, Delays New Selection," *Minneapolis Tribune*, October 1, 1968, 25.

32. Ibid., 25.

33. Ibid., 27.

34. Dave Mona, "Twins Expected to Pick Martin," *Minneapolis Tribune*, October 11, 1968, 31.

35. Griffith quoted in Sid Hartman, *Minneapolis Tribune*, October 12, 1968, 18.

36. Nettles quoted in Peter Golenbock, *Wild, High, and Tight: The Life and Death of Billy Martin* (New York: St. Martin's, 1994), 165.

37. *1969 Minnesota Twins Press Radio TV Guide*, 22, 23.

38. Golenbock, *Wild, High, and Tight*, 167.

39. Joseph Durso, "National League Adds Montreal and San Diego," in *The New York Times Book of Baseball History: Highlights from the Pages of The New York Times* (New York: Arno, 1975), 277.

40. Martin quoted in *Carew*, 109. Emphasis added to point out Martin's interesting choice of adverb. Ironically, Martin "was surprised when Calvin was critical of me having Tony Oliva thrown out stealing eight times during the season with Harmon Killebrew at the bat." This stratagem was justified in Martin's mind because he believed that with a baserunner on the move, Killebrew was more likely to see a good fastball. See Sid Hartman, *Minneapolis Tribune*, October 22, 1969, 28.

41. Tom Briere, "Martin Stands Firm Against Second Guess," *Minneapolis Tribune*, October 7, 1969, 24.
42. Oliva with Fowler, *Tony O!*, 142.
43. Dick Cullum, *Minneapolis Tribune*, October 12, 1969, 2S. The October 14 edition of the newspaper reported that the emotional outpouring of Twins backers ranged from tear-soaked pleas for Martin's return to angry ticket holders swearing off Twins games in 1970. See Dave Mona, "Fan Reaction to Martin's Firing: 'Foul,'" *Minneapolis Tribune*, October 14, 1969, 25.
44. Martin quoted in Sid Hartman, *Minneapolis Tribune*, October 22, 1969, 28.
45. Golenbock, *Wild, High, and Tight*, 176.
46. Rigney quoted in Jon Roe, "Team Must Show Fans and Orioles," *Minneapolis Tribune*, October 2, 1970, 27.
47. Oliva, *Tony O!*, 154. Oliva made his point, but at least the Twins were only down 4–3 going into the top of the ninth inning in Game 2 of the 1970 ALCS before the Orioles exploded for seven runs to clinch the contest.

## *Chapter 5*

1. James Edward Miller, *The Baseball Business: Pursuing Pennants and Profits in Baltimore* (Chapel Hill: University of North Carolina Press, 1990), 27.
2. Ibid., 29.
3. *1953 St. Louis Browns Press Radio TV Guide*, 2. Under a cheeky photograph of the irrepressible Veeck, the owner's statement proclaimed, "Both [manager] Marty Marion and I feel that our 18-month rebuilding job will produce many more victories in 1953." The Browns' 54–100 record that year, however, was twelve games worse than their performance in 1952.
4. Baltimore hosted teams in the National Association, American Association, and Union Association most years from 1872 to 1891. Beginning in 1892, the city had a National League club for eight years, followed by an entry in the new American League in 1901, but that team lasted for only two seasons. Baltimore joined the Eastern League in 1903, which was renamed as the International League in 1912, where it remained until the Browns' transfer in late 1953.
5. Dalton quoted in John Eisenberg, *From 33rd Street to Camden Yards: An Oral History of the Baltimore Orioles* (New York: Contemporary, 2001), 11.
6. Chapter 3 of Eisenberg's *From 33rd Street to Camden Yards: An Oral History of the Baltimore Orioles* provides an interesting collection of firsthand accounts from players and front-office staff on the assets and foibles of Richards, the man who molded the Orioles in this crucial period.
7. Bob Maisel, "The Paul Richards Years," in *The House of Magic, 1922–1991: 70 Years of Thrills and Excitement on 33rd Street*, ed. Bob Brown (Baltimore: French Bray, 1991), 13–14.
8. Brooks Robinson, interview by Dane Ratasky and Ben Nichols, May 6, 2003, Society for American Baseball Research Archives, Cleveland, OH.
9. Brooks Robinson interview; Eisenberg, *From 33rd Street to Camden Yards*, 52–54. Still a raw recruit during his appearances with the Orioles in 1955 and 1956, Robinson admitted to being over-matched at the plate and later acknowledged the wisdom of his decision to spend more time in the minors en route to securing a job in Baltimore. Richards concurred with Staller's opinion regarding the installation of Robinson at third base.
10. Brooks Robinson quoted in Eisenberg, *From 33rd Street to Camden Yards*, 57.
11. Dalton quoted in Miller, *The Baseball Business*, 46.
12. Miller, *The Baseball Business*, 59.
13. Years after this philosophy was put into practice, former Oriole Bobby Grich acknowledged without hesitation that Baltimore's scouting system was the key factor in facilitating the success of its minor league teams. Author telephone interview with Bobby Grich, August 9, 2009.
14. Maisel, "The Paul Richards Years," 16.
15. Miller, *The Baseball Business*, 62.
16. Milt Pappas, oral history, August 28, 1992, Society for American Baseball Research Archives, Cleveland, OH.
17. Eisenberg, *From 33rd Street to Camden Yards*, 85.
18. Roy Terrell, "Eager Young Birds," *Sports Illustrated*, June 13, 1960, 73.
19. Brown quoted in Eisenberg, *From 33rd Street to Camden Yards*, 108.
20. Although ownerships changed over the ensuing decades, the Red Wings continued as the Orioles' top farm club until 2002.
21. "Baltimore Orioles," *Sports Illustrated*, April 10, 1961, 74.
22. Pappas, oral history.
23. MacPhail quoted in Eisenberg, *From 33rd Street to Camden Yards*, 120.
24. Miller, *The Baseball Business*, 87–88.
25. Hitchcock quoted in Eisenberg, *From 33rd Street to Camden Yards*, 124.
26. Bob Brown, "Just Before Dawn," in *The House of Magic*, 29.
27. "Year by Year with the Orioles," *1984 Baltimore Orioles Yearbook*, 29.
28. William Leggett, "A Success Is Killing the American League," *Sports Illustrated*, September 9, 1963, 20. Finley at this time was already focusing on Oakland as a new home, and those in the Kansas City area felt justified in complaining that Finley was negligent in promoting and improving the Athletics. Kansas City's team ERA of 4.74 (1961) and 4.79 (1962) ranked dead-last in the American League during Bauer's one and a half seasons there.
29. William Leggett, "They Went and Got 'Em," *Sports Illustrated*, August 31, 1964, 17–18.
30. The April 13, 1964, seasonal preview of the Orioles by *Sports Illustrated* conflicts with Pappas's recollection of a curfew (Eisenberg, *From 33rd Street to Camden Yards*, 141), but suffice it to say that however Bauer treated his players, the respect he earned was vital to the winning attitude exhibited by the Orioles in 1964.
31. Curt Blefary, interview by Dave Bergman, July 10, 1992, Society for American Baseball Research Archives, Cleve-

land, OH. Blefary had been spiked in spring training of 1963, and when the Orioles claimed him, he was sent to Elmira of the Eastern League.

32. The Orioles catching had been tenuous at best since 1962, so it was understandable that Baltimore was anxious to stabilize that position. It is interesting to speculate what the team would have been like had they been successful in signing Carlton Fisk, their 19th round pick of the inaugural 1965 amateur draft.

33. *1966 Baltimore Orioles Press Radio TV Guide*, 10–13. According to this team publication, Baltimore played better than .500 baseball in every category listed: one-run games, two-run games, day games, night games, extra-inning contests, etc. The focus in this text concerns the closing weeks of the 1965 season. In the case of the Orioles, it was proven, as had been the case in 1964, that they had yet to cross the fine line that separated the good teams from the pennant winners.

34. Eisenberg, *From 33rd Street to Camden Yards*, 146.

35. Dalton and Cashen quoted in Eisenberg, *From 33rd Street to Camden Yards*, 148, 149.

36. Earl Lawson, "Reds Swap Robby — Get Hurler Pappas," *The Sporting News*, December 18, 1965, 9; Doug Brown, "Robinson Deal Gives Oriole Kids Chance to Test Their Wings," *The Sporting News*, January 1, 1966, 8.

37. "Analysis of the Orioles," *Sports Illustrated*, April 10, 1961, 75.

38. Eisenberg, *From 33rd Street to Camden Yards*, 71.

39. Scouting reports, September 21, 1964, Papers of Harry Dalton, 1960–1993, BAMSS40, National Baseball Hall of Fame Library, National Baseball Hall of Fame, Cooperstown, NY, Box 2, Series I, Folder 1, Fall Meetings, 1957, 1962–1966.

40. Blefary interview.

41. Scouting reports, September 21, 1964, Papers of Harry Dalton.

42. Ibid.

43. Ibid.

44. Ibid.

45. Ibid.

46. Ibid.

47. Ibid.

48. Ibid.

49. Ibid. Emphasis added.

50. Ibid.

51. *1975 Baltimore Orioles Press Radio TV Guide*, 6; Newsletters, 1964–1965, Papers of Harry Dalton, 1960–1993, BAMSS40, National Baseball Hall of Fame Library, National Baseball Hall of Fame, Cooperstown, NY, Box 1, Series I, Folder 3.

52. Bob Allen with Bill Gilbert, *The 500 Home Run Club: Baseball's 15 Greatest Home Run Hitters from Aaron to Williams* (Champaign, IL: Sports Publishing, 1999), 194, 195.

53. Morton Sharnik, "The Moody Tiger of the Reds," *Sports Illustrated*, June 17, 1963, 43.

54. Dewitt quoted in Allen and Gilbert, *The 500 Home Run Club*, 200. The Reds president failed to note that Robinson's regimen often included ten hours of sleep each night.

55. Eisenberg, *From 33rd Street to Camden Yards*, 162.

56. Mark R. Millikin, *The Glory of the 1966 Orioles and Baltimore* (Haworth, NJ: St. Johann, 2006), 29–30.

57. Jim Russo with Bob Hammel, *SuperScout: Thirty-Five Years of Major League Scouting* (Chicago: Bonus, 1992), 56.

58. Author telephone interview with Bobby Grich, August 9, 2009.

59. Moe Drabowsky, interview by Leonard Schecter, August 13, 1992, Society for American Baseball Research Archives, Cleveland, OH.

60. Ibid.

61. "Frank Robinson Almost Drowned at Party," *Los Angeles Times*, October 12, 1966, B1.

62. *1966 Baltimore Orioles Press Radio TV Guide*, 20.

63. Frank Finch, "Big D (But It's Drabowsky) Wins, 5–2," *Los Angeles Times*, October 6, 1966, B1.

64. Jim Murray, "Willie D. Played Center Just Like It Owned Him," *Los Angeles Times*, October 7, 1966, B1. Among Murray's sardonic japes was his comment: "The only way Willie can make a sure out is with a bat." One also wonders what could have been going through the minds of some other reporters, one of whom asked Koufax after the game, "Were you disappointed by the play behind you? I specifically mean Willie Davis." This asinine query caused Koufax to explode in anger and defend his teammate with the more astute observation: "Without Willie Davis, we wouldn't be in the World Series." See John Hall, "It's Only a Game," *Los Angeles Times*, October 8, 1966, A3.

65. Eisenberg, *From 33rd Street to Camden Yards*, 175. In reality, Wills' .314 on-base percentage trailed that of Ron Fairly (.380), Wes Parker (.351), Tommy Davis (.345), John Roseboro (.343), Jim Lefebvre (.333), and Lou Johnson (.316).

66. Letter from Joel Chaseman to Harry Dalton, September 26, 1966, Papers of Harry Dalton, 1960–1993, BAMSS40, National Baseball Hall of Fame Library, National Baseball Hall of Fame, Cooperstown, NY, Box 2, Series I, Folder 1, Correspondence.

67. O'Malley quoted in John Hall, "Aftermath: Ecstasy, Indifference," *Los Angeles Times*, October 10, 1966, B1.

68. Eisenberg, *From 33rd Street to Camden Yards*, 184.

69. Brooks Robinson quoted in Eisenberg, *From 33rd Street to Camden Yards*, 185.

# *Chapter 6*

1. *1969 Baltimore Orioles Press Radio Television Guide*, 10, 14. For all major league batters, 1968 was the nadir of

hitting for the decade. Season-ending totals showed a composite .237 average, but this rose to .248 in 1969 after both leagues expanded to twelve teams.

2. Eisenberg, *From 33rd Street to Camden Yards*, 186. When Dalton visited Bauer at the manager's Kansas City home to deliver the news that he was changing managers, so brief was Dalton's stay that he had his taxi waiting at the curb to whisk him back to the airport for his return flight to Baltimore.

3. Bauer quoted in Associated Press article, "Bauer Fired by Baltimore," *Minneapolis Tribune*, July 11, 1968, 27.

4. Transcript of Earl Weaver promotion press conference, July 11, 1968, Papers of Harry Dalton, 1960–1993, BAMSS40, National Baseball Hall of Fame Library, National Baseball Hall of Fame, Cooperstown, NY, Box 1, Series I, Folder 6, Earl Weaver.

5. Ibid.

6. Grich interview.

7. Ibid. Emphasis added.

8. List of 1968 prospects, Papers of Harry Dalton; "Baltimore Oriole Prospects," October 14, 1968, Papers of Harry Dalton, 1960–1993, BAMSS40, National Baseball Hall of Fame Library, National Baseball Hall of Fame, Cooperstown, NY, Box 1, Series I, Folder 1, Team Rosters and Prospects. This list of names included several players who eventually played for Weaver: Dave May, Bobby Grich, Terry Crowley, and Rich Coggins. All were rated "good," as well as John Oates, Jesse Jefferson, and pitcher David C. Johnson, who were rated "fair."

9. Undated handwritten note by Harry Dalton, Papers of Harry Dalton, 1960–1993, BAMSS40, National Baseball Hall of Fame Library, National Baseball Hall of Fame, Cooperstown, NY, Box 1, Series I, Folder 6, Earl Weaver. Accompanying this piece of ephemera is a July 11, 1968, telegram from Rochester Red Wings executive Morie Silver, who congratulated Dalton for hiring Weaver.

10. Jim Elliot, "Umpire Calls O's Manager 'Bush,'" Baltimore *Morning Sun*, September 3, 1968, C4, found in Papers of Harry Dalton, 1960–1993, BAMSS40, National Baseball Hall of Fame Library, National Baseball Hall of Fame, Cooperstown, NY, Box 1, Series I, Folder 6, Earl Weaver.

11. Russo quoted in Jim Henneman, "The Earl of Baltimore," *1982 Baltimore Orioles Yearbook*, 48.

12. Grich interview.

13. Don Buford, oral history, Society for American Baseball Research Archives, Cleveland, OH. Bragging a bit in an interview Buford later gave, he said, "Playing for Earl Weaver enhanced Weaver's career because of the production I provided to the top of the batting order."

14. Doug Brown, "Orioles Fought Well Against Awesome Tiger Lead," *Official 1969 Baseball Guide*, 19.

15. Blefary interview. Blefary indicated his dismay at being traded "because [the Orioles were] ready to go into a dynasty," but this was pure hindsight on his part since there was no way he could anticipate how well Baltimore would perform after his departure. Blefary did not endear himself to the Orioles management when, after filling in at first base for twelve games in 1968, he stated that he would no longer play that position. Regarding the acquisition of Cuellar, the 32-year-old pitcher came with a lengthy resume but had nonetheless drawn the notice of an Orioles scout, the legendary Frank Lane, whose visit to Houston in the summer of 1968 likely generated input that reached Harry Dalton.

16. Harry Dalton, memorandum to players on Baltimore Orioles 40-man roster, January 22, 1969, Papers of Harry Dalton, 1960–1993, BAMSS40, National Baseball Hall of Fame Library, National Baseball Hall of Fame, Cooperstown, NY, Box 1, Series I, Folder 2, Spring Training Programs, 1968–1970. Dalton's missive included Bamberger's check list of tips on what pitchers should do to stay in shape during the winter.

17. In the oral history with SABR, Don Buford erroneously called the action in early 1969 a "lockout," but he was correct in observing that the unifying stance assumed by the players "form[ed] the mindset of the modern Major League Players' Association."

18. Author telephone interview with Jim Bouton, April 2, 2010.

19. Ibid.

20. Jim Elliot, "Weaver Lists Rules for Birds," Baltimore *Morning Sun*, February 19, 1969, C1, found in Papers of Harry Dalton, 1960–1993, BAMSS40, National Baseball Hall of Fame Library, National Baseball Hall of Fame, Cooperstown, NY, Box 1, Series I, Folder 6, Earl Weaver.

21. Harry Dalton, memorandum to Earl Weaver, March 22, 1969, Papers of Harry Dalton, 1960–1993, BAMSS40, National Baseball Hall of Fame Library, National Baseball Hall of Fame, Cooperstown, NY, Box 1, Series I, Folder 2, Spring Training Programs, 1968–1970. In this note, Dalton also stressed the need for Paul Blair to bunt more often because "this helped him hit .293 two years ago."

22. Ibid.

23. Ibid.

24. Earl Weaver, "A Game of Common Sense: Strategy and Managing," in *This Great Game*, ed. Doris Townsend (New York: Rutledge, 1971), 52, 54.

25. Powell quoted in Doug Brown, "Need a Win? See B. & F. Robby-Powell, Inc.," *The Sporting News*, July 19, 1969, 3.

26. For the 1969 season as a whole, Belanger cut his strikeout total in half (from 114 in 1968 to 54) and raised his average nearly 80 points (from .208 to .287).

27. Bauer quoted in Doug Brown, "Fencing with Weaver Can Be Fun," *The Sporting News*, July 26, 1969, 8. Dalton countered such charges by saying that Weaver "built the machine and installed all the buttons." See 1996 Hall of Fame Induction Program excerpt, Papers of Harry Dalton, 1960–1993, BAMSS40, National Baseball Hall of Fame Library, National Baseball Hall of Fame, Cooperstown, NY, Box 1, Series I, Folder 6, Earl Weaver.

28. Ibid. Bauer's sour grapes primarily alluded to Jim Palmer and Frank Robinson, but it was not until Palmer pitched in the recently concluded winter league that he gave any indication of being able to pitch again at the major league level. See Eisenberg, *From 33rd Street to Camden Yards*, 198–199.

29. The figure of just over one million is according to the *1970 Baltimore Orioles Press Radio Television Guide*, but several subsequent team publications list an amended total of 1,062,094.

30. Bamberger quoted in Phil Jackman, "Oriole Wings Thrive Under Dr. Bamberger," *The Sporting News*, April 5, 1969, 9. The rules changes meant to inject more offense into the game served its purpose, but among the American League's better teams, the Orioles' ERA rose only from 1968's 2.66 to 2.83 in 1969, a difference of only 0.17. While the Angels rose just 0.11 and the Senators actually fell 0.15, other AL pitching-staff ERAs increased anywhere from 0.35 (Twins) to 1.46 (White Sox).

31. Ibid.

32. Earl Weaver, interview by Dan Austen, July 3, 1990, Society for American Baseball Research Archives, Cleveland, OH.

33. *1970 Baltimore Orioles Press Radio Television Guide*, 32.

34. Frank Robinson quoted in Ralph Ray, "Twins Get the Message ... It's Orioles Who Rule AL," *The Sporting News*, October 18, 1969, 11.

35. Weaver quoted in "Weaver, Pilot of Orioles, Calls Mets a Worthy Foe for Series," *New York Times*, October 7, 1969, 55.

36. Powell quoted in Murray Chass, "What the Orioles Don't Know About Mets Might Hurt Them," *New York Times*, October 8, 1969, 38.

37. Eisenberg, *From 33rd Street to Camden Yards*, 215.

38. Earl Weaver, *Winning!* (New York: William Morrow, 1972), 97.

39. Arthur Daley, "It Won't Be Quiet," *New York Times*, October 14, 1969, 55.

40. Murray Chass, "Palmer Calls Scouting Report on Gentry as Pitcher and Batter Misleading," *New York Times*, October 15, 1969, 51. Don Buford concurred that Gentry "threw harder than we thought he could ... a surprise." See Buford oral history.

41. Up to this point in time, Weaver had been thrown out of two games in 1968 and four others in 1969. Not until 1973 did Weaver really hit his stride by averaging eight ejections per season for the rest of the 1970s.

42. *1970 Baltimore Orioles Press Radio Television Guide*, 37

43. Murray Chass, "Hendricks Says He Attempted to Wave Richert Off Martin's Deciding Bunt," *New York Times*, October 16, 1969, 59.

44. Weaver quoted in "Weaver Bows Again to Umpire, but Keeps His Seat on Bench," *New York Times*, October 17, 1969, 59.

45. Johnson quoted in Murray Chass, "A Loser Sums It Up: Orioles Had the Reputation, but Mets Had Momentum," *New York Times*, October 17, 1969, 59.

46. Frank Robinson quoted in Eisenberg, *From 33rd Street to Camden Yards*, 218, 219.

47. Earl Weaver, interview by Paul Brown, April, 1990, Society for American Baseball Research Archives, Cleveland, OH.

48. Brad Snyder, *A Well-Paid Slave: Curt Flood's Fight for Free Agency in Professional Sports* (New York: Plume, 2007), 1.

49. Ibid., 9. In his excellent account of Flood's travails, Snyder details the chicanery into which Flood fell regarding the pawning off of some of his work as original paintings.

50. Ibid., 19–26.

51. Ibid., 10–11. Jorgensen and her husband Johnny were, according to Snyder, "progressive and freethinking in an era when most white people their ages could not comprehend the social and political upheaval of the 1960s."

52. Marvin Miller, *A Whole Different Ball Game: The Sport and Business of Baseball* (New York: Birch Lane, 1991), 174.

53. Goldberg quoted in Snyder, *A Well-Paid Slave*, 281.

54. Snyder, *A Well-Paid Slave*, 309.

55. Bowie Kuhn, *Hardball: The Education of a Baseball Commissioner* (New York: Times Books, 1987), 89.

56. Grich interview.

57. This anecdote was told to the author by Curt Flood at a fantasy camp held in Mesa, Arizona, in January 1992.

58. Miller, *A Whole Different Ball Game*, 170.

58. Weaver, *Winning!*, 109.

60. Grich interview.

61. Baltimore Orioles professional prospect report, September 1, 1970, Papers of Harry Dalton, 1960–1993, BAMSS40, National Baseball Hall of Fame Library, National Baseball Hall of Fame, Cooperstown, NY, Box 1, Series I, Folder 4, Scouting Reports, 1961–1970.

62. Weaver quoted in Phil Jackman, "All Earl Does Is Win — Except in Pilot-of-Year Poll," *The Sporting News*, November 7, 1970, 41.

63. Phil Jackman, "Birds Spread-Eagle Field Again," *Official 1971 Baseball Guide*, 15.

64. Weaver, *Winning!*, 111.

65. Ibid., 112.

66. *1971 Baltimore Orioles Media Guide*, 29. Emphasis added.

67. William Leggett, "Flying Start for the Big Bad Birds," *Sports Illustrated*, October 19, 1970, 20.

68. Anderson quoted in *1971 Baltimore Orioles Media Guide*, 29.

69. Brooks Robinson quoted in Eisenberg, *From 33rd Street to Camden Yards*, 229.

70. Frank Deford, "Best Damn Team in Baseball," *Sports Illustrated*, April 12, 1971, 78.

71. Scouting report of Cal Ripken, Sr., September 1, 1970, Papers of Harry Dalton, 1960–1993, BAMSS40, National Baseball Hall of Fame Library, National Baseball Hall of Fame, Cooperstown, NY, Box 1, Series I, Folder 4, Scouting Reports, 1961–1970.

72. Don Buford oral history.

73. Grich interview.

74. Bamberger quoted in Phil Jackman, "O's Hill Aces Never Pampered by Bamberger," *The Sporting News*, October 16, 1971, 29.

75. *1972 Baltimore Orioles Media Guide*, 33.

76. Weaver quoted in David Maraniss, *Clemente: The Passion and Grace of Baseball's Last Hero* (New York: Simon and Schuster, 2006), 251.

77. So encouraged were the commissioner's office and the executives at NBC, the network carrying the World Series, by the estimated 61 million viewers tuning in that Bowie Kuhn announced that all weekday Series games thereafter would be held at night.

78. Weaver quoted in Phil Jackman, "Beaten Birds Take Wing to Try Their Luck on Junket to Japan," *The Sporting News*, October 30, 1971, 8.

79. Weaver, *Winning!*, 131.

80. Ibid.

81. Weaver quoted in Lowell Reidenbaugh, "Champ Bucs Batting 1.000 as Seers," *The Sporting News*, October 30, 1971, 3.

82. *1972 Baltimore Orioles Media Guide*, 42.

83. Weaver, *Winning!*, 125. Johnson's two outings, including a complete-game, 2–1, loss to Baltimore, totaled 11 hits and two runs allowed in 15 and one-third innings, with 5 walks and 15 strikeouts.

84. Wells Twombly, "The Losers Were the Lucky Ones," *The Sporting News*, November 6, 1971, 42.

85. Joe Falls column, *The Sporting News*, November 13, 1971, 44.

## Chapter 7

1. Untitled memorandum of August 6, 1971, Papers of Harry Dalton, 1960–1993, BAMSS40, National Baseball Hall of Fame Library, National Baseball Hall of Fame, Cooperstown, NY, Box 1, Series I, Folder 4, Scouting Reports, 1961–1970. This document speaks of Dalton in the third person, so it seems unlikely that he was the author. However, it reads like a press release, and the enumeration of Dalton's deeds would have made for a suitable attachment to his resume.

2. Harry Dalton, memorandum to Frank Cashen, October 19, 1971, Papers of Harry Dalton, 1960–1993, BAMSS40, National Baseball Hall of Fame Library, National Baseball Hall of Fame, Cooperstown, NY, Box 1, Series I, Folder 4, Scouting Reports, 1961–1970.

3. Ibid.

4. Ibid.

5. Ibid.

6. In an interview Dalton gave to author John Eisenberg, the Orioles executive said he was "a little surprised" by the trade and disingenuously claimed, "I don't know what the inner thinking was, and I've never talked to Frank [Cashen] about it." Dalton may never have literally spoken to Cashen about a trade, but he certainly committed his thoughts to paper for the man who would replace him. See Eisenberg, *From 33rd Street to Camden Yards*, 256–257.

7. Miller, *The Baseball Business*, 184–185.

8. Miller, *A Whole Different Ball Game*, 204; Miller, *The Baseball Business*, 185.

9. Miller, *A Whole Different Ball Game*, 204.

10. Ibid., 209. No endnotes or citations accompany Miller's recollection, but there is reason to suspect that the number of players voting against a strike might have been greater than ten. In the Orioles' case, Jim Palmer blasted Miller for having "'brainwashed' the players," while Bobby Grich in a later interview recalled a vote that was almost evenly split among his teammates. In any event, the preponderance of players such as those on the White Sox, Dodgers, and Red Sox strongly favored a strike. See Miller, *A Whole Different Ball Game*, 217.

11. Kuhn, *Hardball*, 107.

12. Ibid.

13. *1973 Baltimore Orioles Media Guide*, 24.

14. Don Baylor, *Don Baylor — Nothing but the Truth: A Baseball Life* (New York: St. Martin's, 1989), 59.

15. Grich interview. The naming of Grich to the All-Star squad was not without controversy. Luis Aparicio had been voted by the fans to be the starting shortstop, but he and the Texas Rangers' Toby Harrah were forced out with injuries. With veteran Bert Campaneris as the only other shortstop on the AL team, Weaver not only took Grich as a last-minute addition but chose to play him for the entire game.

16. Earl Weaver with Berry Stainback, *It's What You Learn After You Know It All That Counts* (Garden City, NY: Doubleday, 1982), 203.

17. Ibid., 205.

18. Ibid.

19. Joseph Durso, "American League to Let Pitcher Have a Pinch-Hitter and Stay In," in *The New York Times Book of Baseball History*, 308.

20. Jerome Holtzman, "*The Sporting News* Praises Cronin," *Official 1974 Baseball Guide*, 281.

21. Ibid., 282.

22. Weaver, *It's What You Learn After You Know It All That Counts*, 213.

23. Miller, *A Whole Different Ball Game*, 109.

24. *1973 Baltimore Orioles Media Guide*, 54.

25. *1974 Baltimore Orioles Media Guide*, 19.

26. Cashen quoted in Robert H. Boyle, "Doing the Oriole Cha-cha," *Sports Illustrated*, July 23, 1973, 54.

27. Baylor, *Nothing but the Truth*, 76.

28. Weaver, *It's What You Learn After You Know It All That Counts*, 213.

29. Former Oriole — and now former Dodger — Frank Robinson was back in the American League, reunited with Harry Dalton in Anaheim with the California Angels. Frank's .266 average, 30 homers, and 97 RBIs, perhaps the best overall DH statistics, would also have been welcome at Memorial Stadium. One of his clouts beat his former mates in Anaheim in late April, and when he returned to Baltimore ten days later, at which time his uniform number 20 was retired by the Orioles, he scored the lone run in the Angels' 1–0 victory over McNally.

30. Jim Palmer and Jim Dale, *Together We Were Eleven Foot Nine: The Twenty-Year Friendship of Hall of Fame Pitcher Jim Palmer and Orioles Manager Earl Weaver* (Kansas City: Andrews and McMeel, 1996), 44–45.

31. Weaver, *It's What You Learn After You Know It All That Counts*, 214.

32. Ibid.

33. Baylor, *Nothing but the Truth*, 78.

34. Ibid., 79.

35. Palmer, *Together We Were Eleven Foot Nine*, 51.

36. Weaver was still browbeating Williams for the team's misfortunes and ascribed the September surge to the divisional title to great pitching by his starters. See *It's What You Learn After You Know It All That Counts*, 214–217.

37. *1975 Baltimore Orioles Media Guide*, 32.

38. Baylor, *Nothing but the Truth*, 80.

39. Weaver, *It's What You Learn After You Know It All That Counts*, 217.

40. Ibid.

41. Eisenberg, *From 33rd Street to Camden Yards*, 265.

42. Russo, *SuperScout*, 79.

43. Jim Henneman, "Orioles Stumble at Wire," *Official 1976 Baseball Guide*, 139.

44. Hendricks's stay with the Cubs was short-lived. He had been re-acquired after the 1972 season and was the Orioles backup catcher.

45. Grich interview.

46. Weaver's return to the Baltimore dugout in 1985 and 1986 was less than spectacular. His teams in those years finished fourth and seventh, respectively.

47. Boyle, "Doing the Oriole Cha-cha."

## Chapter 8

1. John E. Peterson, *The Kansas City Athletics: A Baseball History, 1954–1967* (Jefferson, NC: McFarland, 2003), 39. Peterson's excellent account gives a review of the financial details surrounding the transaction, including the relationships Johnson had with Yankees owners Dan Topping and Del Webb.

2. Ibid., 277–288.

3. Ibid., 109.

4. Finley quoted in Joe McGuff, "Decision Due on Control of A's," *Kansas City Times*, December 15, 1960, 39.

5. Ernest Mehl, "Sporting Comment," *Kansas City Times*, December 16, 1960, 35.

6. Lane quoted in Cleon Walfoort, "Pips and Pearls Picked Up Along Big-Time Beat," *The Sporting News*, April 5, 1961, 10; *1961 Kansas City Athletics Official Guide for Press-Radio-TV*, 4.

7. Author John Peterson includes a detailed account of trading activity of the Athletics during their time in Kansas City. The most egregious of the swaps in this era was the trade sending Roger Maris to the Yankees, where he blossomed into an MVP in 1960 and 1961.

8. Rex Lardner, "Charlie Finley and Bugs Bunny in K.C.," *Sports Illustrated*, June 5, 1961, 24; "Baseball Thrills ... Elsewhere," *Kansas City Star*, August 16, 1961, 10F.

9. Lane quoted in Ernest Mehl, "Lane Tells A's Plan to Move," *Kansas City Star*, August 23, 1961, 1.

10. Finley quoted in Peterson, *Kansas City Athletics*, 190.

11. "Farmer's Night Prize Winners," *Kansas City Athletics American League News*, Volume 1, Number 5 (July 1967), 8.

12. Drabowsky interview; author telephone interview with Sal Bando, September 28, 2008.

13. Finley quoted in Burton A. Boxerman and Benita W. Boxerman, *Ebbets to Veeck to Busch: Eight Owners Who Shaped Baseball* (Jefferson, NC: McFarland, 2003), 155.

14. "New Shoes, Sox, Helmets to Enhance Colorful Uniforms," *Kansas City Athletics American League News*, Volume 1, Number 2 (March 1967), 3. In a nod toward practicality, Finley also issued standard black shoes to be worn when field conditions were muddy.

15. Charles T. Powers, "A Few Don't Leave A's in Cold," *Kansas City Star*, September 28, 1967, 1.

16. "Oakland Move for A's Owner," *Kansas City Times*, October 12, 1967, 1. As early as the spring of 1965, a proposal to construct a domed stadium in downtown Kansas City was made, but the idea drew no comment from Finley. Even by this time Finley had made it abundantly clear that he wanted nothing to do with keeping his team in Kansas City. See Peterson, *Kansas City Athletics*, 208–209.

17. Boxerman and Boxerman, *Ebbets to Veeck to Busch*, 160.

18. Jerome Holtzman, "Finley Gets Okay to Leave Kansas City," *Official 1968 Baseball Guide*, 178; "Martin Boosted for KC," *Minneapolis Tribune*, October 2, 1967, 36.

19. Peterson, *Kansas City Athletics*, 263. This quote comes from the title Peterson chose for Chapter 28 of his book.

20. Rick Monday, interview by Walter Langford, May 9, 1989, Society for American Baseball Research Archives, Cleveland, OH.

21. Bando interview.

22.  Krausse drew a staggering bonus of $125,000 as a premier prospect signed shortly after Finley bought the Athletics. As the son of Kansas City scout and former Athletics pitcher Lew Krausse, Sr., he seemed destined for stardom when he tossed a three-hit shutout in his major league debut. Unfortunately, Krausse soon found himself overmatched and spent most of the next four years in the farm system. At six feet, five inches tall, the imposing Nash became a study in frustration. After bursting on the American League scene with a 12–1 record with a 2.06 ERA to win the AL Rookie Pitcher of the Year award, Nash never again approached that level of performance.

23.  Dick Williams, interview by Dan Dinardo, August 8, 1992, Society for American Baseball Research Archives, Cleveland, OH.

24.  *Official 1976 Baseball Register*, 310.

25.  Finley quoted in Jim "Catfish" Hunter and Armen Keteyian, *Catfish: My Life in Baseball* (New York: McGraw-Hill, 1988), 33.

26.  Ibid., 3.

27.  *The Baseball Draft*, 35.

28.  Bill Libby and Vida Blue, *Vida: His Own Story* (Englewood Cliffs, NJ: Prentice-Hall, Inc., 1972), 28.

29.  Bill James, *The New Bill James Historical Baseball Abstract* (New York: The Free Press, 2001), 267–268.

30.  Reggie Jackson and Mike Lupica, *Reggie: The Autobiography of Reggie Jackson* (New York: Villard, 1984), 55. Jackson emphasized the prevailing racial attitude by titling the chapter in which this passage appears, "Birmingham: Just the Kind of Nigger Boy They Needed."

31.  Finley quoted in "Cullum's Column," *Minneapolis Tribune*, July 19, 1965, 27.

32.  *1968 Oakland A's Premier Yearbook*, 59.

33.  Ibid. This is a typical example of Finley never passing up an opportunity for self-aggrandizement.

34.  Harrelson quoted in Peterson, *Kansas City Athletics*, 244. Harrelson, just shy of his 26th birthday, was picked up by the Boston Red Sox and filled their void in right field created by ghastly beaning of Tony Conigliaro.

35.  Peterson, *Kansas City Athletics*, 246. Finley's knowledge of player pranks came courtesy of private detectives who tailed some of the Athletics. See Hunter, *Catfish*, 53.

36.  Miller, *A Whole Different Ball Game*, 236.

37.  "Censor of All He Surveys," *The Sporting News*, April 13, 1968, 16.

38.  "A's Play 'First Baseball Ever' in Coliseum," *Oakland A's 1968 Press Radio TV Guide*, 2–3.

39.  Bando interview. Bando listed DiMaggio's presence in Oakland as vice-president/coach as one of his career highlights.

40.  Rudi quoted in Hunter, *Catfish*, 80.

41.  Hunter, *Catfish*, 83.

42.  Monday interview.

43.  Ron Bergman, "Finley Decided Last June to Give Kennedy the Axe," *The Sporting News*, October 12, 1968, 24.

44.  Ibid.

45.  *1969 Oakland A's Press Radio TV Guide*, 6.

46.  Hunter, *Catfish*, 86.

47.  William Leggett, Mark Mulvoy, Peter Carry, and Roy Blount, "Two Managers and Two Teams," *Sports Illustrated*, April 14, 1969, 82.

48.  Bando quoted in Jack Clary, *The Captains: The Qualities, Duties, and Responsibilities of Sports Leadership* (New York: Atheneum, 1978), 71.

49.  Jackson, *Reggie*, 74.

50.  Bando interview. Finley had been denied permission by the city of Oakland to use full-scale pyrotechnics during a particular game and ordered his men to be ready to stride to the plate bearing sparklers in the event a ball cleared the fence. Bando said the players hoped they would be spared the embarrassment, and their hopes were realized when no Oakland batter hit one out.

51.  Bando interview.

52.  Duncan quoted in Ron Bergman, "Dick Williams on Finley's Firing Line; McNamara Axing Blamed on Duncan," *The Sporting News*, October 17, 1970, 25.

53.  Ibid.

54.  Grant interview.

55.  Kuhn, *Hardball*, 126–127.

56.  Leonard Koppett, "Kuhn Would Have Czar Power If Planners' Ideas Win Okay," *The Sporting News*, 29; Jerome Holtzman, "Two Division, Rules, Player Demands, Etc.," *Official 1970 Baseball Guide*, 263.

57.  Kuhn, *Hardball*, 127.

58.  Email correspondence to author from Ed Edmonds, June 9, 2009. Other notable players who began a season playing with a renewed contract included Ted Simmons (1972), Jim Kaat (1973), and Sparky Lyle (1974).

59.  Hunter, *Catfish*, 91. Emphasis in original.

60.  Dick Williams and Bill Plaschke, *No More Mr. Nice Guy: A Life of Hardball* (New York: Harcourt, Brace, Jovanovich, 1990), 121. Williams also credited his baseball rearing in the Brooklyn Dodgers organization for instructing him in the game's critical fundamentals.

61.  Williams interview by Dinardo.

## *Chapter 9*

1.  Blue, *Vida*, 66.

2.  Williams quoted in Ron Bergman, "White Sox Unload, Spoil Home Debut," *Oakland Tribune*, April 8, 1971, 37.

3. Jackson quoted in Ed Levitt, "Pre-Game Show," *Oakland Tribune*, April 8, 1971, 37.

4. Blue, *Vida*, 76.

5. Williams, *No More Mr. Nice Guy*, 128–129. Blue's final start drew under 11,000 fans to the Coliseum. Augmenting his role of interloper, Finley also managed to raise fans' hackles by canceling a late-season Fan Appreciation Day, then trying to reschedule it. Williams remarked that the blunder prompted a total attendance of less than 2,700 for the final two home games. Catfish Hunter also noted that some promotions intended to increase the gate, such as Shriners Night and Hot Pants Night, did not produce the desired results. See Hunter, *Catfish*, 97.

6. Tom Clark, *Champagne and Baloney: The Rise and Fall of Finley's A's* (New York: Harper & Row, 1976), 71–72.

7. Blue, *Vida*, 9.

8. Ron Bergman, "MVP Next for Vida?" *Oakland Tribune*, October 27, 1971, 41. Mickey Lolich of the Detroit Tigers posted a 25–14 record with a 2.92 ERA while leading the AL in strikeouts (308), games started (45), complete games (29), and innings pitched (an astonishing 376). Lolich's feats were accomplished under Detroit manager Billy Martin.

9. Williams, *No More Mr. Nice Guy*, 130. The season was also fun for players with slim wallets; during his first season in Oakland and through the spring of 1972, Williams had fined a total of just three players.

10. Blue, *Vida*, 76.

11. Williams, *No More Mr. Nice Guy*, 151. Williams said that he limited Mangual's playing time in the field because "every fly ball hit to him was an adventure."

12. Hunter, *Catfish*, 95.

13. Ron Bergman, "Epstein, Knowles to A's," *Oakland Tribune*, May 8, 1971, 9.

14. Hunter, *Catfish*, 95; Bruce Markusen, *A Baseball Dynasty: Charlie Finley's Swingin' A's* (Haworth, NJ: St. Johann, 2002), 26.

15. Markusen, *A Baseball Dynasty*, 41.

16. Dobson quoted in Ron Bergman, "Victorious A's Focus on Baltimore," *Oakland Tribune*, September 16, 1971, 39.

17. Ed Levitt, "Why A's Playoff?" *Oakland Tribune*, September 28, 1971, 37.

18. Williams, *No More Mr. Nice Guy*, 132.

19. Hunter quoted in Ron Bergman, "I Lost It," *Oakland Tribune*, October 5, 1971, 37.

20. Ibid.

21. Williams, *No More Mr. Nice Guy*, 132.

22. Williams quoted in Ed Levitt, "O's Prove the Best," *Oakland Tribune*, October 6, 1971, 41.

23. Jackson, *Reggie*, 77.

24. As a contemporaneous reference point, Hank Aaron of the Atlanta Braves, who continued his drive to top Babe Ruth as baseball's all-time home run king, was the game's highest-paid player, drawing $200,000. Among front-line pitchers of the day, the St. Louis Cardinals' Bob Gibson was paid $150,000.

25. In the five years leading up to 1972, the cost of living in the United States had increased 25 percent, but the federal Pay Board ultimately ruled that the salaries of professional athletes would not be held to the inflationary guidelines. See William Manchester, *The Glory and the Dream: A Narrative History of America, 1932–1972* (New York: Bantam, 1974), 1225; *Official 1973 Baseball Guide*, 288.

26. Gerst quoted in Dick Miller, "'Finley Lied,' Blue's Lawyer Claims," *The Sporting News*, March 4, 1972, 16.

27. Dick Miller, "Blue's Pact Under Question," *The Sporting News*, March 11, 1972, 34.

28. Ibid. A situation eerily similar to Blue's would release Catfish Hunter from Finley's clutches in less than three years.

29. Ron Bergman, "Finley Pitch Too Low—and Vida Walks," *The Sporting News*, April 1, 1972, 29.

30. Bando interview.

31. Finley quoted in "Big League Confusion," *Oakland Tribune*, April 1, 1972, 13-E.

32. Ed Levitt, "Strike Three," *Oakland Tribune*, April 2, 1972, 51.

33. Ed Schoenfeld, "Walkout Near End—Finley," *Oakland Tribune*, April 7, 1972, 52.

34. "Finley Calls for Compromise," *Oakland Tribune*, April 10, 1972, 37. This story originated from the Associated Press.

35. "Players Insist on Full Pay," *Oakland Tribune*, April 11, 1972, 37. This story originated from the Associated Press.

36. Ibid, 33.

37. Oscar Kahan, "Strong Clubs Yield to Help the Weak," *The Sporting News*, April 29, 1972, 8.

38. Ibid. Emphasis added.

39. "End of the Baseball Strike," *Oakland Tribune*, April 14, 1972, 20.

40. Kuhn, *Hardball*, 132.

41. Ron Bergman, "New Bando's Hair to Cover His Ears," *The Sporting News*, February 5, 1972, 44.

42. Finley, notorious as an absentee owner, was in town for only his second home series of the season, yet he chose instead to tend to insurance business at the American Medical Association convention being held that same weekend in San Francisco.

43. Ron Bergman, "Wild and Wooly A's Win It All," *Official 1973 Baseball Guide*, 15.

44. Bando interview.

45. Williams, *No More Mr. Nice Guy*, 135.

46. Finley quoted in Ed Levitt, "Charlie's Pep Talk," *Oakland Tribune*, October 6, 1972, 45.

47. Fingers quoted in Richard Keller, "Rollie Rolls into Cooperstown," *Oakland Athletics Magazine*, 1992, Vol. 12, No. 3, 22.

48. Bando interview.

49. Hunter, *Catfish*, 100–101; Keller, "Rollie Rolls into Cooperstown," 22.

50. Jackson, *Reggie*, 95. In his own autobiography, Hunter quoted Hendrick as saying he "wanted to see Epstein kick the [crap] out of Reggie." See Hunter, *Catfish*, 107.

51. Jackson quoted in Ed Levitt, "Pop Goes the Flag," *Oakland Tribune*, September 29, 1972, 45.

52. Williams interview by Dinardo.

53. Williams quoted in Ron Bergman, "A's Win, Boost Lead," *Oakland Tribune*, September 2, 1972, 10. The Oakland manager was working with the same mindset as his National League counterpart in the 1972 World Series, Sparky Anderson, who was known for pulling his starting pitchers at the first sign of trouble. Speaking confidently of the quality of the arms in his bullpen, Williams said, "If you've got them, use them."

54. John Porter, "Fist-Swinging A's Win," *Oakland Tribune*, August 23, 1972, 41.

55. Chylak quoted in Murray Chass, "A's Conquer Tigers, 5 to 0, for 2–0 Playoff Margin," *New York Times*, October 9, 1972, in *New York Times History of Baseball*, 306.

56. Suspension notwithstanding, Williams explained away the league's disciplinary action by claiming that Campaneris would not have played in any more playoff games because of the condition of his ankle.

57. Blue quoted in Ed Levitt, "Vida Fires at Charlie O, Williams," *Oakland Tribune*, October 11, 1972, 41.

58. Ed Levitt, "Tiger Town," *Oakland Tribune*, October 12, 1972, 39.

59. Kuhn, *Hardball*, 139.

60. The "bonuses" awarded by Finley became another point of contention with Bowie Kuhn. Finley equivocated as to whether his awards were bonuses or salary increases, while the commissioner argued that major league rules prohibited any such payment during or after the World Series. See "Finley, Kuhn Dispute 'Bonus' to A's Players," *Oakland Tribune*, October 17, 1972, 41.

61. Blue quoted in Ron Bergman, "Vida's Remarks Anger Reds," *Oakland Tribune*, October 17, 1972, 41.

62. Dick Williams, interview by Ed Attansio, 2006, Society for American Baseball Research Archives, Cleveland, OH; Williams interview by Dinardo. Williams, who drew inspiration for the scheme from a similar incident he witnessed in a 1940s Cardinals-Braves game, claimed he twice had to tell Tenace what he wanted him to do on the pitch to Bench.

63. Ed Levitt, "A's Still Can Do It," *Oakland Tribune*, October 22, 1972, 49.

64. Ibid.

65. Pat Frizzell, "Wild Crowds Fill Streets, Stall A's Victory Parade," *Oakland Tribune*, October 23, 1972, 1. The joy among the team members apparently was not universal. In his autobiography, Williams noted that Vida Blue was the pageant's most prominent no-show.

66. Dave Condon, "Charlie O.: Amazing Sports Maverick," *The Sporting News*, January 6, 1973, 32.

67. Clark, *Champagne and Baloney*, 143. By the spring of 1973, Tenace's shoulder issues had curiously disappeared.

68. Davis landed with Baltimore and Cepeda was signed by Boston, both excelling as DHs. The former hit .306 with seven home runs and 89 RBIs, the latter belted 20 homers, drove in 86 runs to go with a .289 average. Nearing the end of his career, Alou (.296, 2 home runs, 28 RBIs) still played in right field (85 games) and at first base (40 games) for the Yankees.

69. Ron Bergman, "Reggie's Indoor Fireworks," *Oakland Tribune*, July 5, 1973, 39.

70. Markusen, *A Baseball Dynasty*, 228–229. Where Williams saw an aggressive attitude in North, opponents viewed this same trait as an irritation, thus making North one of the least liked players in the league.

71. Ron Bergman, "Blue, 20-Winner 2nd Time, Did It Only for Long Green," *The Sporting News*, October 13, 1973, 7.

72. Hunter, *Catfish*, 117. Emphasis in original.

73. Jackson quoted in Ron Bergman, "2 'Miracle' Teams Set for Series," *Oakland Tribune*, October 12, 1973, 1.

74. Williams, *No More Mr. Nice Guy*, 166.

75. Leonard Koppett, "A's Major Annoyances: Bright Sun, Haze, Glare," *New York Times*, October 15, 1973, 44. Koppett advanced the argument that had Manny Trillo been allowed a place on the Oakland roster, it is quite likely that he rather than Andrews would have been in the field during the twelfth inning. Trillo would later win three Gold Gloves as a second baseman.

76. In an interview with the author, Bando indicated that Andrews had been hampered by a shoulder ailment for several weeks. It was not until the fateful second World Series game that, at least in Finley's opinion, Andrews' condition required the attention, that is to say punishment, doled out by the owner.

77. Ron Bergman, "Was Andrews Fired?," *Oakland Tribune*, October 15, 1973, 34.

78. Kuhn, *Hardball*, 136.

79. Finley quoted in Ron Bergman, "Kuhn Reinstates Andrews," *Oakland Tribune*, October 16, 1973, 33.

80. Williams, *No More Mr. Nice Guy*, 159.

81. Odom quoted in Ron Bergman, "Dissension Helped A's," *Oakland Tribune*, October 17, 1973, 41.

82. Dave Anderson, "Torture for the Summer Game," *New York Times*, October 20, 1973, 21.

83. Ron Bergman, "Dissension Helped A's," *Oakland Tribune*, October 17, 1973, 41.

84. Jackson quoted in Ed Levitt, "Reggie: We're Losing Best," *Oakland Tribune*, October 18, 1973, 37.

## *Chapter 10*

1. Dark quoted in Ron Bergman, "Dark Named A's Manager," *Oakland Tribune*, February 20, 1974, 33.

2. Herbert Michelson, *Charlie O: Charles Oscar Finley vs. the Baseball Establishment* (Indianapolis: Bobbs-Merrill, 1975), 314–320.

3. Rudi quoted in Michelson, *Charlie O*, 320.

4. Reggie Jackson with Bill Libby, *Reggie: A Season with a Superstar* (Chicago: Playboy, 1975), 37.

5. Finley quoted in Ron Bergman, "Finley Rips into Alvin," *Oakland Tribune*, May 19, 1974, 37. A sober anecdote to Finley's bluster came in the next day's edition of the *Tribune*, which quoted an anonymous player as saying, "I really

felt sorry for Alvin. No one should be talked to that way." See Ron Bergman, "Angel Gives Dark Respite," *Oakland Tribune*, May 20, 1974, 29,

6. Bando interview.

7. Ron Bergman, "Clubhouse Fist Fight Costly to Slumping A's," *The Sporting News*, July 6, 1974, 5. Trying to make light of the damage to Fosse, Jackson claimed in his version of the story that the catcher was still suffering the affects of his collision with Pete Rose in the 1970 All-Star Game and was not hurt trying to separate Jackson and North. Jackson's contemporaneous account is hard to fathom considering that a healthy Fosse had caught in a career-high 141 games for Oakland the year before. See Jackson, *Reggie: A Season with a Superstar*, 173.

8. Ron Bergman, "A's Swinging Fists and Bats," *Oakland Tribune*, June 6, 1974, 39.

9. Bando quoted in Ron Bergman, "Sal Says Dark Can't Manage," *Oakland Tribune*, June 20, 1974, 37. In a subtle jab at Dark, the jump page of this story called the defeat "a curious, curious loss."

10. Some players treated out-of-town reporters better than the local correspondents. Beat writer Ron Bergman of the *Oakland Tribune* later noted in his *Sporting News* column, "The unfavored press ... constitute the main bulk of the Bay Area baseball writers." See Ron Bergman, "Jitters Run Rampant When Charlie Visits A's," *The Sporting News*, September 7, 1974, 15.

11. Dark quoted in Ron Bergman, "New A's Fireworks as Coaches Ousted," *Oakland Tribune*, July 10, 1974, 39.

12. Jackson, *Reggie: A Season with a Superstar*, 143.

13. Hunter quoted in Ron Bergman, "New A's Fireworks as Coaches Ousted," *Oakland Tribune*, July 10, 1974, 35.

14. Williams gave credence to the World Series rumors of his move to the Yankees when he signed a three-year contract in December 1973. But Finley objected over Williams's flight to New York, and his protest was upheld by league president Joe Cronin. Finley claimed he was entitled to some form of compensation since Williams was technically under contract with Oakland, and when the Yankees refused to part with two of their best minor league prospects — pitcher Scott McGregor and outfielder Otto Velez — to secure Williams's services, Williams at last brokered a deal with Angels owner Gene Autry. Finley also netted a tidy sum of $100,000 from Autry as compensation, of sorts, for allowing him the privilege of signing Williams.

15. George Ross, "The Designated Manager," *Oakland Tribune*, July 16, 1974, 25.

16. Jackson, *Reggie: A Season with a Superstar*, 213–214.

17. Bando interview.

18. Jackson, *Reggie: A Season with a Superstar*, 228.

19. Ibid, 230.

20. Ron Bergman, "Jackson Emphatic He'll Play," *Oakland Tribune*, October 10, 1974, 41.

21. Ron Bergman, "A's Have Series Axe to Grind," *Oakland Tribune*, October 10, 1974, 39.

22. Jackson, *Reggie: A Season with a Superstar*, 235.

23. Clark, *Champagne and Baloney*, 248.

24. George Ross, "A Little Silence Pleases A's," *Oakland Tribune*, October 17, 1974, 37.

25. North quoted in Ross Newhan, "Maturity, Poise Made Difference, A's Claim," *Los Angeles Times*, October 18, 1974, 2; Jeff Prugh, "Buckner Rips A's Fans, Says Dodgers Still Best Team," *Los Angeles Times*, October 18, 1974, 8. Buckner also was understandably upset about the treatment he received when some Oakland fans tossed objects at him while he was in the field late in the last game of the Series.

26. Bobby Bonds quoted in Ed Levitt, "Bonds on Brawling," *Oakland Tribune*, June 7, 1974, 47.

27. "Tribune Editorial," *Oakland Tribune*, October 18, 1974, 1. The publication may have also asked some of the Athletics themselves for better attendance at the parade to commemorate the World Series victory. Vida Blue sat out the festivities, as did Gene Tenace, who took a seat on the bench for most of the last two contests of the Series.

28. Herb Michelson, "Charles O. Finley ... a Genius or Jerk?" *The Sporting News*, October 19, 1974, 17–18.

29. Clark, *Champagne and Baloney*, 253.

20. Ron Bergman, "Dark Signs for '75," *Oakland Tribune*, October 20, 1974, 45.

31. Ibid.

32. Moss quoted in Jerome Holtzman, "Year in Review," *Official 1975 Baseball Guide*, 287.

33. Hunter, *Catfish*, 131.

34. Contract wording quoted in *Official 1975 Baseball Guide*, 287.

35. Seitz quoted in *Official 1975 Baseball Guide*, 292.

36. Kuhn, *Hardball*, 140.

37. Holtzman, "Year in Review," *Official 1975 Baseball Guide*, 293. Mike Corkins of the San Diego Padres sought a nullification of his contract when he claimed the Padres reneged on $334.68 in moving expenses, but Seitz said that Corkins's "dispute did not penetrate to the heart of [his] contract, as was the case with Hunter."

38. Miller, *A Whole Different Ball Game*, 236. In this book, Miller expressed his disappointment with Hunter when the pitcher later credited George Steinbrenner with affording him the "economic security" that Miller said was the result of all the effort put forth on Hunter's behalf by the union in his dispute with Finley and the ensuing freedom Hunter had won. An undercurrent of bitterness is evident in the tone of a rhetorical question Miller posed: "Had Hunter forgotten all that the Players Association did for him?"

39. In his autobiography, Hunter's own accounting of the contract totaled $2.88 million, while Yankees beat writer Phil Pepe's calculation came to $3.2 million. In any event, Hunter was correct when he assessed the deal as "phenomenal."

40. Neil Papiano quoted in "A Counter Suit Filed by Finley," *Oakland Tribune*, January 1, 1975, 41. This story was sourced from the Associated Press.

41. "Catfish Feels Like Million, or Three," *Oakland Tribune*, January 1, 1975, 41. This story was sourced from the Associated Press.

42. Salary data gleaned from Clark, *Champagne and Baloney*, 287–294.

43. Finley quoted in Miller, *A Whole Different Ball Game*, 374.

44. Finley quote from numerous sources.

45. Clark, *Champagne and Baloney*, 413.

46. Hunter probably wished that he could have faced his old team more often than he did. He was undefeated in his four complete-game victories versus Oakland in 1975, allowing a total of just three runs on 16 hits in 36 innings.

47. Dark quoted in Clark, *Champagne and Baloney*, 413.

48. Slogan as printed on the cover of the *1976 Oakland A's Press–Radio–TV Guide*.

49. Stew Thornley, "The Demise of the Reserve Clause," *Baseball Research Journal*, No. 35 (2006), 115. Emphasis added.

50. Ibid., 119.

51. Miller, *A Whole Different Ball Game*, 246.

52. Seitz served at the pleasure of both the Players Association and the owners, either group having the option to dismiss him.

53. Roger I. Abrams, "Arbitrator Seitz Sets the Players Free," *Baseball Research Journal*, Volume 38, Number 2 (Fall 2009), 81. Emphasis added.

54. Grich interview.

55. Thornley, "The Demise of the Reserve Clause," 120.

56. Kuhn, *Hardball*, 160.

57. Miller, *A Whole Different Ball Game*, 250. The owners tried to resist the enforcement of Seitz's ruling by locking players out of spring training camps in February and March of 1976, but they relented in mid–March.

58. Billy North led the AL in stolen bases with 75, while Bert Campaneris (54) and Don Baylor (52) also contributing greatly. Among other regulars, Claudell Washington stole 37, Phil Garner swiped 35, and Sal Bando set a career-high with 20 steals, while pinch-runners Larry Lintz stole 31 and Matt Alexander had 20.

59. Markusen, *A Baseball Dynasty*, 395. "Oakland Seven" was Billy North's term for his soon-to-be-former teammates.

60. *Official 1978 Baseball Guide*, 316; Campaneris salary found at baseball-reference.com.

61. *Official 1978 Baseball Guide*, 316.

62. In another of Finley's bizarre moves, the owner acquired Sanguillen from the Pittsburgh Pirates in exchange for manager Chuck Tanner, who later guided the Bucs to the 1979 World Series title.

# Bibliography

Allen, Bob, with Bill Gilbert. *The 500 Home Run Club: Baseball's 15 Greatest Home Run Hitters from Aaron to Williams.* Champaign, IL: Sports Publishing, 1999.

Anderson, David, ed. *Before the Dome: Baseball in Minnesota When the Grass Was Real.* Minneapolis: Nodin, 1993.

Aschburner, Steve. *The Good, the Bad, and the Ugly: Heart-pounding, Jaw-dropping, and Gut-wrenching Moments from Minnesota Twins History.* Chicago: Triumph, 2008.

*The Baseball Encyclopedia.* 9th ed. New York: Macmillan, 1993.

Baylor, Don, with Claire Smith. *Don Baylor—Nothing but the Truth: A Baseball Life.* New York: St. Martin's, 1989.

Berney, Louis. *Tales from the Orioles Dugout.* Champaign, IL: Sports Publishing, 2004.

Boxerman, Burton A., and Benita W. Boxerman. *Ebbets to Veeck to Busch: Eight Owners Who Shaped Baseball.* Jefferson, NC: McFarland, 2003.

Branch, Taylor. *At Canaan's Edge: America in the King Years, 1965–1968.* New York: Simon and Schuster, 2006.

Brown, Bob, ed. *The House of Magic, 1922–1991: 70 Years of Thrills and Excitement on 33rd Street.* Baltimore: French Bray, 1991.

Butler, Hal. *The Bob Allison Story.* New York: Julian Messner, 1967.

Carew, Rod, and Ira Berkow. *Carew.* New York: Simon and Schuster, 1979.

Clark, Tom. *Champagne and Baloney: The Rise and Fall of Finley's A's.* New York: Harper & Row, 1976.

Clary, Jack. *The Captains: The Qualities, Duties, and Responsibilities of Sports Leadership.* New York: Atheneum, 1978.

Cohen, Richard M., David S. Neft, and Jordan A. Deutsch. *The World Series.* New York: Dial, 1979.

Cohen, Robert W. *The Lean Years of the Yankees, 1965–1975.* Jefferson, NC: McFarland, 2004.

Devaney, John, and Burt Goldblatt. *The World Series: A Complete Pictorial History.* Chicago: Rand McNally, 1981.

Eisenberg, John. *From 33rd Street to Camden Yards: An Oral History of the Baltimore Orioles.* New York: Contemporary, 2001.

Enright, Jim, ed. *Trade Him!: 100 Years of Baseball's Greatest Deals.* Chicago: Follett, 1976.

Gillette, Gary, and Pete Palmer. *The ESPN Baseball Encyclopedia,* 4th ed. New York: Sterling, 2007.

Golenbock, Peter. *Dynasty: The New York Yankees, 1949–1964.* Englewood Cliffs, NJ: Prentice-Hall, 1975.

_____. *Wild, High, and Tight: The Life and Death of Billy Martin.* New York: St. Martin's, 1994.

Halberstam, David. *October 1964.* New York: Villard, 1994.

_____. *The Fifties.* New York: Villard, 1993.

Hanssen, Andrew. "The Cost of Discrimination: A Study of Major League Baseball." *Southern Economic Journal,* Vol. 64, No. 3 (January 1998), 603–627.

Hunter, Jim "Catfish," and Armen Keteyian. *Catfish: My Life in Baseball.* New York: McGraw-Hill, 1988.

Jamail, Milton. *Full Count: Inside Cuban Baseball.* Carbondale: Southern Illinois University Press, 2000.

Jackson, Reggie, with Bill Libby. *Reggie: A Season with a Superstar.* Chicago: Playboy, 1975.

_____, and Mike Lupica. *Reggie: The Autobiography of Reggie Jackson.* New York: Villard, 1984.

James, Bill. *The New Bill James Historical Baseball Abstract.* New York: Free Press, 2001.

Kaat, Jim, with Phil Pepe. *Still Pitching: Musings from the Mound and the Microphone.* Chicago: Triumph, 2003.

Katz, Jeff. *The Kansas City A's and The Wrong Half of the Yankees.* Hingham, MA: Maple Street, 2007.

Kerr, Jon. *Calvin: Baseball's Last Dinosaur—An Authorized Biography.* Dubuque, IA: Wm. C. Brown, 1990.

Kuhn, Bowie. *Hardball: The Education of a Baseball Commissioner.* New York: Times Books, 1987.

Lang, Jack, and Peter Simon. *The New York Mets: Twenty-Five Years of Baseball Magic.* New York: Henry Holt, 1986.

Libby, Bill, and Vida Blue. *Vida: His Own Story.* Englewood Cliffs, NJ: Prentice-Hall, 1972.

Little, Rick, and Bill Morlock. *Split Double Header: An Unauthorized History of the Minnesota Twins.* Minneapolis: Morick, 1979.

Lowry, Philip J. *Green Cathedrals: The Ultimate Celebration of All 271 Major League and Negro League Parks Past and Present.* Reading, MA: Addison-Wesley, 1992.

Mahl, Tom E. *The Spitball Knuckleball Book.* Elyria, OH: Trick Pitch, 2009.

Manchester, William. *The Glory and the Dream: A Narrative History of America, 1932–1972.* New York: Bantam, 1974

Maraniss, David. *Clemente: The Passion and Grace of Baseball's Last Hero.* New York: Simon and Schuster, 2006.

Markusen, Bruce. *A Baseball Dynasty: Charlie Finley's Swingin' A's.* Haworth, NJ: St. Johann, 2002.

McLain, Denny, with Eli Zaret. *I Told You I Wasn't Perfect.* Chicago: Triumph, 2007.

Michelson, Herbert. *Charlie O: Charles Oscar Finley vs. the Baseball Establishment.* Indianapolis: Bobbs-Merrill, 1975.

Miller, James Edward. *The Baseball Business: Pursuing Pennants and Profits in Baltimore.* Chapel Hill: University of North Carolina Press, 1990.

Miller, Marvin. *A Whole Different Ball Game: The Sport and Business of Baseball.* New York: Birch Lane, 1991.

Millikin, Mark R. *The Glory of the 1966 Orioles and Baltimore.* Haworth, NJ: St. Johann, 2006.

*The New York Times Book of Baseball History: Highlights from the Pages of The New York Times.* New York: Arno, 1975.

Nichols, Fred. *The Final Season: 1953 St. Louis Browns.* St. Louis: St. Louis Browns Historical Society, 1991.

Oliva, Tony, with Bob Fowler. *Tony O!: The Trials and Triumphs of Tony Oliva.* New York: Hawthorn, 1973.

Palmer, Jim, and Jim Dale. *Together We Were Eleven Foot Nine: The Twenty-Year Friendship of Hall of Fame Pitcher Jim Palmer and Orioles Manager Earl Weaver.* Kansas City: Andrews and McMeel, 1996.

Palmer, R.R., Joel Colton, and Lloyd Kramer. *A History of the Modern World.* 10th ed. New York: McGraw-Hill, 2007.

Patterson, James T. *Grand Expectations: The United States, 1945–1974.* New York: Oxford University Press, 1996.

Peterson, John E. *The Kansas City Athletics: A Baseball History, 1954–1967.* Jefferson, NC: McFarland, 2003.

Pluto, Terry. *The Earl of Baltimore: The Story of Earl Weaver, Baltimore Orioles Manager.* Piscataway, NJ: New Century, 1982.

Russo, Jim, and Bob Hammel. *SuperScout: Thirty-Five Years of Major League Scouting.* Chicago: Bonus, 1992.

Schoor, Gene. *Billy Martin.* Garden City, NY: Doubleday, 1980.

Simpson, Allan, ed. *The Baseball Draft: The First 25 Years.* Durham, NC: American Sports Publishing, 1990.

Snyder, Brad. *A Well-Paid Slave: Curt Flood's Fight for Free Agency in Professional Sports.* New York: Plume, 2007.

Terzian, James. *The Kid from Cuba: Zoilo Versalles.* Garden City, NY: Doubleday, 1967.

Thielman, Jim. *Cool of the Evening: The 1965 Minnesota Twins.* Minneapolis: Kirk House, 2005.

Thornley, Stew. "The Demise of the Reserve Clause. *Baseball Research Journal,* No. 35 (2006), 115–123.

Thorpe, Laura, ed. *Oakland A's: The First Twenty-Five Years.* San Francisco: Woodford, 1992.

Townsend, Doris, ed. *This Great Game.* New York: Rutledge, 1971.

Urdahl, Dean. *Touching Bases with Our Memories: The Players Who Made the Minnesota Twins, 1961–2001.* St. Cloud, MN: North Star, 2001.

Weaver, Earl. *Winning!* New York: William Morrow, 1972.

_____, with Berry Stainback. *It's What You Learn After You Know It All That Counts.* Garden City, NY: Doubleday, 1982.

Williams, Dick, and Bill Plaschke. *No More Mr. Nice Guy: A Life of Hardball.* New York: Harcourt, Brace, Jovanovich, 1990.

Zinn, Howard. *A People's History of the United States, 1492–Present.* New York: Harper Collins, 2003.

## Interviews and Oral Histories

Bando, Sal. Telephone interview with author, September 28, 2008.

Blefary, Curt. Interview by Dave Bergman, July 10, 1992. Society for American Baseball Research Archives, Cleveland, OH.

Bouton, Jim. Telephone interview with author, April 2, 2010.

Buford, Don. Oral history. Society for American Baseball Research Archives, Cleveland, OH.

Dark, Alvin. Interview by Dan Dinardo, August 8, 1992. Society for American Baseball Research Archives, Cleveland, OH.

Drabowsky, Moe. Interview by Leonard Schecter, August 13, 1992. Society for American Baseball Research Archives, Cleveland, OH.

Grant, Jim "Mudcat." Interview by Joseph P. Keaney, Jr., compact disk recording, February 12, 1991. National Baseball Hall of Fame Archives, Cooperstown, NY.

Grich, Bobby. Telephone interview with author, August 9, 2009.

Killebrew, Harmon. Interview by Jon Pessah, compact disk recording, February 21, 2002. National Baseball Hall of Fame Archives, Cooperstown, NY.

Kindall, Jerry. Oral history, March 18, 2003. Society for American Baseball Research Archives, Cleveland, OH.
_____. Telephone interview with author, September 9, 2008.

Klippstein, Johnny. Oral history. Society for American Baseball Research Archives, Cleveland, OH.

Mele, Sam. Oral history. Society for American Baseball Research Archives, Cleveland, OH.

Monday, Rick. Interview by Walter Langford, May 9, 1989. Society for American Baseball Research Archives, Cleveland, OH.

Pappas, Milt. Oral history, August 28, 1992. Society for American Baseball Research Archives, Cleveland, OH.

Robinson, Brooks. Interview by Dane Ratasky and Ben Nichols, May 6, 2003. Society for American Baseball Research Archives, Cleveland, OH.

Weaver, Earl. Interview by Dan Austen, July 3, 1990. Society for American Baseball Research Archives, Cleveland, OH.
_____. Interview by Paul Brown, April 1990. Society for American Baseball Research Archives, Cleveland, OH.

Williams, Dick. Interview by Ed Attanasio, 2006. Society for American Baseball Research Archives, Cleveland, OH.
_____. Interview by Dan Dinardo, August 8, 1992. Society for American Baseball Research Archives, Cleveland, OH.

## Archives

Papers of Harry Dalton, 1960–1993, BAMSS40, National Baseball Hall of Fame Library, National Baseball Hall of Fame, Cooperstown, NY.

## Baseball Publications

*Baltimore Orioles Press Radio TV Guide*, 1962, 1965–1971, 1979
*Baltimore Orioles Yearbook*, 1980–1986
*Kansas City Athletics American League News*, 1967
*Kansas City Athletics Press Radio TV Guide*, 1961, 1965–1967
*Minnesota Twins Press Radio TV Guide*, 1961, 1963, 1966–1972, 1984
*Minnesota Twins Yearbook*, 1991
*Minnesota Twins Record and Information Book*, 2001
*Oakland Athletics Magazine*, 1992
*Oakland Athletics Yearbook*, 1968
*Oakland A's Press–Radio–TV Guide*, 1968–1977, 1984
*Official Baseball Register*, 1967–1979
*St. Louis Browns Press Radio TV Guide*, 1953
*The Sporting News*, 1959–1974
*Sports Illustrated*, 1963–1971

## Newspapers

*Baltimore Morning Sun*          *Los Angeles Times*          *Oakland Tribune*
*Kansas City Star*               *Minneapolis Tribune*        *Washington Post*
*Kansas City Times*              *New York Times*

# *Index*

Numbers in *bold italics* indicate pages with photographs.